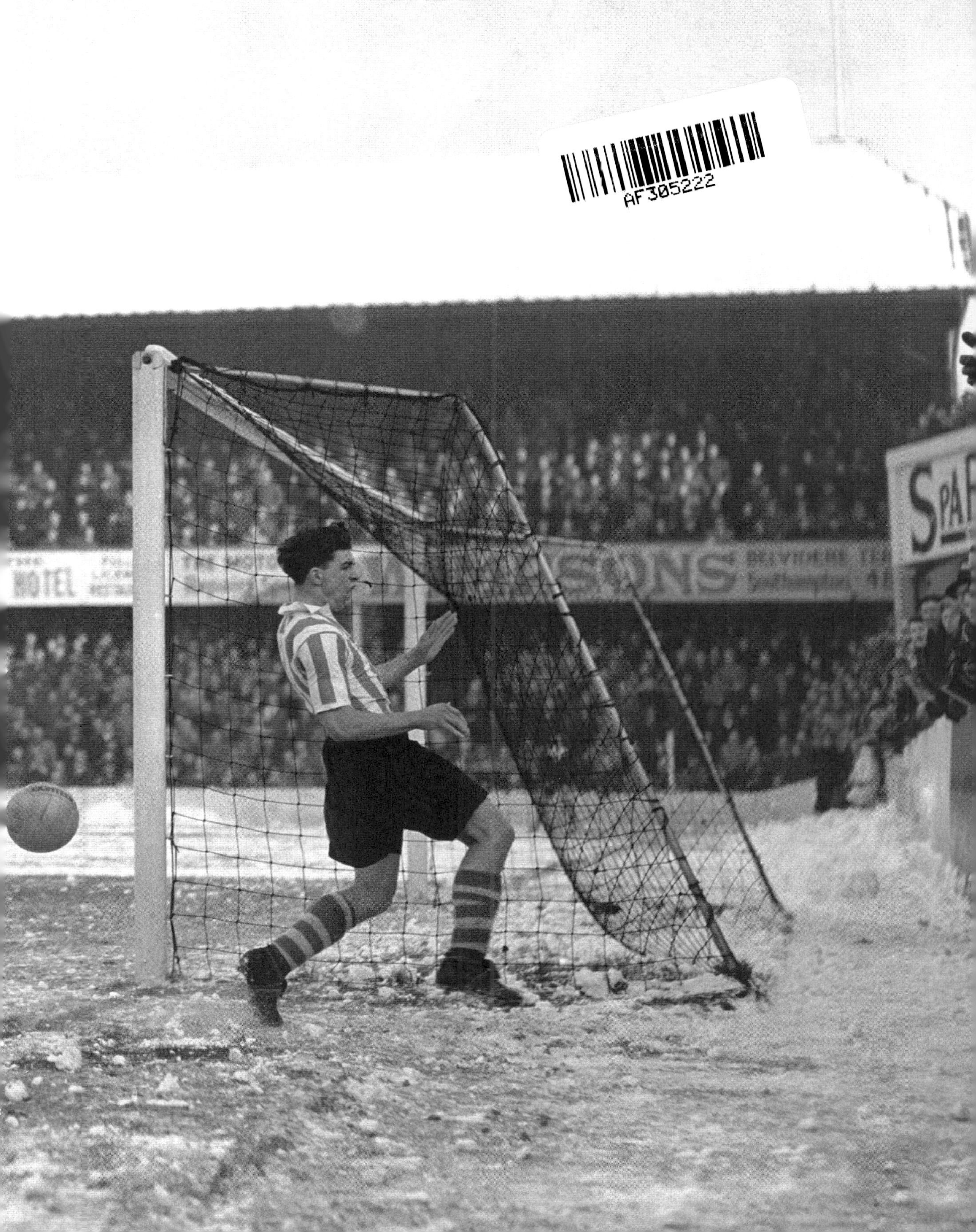
MOTEL
SONS
SPA

Pitch Publishing Ltd
A2 Yeoman Gate
Yeoman Way
Durrington
BN13 3QZ

Email: info@pitchpublishing.co.uk
Web: www.pitchpublishing.co.uk

First published by Pitch Publishing 2021
Text © 2021 Matthew Bazell

1

A CIP catalogue record for this book is available from the British Library.

13-digit ISBN: 9781801500067
Design and typesetting by Olner Pro Sport Media. Visit www.olnerpsm.co.uk
Printed in India by Replika Press Pvt. Ltd.

Soul & Glory

English Football: 1950–1989

Matthew Bazell

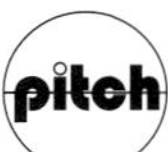

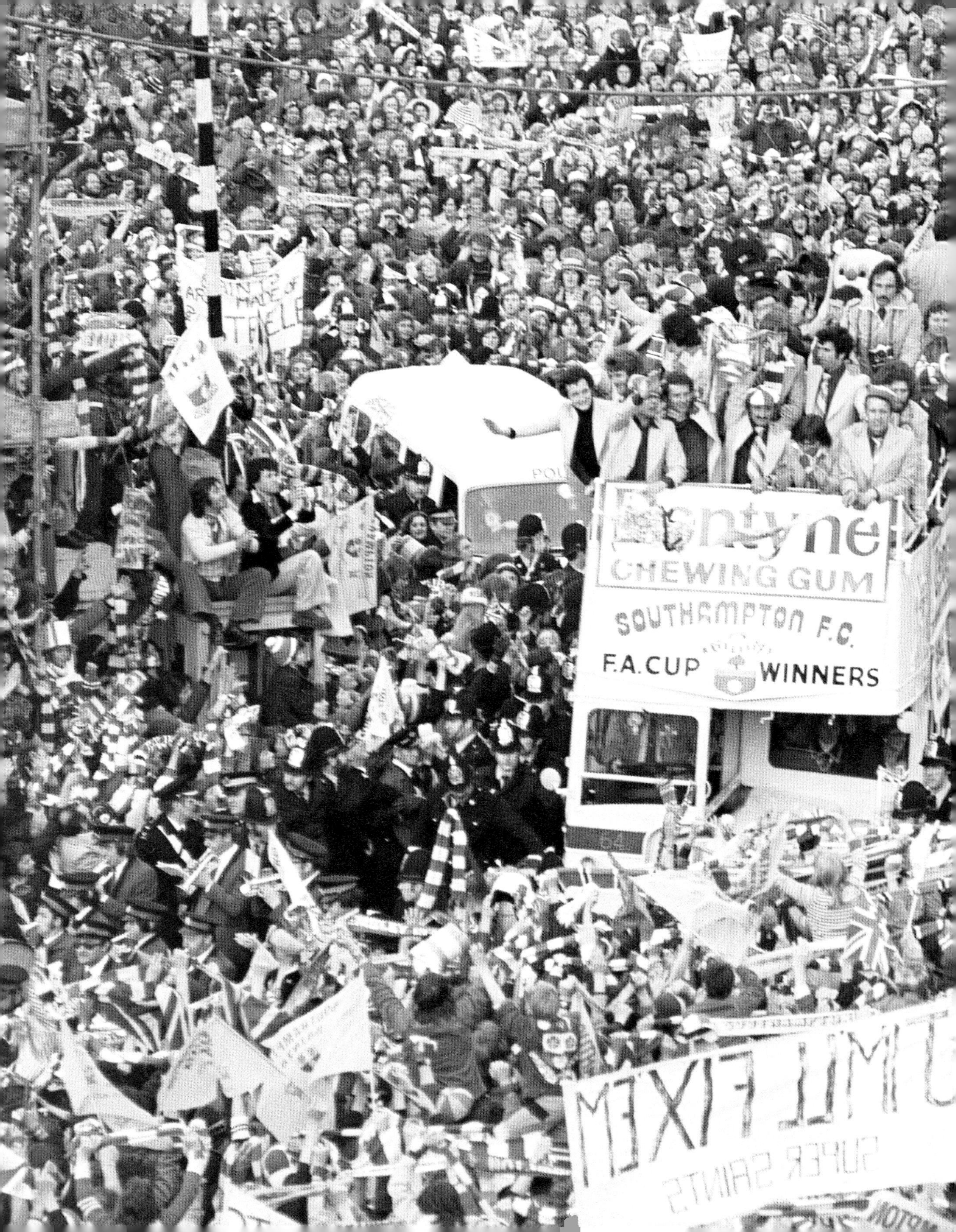
SAINTS MADE OF
STEEL
Bntyne
CHEWING GUM
SOUTHAMPTON F.C.
F.A. CUP WINNERS
WE'LL FIX 'EM
SUPER SAINTS

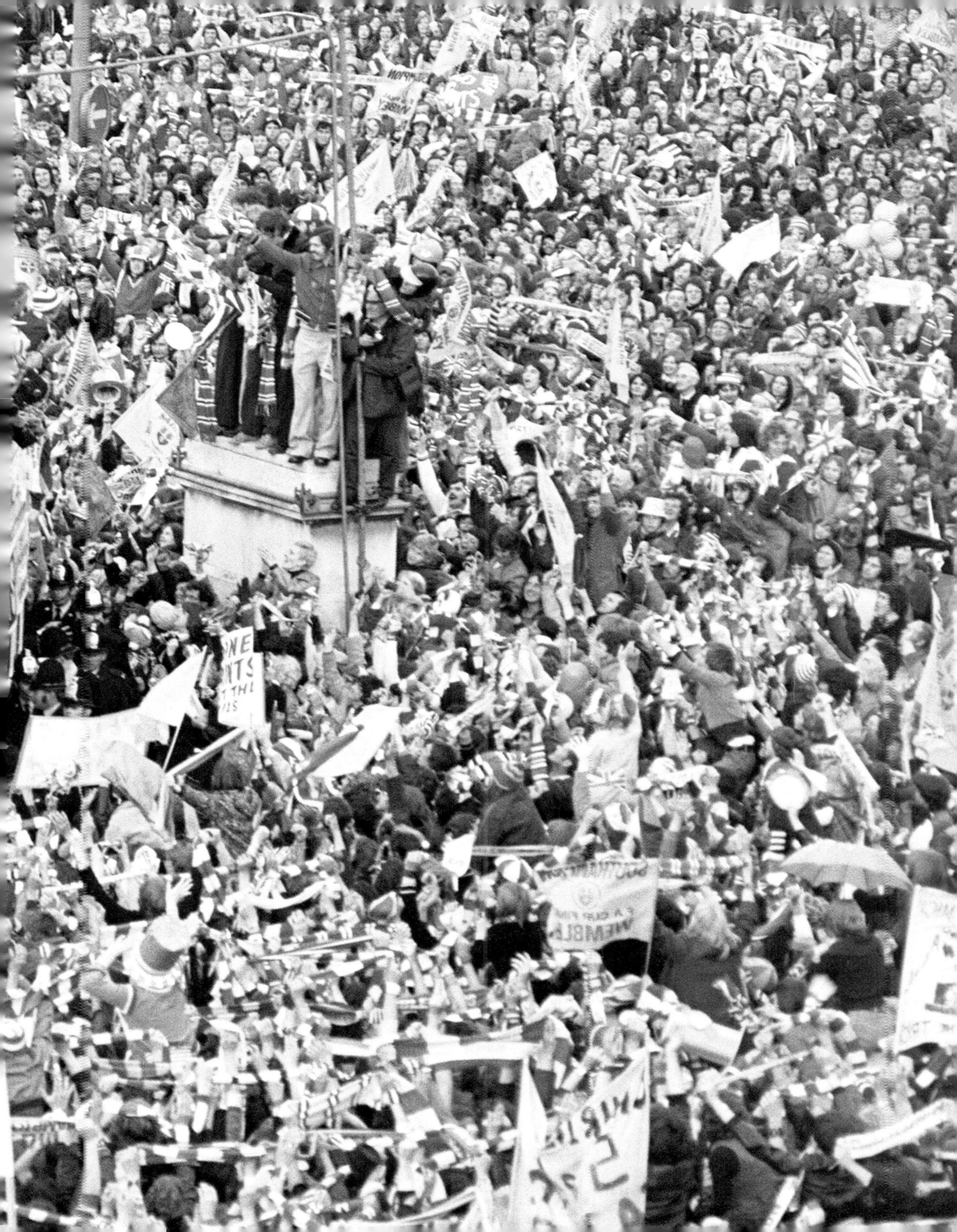

What Changed? Everything!

I love the purity of old football images and what they tell us about how the game has changed. It's interesting to look at an older football photograph and ask yourself a question: what's different about this scene compared to now?

On pages 80–81 in Chapter Two, there is a photo of Blackburn's Derek Dougan celebrating a goal in an FA Cup semi-final against Sheffield Wednesday in 1960. In just one image you see something that's so recognisable and familiar to today's game. It's a footballer thrilled at scoring a goal and celebrating in front of joyous fans in a packed out stadium. When you study the photo, everything is different, every nuance. Apart from the essence of what football is as a game, what the competition is, what the thrill is, you can look at this photo and conclude that pretty much everything has changed; the better or worse aspect of it is down to each person's opinion.

One of the most striking differences is the lack of clutter and the minimalism that surrounds everything in this scene. Dougan is in front of the barrier where the fans are, which is just a long white concrete slab. Today that would be the site of a digital, and some would say very intrusive, advertising hoarding flashing out messages for global products and betting companies. In-between Dougan and the fans there are no stewards. The same scene today would have people in high visibility jackets trying to prevent player and fan contact, as well as general security. If this scenario was from the 1980s, a steward would be visible, but they would look different. Their uniform would blend in more, and they were usually fans who were employed directly by the club. They would think nothing wrong in jumping up and celebrating a goal with the fans.

As Dougan celebrates one of his two goals that day, it was a time before the English game was enriched by black players. By the 1960s the first wave of mass migration from the Caribbean was in its infancy. There had been a handful of black players in the English game, but for the most part it was very uncommon. On the pitch in this semi-final, everyone, like Dougan, was white. Not just white, but white British, with Irish players being the one exception of overseas players.

Dougan's days of glory didn't earn him thousands, let alone millions. His wages were capped at £20 a week, and the maximum wage was a huge issue in the game until it was scrapped a year after he scored this goal. Even if Dougan were on the maximum of £20 a week, he would barely make £1,000 a year as the wage was capped at £17 a week during the summer off season. It was an amount of money that was a lot higher than the average worker, and it meant the best paid footballers could live in a nice house in a middle-class street, but certainly a far cry away from the kind of wages that meant you could buy a middle-class house on just one week's pay packet, which is a realistic scenario today. On the 1970s football show, *The Big Match*, the presenter Brian Moore used to do a feature called 'where are they now?', which looked at what some former stars were doing since their career ended. Most typically, players just went on to humble day jobs; the money they earned from the game sometimes allowing them the means to open up a business, with the stereotype image being quitting football and opening up a pub. To give one example, *The Big Match* featured Spurs' 1960/61 double winner Maurice Norman and found out that he was running a shop in Essex that sold wool and baby clothes, to which Brian Moore concluded 'he's doing pretty well'. There was no expectation for anyone to be rich, just because they used to play football at a high level, so running your own shop or pub was 'doing pretty well'. In a lot of cases once players retired, they went to the labour exchange and signed on the dole, having no direction on what to do, or how to do it.

The kit Dougan wears is so different to the same scenario today. Again, for better or worse depending on your point of view. There is no team badge in this photo, just a blue shirt with a white collar. As the years went on, a badge would appear, then in some cases by the 1970s a manufacturer symbol by the badge, then by the late 70s to early 80s a sponsor on the front, to where we are now – which is a sponsor on the sleeves and the stadium itself named after a brand. The shirt Dougan wears is cotton, not polyester. The boots alone exemplify a better and worse scenario: better today, in that the boots are lighter, allowing for a faster game and trickery. Worse, in that they are a variety of pastel colours! Football boots in the modern era are eyesores, but like Dougan everyone on the pitch in 1960 wore dark footwear. In 2021, Raheem Sterling caught the eye for the boots he was wearing which really stood out from the crowd, in that they were black. It looked so formal and elegant, as everyone else ran around in yellow, pink, blue and bright green. Speaking of green, the goalkeeper who Dougan scored against would have been wearing that colour jersey. All keepers did until recent years, the reason being that a goalkeeper had to look different to the rest of his team-mates; and in the very early years of football they would be distinguishable by an accessory such as a cap. As the years went on, the colour green was thought of as a safe bet for keepers, as hardly any teams wore green for their home or away colours. Unless you were playing Plymouth Argyle then your goalkeeper's green jersey was unlikely to clash with the opposition. If Dougan's shot had been palmed away by the keeper that day it would have been with a bare hand; gloves wouldn't come in for a couple more decades, for goalkeepers let alone outfield players the minute September hits.

The ball Dougan kicked into the net could get heavier on a wet day. On a dry day the balls were not that much heavier than they are now (though modern footballs move faster), and had been that way since new regulations in 1937, but they would still absorb water, and you wouldn't want to head one from a high goal kick on a soggy day. What the ball looked like was dependent on whose home ground it was. In the Premier League, the ball is standardised among all clubs, whereas before, it was up to the club what make of football they would use as long as it met the size and weight requirements. In the 1980s Mitre was a popular choice, but clubs whose team kits were made by Adidas would use the iconic Adidas Tango ball. The pitch that Dougan scored on would not be the smooth carpet that we are used to today, and muddy cut-up pitches were a normal part of the game, highlighted more so when colour TV showed up. You'll certainly see a few muddy pitches throughout this collection of photographs, not least the Swindon v Arsenal League Cup Final of 1969 when Wembley resembled Glastonbury on day three of a soaked-out festival. From uniform to playing surfaces, the challenges footballers were faced with points us to why the game speeded up so much over the years, not to mention different standards of nutrition and training.

The net and goalposts Dougan put the ball into looked different to today. Metal stanchions were attached, sometimes in distinctive shapes. The actual goals themselves did look different depending on the stadium. The goal shapes at Highbury looked different to the goal shapes at White Hart Lane, as they were deeper and had green painted stanchions. In the 80s, Goodison Park stood out because it didn't have stanchions at all as the net gracefully drooped down like a half moon. The goal nets at Anfield were distinct and coloured red, compared to a club like Manchester City who had blue nets. Chelsea's Stamford Bridge had the deepest sized goals to the point where you could have a cup of tea in the time it took for the ball to leave the foot and hit the back of the net. The opposite to that was Southampton, whose goals were so shallow that by the time the ball crossed the line, it was virtually hitting the net. You could recognise a game being played at Wembley just from the goal designs, which were the most distinguishable and regal looking in football. Today the goalposts and nets are universal in appearance; the same box shape, same colour, same depth, same personality. For the stadiums themselves, Southampton's Dell looked very different to Derby's Baseball Ground. I use those two clubs as examples, because they now both play in the quintessential modern arena, based on the same design. If you took away colouring and branding it would be hard to guess which one is Pride Park and which one is St. Mary's. The first club to build this style stadium was Middlesbrough who opened up the Riverside in 1995. At the time it was very original, but then the design plan became the blueprint and everyone copied it. This book celebrates the eras when rivals and neighbours looked different to one another. When stadiums had terraces and stands that became famous for look and personality.

As Dougan stands in front of the fans with his arms raised in triumph, many of them in the picture are not his own, but rather fans of Sheffield Wednesday. Some are less than happy, whilst they stand next to elated Rovers fans. There was no segregation until the 1970s, when hooliganism began to get out of control. Football would become very unique in this, with its image tainted as being the one sport where fans had to be separated because the passion ran too high. The segregation would not be an English disease, as all over the world, home and away fans just couldn't mix (though you could argue that most could and it was a minority that couldn't). Every fan in this photo was already standing up before the ball hit the net. Every stadium had wooden seats, but the majority of a ground would be made up of terraces, leading to huge capacities, far larger than today. Charlton's Valley stadium was famous for having the biggest terraced end in the country, as the huge East Terrace, like so many other ends, stretched from one length of the pitch to the other. This book ends in 1989, which would be a tragic and pivotal year for terracing, spelling the end of the culture of standing up at football.

Dougan looks in the direction of the camera with a beaming smile. The person taking this shot was one of very few photographers in the stadium. The same scene today would include a sea of smartphones in the air, and that's just the fans. There are no TV cameras in this shot. This game would not have been televised and like every other match was played at 3pm on a Saturday; after lunch and after weekend workers finished their midday shifts. A couple of film cameras from British Pathe would have filmed the game and the highlights then shown to a cinema audience during the news footage that was shown before the main feature film. As Dougan scores, there's no dispute that the goal stands because the referee has given it, and no flags were raised. No fan in this photo has any doubt whatsoever that this was a goal. As the players walk back to the halfway line there is no fear that the decision will be reversed by a third party. Blackburn know they can celebrate the goal without being made to look foolish two minutes later, as technology did a thorough investigation and found that a boot lace was offside. There was a disallowed goal in this game from Sheffield Wednesday, and as the Pathe commentator noted 'for some seconds the crowd didn't realise that it was no goal'.

Dougan's goal allowed Blackburn to win 2-1 and progress to a Wembley final, the FA Cup – the trophy that every English player wanted to win. For this semi-final to have been played at Wembley would have been unthinkable. Part of the prestige of an FA Cup Final was playing at Wembley. It was an occasion, and something to be earned. This game was played in front of 74,135 fans at Maine Road, home of Manchester City, 26 miles from Blackburn and 38 miles from Sheffield. Today both sets of fans would be Wembley bound, with a feeling of 'can't we play this closer to home?' Two teams playing at another club's home ground, for

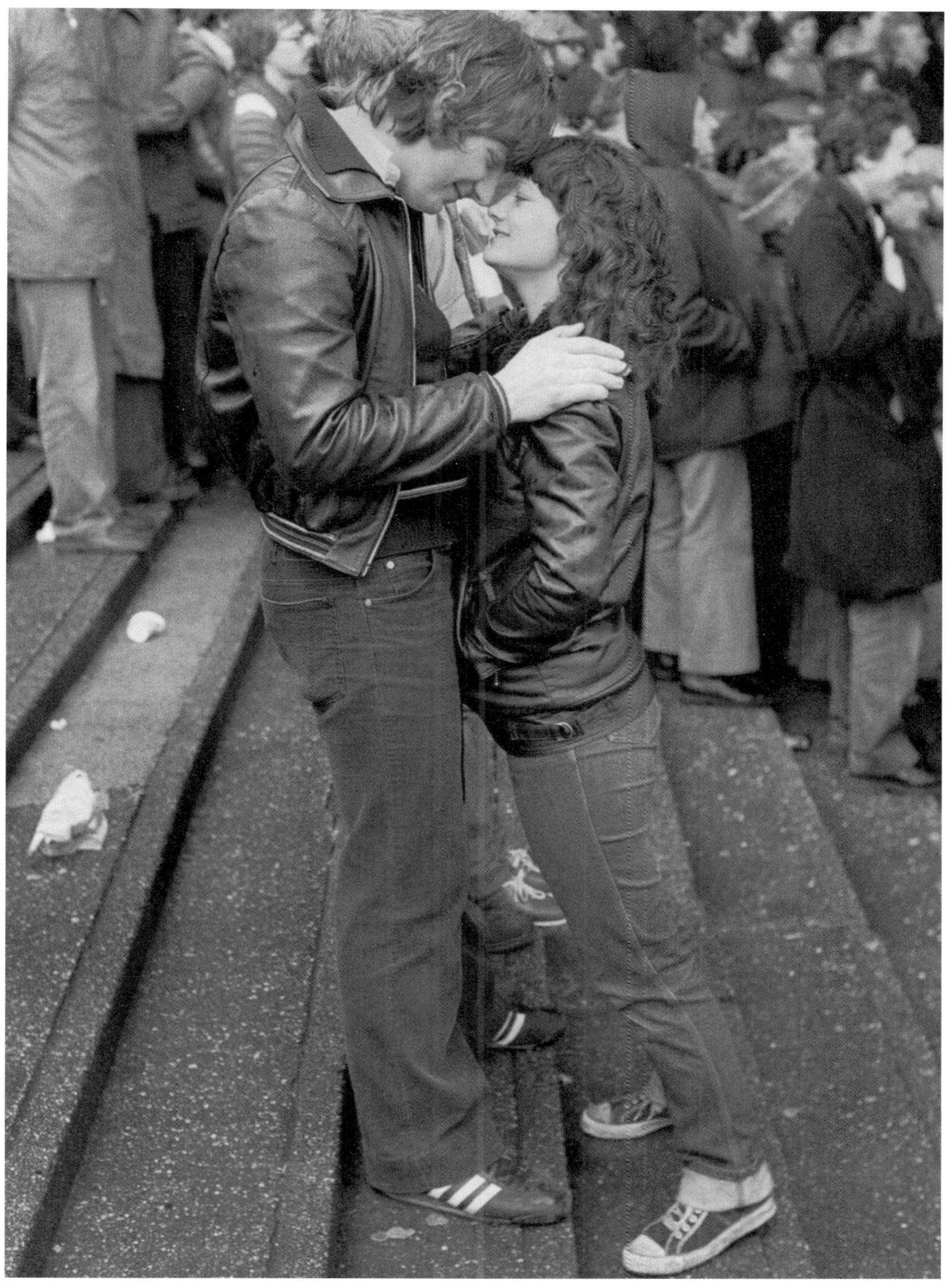

Highfield Road, 1981
In love with the game or just
in love with each other?

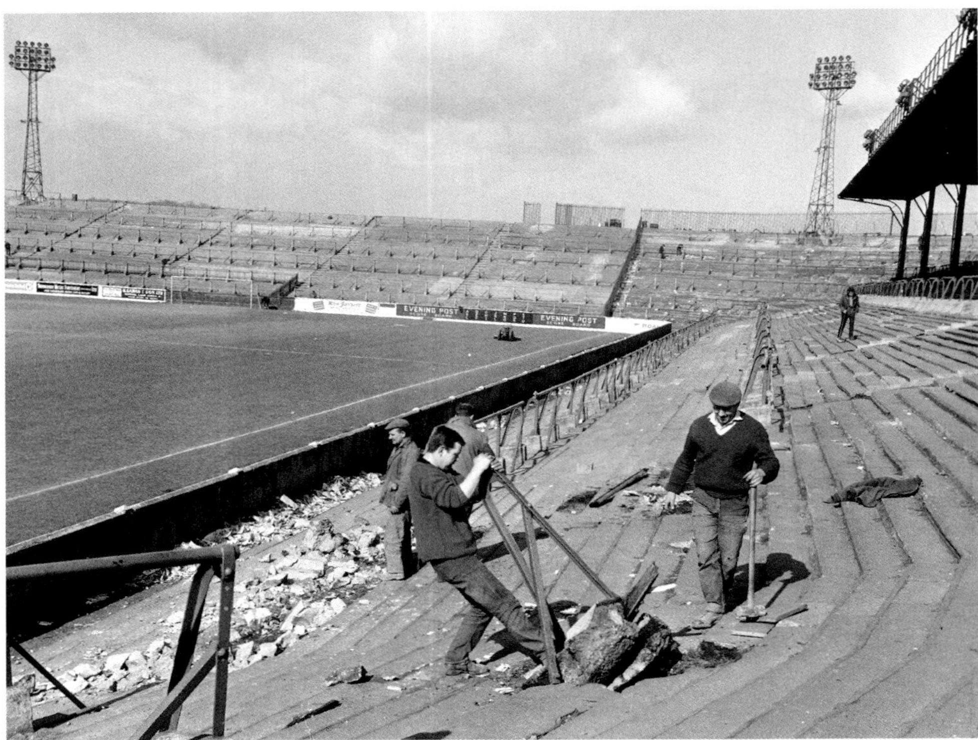

Elland Road,1967 The Chief Constable of Leeds inspects damage after the FA Cup fifth round replay between Leeds United and Sunderland. The record attendance of nearly 58,000 fans led to barrier collapses and fans being injured on the terraces.

example Arsenal v Manchester United at Villa Park, was a really intriguing and unique element of the FA Cup which got dropped two decades ago, in favour of something that looks the same every year. Many of the fans at Maine Road on this day would have got into the ground at least an hour before kick-off to get the best spot on the terrace they could. The ones in this photo near Dougan are most likely to have done this, as getting to the front, especially for kids was vital so you weren't stuck behind anyone tall. Being a kid on a football terrace was great, but it was also hard to see, so getting near the front was essential. Apart from a few exceptions, the 74,000 fans would have stayed until the final whistle. The masses leaving ten minutes early is something that has only crept into fan culture over the past two decades. One explanation is that home crowds, especially at the big clubs, are not as localised anymore, and travel further to games. Another explanation is that when you get to a ground an hour early to get the best view, you are more invested in being there and wouldn't consider missing any of the game, no matter what the score was. Like a theatre show, why would you leave before the end when you don't know what's going to happen?

The fans in this photo were no doubt largely from working-class communities. That had always been the case from the rise of the professional clubs in the late 1800s. The game's founding fathers, who were from the elite private schools, could not compete with the size of these new clubs. Suddenly football was the People's Game, with the FA Cup being won by teams from highly populated industrial towns and cities. There were more

 Soul & Glory English Football: 1950–1989

poor people than the rich elite, so when it came to filling a stadium with fans there was no competition between Blackburn and Charterhouse. That working class social demographic is a consistent presence throughout the time period that this book covers. It's present in the faces of the crowd, the enthusiasm, the way that football was a wonderful distraction from daily life. By the turn of the millennium however, being a supporter would start to become a costly business, and now you would conclude that the majority of people in a top-tier football stadium are no longer from working-class communities. Rather than going to football as a form of escapism, work came to football; for example Spurs recently had an advert on the London underground that said 'come to Spurs to network'. The change of demographic, to the point where one group is excluded, is probably the starkest and most questionable change in football from this photo in 1960, to now.

Along with how different things used to look, a motivation for this book is to celebrate the diversity and parity of English football history with regards to success. In recent years we have become so used to seeing the same winners who are dependent on being in the financial elite, that it's easy for younger fans to think that it's always been this way, or to not care about what came before. You judge a person by their entire life, and the good things they did when they were younger and it's the same with football clubs. History matters, glory is everlasting and shouldn't be brushed aside. As well as living for the moment, what is strived for today is for the purpose of being remembered and celebrated for years to come. Football is often mocked today for acting like the game never existed before 1992 and the formation of the Premier League. After all, the format of competition never changed, just the ownership of the league. The three major honours on offer in domestic football are no different in structure than they were pre-Premier League. The covering of games does point towards this obsession that stats and records only count if they came after 1992. To give the classic example, in January 2021 West Ham's Michail Antonio scored for West Ham against West Brom in a 2-1 win: and the commentator revealed that the striker was now the third highest West Ham goalscorer in history – in the Premier League. In real terms that made him West Ham's third highest scorer in a 29-year period (or less, considering West Ham spent several seasons outside the top division). To put that in context, Antonio was not even in the top 30 West Ham goalscorers at the time of this stat. Again, in early 2021 a commentator covering a match at St James' Park told us, 'And this is the ninth time that Newcastle and Wolves have drawn a match in the Premier League.' Newcastle were founded in 1892, 100 years before that stat comes into effect! Wolves were founded earlier, in 1877, one of the oldest clubs in the world. Surely the overall record between the two teams is the more interesting stat than games played since 1992, not to mention that Newcastle and Wolves didn't play against one another for the majority of Premier League seasons. Without overall history, the reputations of both mentioned clubs are totally diminished. This book starts in the 50s, an era when both Wolves and Newcastle were dominant and successful. Their 'big club' tag was cemented by total history, not a snippet over the past 30 years.

English football history is too vast for a photography book to cover its origins, to where we are now, and give enough fair time to each decade. I felt this collection would be better condensed to just four decades that all had different identities and personalities and tell a story of how football changed as the years went on. The change was fascinating; going to a game in 1950 was such a different experience to one in 1989, both on and off the pitch. Everything looked different. From 1989 to now you could ask what has changed. Once again, the answer is pretty much everything!

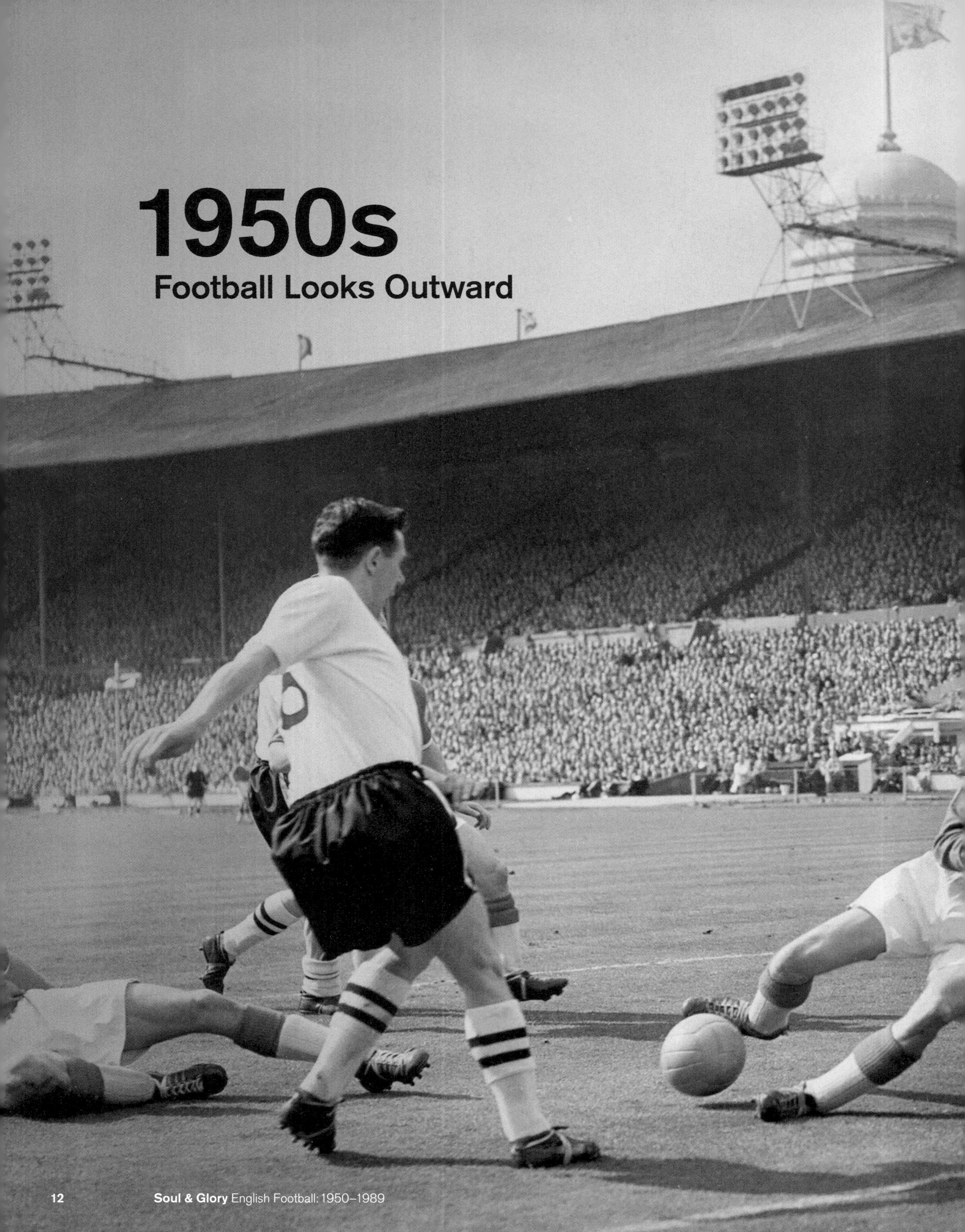

1950s
Football Looks Outward

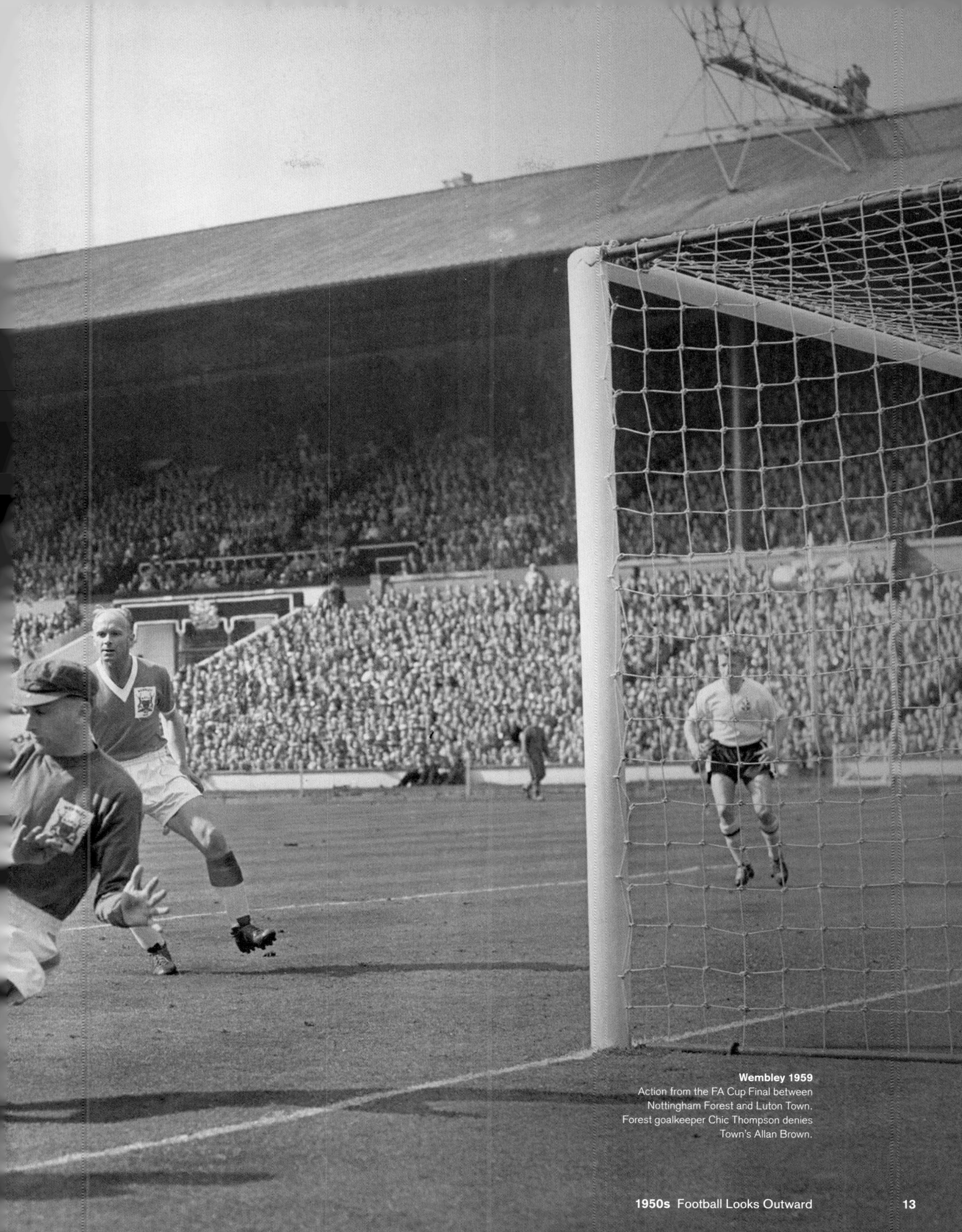

Wembley 1959
Action from the FA Cup Final between
Nottingham Forest and Luton Town.
Forest goalkeeper Chic Thompson denies
Town's Allan Brown.

1950s: Football Looks Outward

The identity the 1950s perhaps takes on is the decade that bridges the gap between the early years of the game and modern football, in both appearance and outward-looking culture. Not as glamorous and charismatic as the 1960s, but a step forward from the pre-war game with the emergence of more floodlit matches and international club football. A forward-thinking sport beyond borders. The era when UEFA was first formed and the beginning of European club competition such as the European Cup – now known as the Champions League. The decade where the FA settled a dispute with FIFA, allowing England to enter the 1950 World Cup. England's absence from the three World Cups of the 1930s denied future generations of Three Lions fans the chance of more than one lonely star above the badge, as England would have been strong contenders in that era. The 1940s was put into blackout by WW2, and by the time it was all over, and the world began to heal, all the decade had left was three full league seasons to its name giving the 40s little chance of acquiring a rich football identity. It's the only decade that never hosted a World Cup, but when the conflict was over and freedom was won, all that really mattered was that football crowds couldn't wait to flock back to the terraces in their droves.

The 50s started how the 40s ended, with a surprise winner of the league title from a little-fancied club on the south coast. Portsmouth won back-to-back championships with average attendances of 37,000; a figure far lower than most teams in Division One at that time. Other clubs had bigger reputations, bigger stadiums, bigger crowds, and bigger stars, but Pompey held off a challenge from Wolves and Sunderland to win the 1950 title on goal difference, and to this day are one of only five clubs to win consecutive post-war championships.

Pre-war, Arsenal had definitively ruled English football in the 1930s with five league titles and two FA Cups, giving the club an identity with the decade. When the Gunners won the second post-war title in 1946/47, it indicated that they would continue their league dominance for years. However, in the 1950s Arsenal won just the solitary championship and Division One would develop into a power struggle between Wolverhampton Wanderers and Manchester United, both teams winning the league three times each during that ten-year period. Today, Wolves would be viewed as the underdog going to play the mighty Manchester United, but back then 'Old Gold' were the club that carried that sense of awe. The standard-bearer of English football, led by the legendary England international Billy Wright. A young kid growing up in from Belfast called George Best supported Wolves, and Bobby Charlton spoke of the prestige he felt that his young Manchester United team were going to play the mighty Wolverhampton Wanderers. How things would change over the years, as one club would become a global brand whilst the other got labelled a sleeping giant and would sink to the depths of Division Four.

The birth of Manchester United as a world-famous superclub happened in the 50s through triumph and tragedy as the European Cup-challenging Busby Babes, the champions of England, were cut down in their prime by the Munich air disaster in February 1958 when the plane skidded on an icy runway after trying to take off in freezing conditions. The crash killed 23 people including the biggest star of the team, Duncan Edwards. Five days before

'Football was described as the opiate of the masses. The relief from the horrors of war and the privations of the postwar years. People went to football to get away from that.'

Jeff Powell – Journalist

'Over the years people called several players the new Duncan Edwards... but none of them came close. He was the only player that made me feel inferior.'

Matt Busby

'You're 32, do you think you can make it for another couple of years?'

Blackpool manager Joe Smith to Stanley Matthews in 1947

the disaster, Edwards had scored in a thrilling 5-4 United win at Highbury in front of 63,578 supporters. Edwards was capped by England at the age of 18, making him the youngest England international since the previous century, and today a statue stands in his home town of Dudley, ironically only six miles away from his biggest rival Wolverhampton. The sympathy that the country and the world felt for the club coincided with the surviving Matt Busby building more great United sides – leading to one of the biggest fan bases in world football. United were second in the league at the time of the disaster and would not go on to win the title that season. However, thanks to an incredible effort from an assortment of reserve and youth team players they got to the 1958 FA Cup Final to face Bolton Wanderers. United had the support of most people outside of Bolton. If life were a Hollywood script then they would have won, but Wanderers had a history of cup success and thanks to two goals from Nat Lofthouse, won their fourth FA Cup in front of a crowd of 99,756. Lofthouse's controversial second goal would go some way to changing football, as he scored by way of colliding with United keeper Harry Gregg, virtually bundling Gregg over the line at the moment the keeper caught the ball from a cross. In the coming years the pendulum would swing massively in the opposite direction. Accepted contact with the goalkeepers would mirror a game like basketball, which is minimal contact at best, leading to TV presenter and former England striker Gary Lineker jokingly referring to them as 'an overprotected species'. However, in 1958 the attitude is nicely summed up by the TV commentator's unassuming reaction as Gregg lay motionless in the goalmouth. 'That charge seemed fair enough, but it's floored Harry Gregg and play is held up.' Along with Harry Gregg, Bobby Charlton was one of only four players to compete in that game who were on the fated flight from Munich.

Throughout the 50s, neither United nor Wolves had applied their league dominance to the FA Cup, even though it was the biggest prize of the day. It's one of the most fundamental changes related to ambition in the game, in how the old trophy was viewed compared to now. The most prominent stars of the decade such as Nat Lofthouse, Tom Finney (Preston) and Stanley Matthews (Stoke and Blackpool) desired an FA Cup medal above all else. Winning the cup was bigger than winning the league, let alone comparing it with today's question of 'Would you rather win the FA Cup or finish fourth in the league?' or resting your players on a cup weekend so they're fresher for a midweek league game. On the BBC's *606* radio phone-in during the 2019/20 season, a Burnley fan was asked if he would rather stay in the Premier League or win the FA Cup. The answer given by the fan was to stay in the Premier League, to which one might point out that one day Burnley will most likely get relegated anyway in the near future. On the other hand, glory is cemented in the history books forever. This question was never so prevalent as in 2013 when Wigan beat Manchester City in the FA Cup Final, only to be relegated from the Premier League just days later. One day Wigan will be back in the top tier, but never again will they be known as a club that never won a major trophy. Many clubs bigger than Wigan have no major honours to their name. The Latics however, will always be FA Cup winners and will always have the photographic images of their victory within the corridors of the stadium. That matters. In a photographic football book that gets released decades from now, Wigan's FA Cup win in 2013 is more likely to be featured as a great nostalgic moment, as opposed to any top-flight league game they played before relegation.

Fifties icons Nat Lofthouse and Stanley Matthews would compete against one another in 1953 in one of the most defining finals of all time, as Blackpool beat Bolton 4-3 in what got labelled the 'Matthews Final', such was the winger's dominance of the game, despite not making it on to the scoresheet. Matthews had been on the losing side of the 1948 and 1951 finals, and desperately wanted an FA Cup winners' medal, not least as it was his father's wish for him whilst on his deathbed. With Bolton ahead 3-1 and just 22 minutes to go, the winger played like a man possessed, and destroyed the Bolton defence on the right wing. With ease he got behind them and played ball after ball into the penalty area as the Seasiders scored three more times to win their first and only major honour, the winning goal coming in the 92nd minute from Bill Perry, who tucked the ball away from a Matthews run and cross. It was the highest goal tally in an FA Cup Final since 1890, and that game was a one-sided 6-1 drubbing from Blackburn Rovers upon Sheffield Wednesday, as opposed to a back-and-forth thriller. Since 1953, no FA Cup Final has had seven goals with Man United 3-3 Crystal Palace (1990), Liverpool 3-3 West Ham (2006) and Manchester City 6-0 Watford (2019) coming the closest to that record. Matthews would continue his playing career for another 12 years after the 53 final.

Along with the Matthews Final, the most iconic FA Cup moment of the 50s came in the 56 final between Manchester City and Birmingham City. Signing for Manchester City in 1949, the German goalkeeper Bert Trautmann was one of very few foreign players to make their name in the English game up to that point. He had been in England since 1945, having been captured in France by British soldiers and transferred to a Prisoner of War camp in Essex. Being a German in 1950s Britain wasn't easy, but Trautmann was resilient to say the least. In fact, so resilient that he broke his neck in the 56 final but played on, after Peter Murphy's knee had smashed into his neck as he dived for the ball. He was treated on the pitch, and in the most incredible show of bravery got up and saw out the last 15 minutes of the match, even making a save. Just watching the ball fly high over the goal was excruciating for the keeper as he looked in agony at just being alive. Trautmann did not go to see a doctor until the next day, and was told that it was just a crick in his neck and he'd be fine. Severe pain forced the German to get a second opinion and the X-ray showed that he could have lost his life. He had five dislocated vertebrae, one of which was cracked, and was only being held together by one of the dislocated ones. In the collision, the Birmingham striker was also injured which shows you just how tough Trautmann's neck must have been, and as the two men lay on the floor Kenneth Wolstenholme commented, 'It looks like Murphy's knee, and Trautmann's head' before going on to say that the German had already had neck issues, which he had treatment for two weeks earlier.

Considering the prestige in which the old cup was viewed, you could perhaps form an argument that Newcastle United achieved the most glory in the 1950s and were the team of the decade, as the Magpies won FA Cups in 1951, 52, and 55, equalling Aston Villa's record of six overall FA Cup triumphs. Jackie Milburn, whose statue currently stands outside St James' Park, played in all three winning finals, and scored in the 1955 final after just 45 seconds – a record for the fastest goal in the occasion, which would stand until 1997. As a club, Newcastle United must have felt pretty good about themselves by 1955, being six times FA Cup winners as well as league champions on four occasions. They had every right to view themselves as masters when it came to winning silverware. Who could have predicted the drought to follow? What odds would you have got for Newcastle to go 66 years and counting with no domestic major honour? It just shows how reputations change over time. In the 50s, the hierarchy we're now used to had not been cemented. A number

'Hello Fritz fancy a cup of tea?'

British soldier who captured German soldier and future Man City keeper Bert Trautmann

of teams would view themselves as successful big clubs including West Brom and Bolton, and when combining all-time league and FA Cup wins by the end of the 1950s, Aston Villa had the right to proclaim themselves as the most successful team in English football history with six league titles and seven FA Cups. It was a meaningful claim, because the game was not in its infancy in the middle of the 20th century. The Football League had been set up for around 70 years, the FA Cup even longer. That's a longer timescale than the entire history of the Super Bowl which began in 1967. The NFL's two most successful teams today are New England Patriots and Pittsburgh Steelers both with six Super Bowl wins (although if Tom Brady were a team, he'd be on top with seven). In 70 years' time we may view both those teams as pioneers of early NFL, but no longer part of the hierarchy as other clubs eclipse their records.

'I had secured my finest signing for ten quid and a couple of rounds of Newcastle Brown Ale.'

Newcastle manager Stan Seymour signs up 19-year-old Jackie Milburn in 1938

No sooner had Newcastle equalled Villa's record of six FA Cups than the Birmingham club regained the record, beating Manchester United in 1957. Villa's first win had dated as far back as 1887 but since that 1957 victory they are yet to make it eight at the time of writing. Like Newcastle, the club has won more trophies than most English teams, but the vast bulk of their glory came in football's early days. How incredible to think that the 1950s established both Newcastle and Villa as the undisputed FA Cup kings, yet neither team has regained the cup since Elvis first sung 'Jailhouse Rock'. Several years ago, the BBC aired a programme that analysed the 1957 FA Cup Final between Villa and United to see how it compared to today's game. Apart from the fact that in those days the final was the only match of the season aired on television, one of the most noticeable factors was the respect the players had for the referee's calls. There was virtually no dissent. The referee made a decision and that was the end of the matter. No arguing, just play the game. Even the supporters were expected to be sporting and polite as the commentator described 'some rather silly booing' by fans on a player who they felt had made a dangerous tackle.

Before the 1950s, Tottenham Hotspur had only two FA Cups on their honours list, 1901 and 1921, thus being the starting point for Lilywhites' claim that it's lucky for Spurs when the year ends in the number one. In 1950/51 they won their first league title, becoming only the second London club to do so. A huge achievement considering it had only been a year since they had been promoted from Division Two. Even to this day, only three London teams have won the title, and Chelsea would be the third capital city championship team when they won the league in 1955. The west Londoners would then go on a 50-year title drought until the Roman Abramovich era, which at the time of writing has led to another five championships making their way to Stamford Bridge. Chelsea's 1955 title win was the lowest points tally since the expansion to 22 teams in Division One in 1919. Even taking into account that it was two points for a win in those days, their 52 points is incredibly low, with the Blues winning 20 games, drawing 12 and losing ten. But despite being the lowest points total to win a league, winning the championship with fewer than 60 points was normal in the 1950s and happened on four other occasions, Portsmouth (1950, 53 points), Manchester United (1952, 57 points), Arsenal (1953, 54 points) and Wolverhampton (1954, 57 points).

Part of Spurs' 1950/51 title-winning side was a centre-forward called Len Duquemin. Known as 'The Duke', he was the first player of note to come from the Channel Islands, and scored 114 goals for Spurs over a nine-year period. His story is the most poetic example of the humble everyday lifestyle most footballers went on to after retirement. Duquemin set up a newsagent in Northumberland Park, right next to White Hart Lane. He bought a season ticket at the ground where he used to be a star, and would have to leave the stadium before the final whistle so that he could get back to his shop on time to sell the classified evening papers. The very same evening papers that used to report the goals he scored. Imagine in a few years' time, popping into a north London newsagent and being sold a newspaper by Son Heung-min.

On an international front the 1950s had been a horrible wake-up call for the England national side. The 1950 World Cup was supposed to mark England's grand entrance to the competition. After all, in 1948 England had thrashed world champions Italy 4-0 in Turin, a year after smashing Portugal 10-0, all of which reinstated the view that the game's inventors were still number one, and were being kind and sympathetic to other countries by not entering tournaments. Instead of glory, England got a grand elimination in the group stages, as a 1-0 defeat by USA went down into all-time shock win folklore. The 1954 World Cup wasn't that much better, with second-round elimination – but at least it spared England from facing Hungary again who had dealt a hammer blow at Wembley a year earlier, winning 6-3 and in one single iconic game destroying the culture of complacency. Up to that point, Ireland had been the only overseas team to have ever beaten England on home soil, but the Hungarians had brought a superior level of tactics to the home of football to which England captain Billy Wright admitted, 'We completely underestimated the advances that Hungary has made.'

'We should be all right here Stan, they haven't got the proper kit.'

Waiting in the Wembley tunnel before England v Hungary in 1953, Billy Wright assures team-mate Stan Mortensen that their opponents had 'lightweight boots' on.

Billy Wright had the chance to avenge Hungarian football with his club side Wolverhampton who pioneered the return of floodlit night games and international club friendlies in the days before any competitive tournament had been set up. When the legendary and feared Honved from Budapest came to Molineux in December 1954 it was seen by many as a battle between the two best club sides in world football, and the most high profile of a series of Wolves home games known as the 'Floodlit Friendlies'. Honved brought with them Ferenc Puskas and took an early 2-0 lead. Wolves came back to win 3-2 in one of the earliest big European triumphs for an English club as the *Birmingham Gazette* roared 'WOLVES. CLUB CHAMPIONS OF THE WORLD'. A French newspaper called *L'Equipe* was more sceptical and wrote, 'Before we declare that Wolverhampton are invincible, let them go to Moscow and Budapest. And there are other internationally renowned clubs: Milan and Real Madrid to name but two. A club world championship, or at least a European one – larger, more meaningful and more prestigious than the Mitropa Cup and more original than a competition for national teams – should be launched.'

1950s Domestic Honours

Division One Champions

1950: Portsmouth (overall title wins 2)
1951: Tottenham Hotspur (overall wins 1)
1952: Manchester United (overall wins 3)
1953: Arsenal (overall wins 7)
1954: Wolverhampton Wanderers (overall wins 1)
1955: Chelsea (overall wins 1)
1956: Manchester United (overall wins 4)
1957: Manchester United (overall wins 5)
1958: Wolverhampton Wanderers (overall wins 2)
1959: Wolverhampton Wanderers (overall wins 3)

FA Cup Winners

1950: Arsenal (overall wins 3)
1951: Newcastle United (overall wins 4)
1952: Newcastle United (overall wins 5)
1953: Blackpool (overall wins 1)
1954: West Bromwich Albion (overall wins 4)
1955: Newcastle United (overall wins 6)
1956: Manchester City (overall wins 3)
1957: Aston Villa (overall wins 7)
1958: Bolton Wanderers (overall wins 4)
1959: Nottingham Forest (overall wins 2)

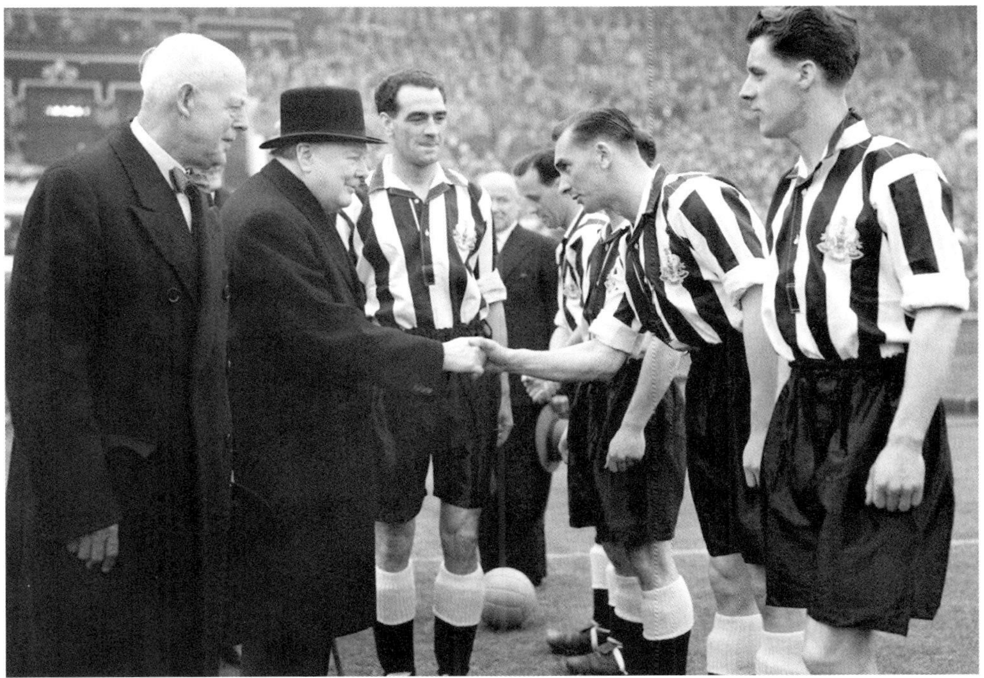

Wembley 1952
Newcastle captain Joe Harvey
introduces Winston Churchill to
Jackie Milburn.

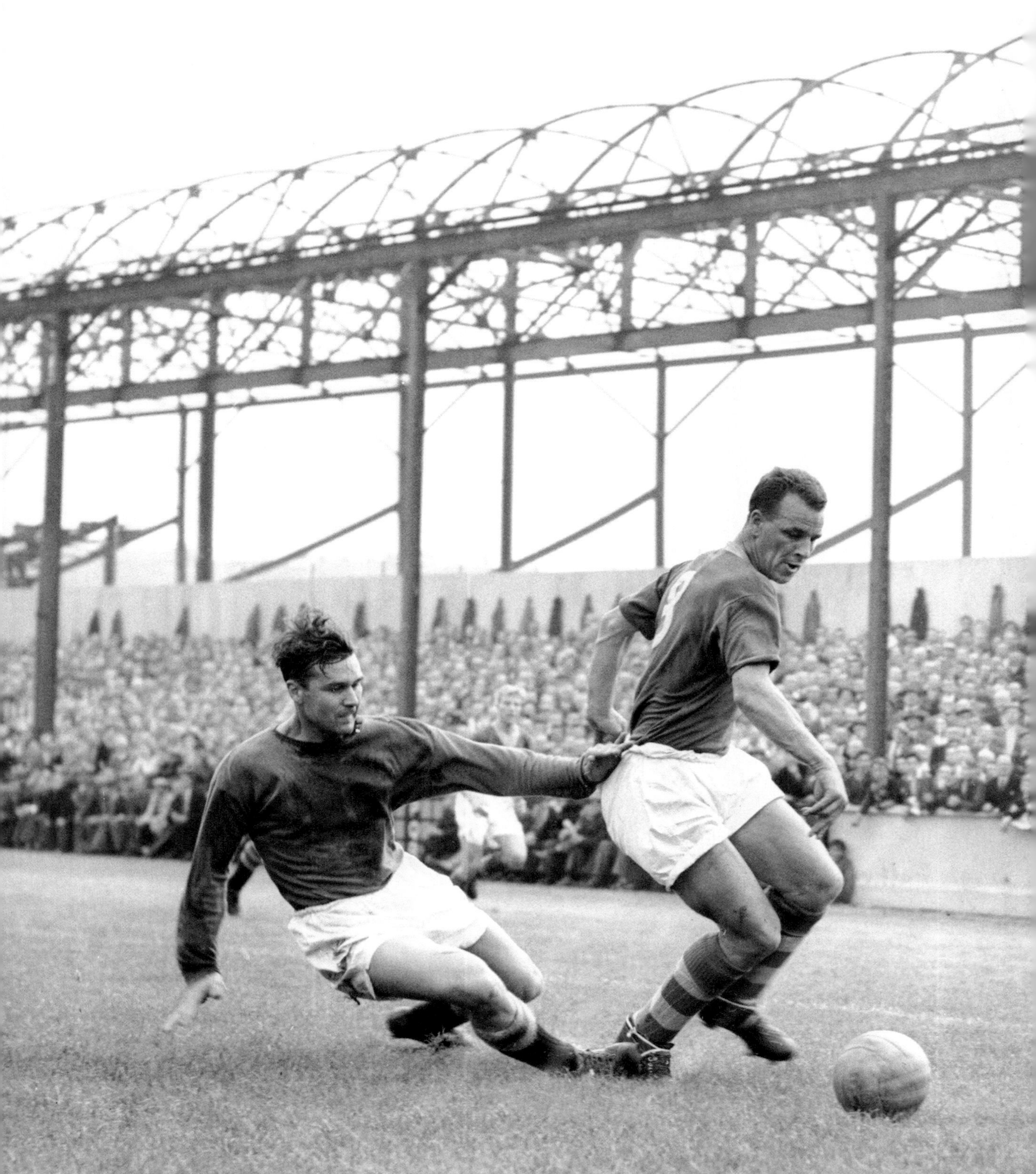

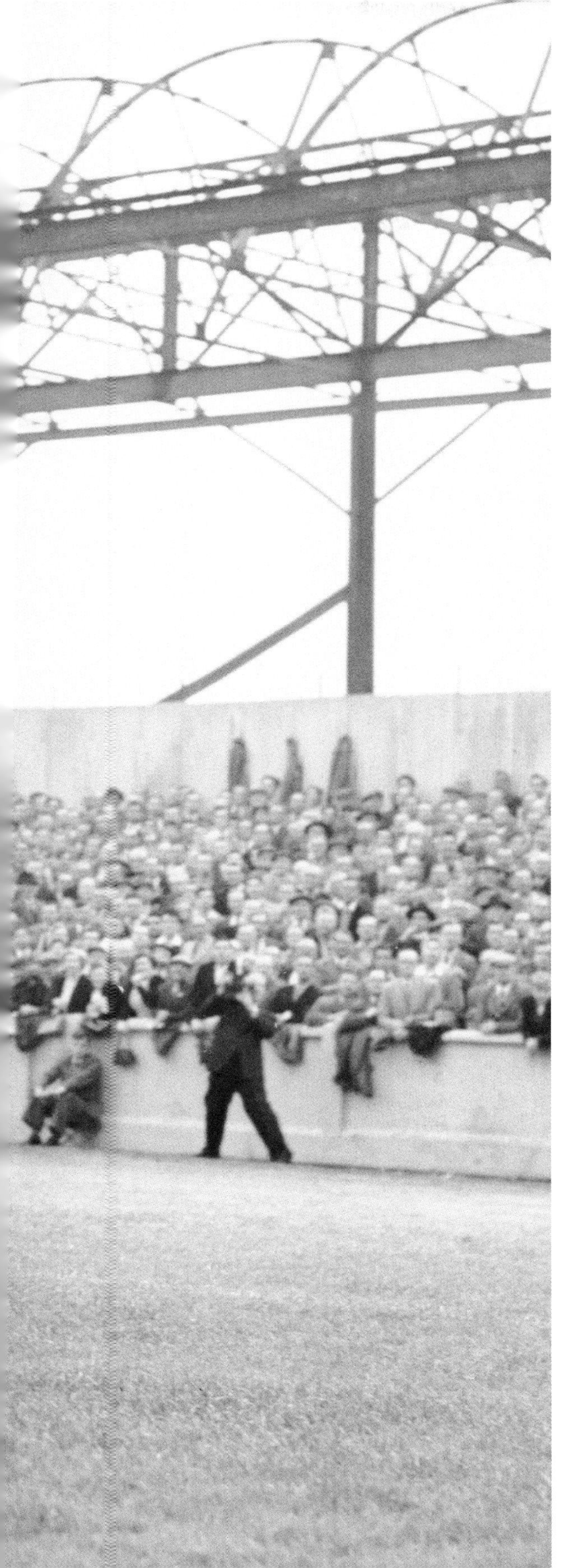

Elland Road 1956
With a makeshift stand in the background,
Leeds United's John Charles takes on the
Aston Villa defence in a 1-0 win.

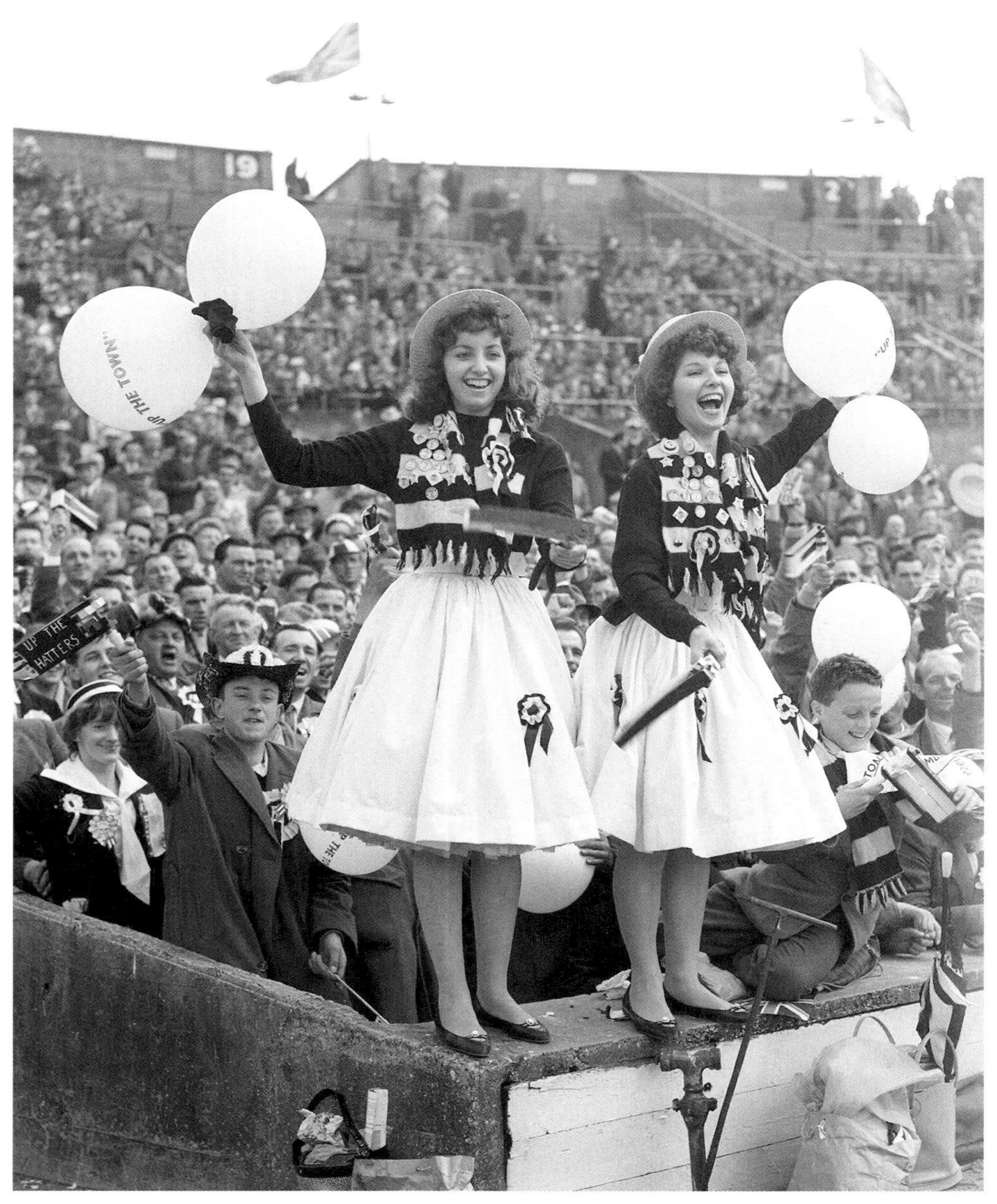

Wembley 1959
Hatters fans from Luton are at the
ground early for their team's one and
only FA Cup Final appearance.

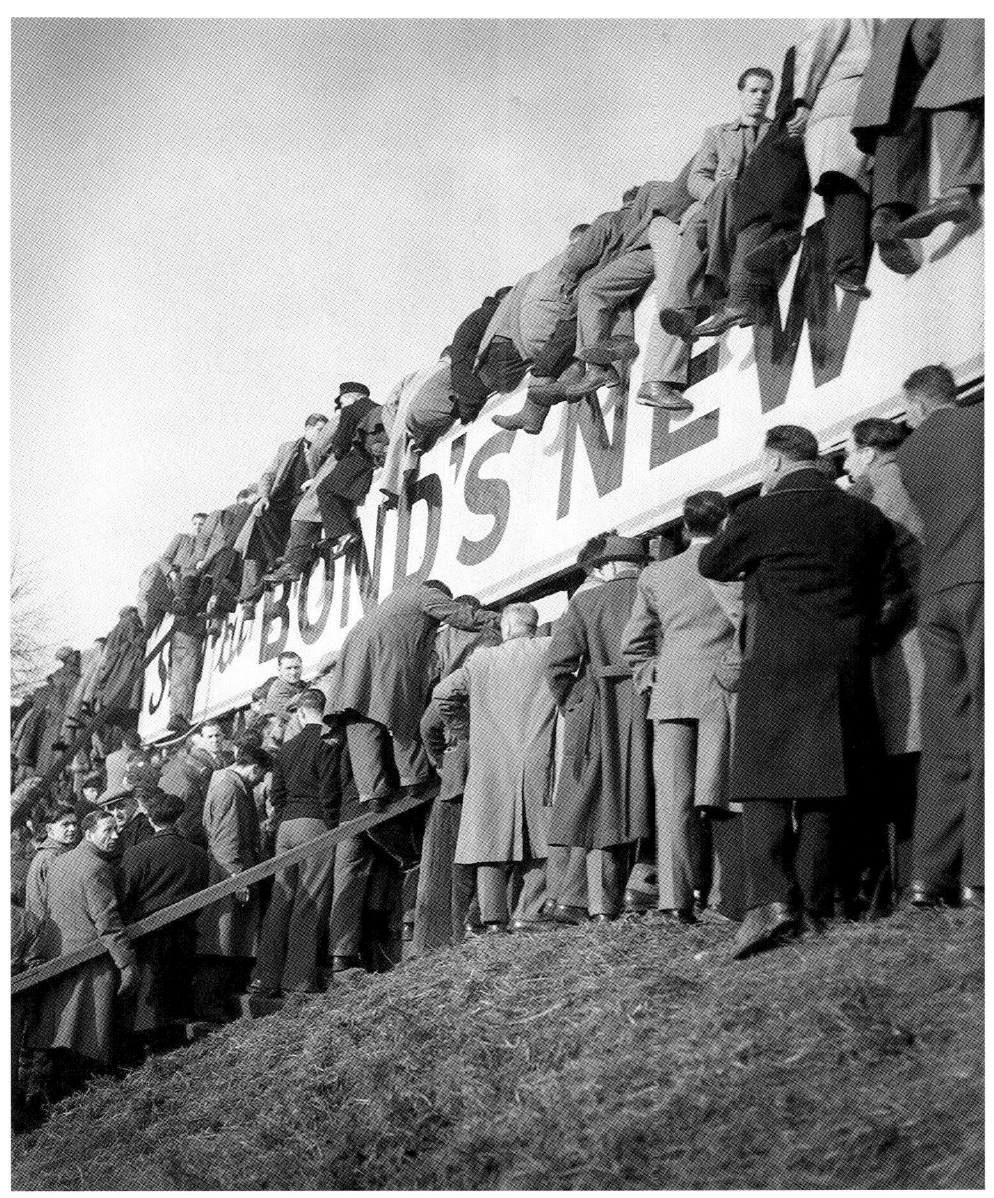

Carrow Road 1950
Fans of Division Three side Norwich City struggle
to get in the ground during their team's FA Cup
clash against English champions elect Portsmouth.

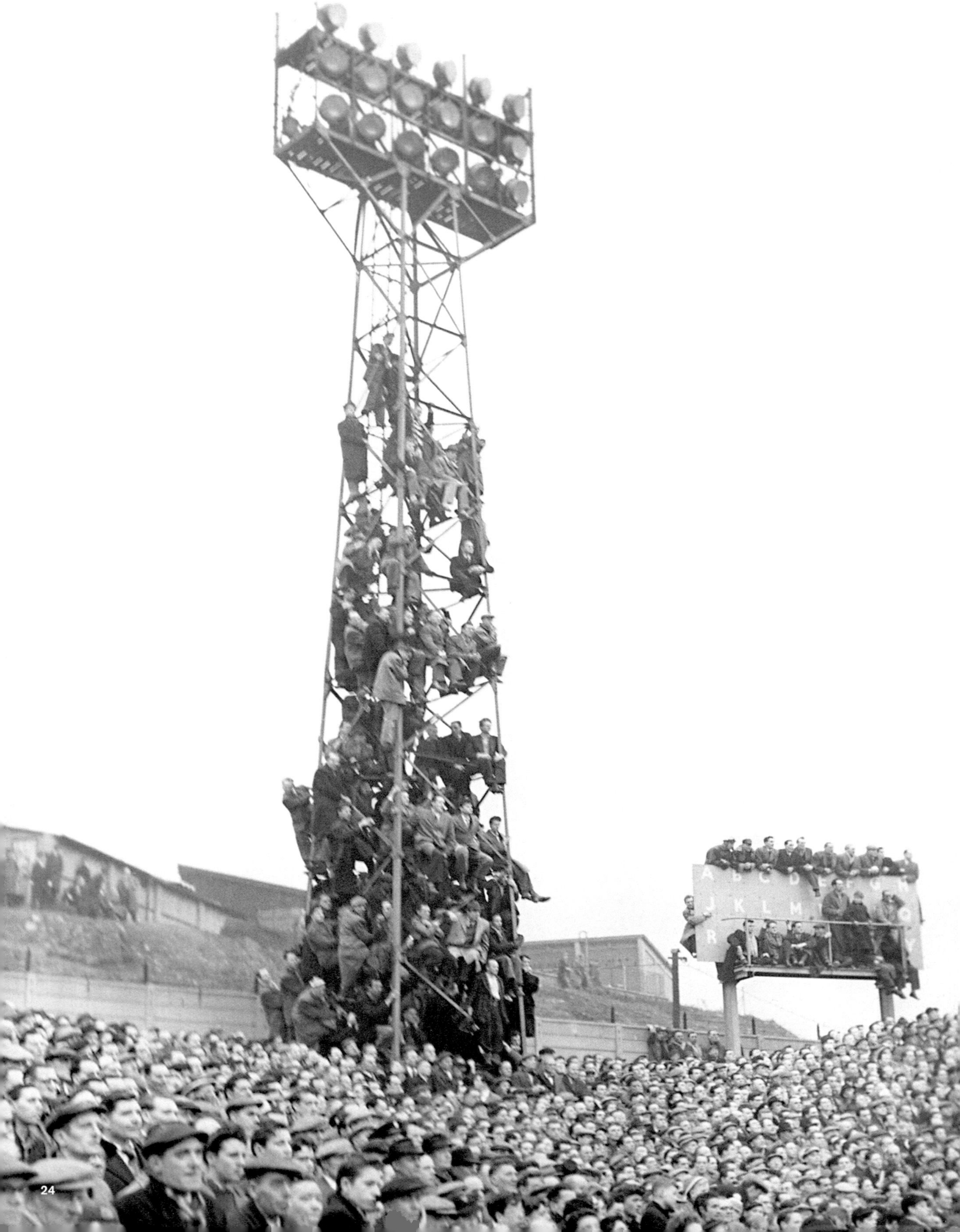
A B C D E F G H
J K L M N O
R

The Den 1957
Millwall fans get the best view in
the house for their side's FA Cup
tie with Newcastle.

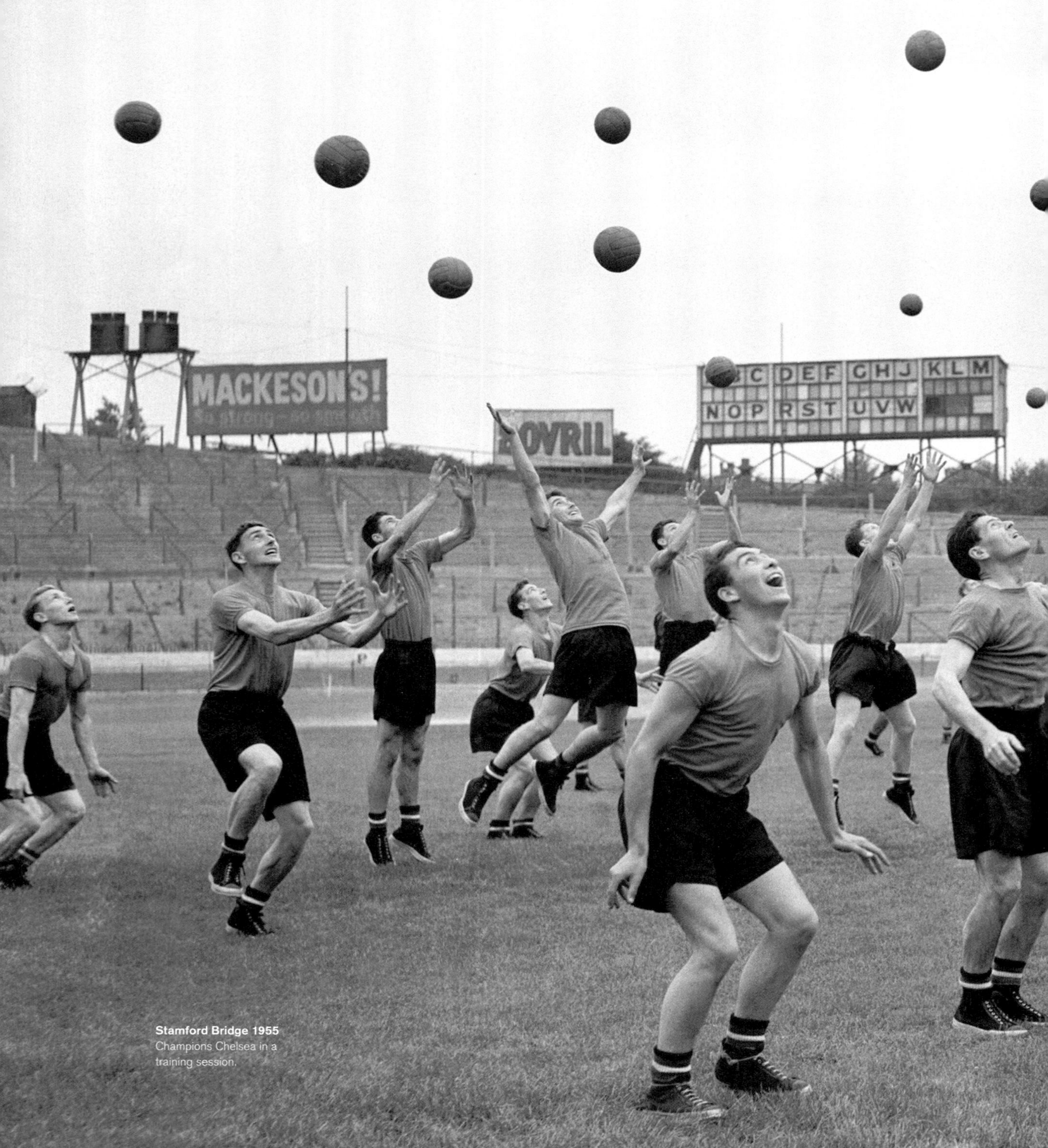

Stamford Bridge 1955
Champions Chelsea in a
training session.

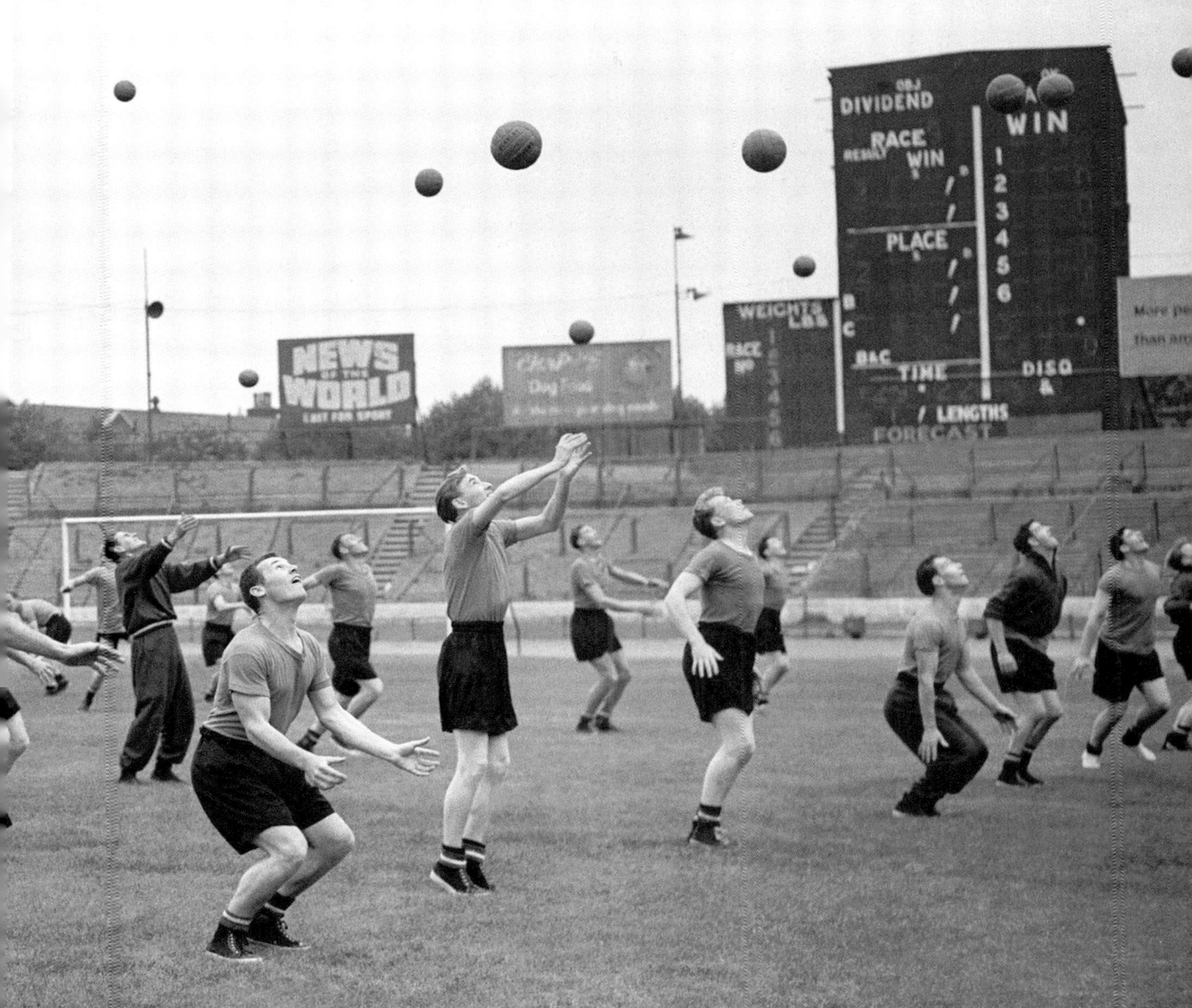

NEWS
OF THE
WORLD
BEST FOR SPORT
OBJ
DIVIDEND
RACE
RESULT
WIN
WIN
1
2
3
4
5
6
PLACE
WEIGHTS
LBS
TIME
DISQ
LENGTHS
FORECAST

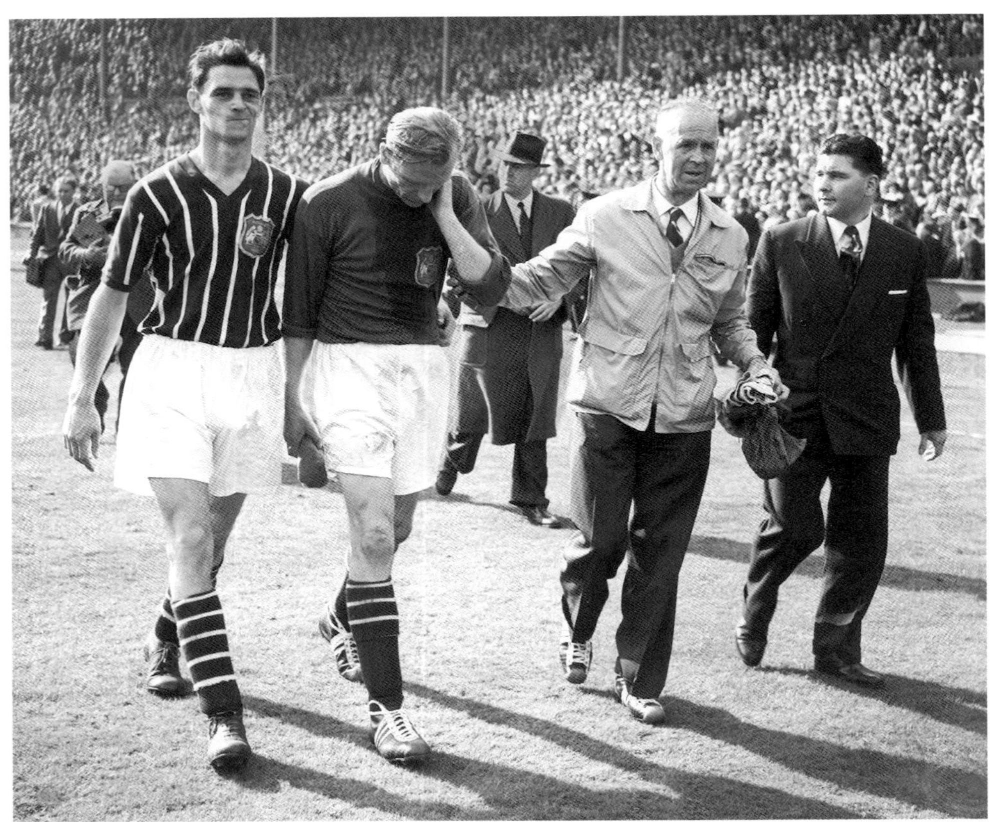

Wembley 1956
Manchester City goalkeeper
Bert Trautmann suffers a
broken neck during his side's
2-1 win over Birmingham City.

1953
Blackpool's victorious FA Cup winning
team parade the cup to the town, as they
are driven along the promenade with the
Blackpool Tower in the background.

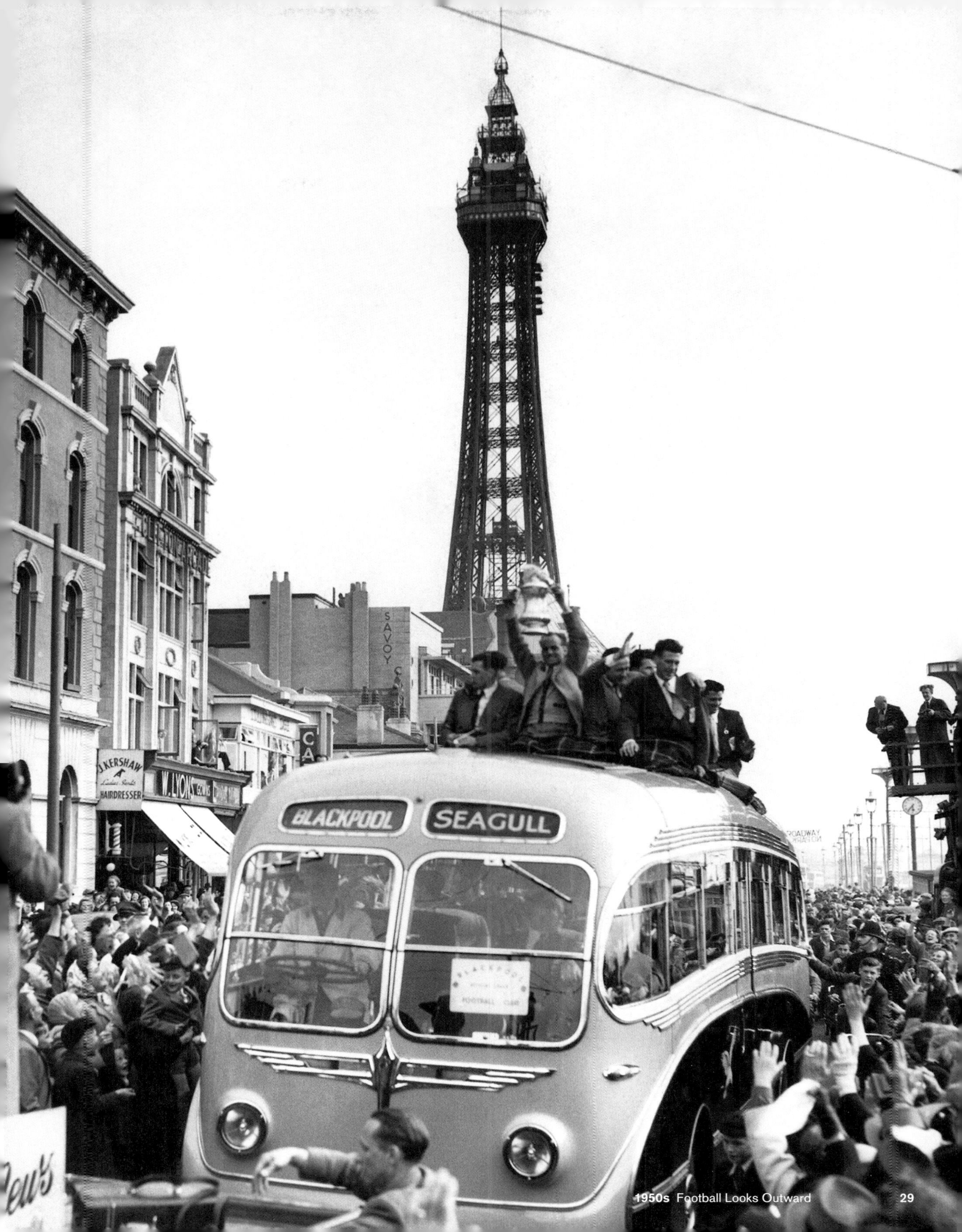

J KERSHAW
HAIRDRESSER
W. LYONS
SAVOY
BLACKPOOL SEAGULL
BLACKPOOL FOOTBALL CLUB

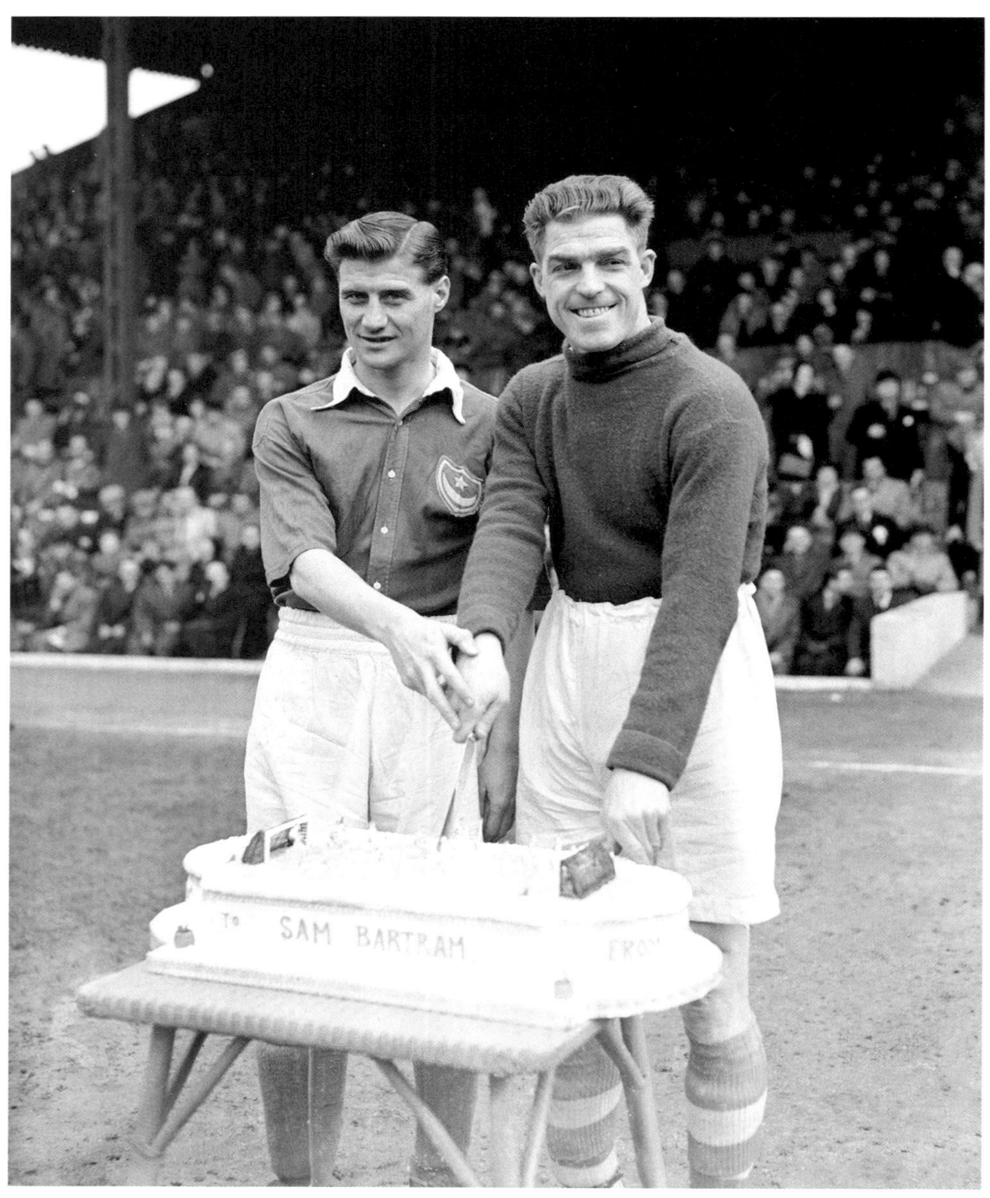

The Valley 1954
Goalkeeper Sam Bartram celebrates 500
appearances for Charlton with a cake
decorated as a football pitch. Next to him
is Portsmouth's Jimmy Dickinson.

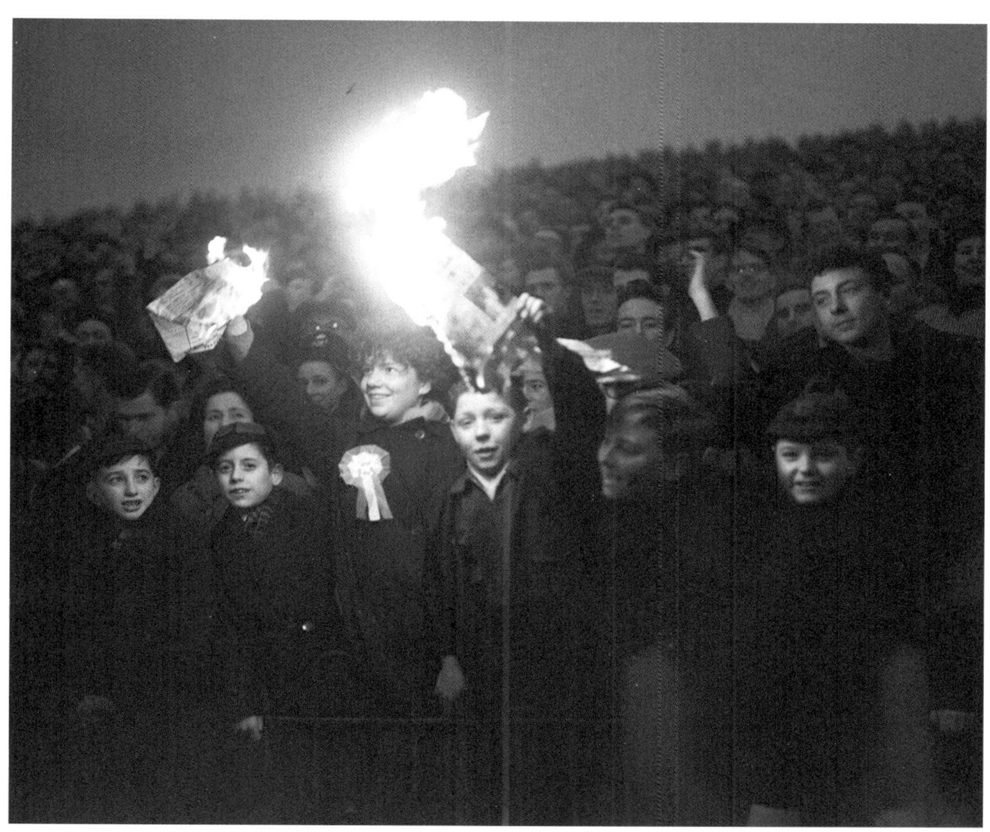

The Valley 1956
Young Charlton fans set fire to
newspaper in the days before
floodlights, as their side beats
Burton Albion 7-0.

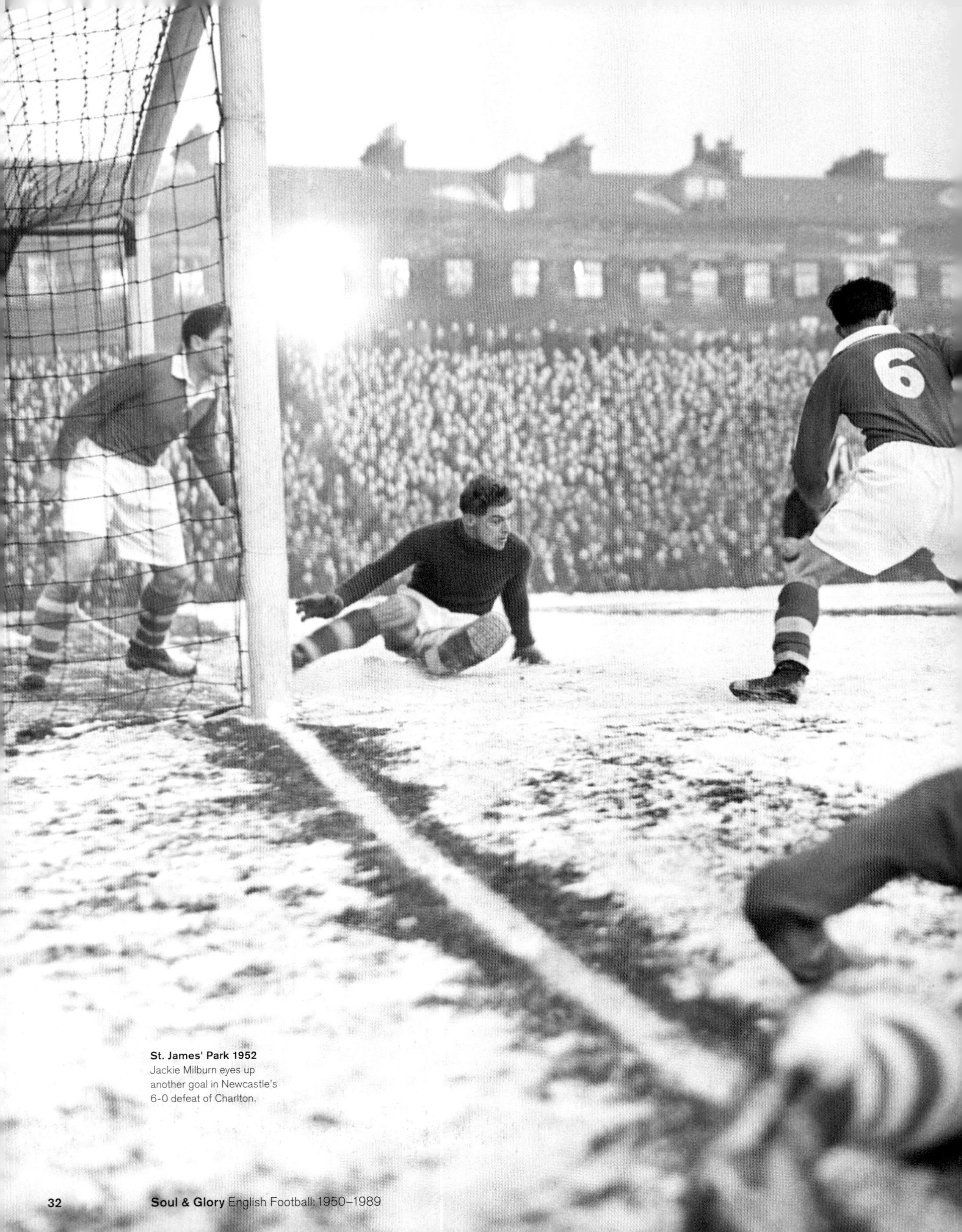

St. James' Park 1952
Jackie Milburn eyes up
another goal in Newcastle's
6-0 defeat of Charlton.

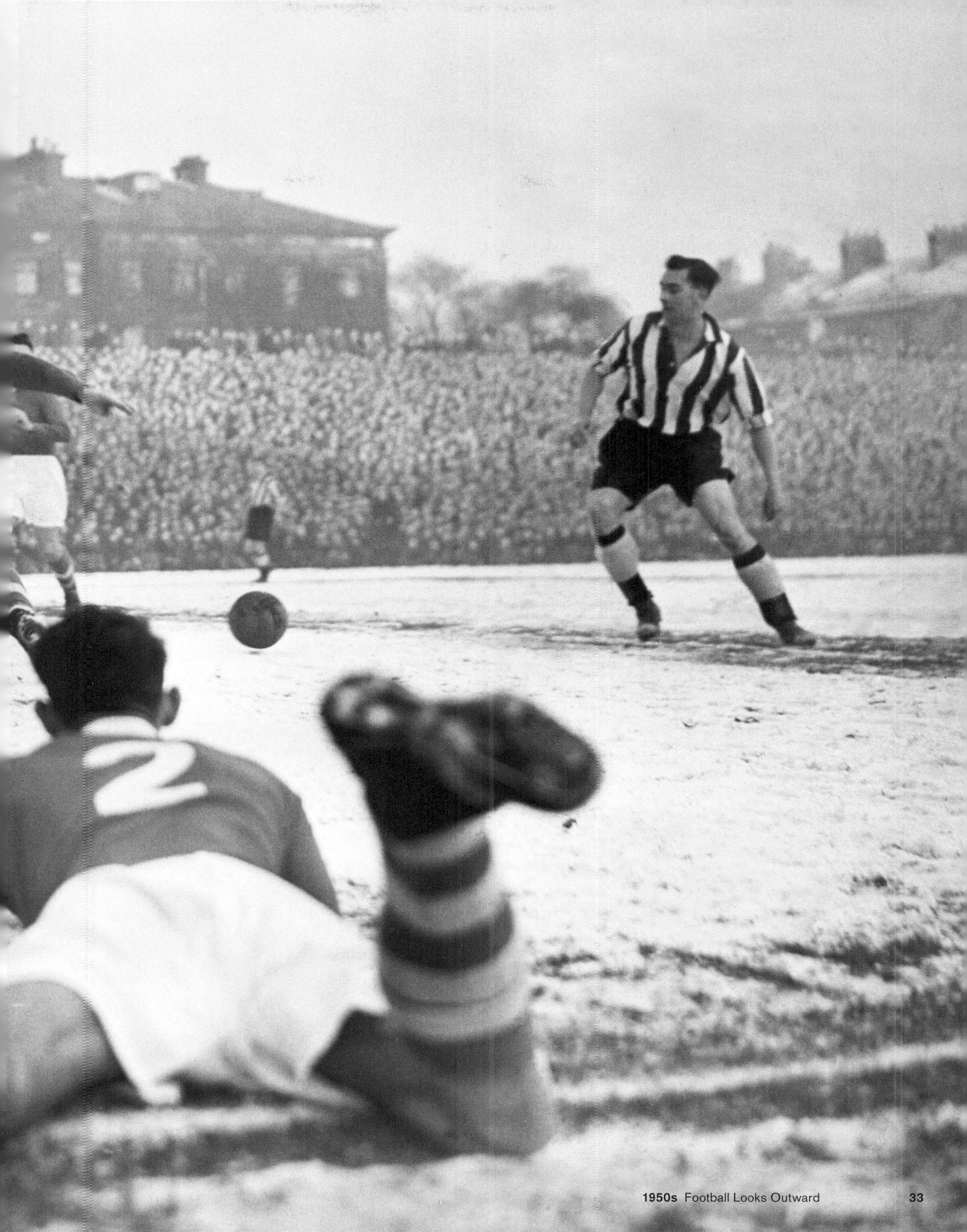

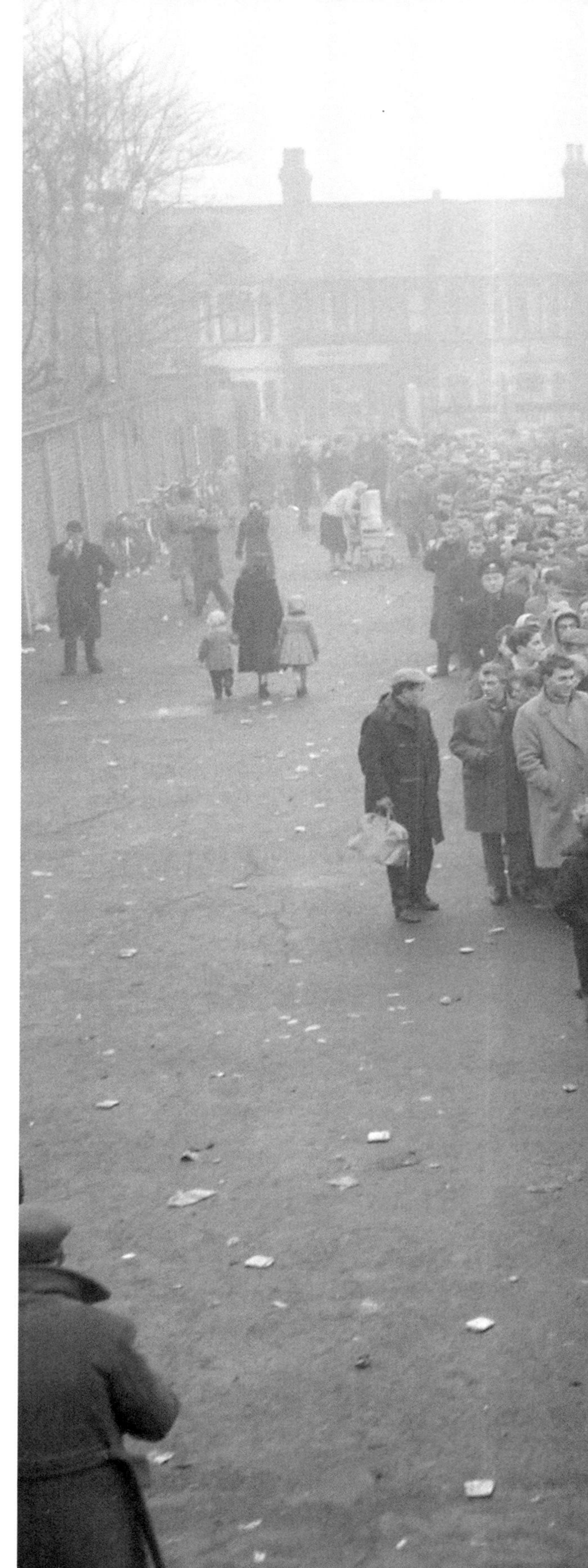

Upton Park 1958
West Ham fans queue up to
get tickets for their FA Cup
clash against Fulham.

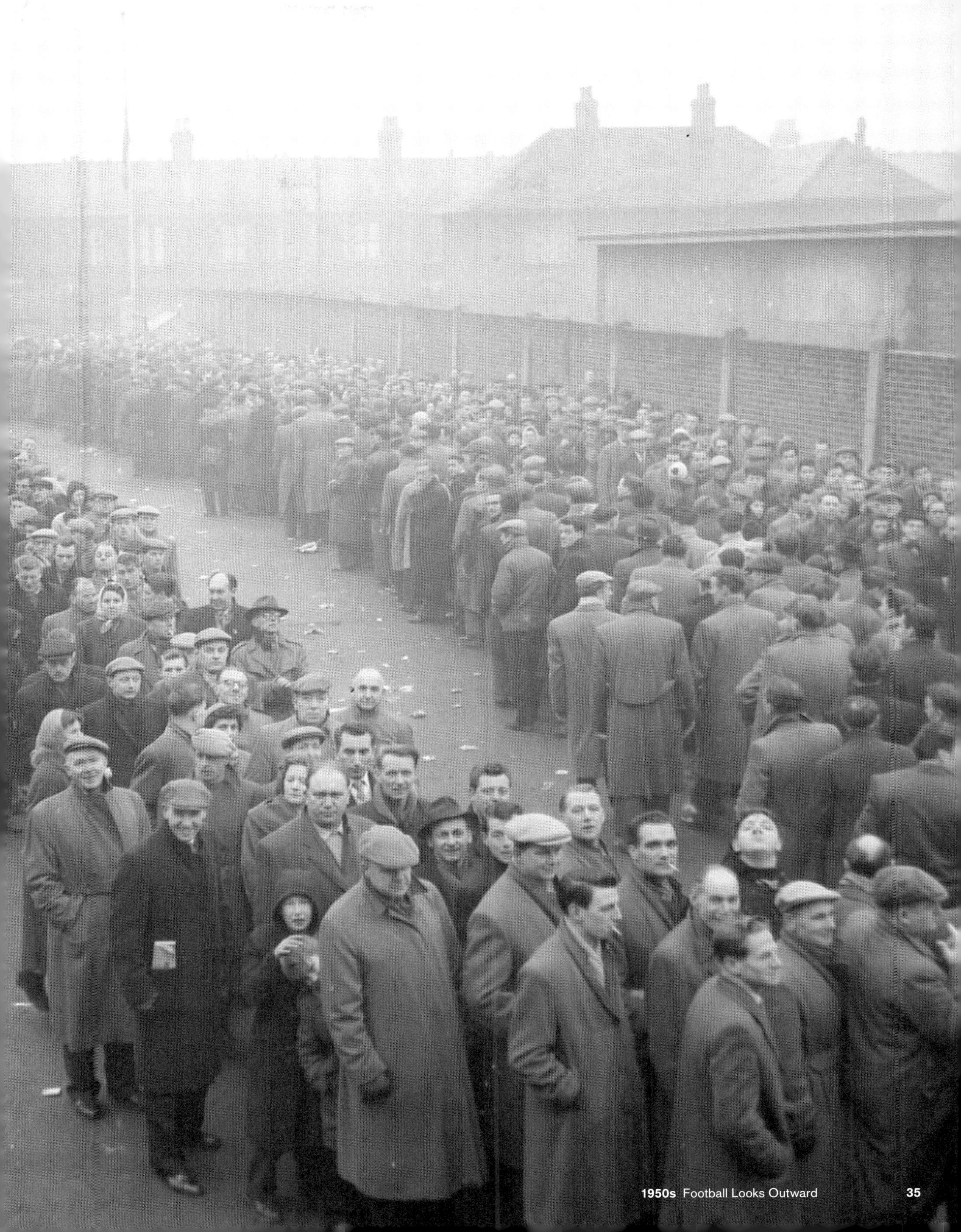

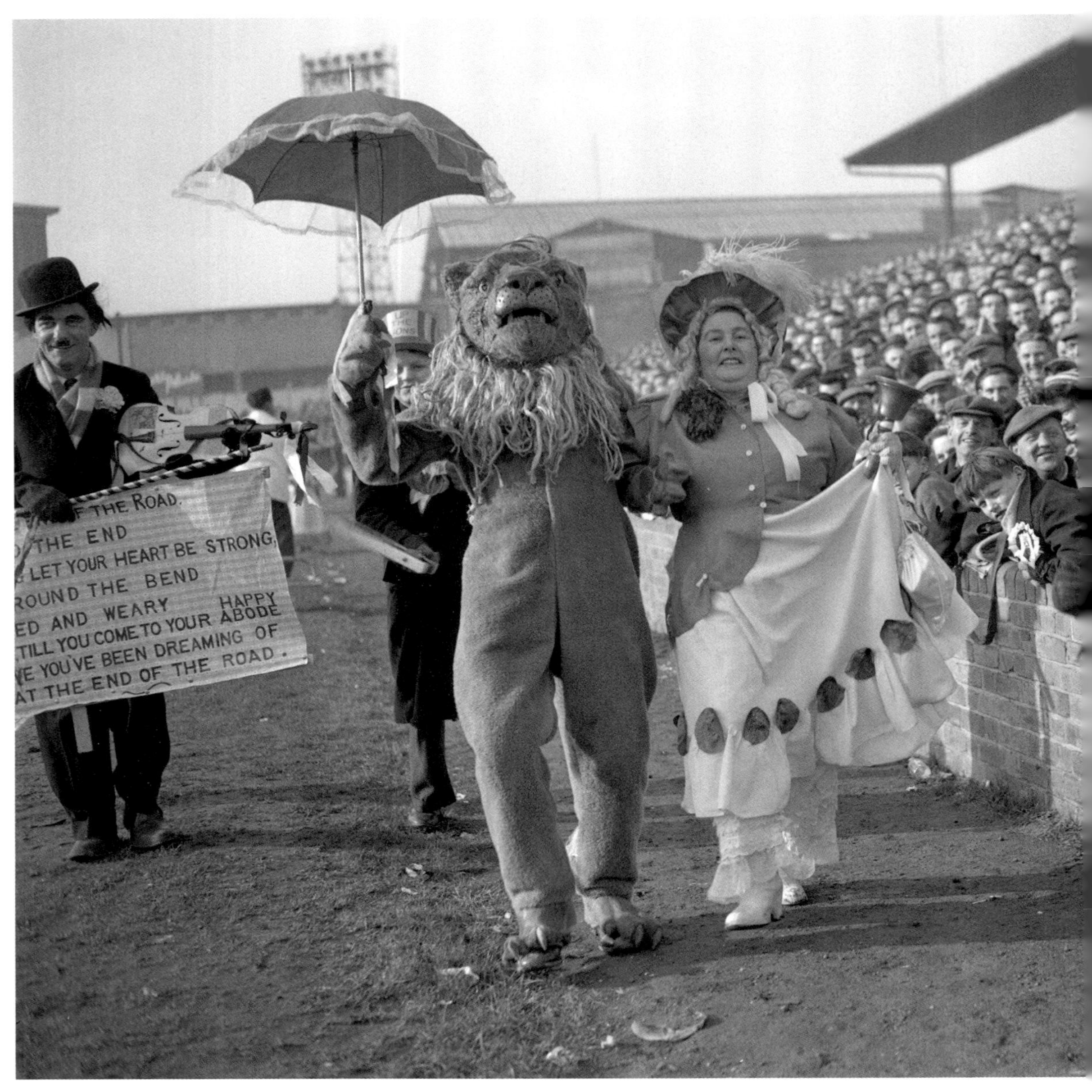

The Den 1957
In 50s football, cheerleaders and mascots would help get the
crowds going before matches. Here, Millwall's Zampa the Lion
and Birmingham's Gainsborough Lady are getting on swimmingly.
To the left, the violin-playing Charlie Chaplin was also one of
Birmingham's mascots.

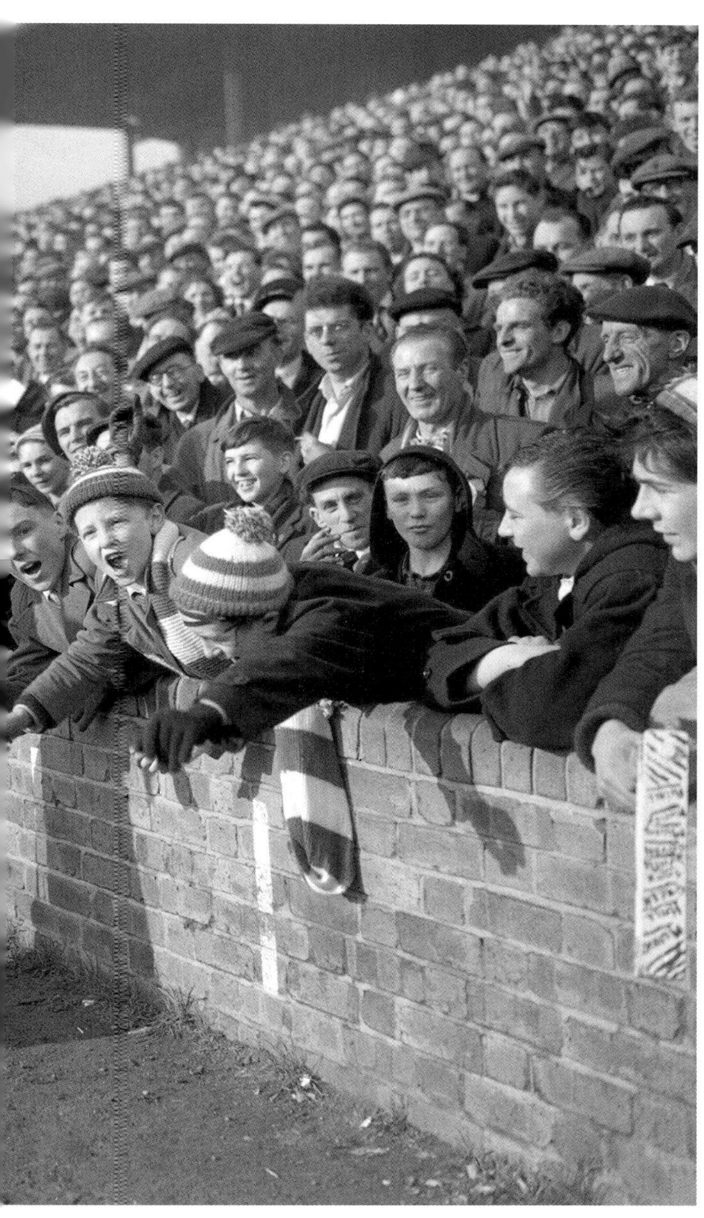

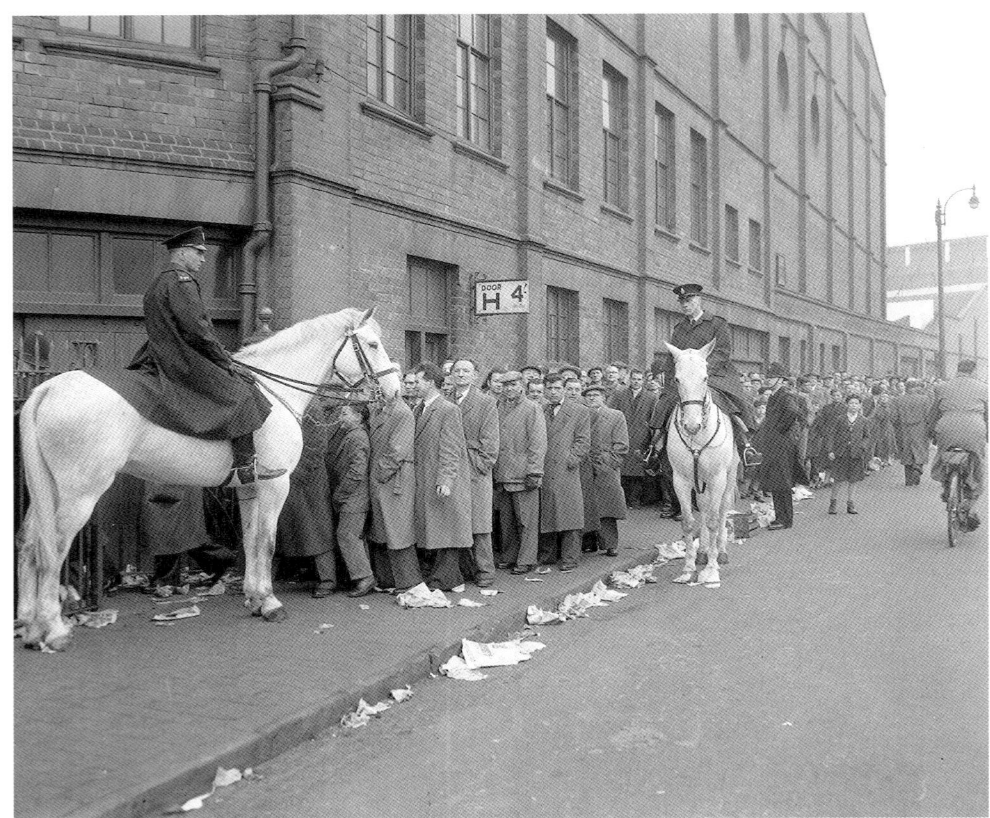

St Andrew's 1957
Fans of Birmingham City queue for tickets for their FA Cup tie against Manchester United.

Goodison Park 1958
Everton's Dave Hickson in mid air during a 6-1 defeat to Arsenal.

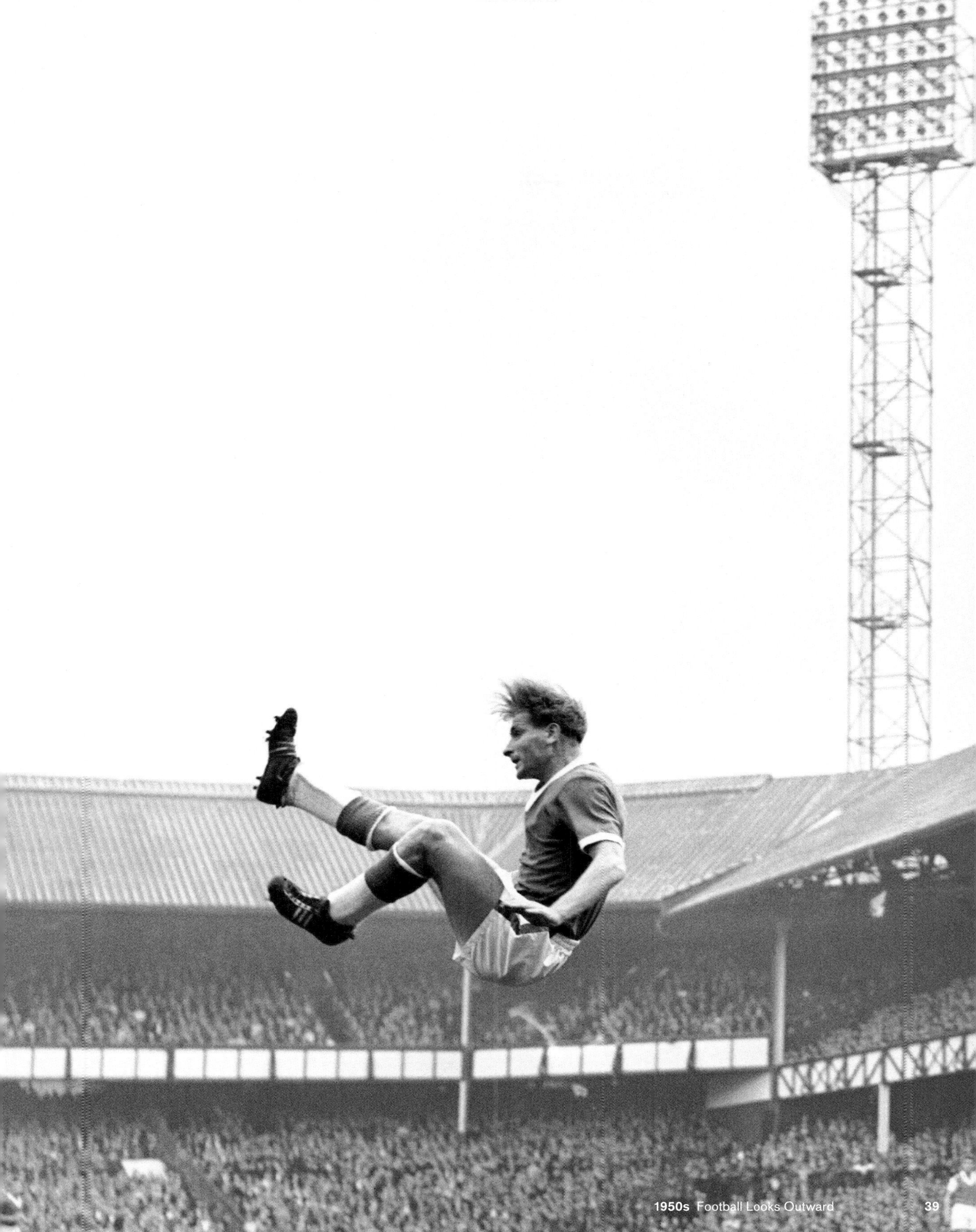

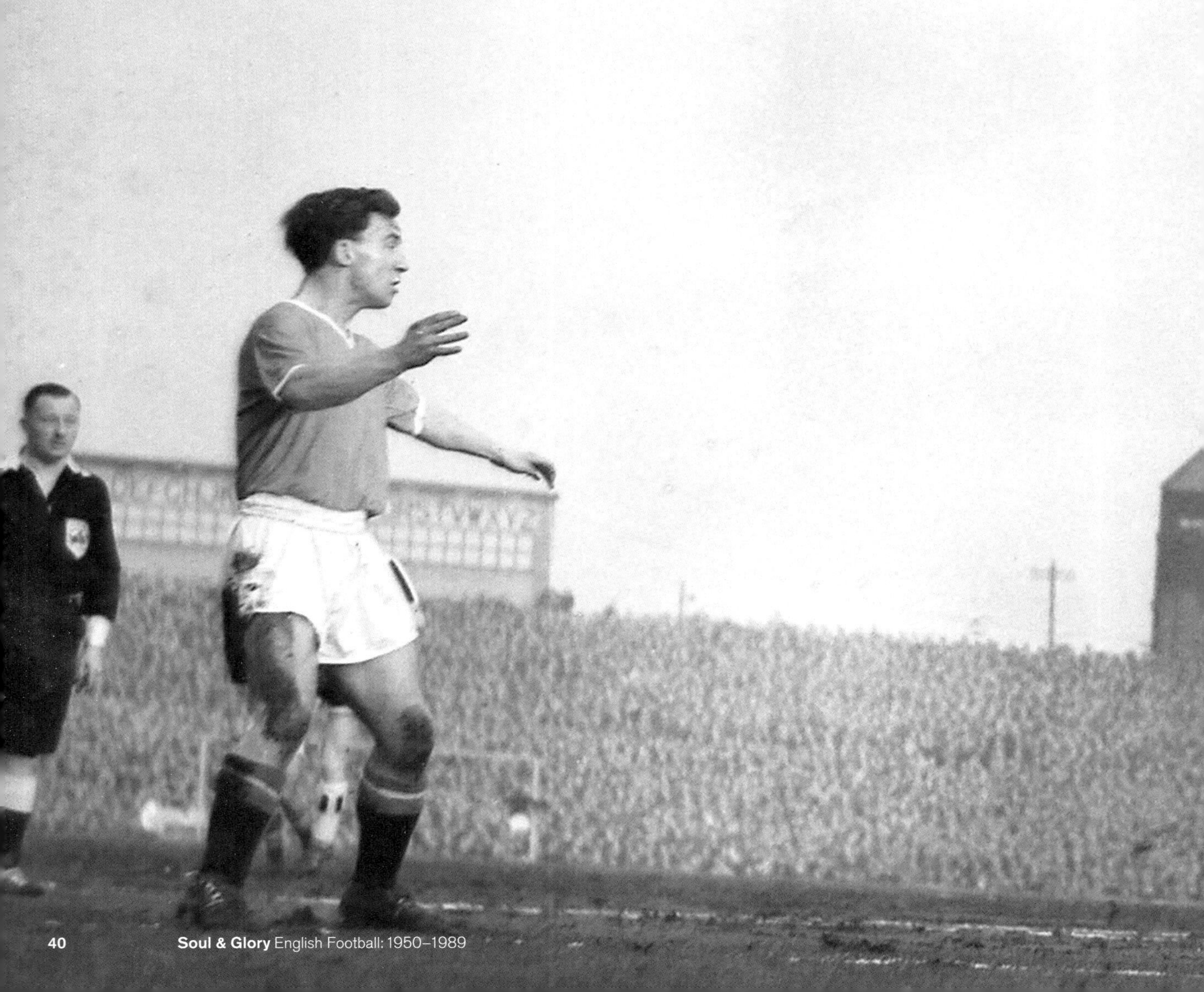

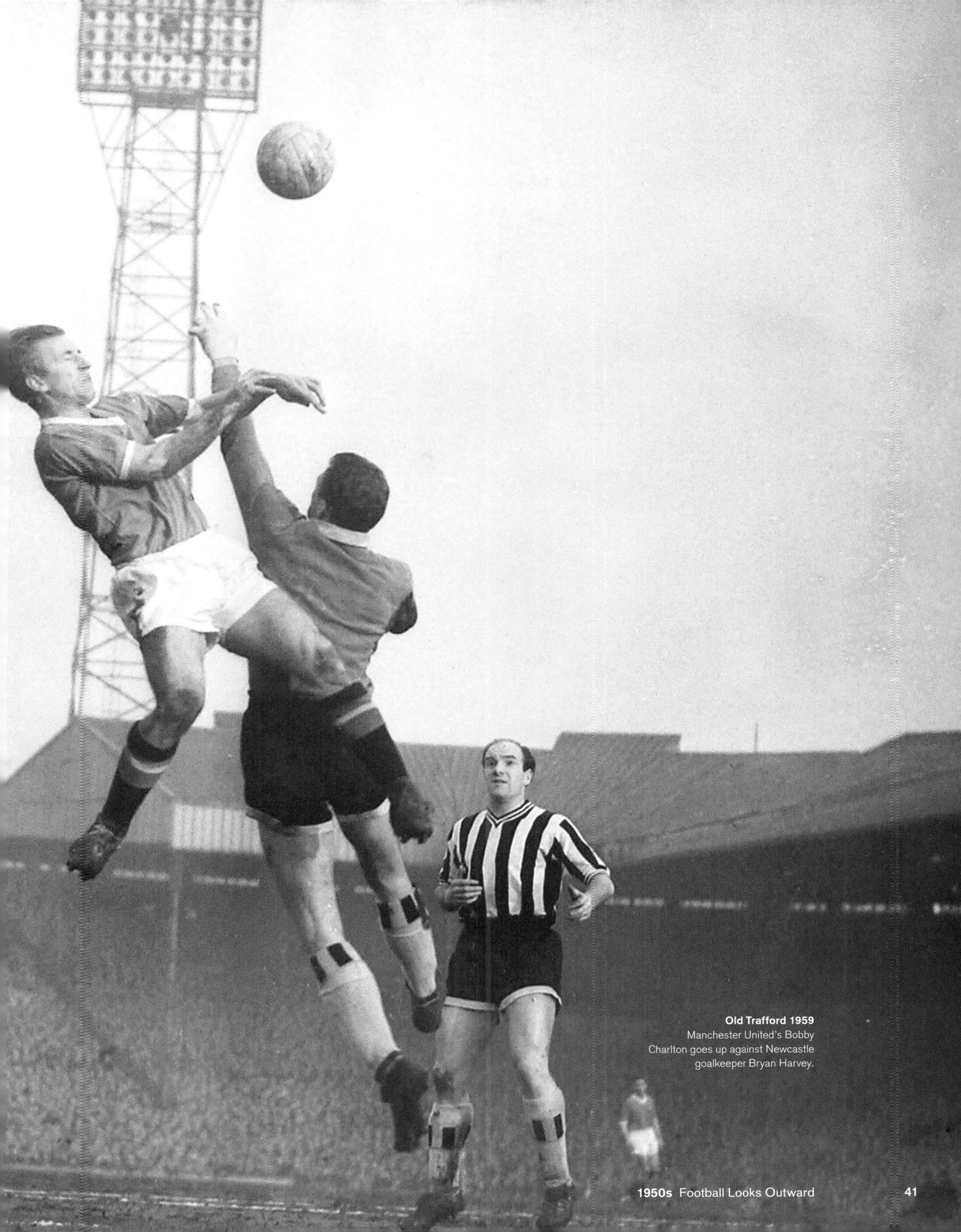

Old Trafford 1959
Manchester United's Bobby
Charlton goes up against Newcastle
goalkeeper Bryan Harvey.

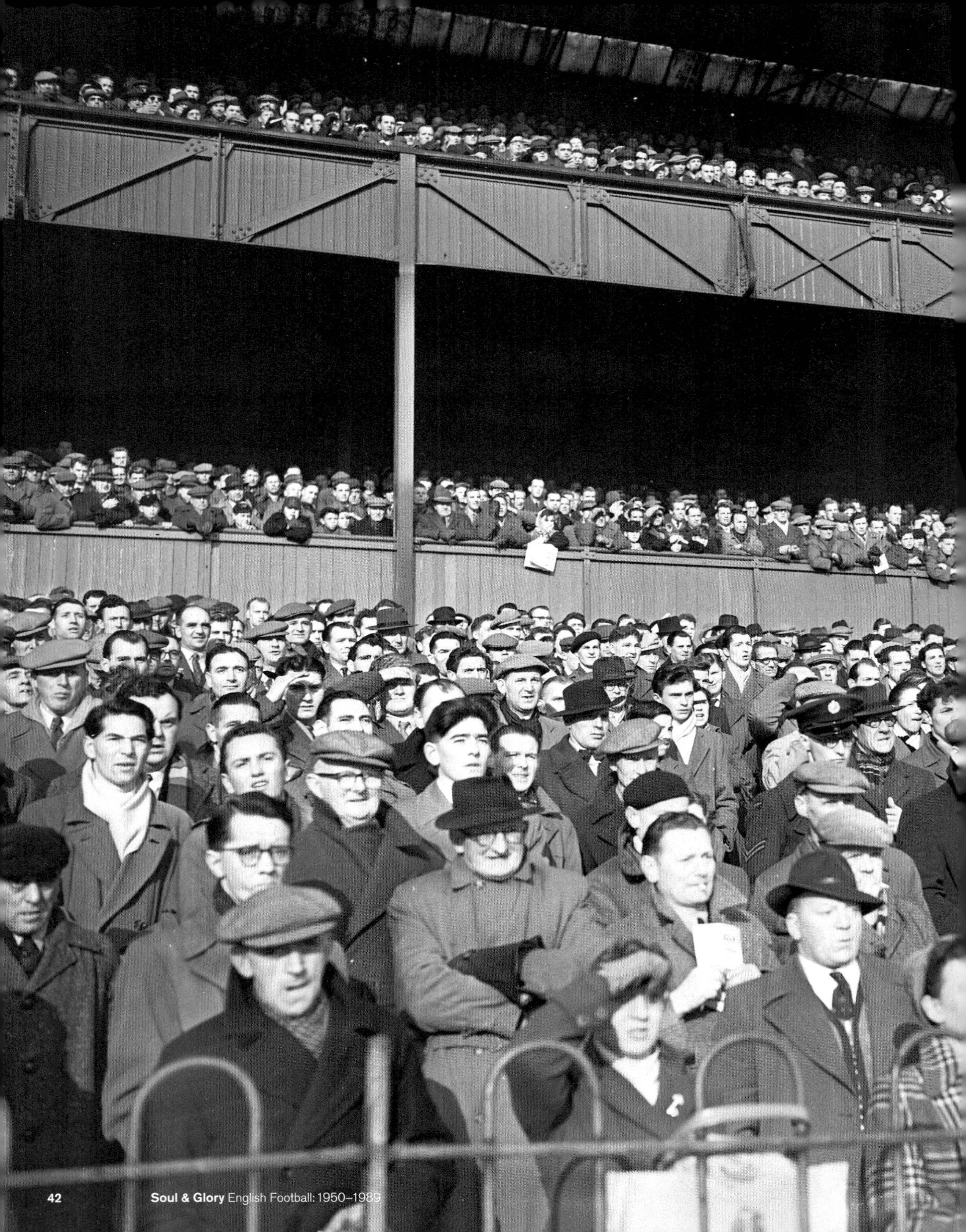

 Soul & Glory English Football: 1950–1989

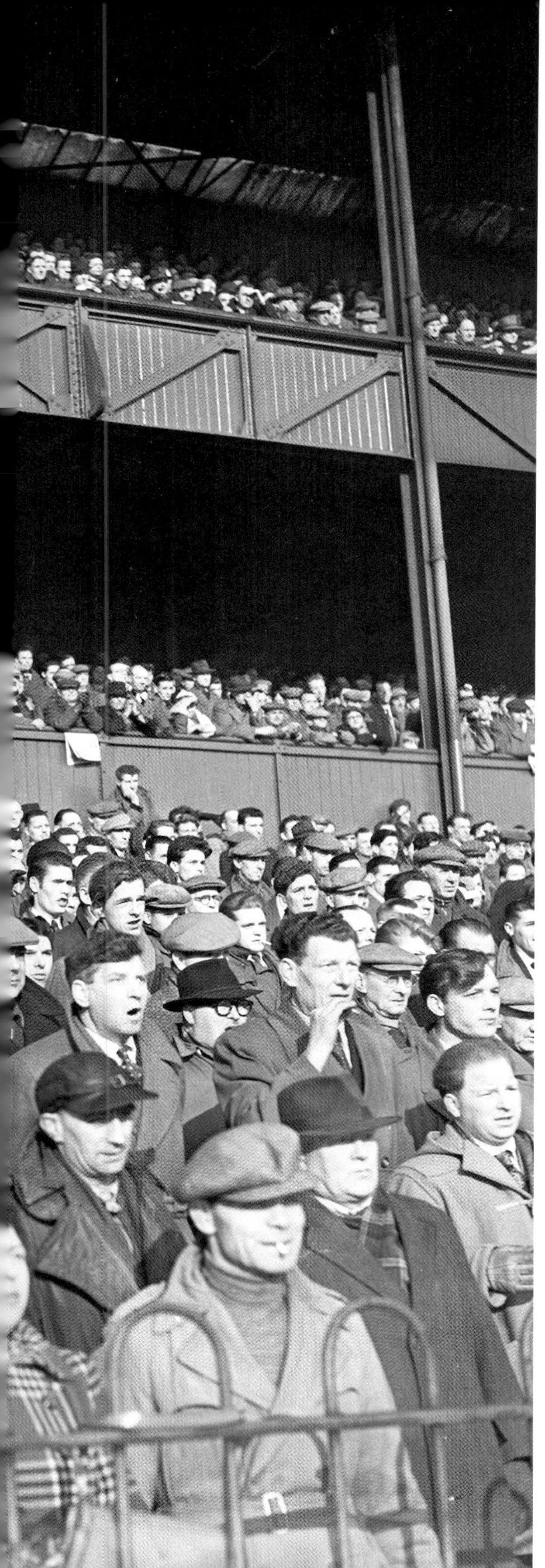

Baseball Ground 1955
Derby County fans watch
on from the three-tiered
Osmaston End.

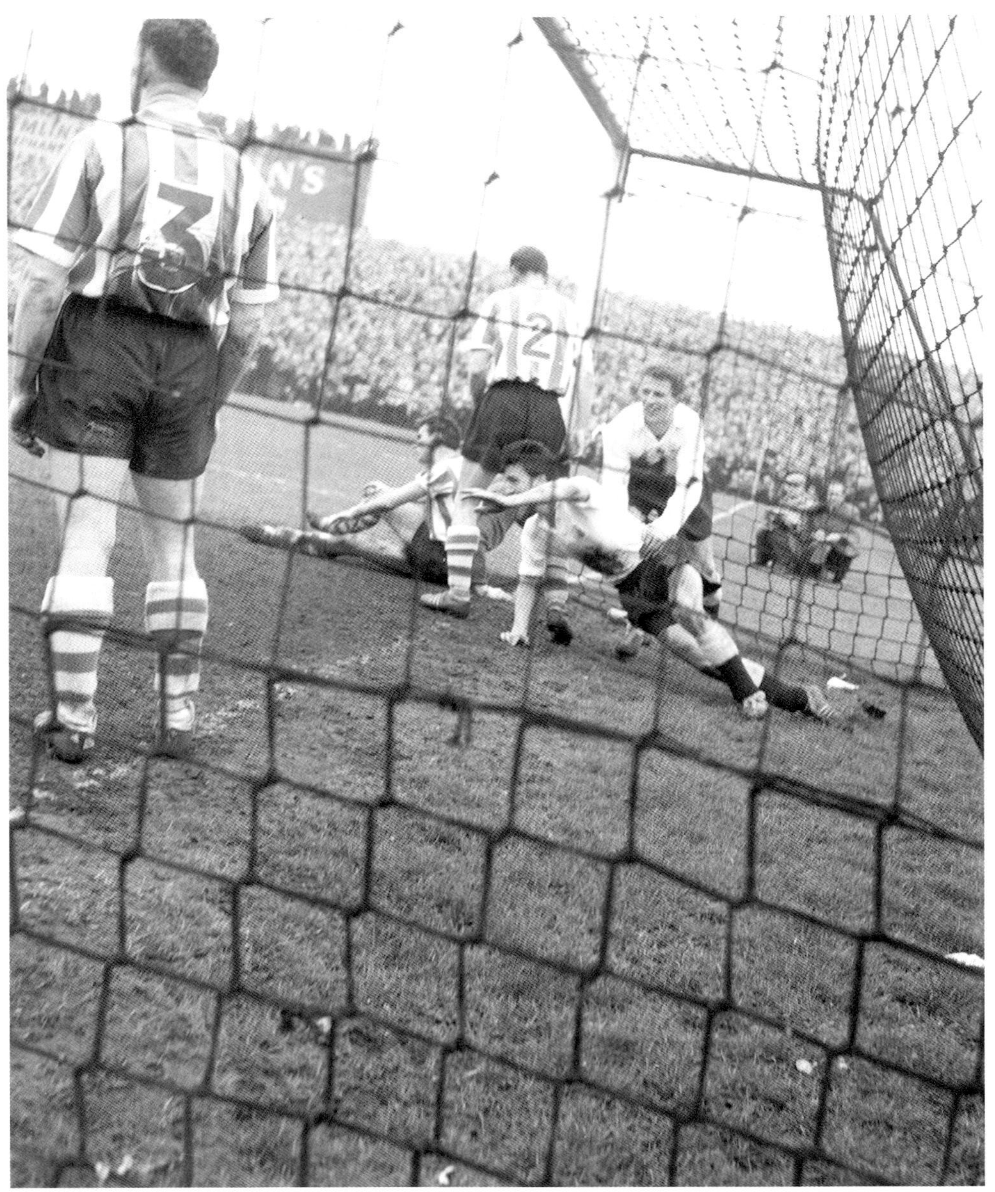

Craven Cottage 1959
Fulham's Jimmy Hill scores his hat-trick as
the Cottagers beat Sheffield Wednesday
6-2. Notice in the background the fans on
the advertising boards.

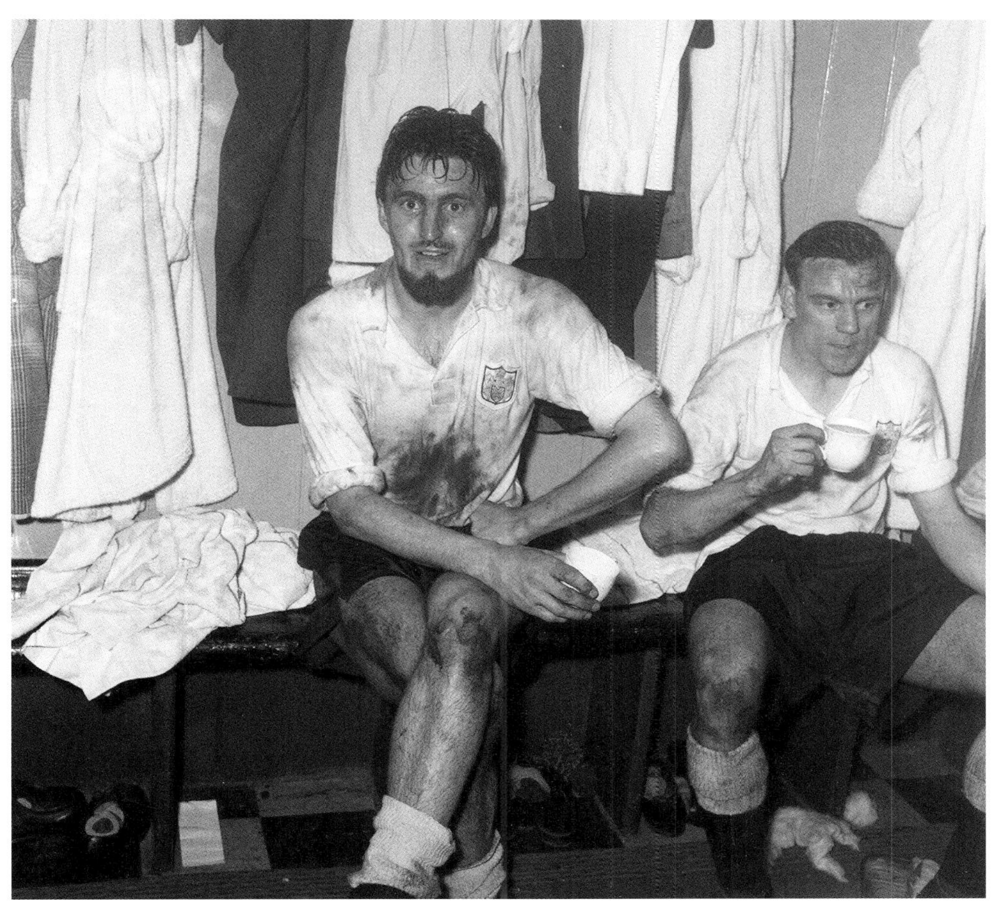

Craven Cottage 1959
After the 6-2 drubbing of
Wednesday, the hat-trick hero
celebrates with a cup of tea.

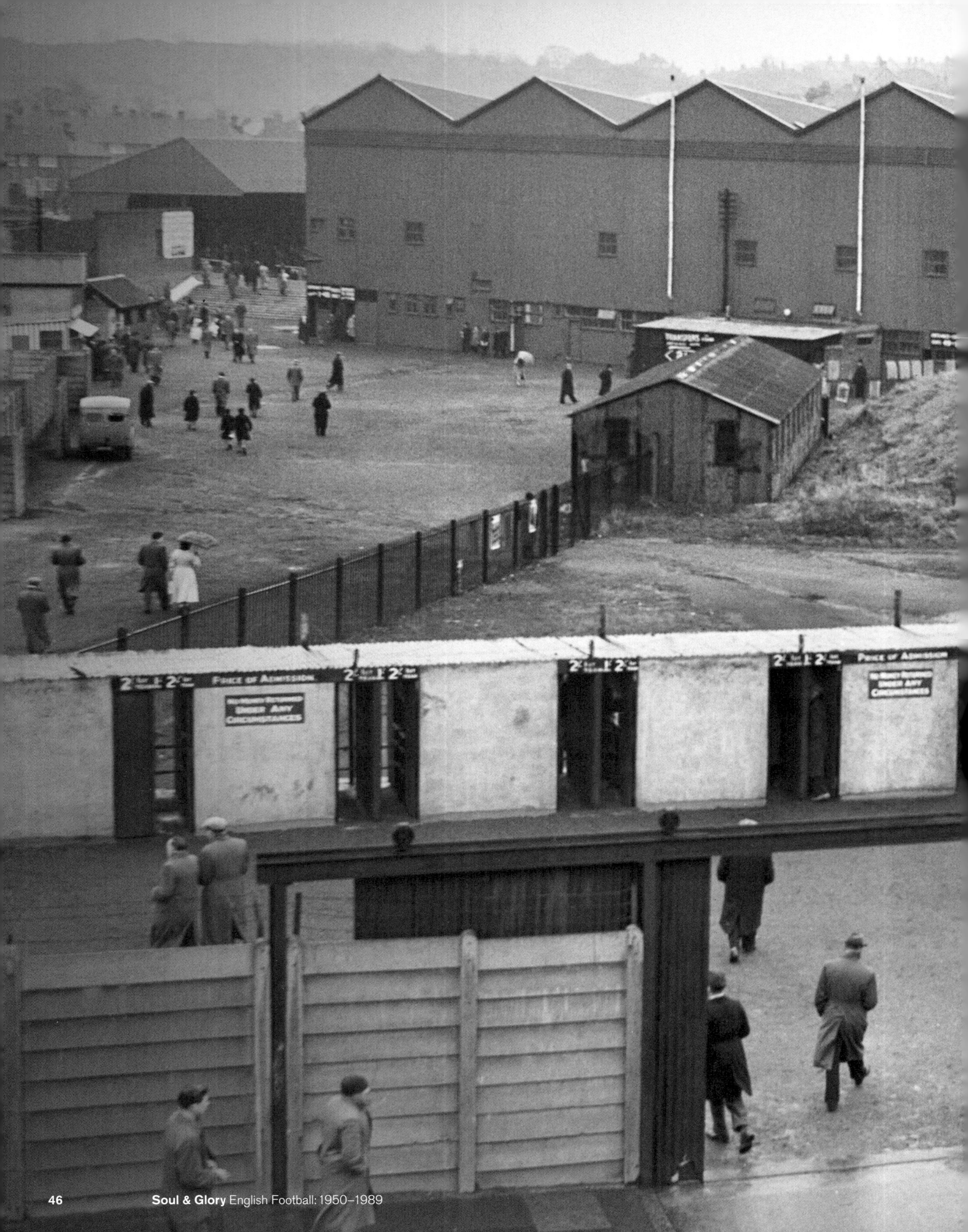
PRICE OF ADMISSION
2/- 1/2/-
NO MONEY RETURNED UNDER ANY CIRCUMSTANCES
PRICE OF ADMISSION
2/- 1/2/-
NO MONEY RETURNED UNDER ANY CIRCUMSTANCES

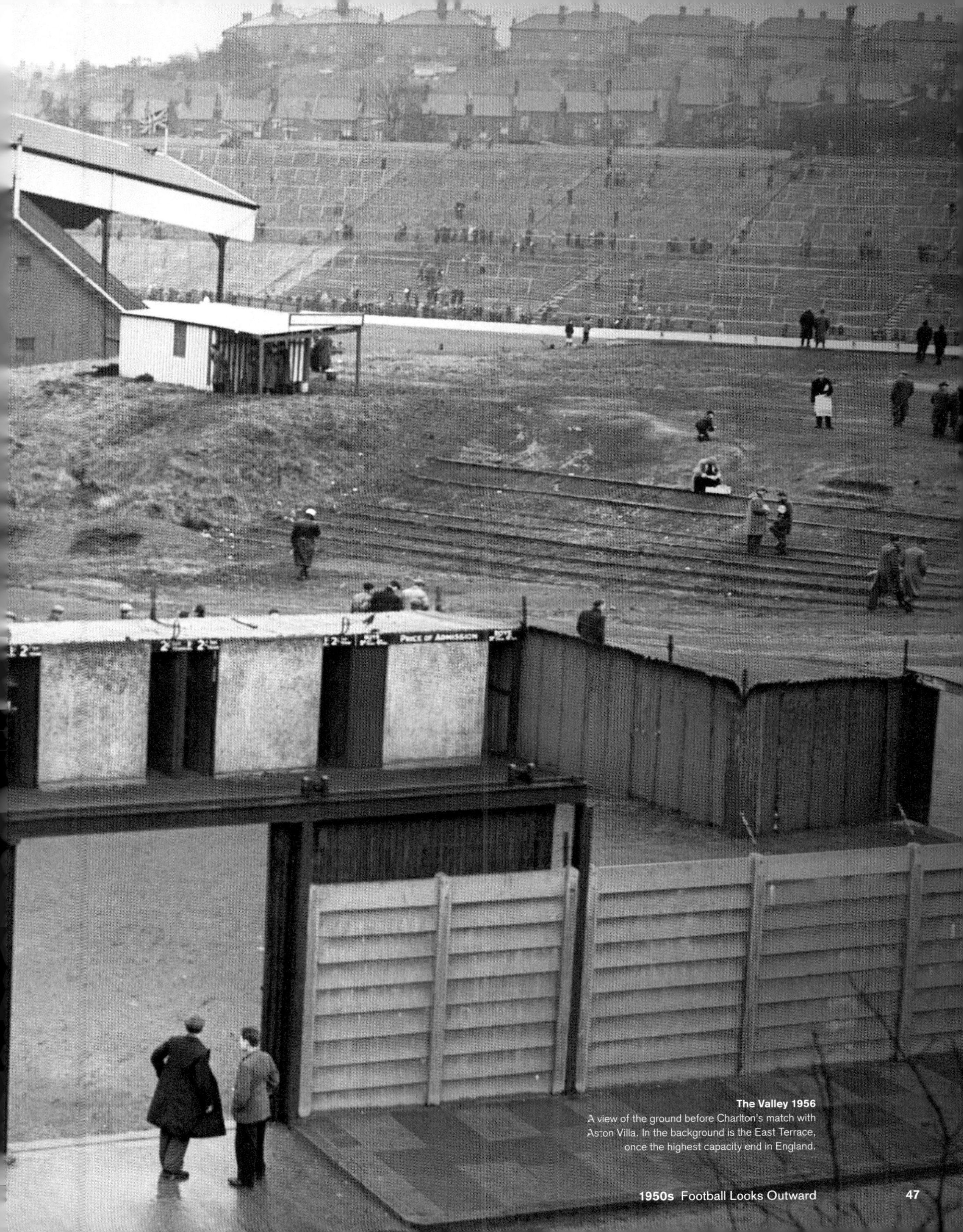

The Valley 1956
A view of the ground before Charlton's match with
Aston Villa. In the background is the East Terrace,
once the highest capacity end in England.

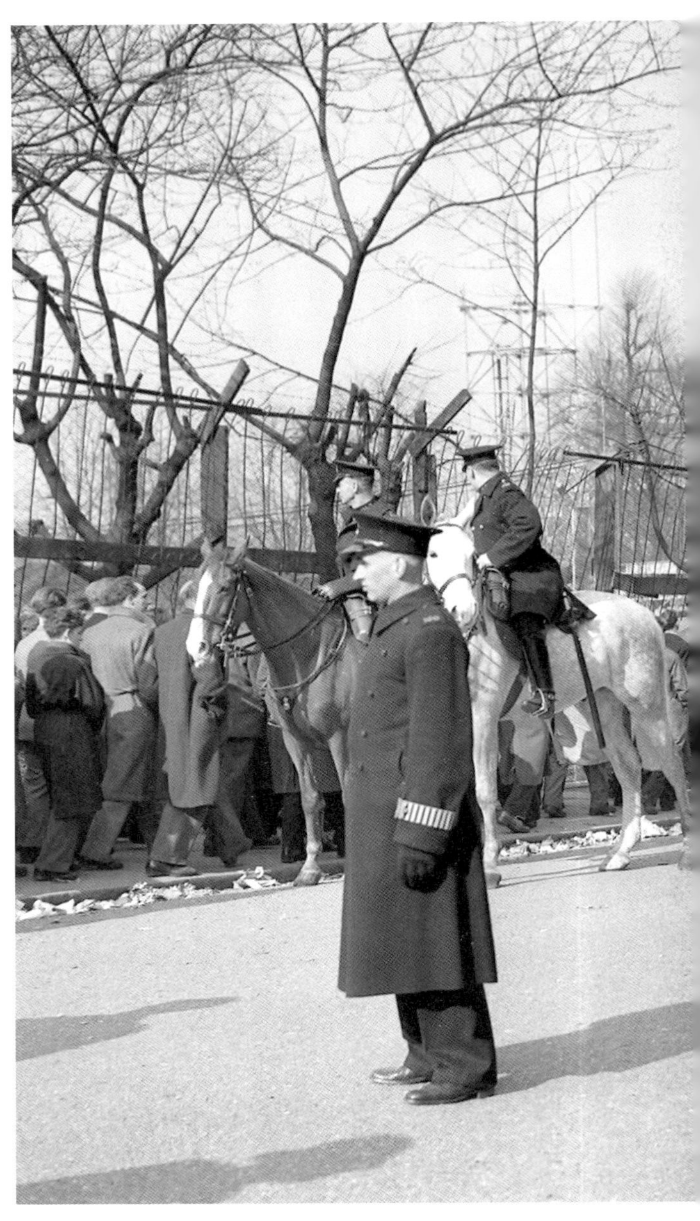

Highbury 1950
Arsenal fans queue all the way up the hill,
in order to get FA Cup semi-final tickets,
with the stadium in the background.

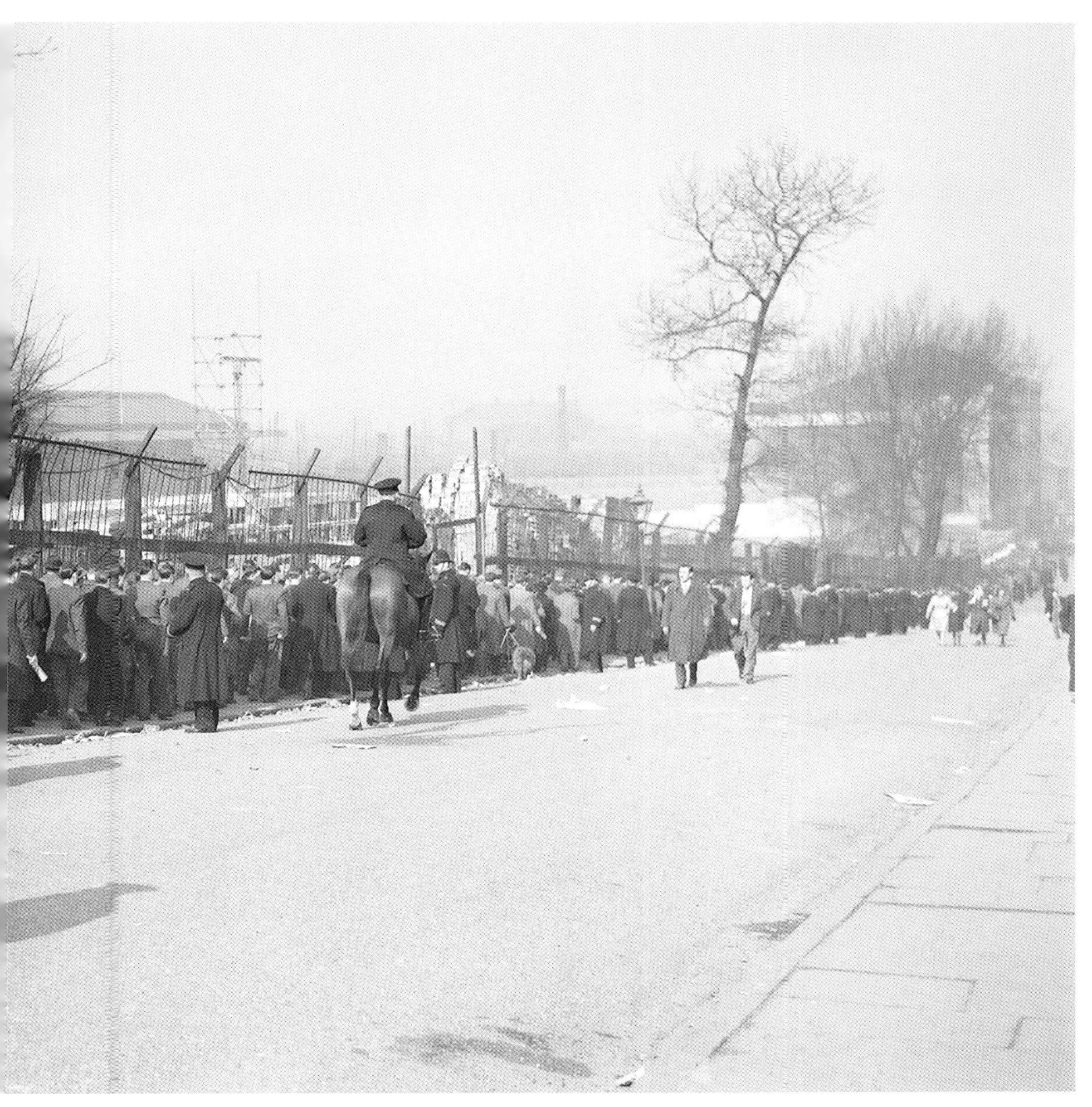

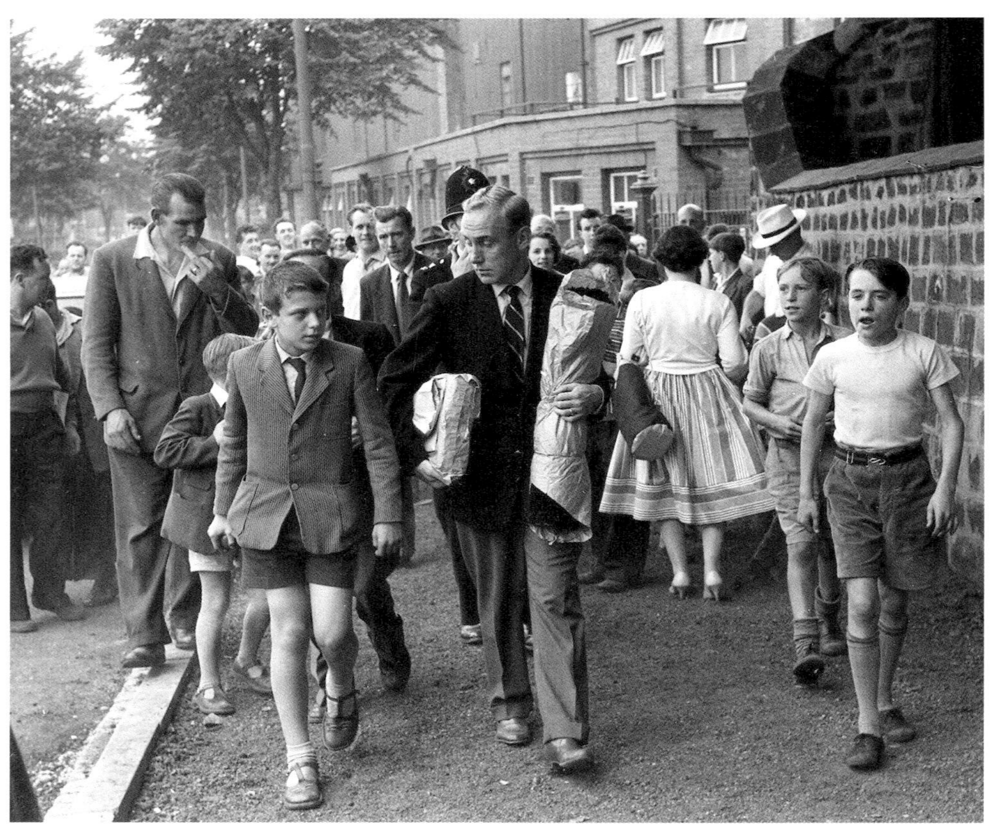

1959

Billy Wright is surrounded
by Wolves fans as he walks
home, after playing his final
match at Molineux.

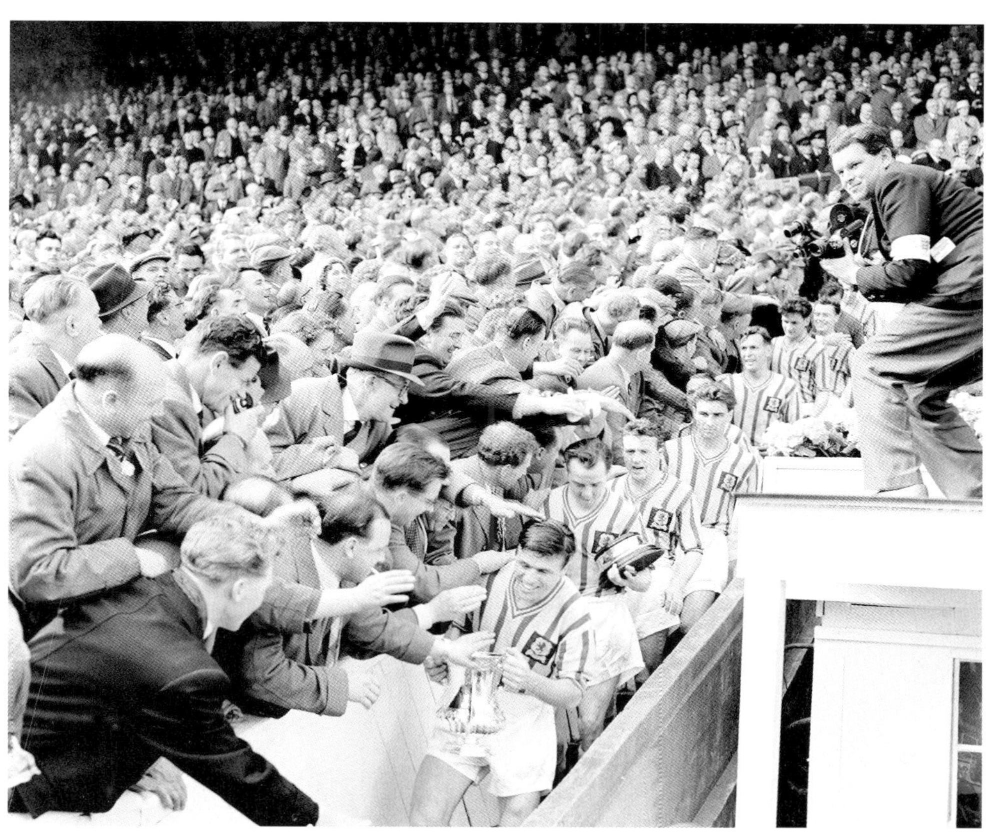

Wembley 1957
Aston Villa captain Johnny Dixon carries the FA Cup in his hands. At the time this was a record seventh win for Villa, but also the last time to date that the Birmingham club has won the famous old trophy.

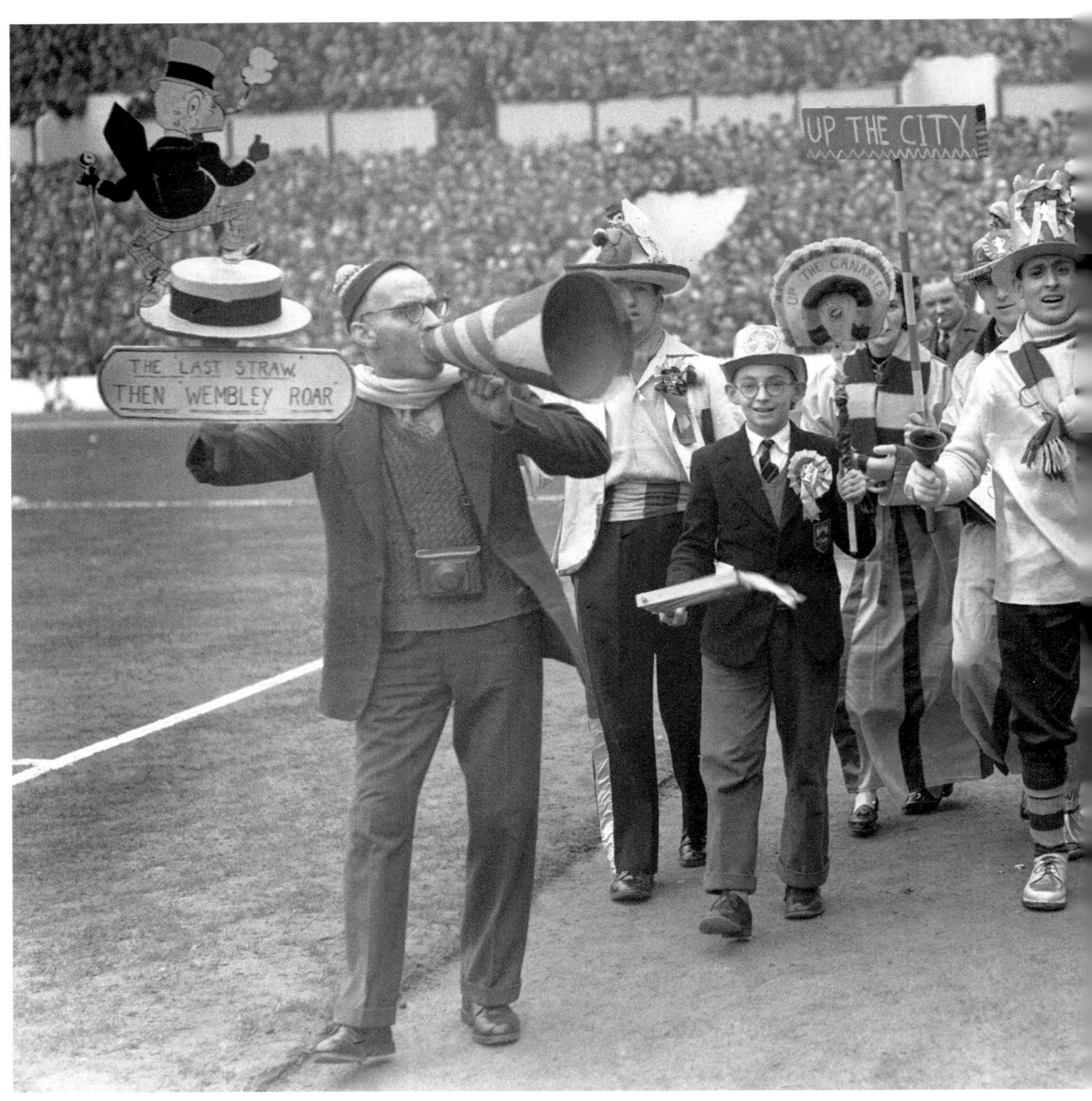

St Andrew's 1959
Cheerleaders and mascots from both Luton
Town and Norwich City whip up the crowd before
the FA Cup semi-final. Norwich were in Division
Three at the time, and lost 2-1.

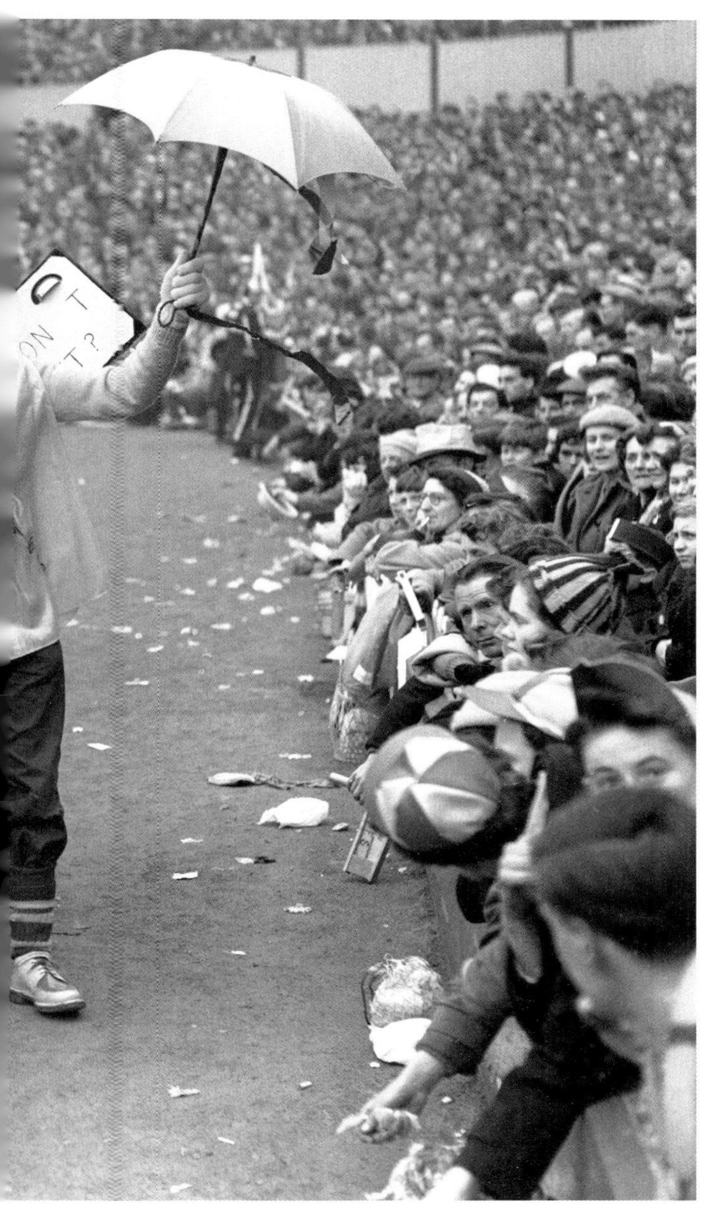

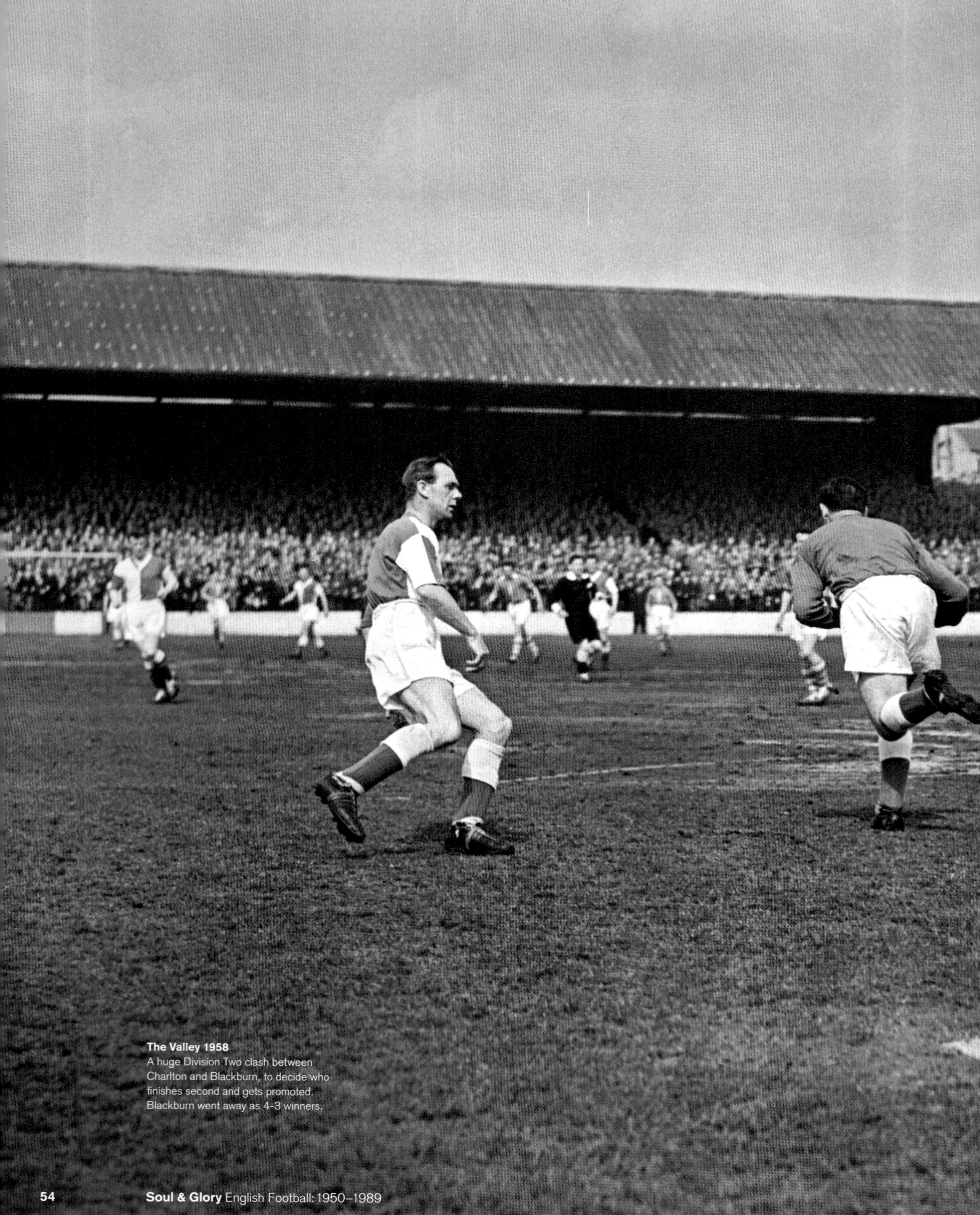

The Valley 1958
A huge Division Two clash between
Charlton and Blackburn, to decide who
finishes second and gets promoted.
Blackburn went away as 4–3 winners.

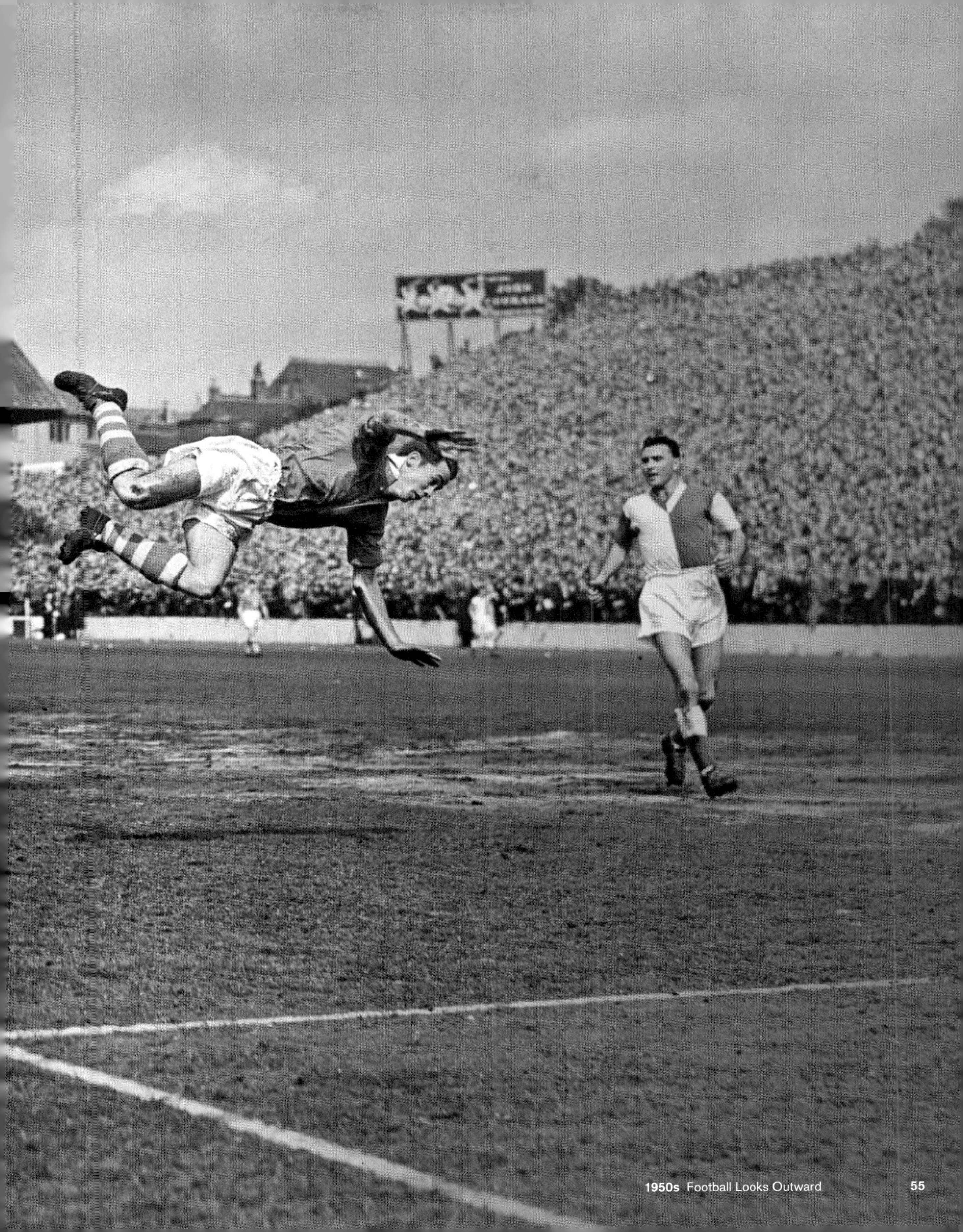

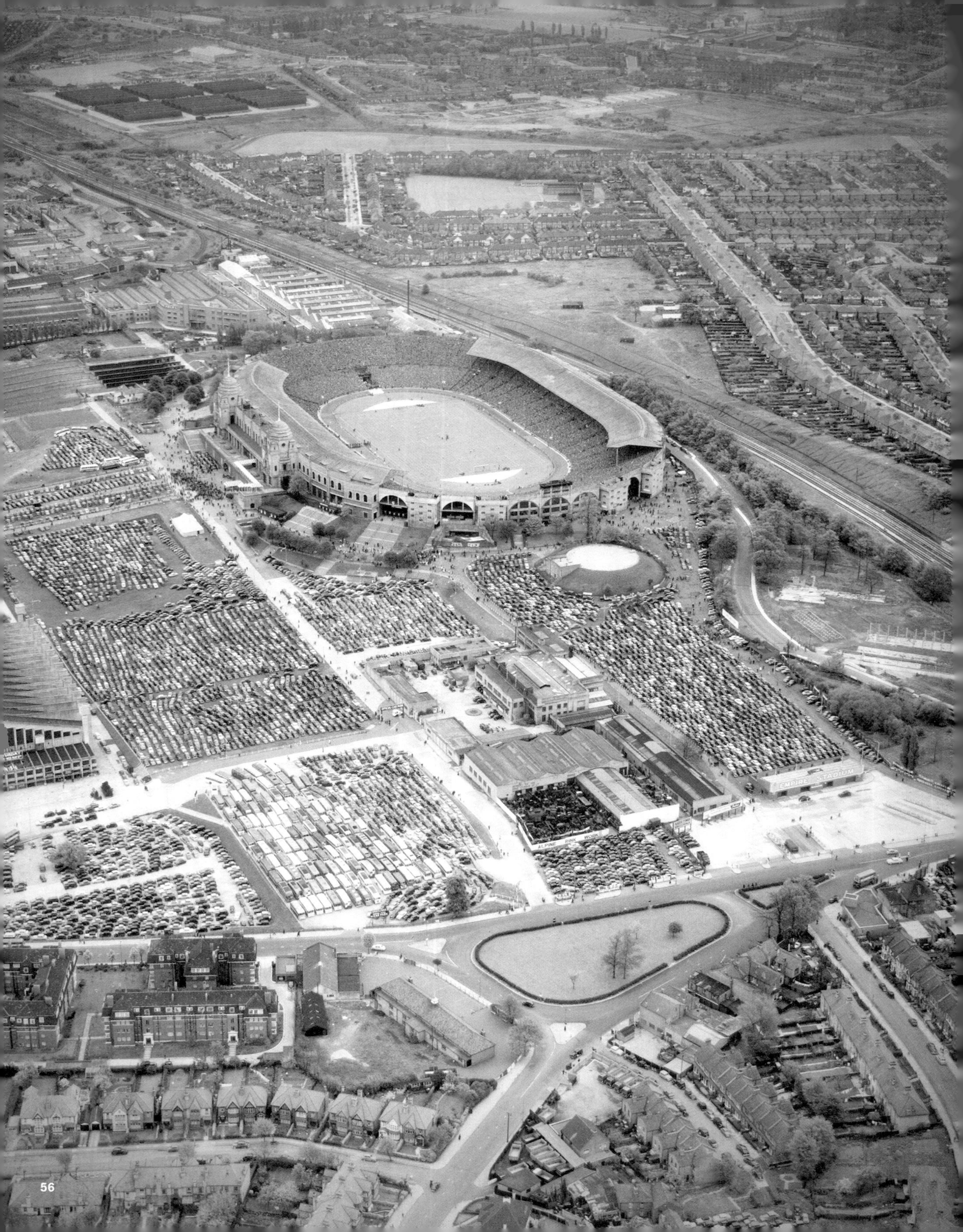

Wembley 1955

Hundreds of buses and coaches sit outside
Wembley Stadium as 100,000 fans watch
the 1955 FA Cup Final between Newcastle
United and Manchester City.

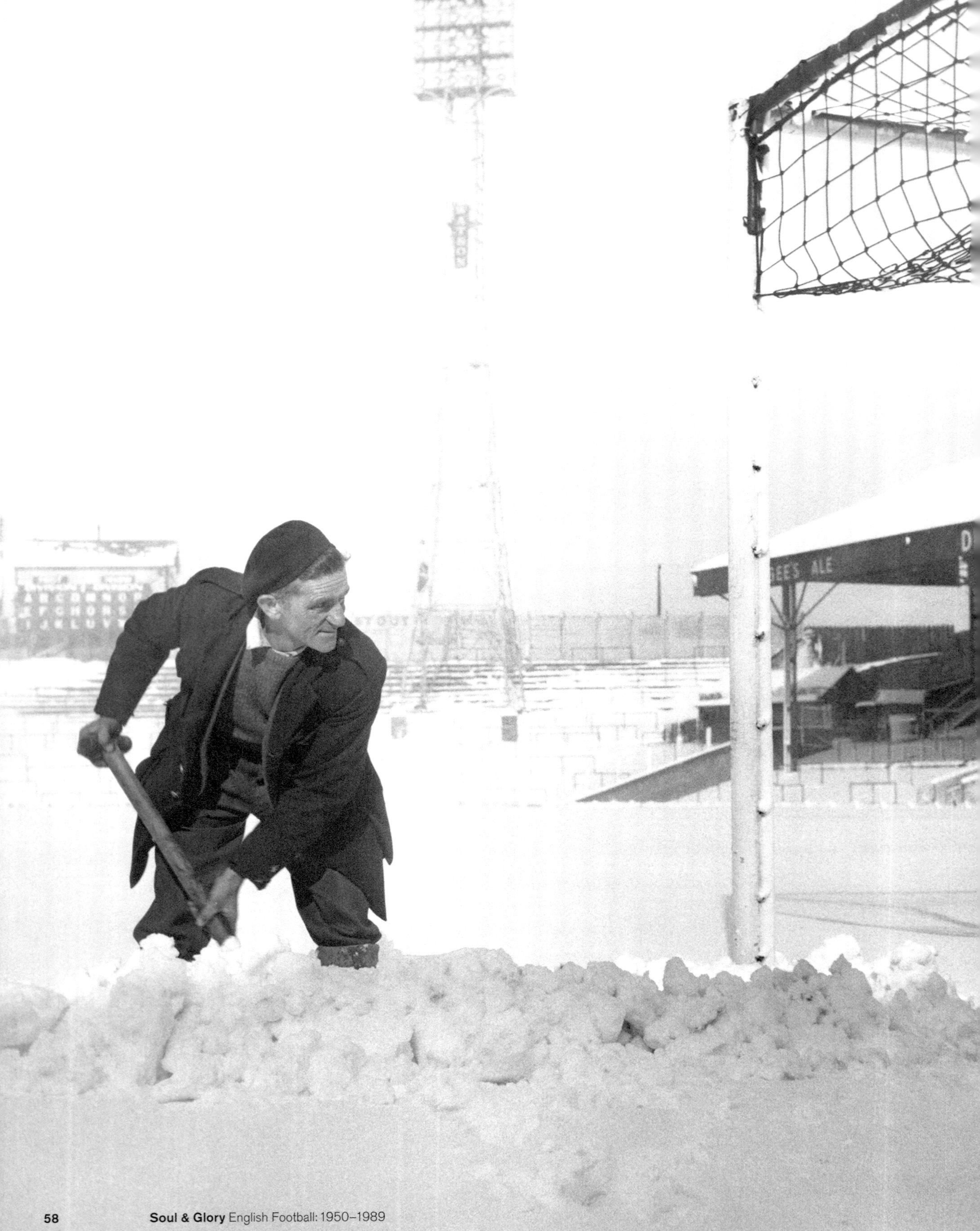

   Soul & Glory English Football: 1950–1989

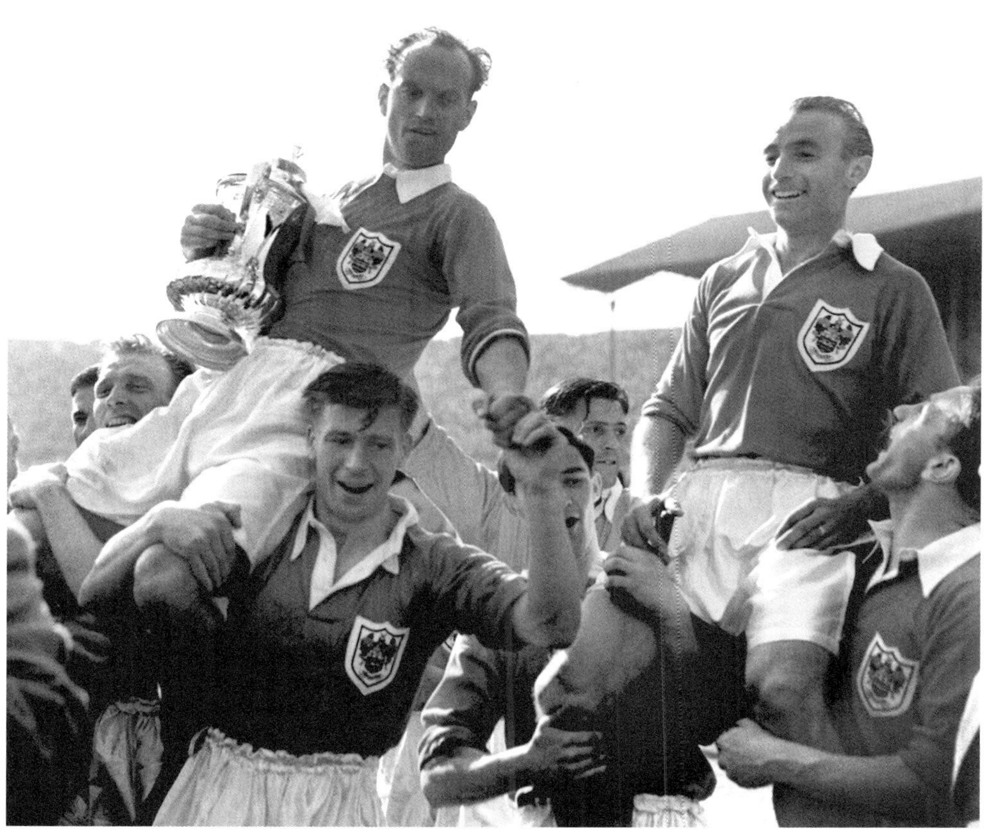

Burnden Park 1958

Bolton's groundsman Fred
Eckersley has a job on his hands
in clearing the snow in time for
an FA Cup tie against Wolves.

Wembley 1953

Stanley Matthews (r) and team captain
Harry Johnston (l) are lifted in the air by their
Blackpool team-mates after the famous 4-3
FA Cup Final win against Bolton.

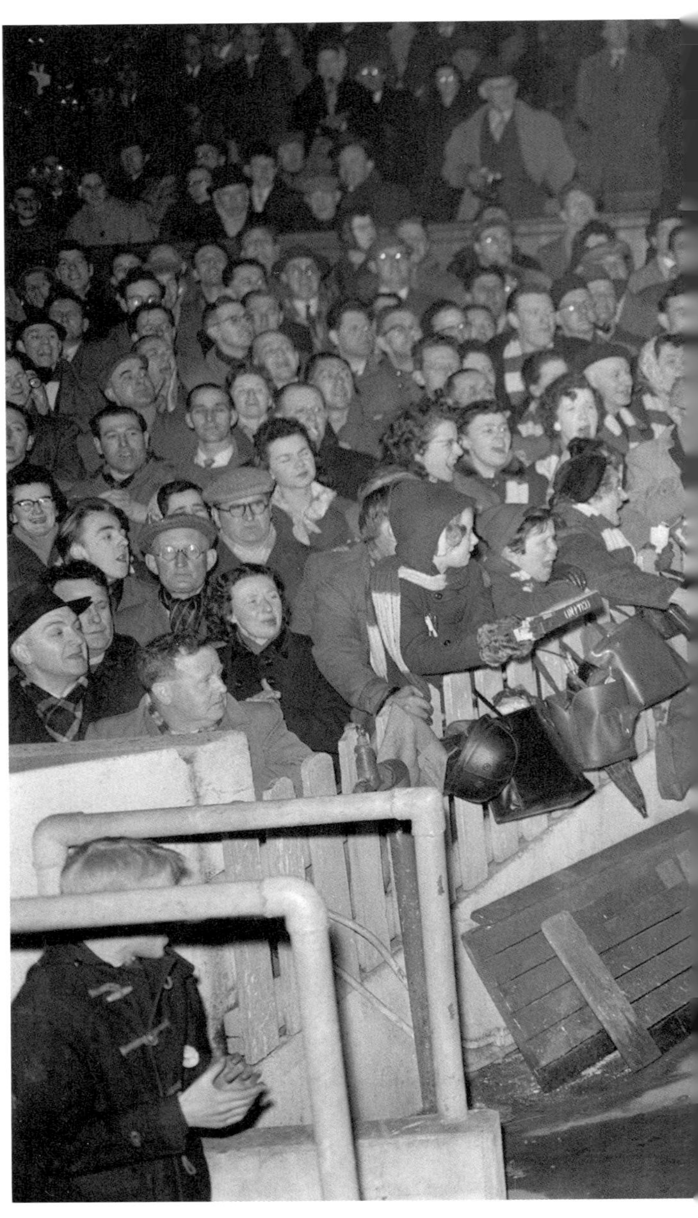

Bramall Lane 1958
Away at Sheffield United was Manchester United's first game after the Munich air disaster. Here, captain Bill Foulkes leads out a makeshift team.

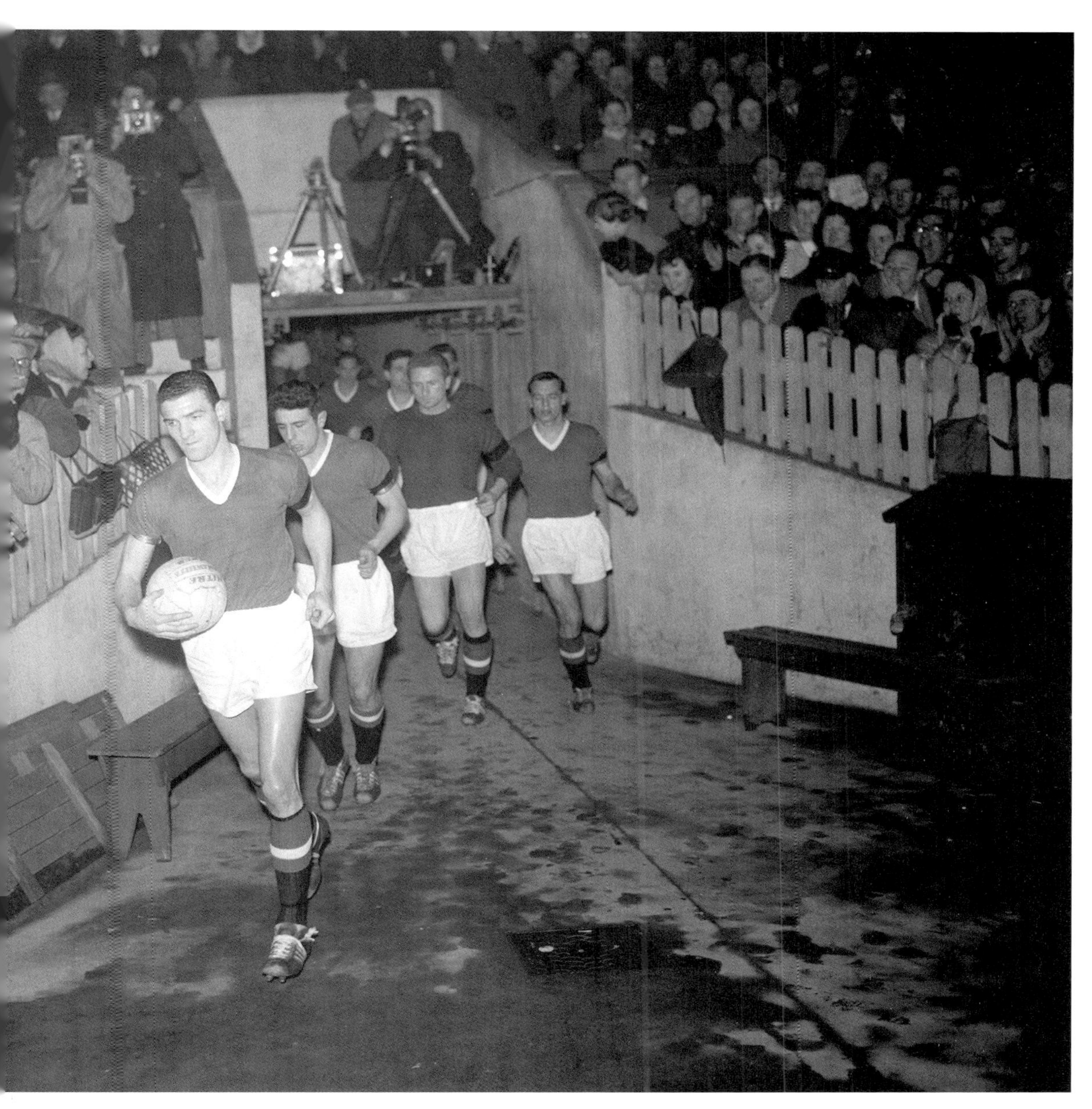

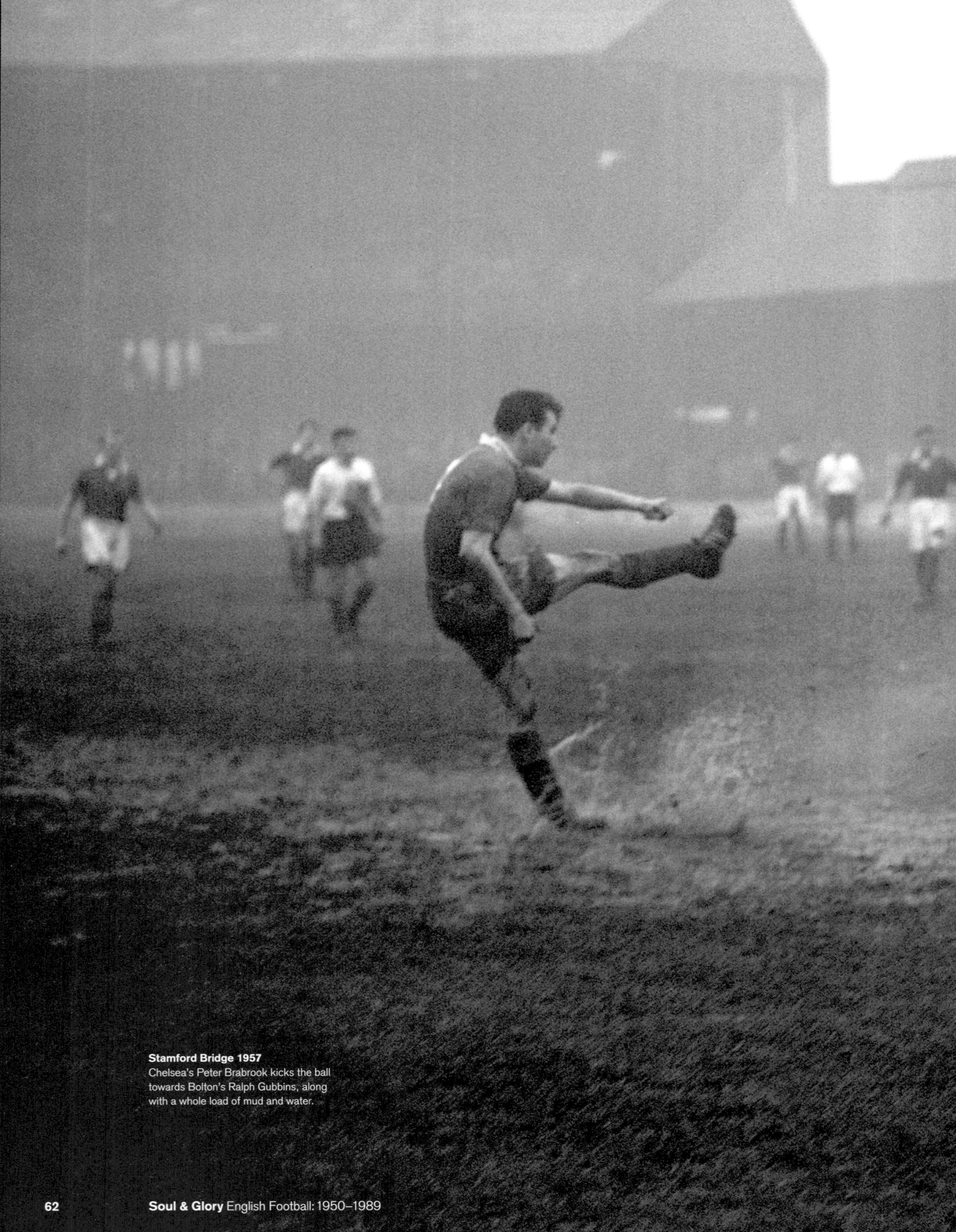

Stamford Bridge 1957
Chelsea's Peter Brabrook kicks the ball
towards Bolton's Ralph Gubbins, along
with a whole load of mud and water.

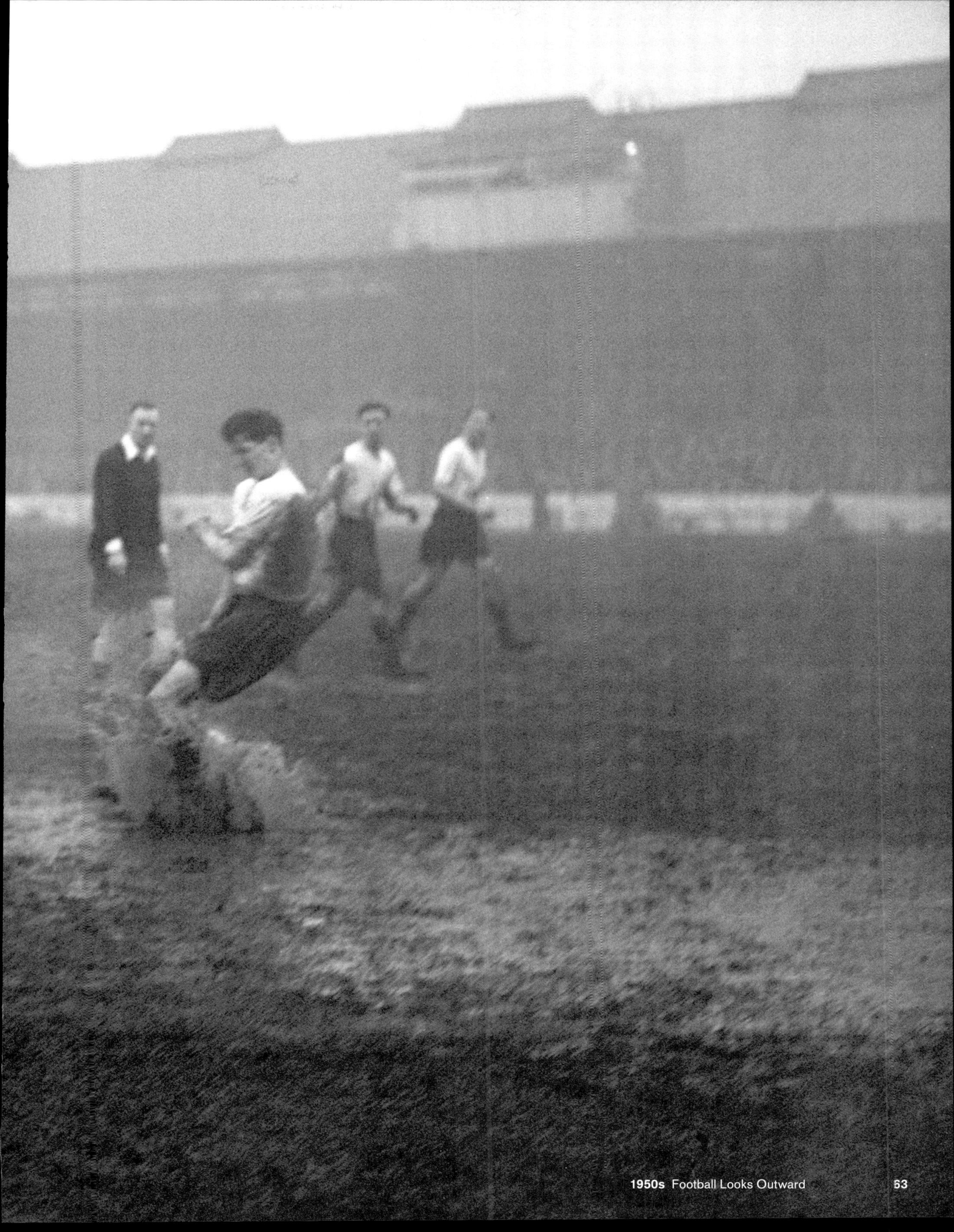

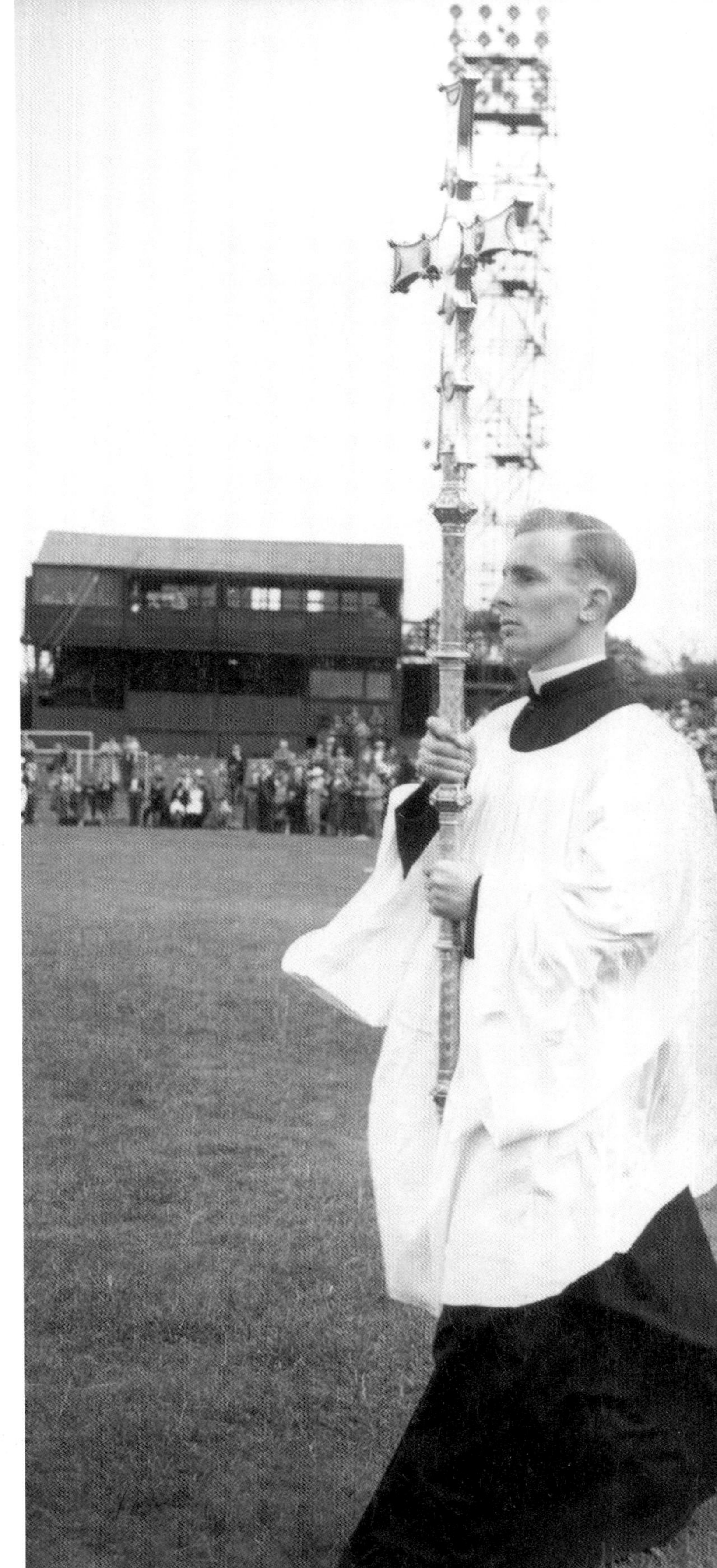

Home Park 1954
Cardinal Bernard Griffin, Archbishop of
Westminster, commemorates 'the simple
son of a Wessex land-owner' with a
colourful pageant at Plymouth Argyle in
front of 15,000 Roman Catholics.

　Soul & Glory English Football: 1950–1989

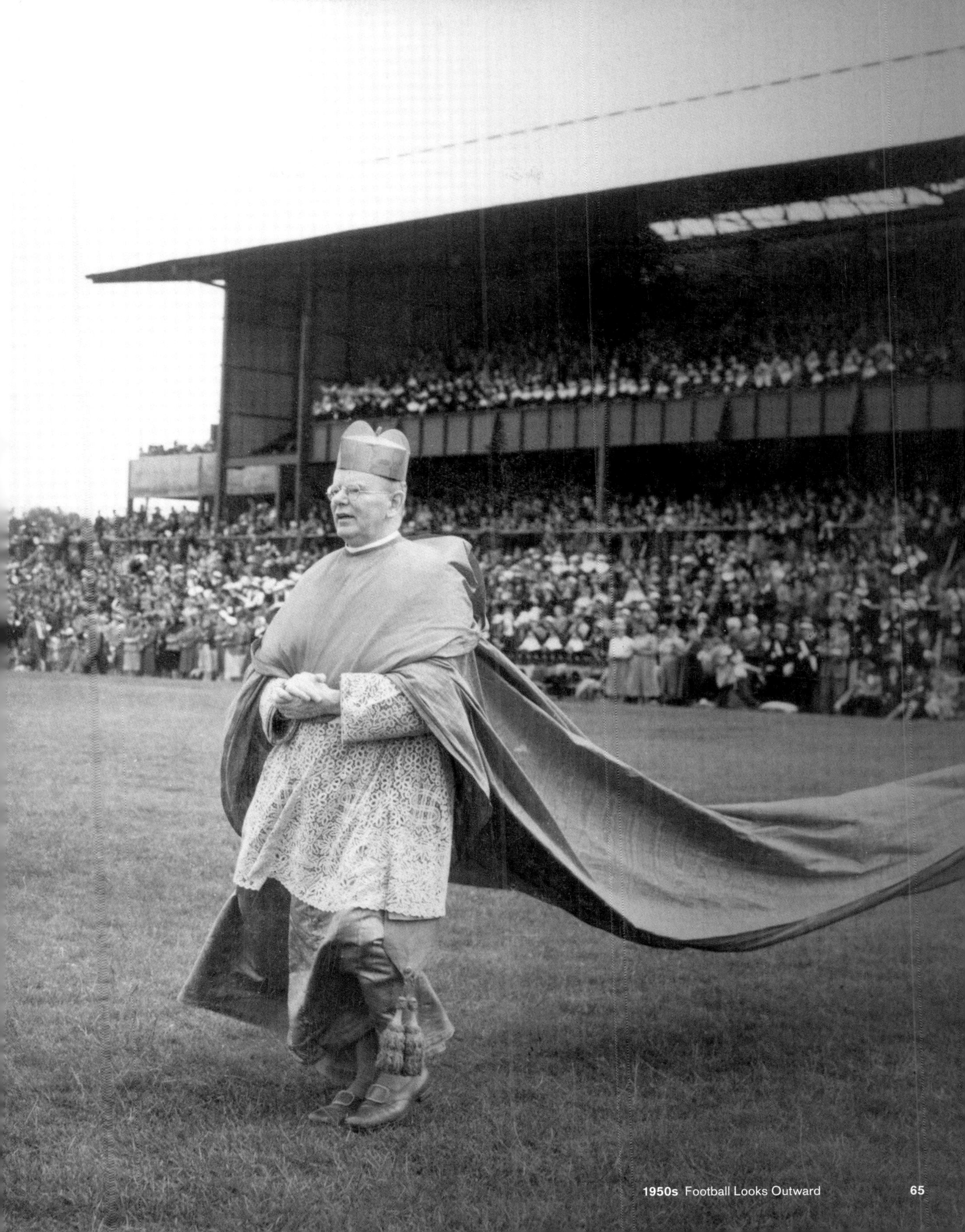

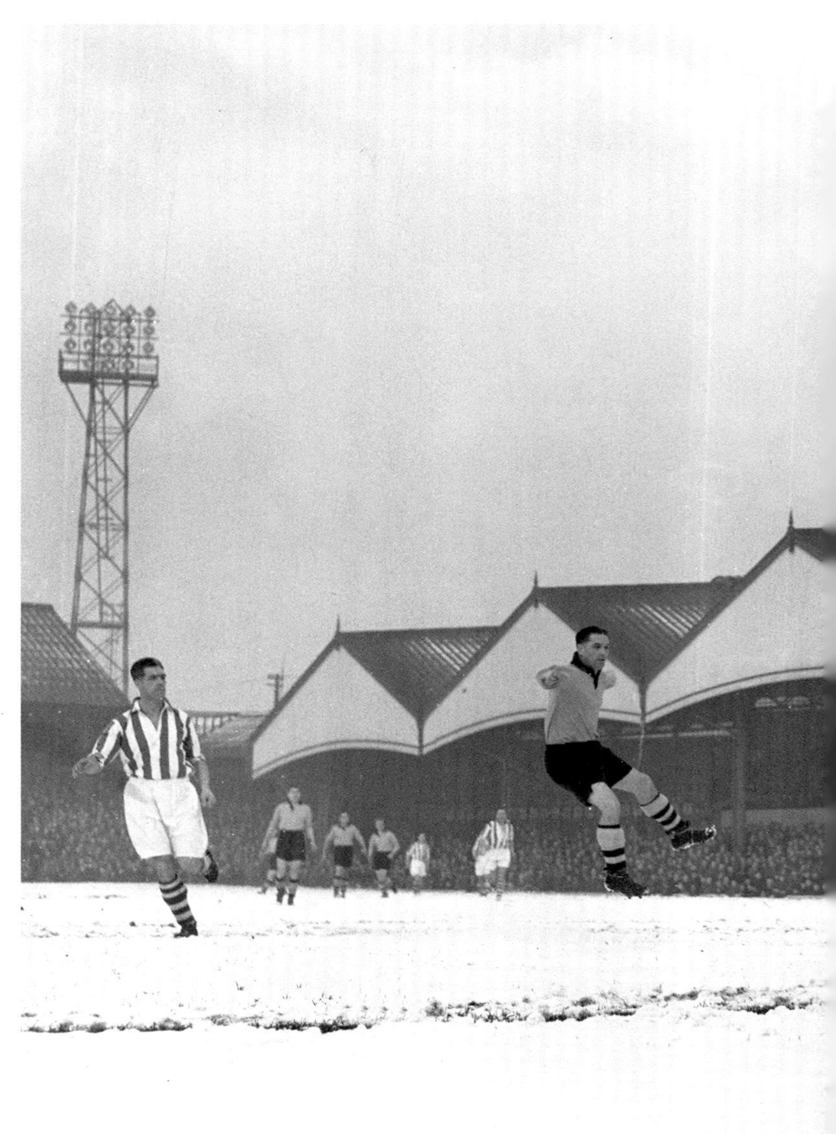

Molineux 1955
After just 90 seconds, Wolverhampton's Johnny Hancocks scores the first of his three goals against Huddersfield Town.

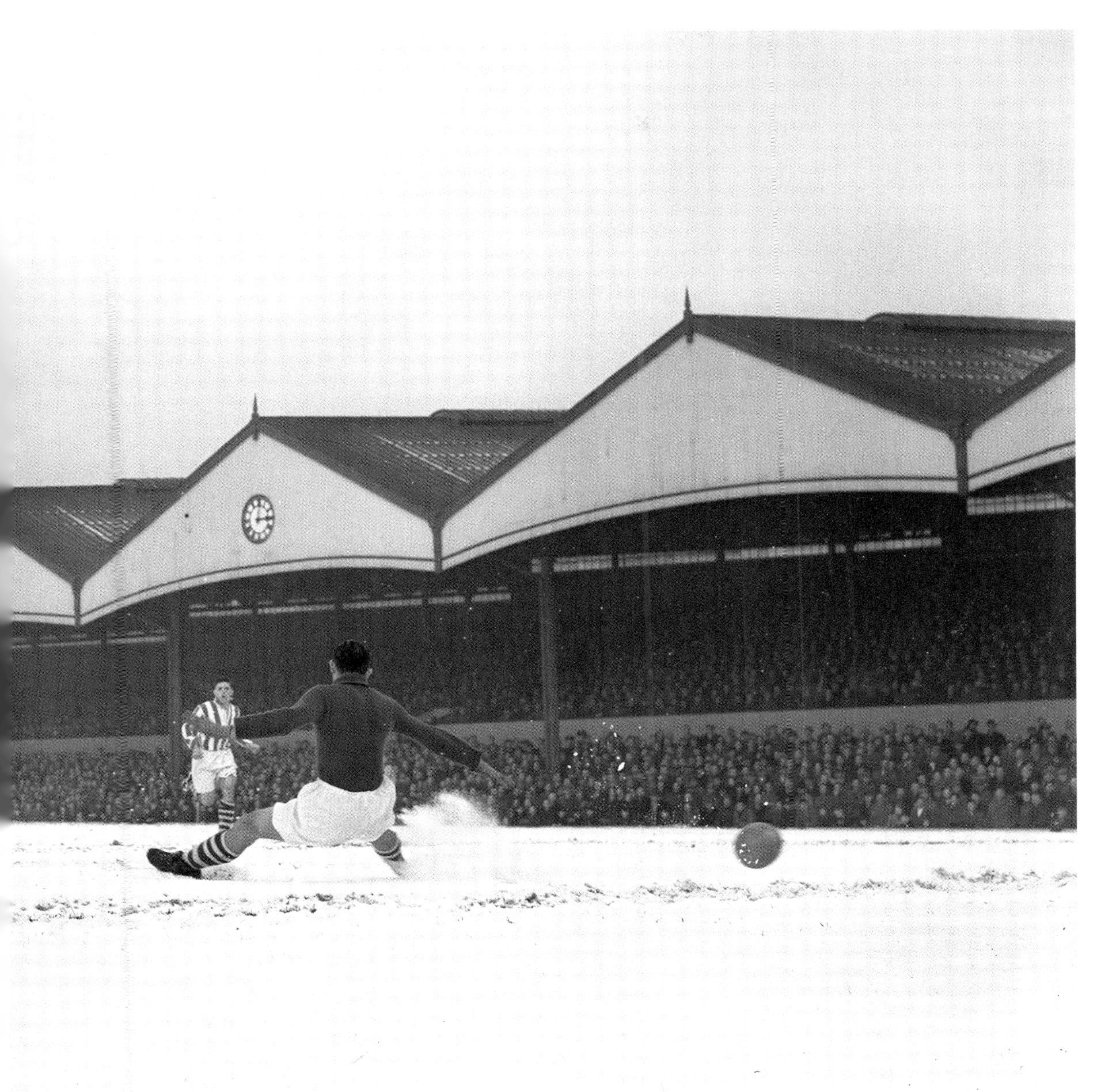

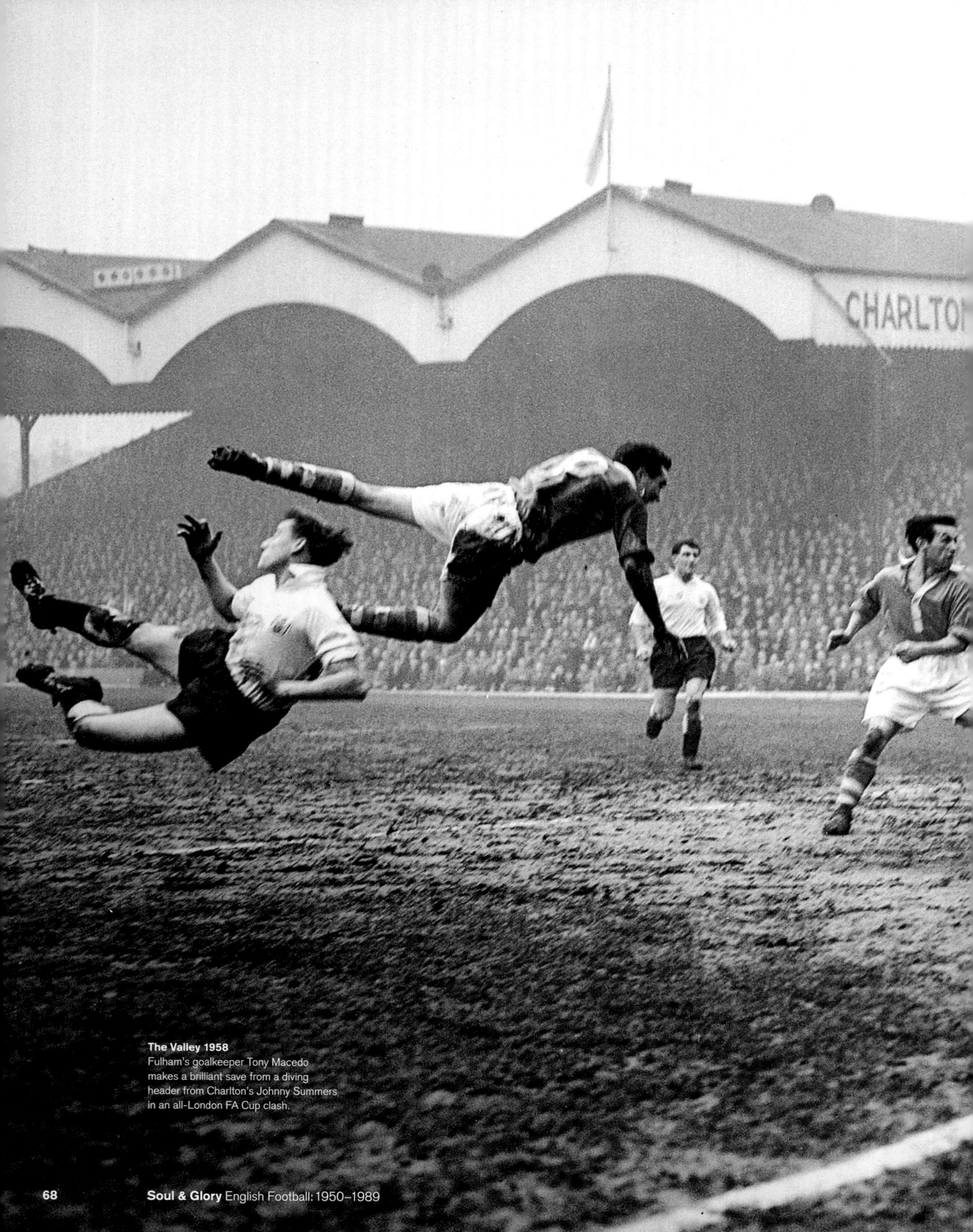

The Valley 1958
Fulham's goalkeeper Tony Macedo
makes a brilliant save from a diving
header from Charlton's Johnny Summers
in an all-London FA Cup clash.

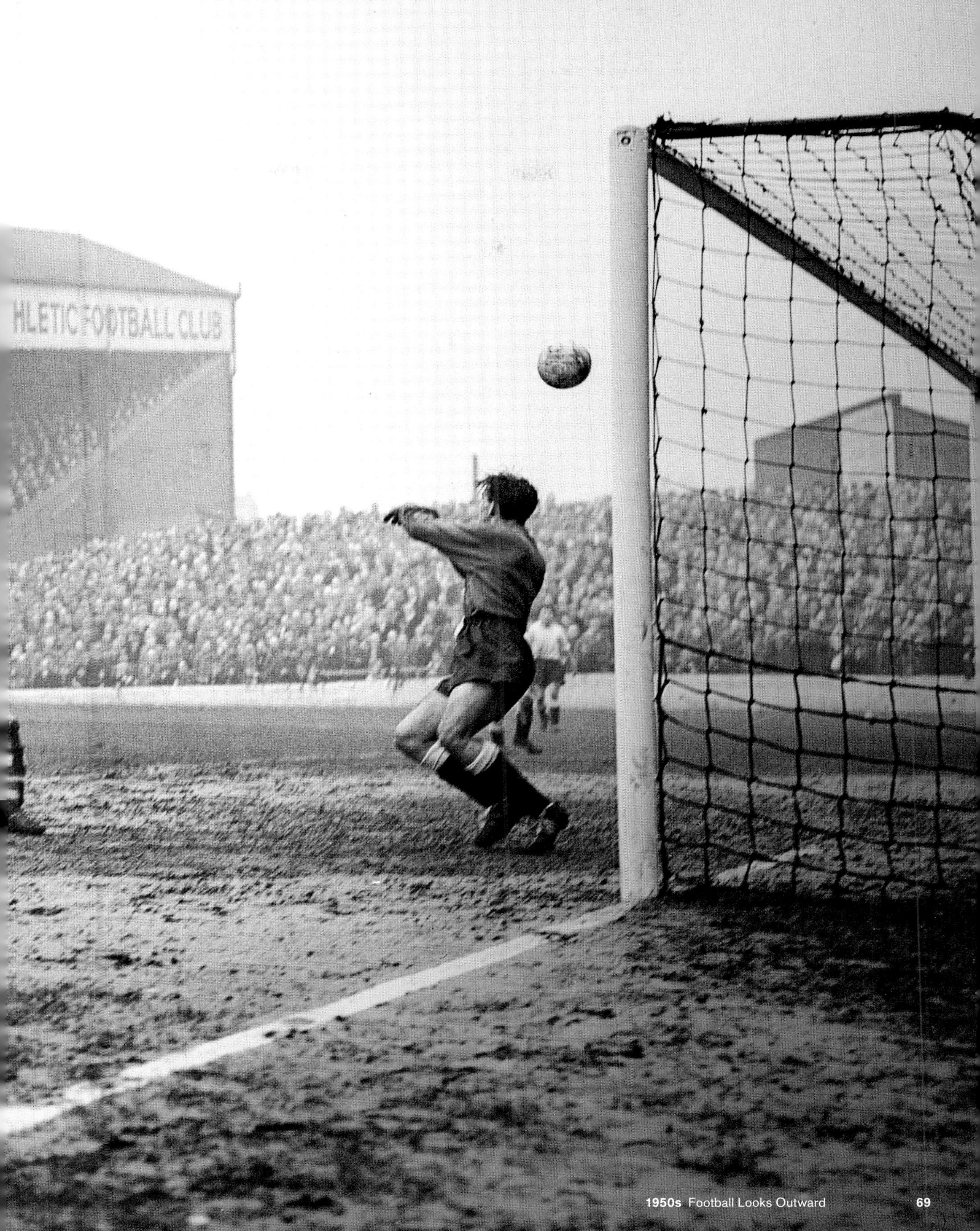
HLETIC FOOTBALL CLUB

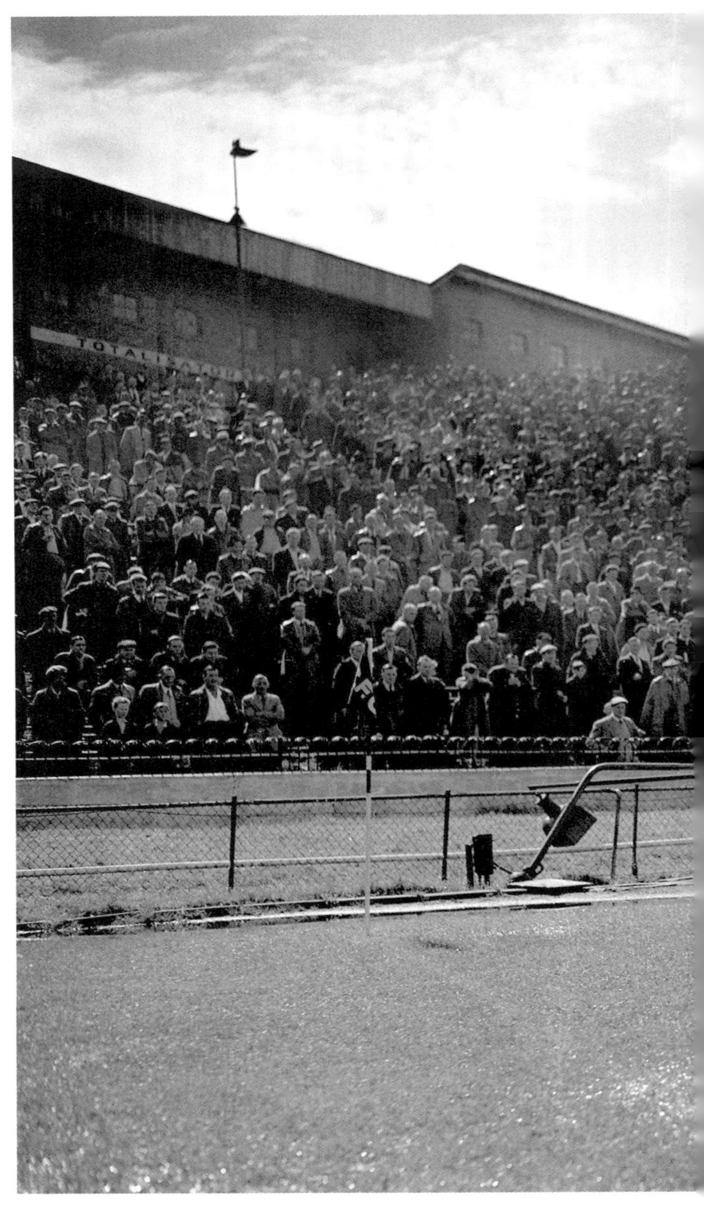

Stamford Bridge 1959
Preston North End legend Tom Finney slides
for a tackle with Chelsea's Wally Bellett who
is completely hidden in this shot due to the
spray of the waterlogged pitch.

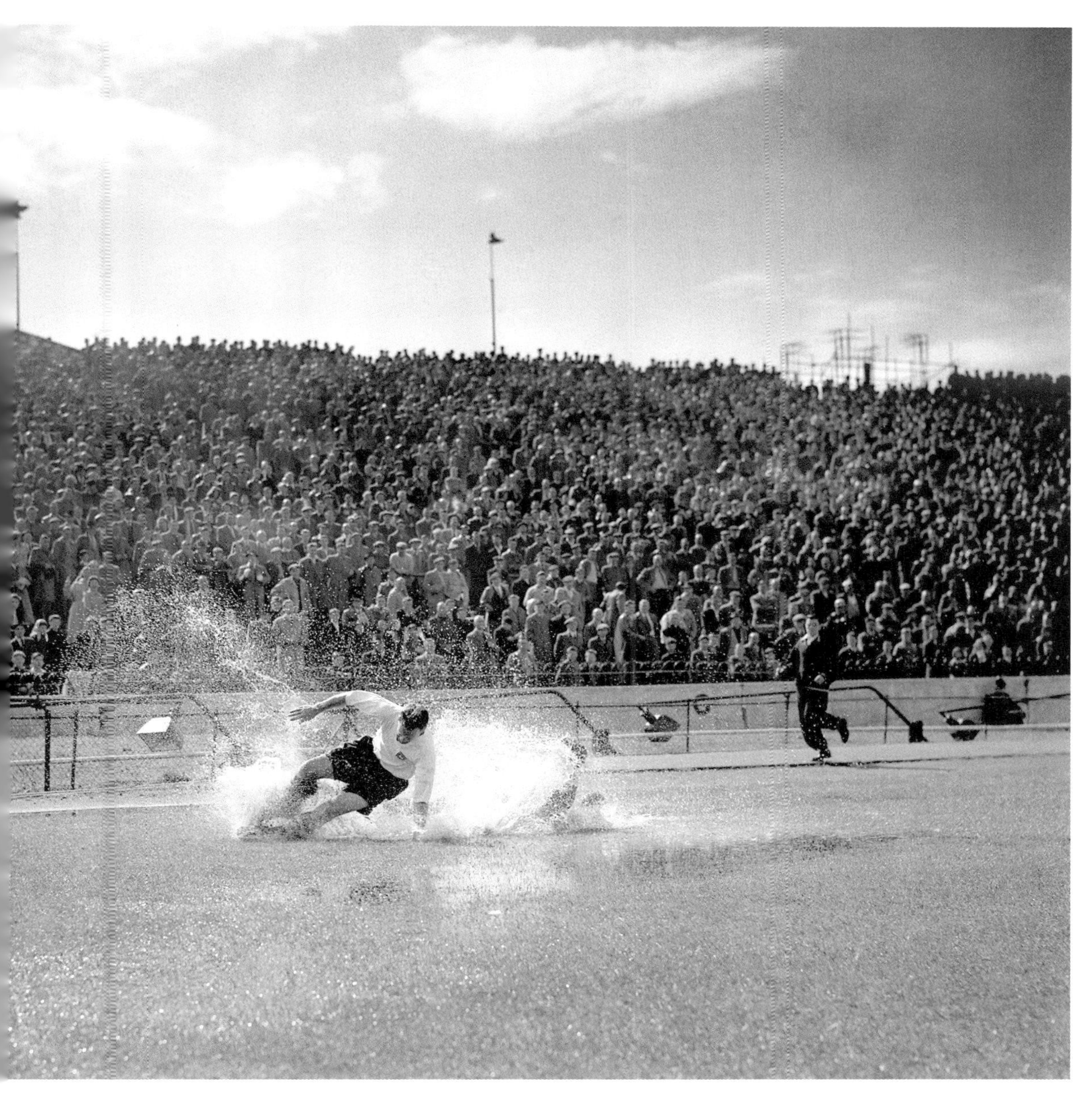

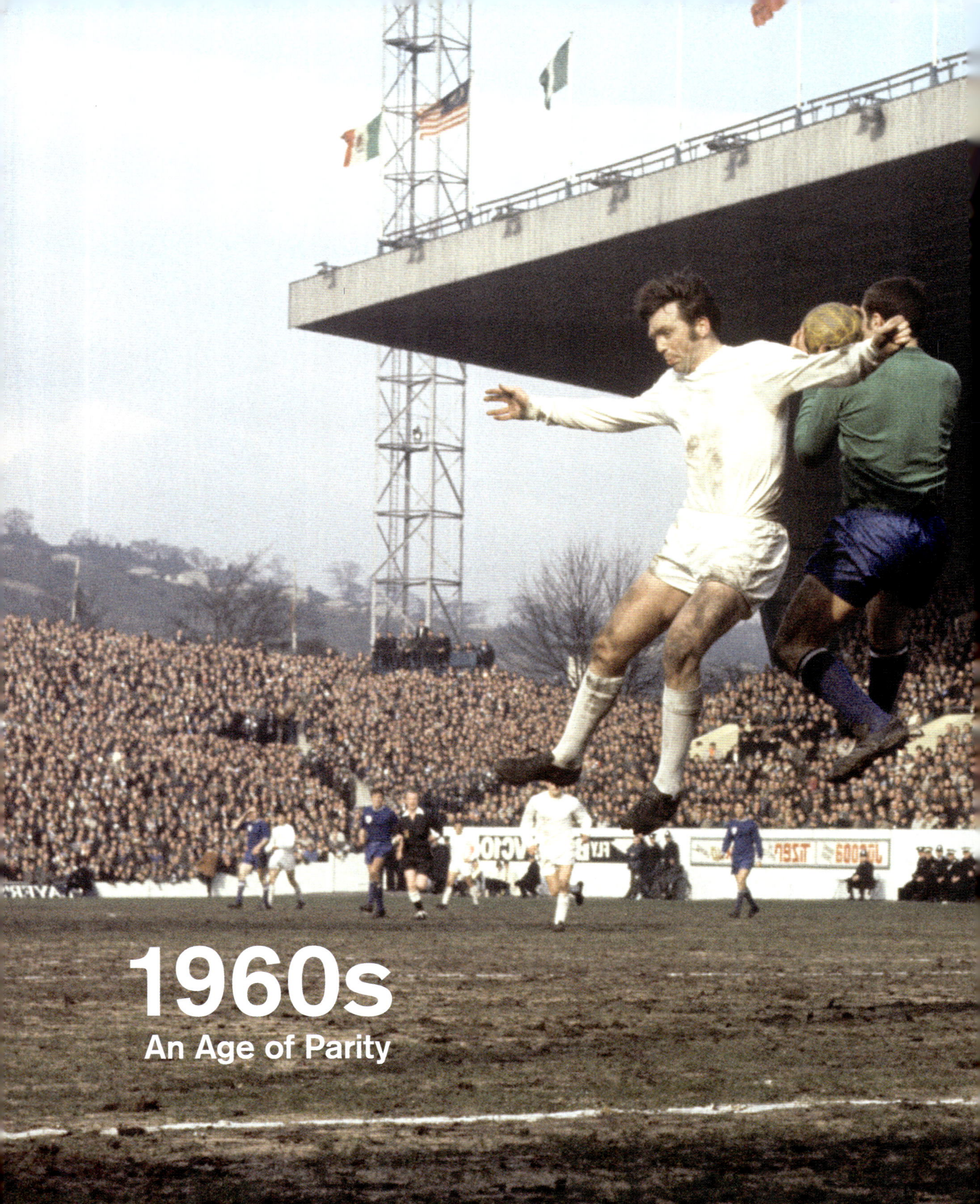

1960s
An Age of Parity

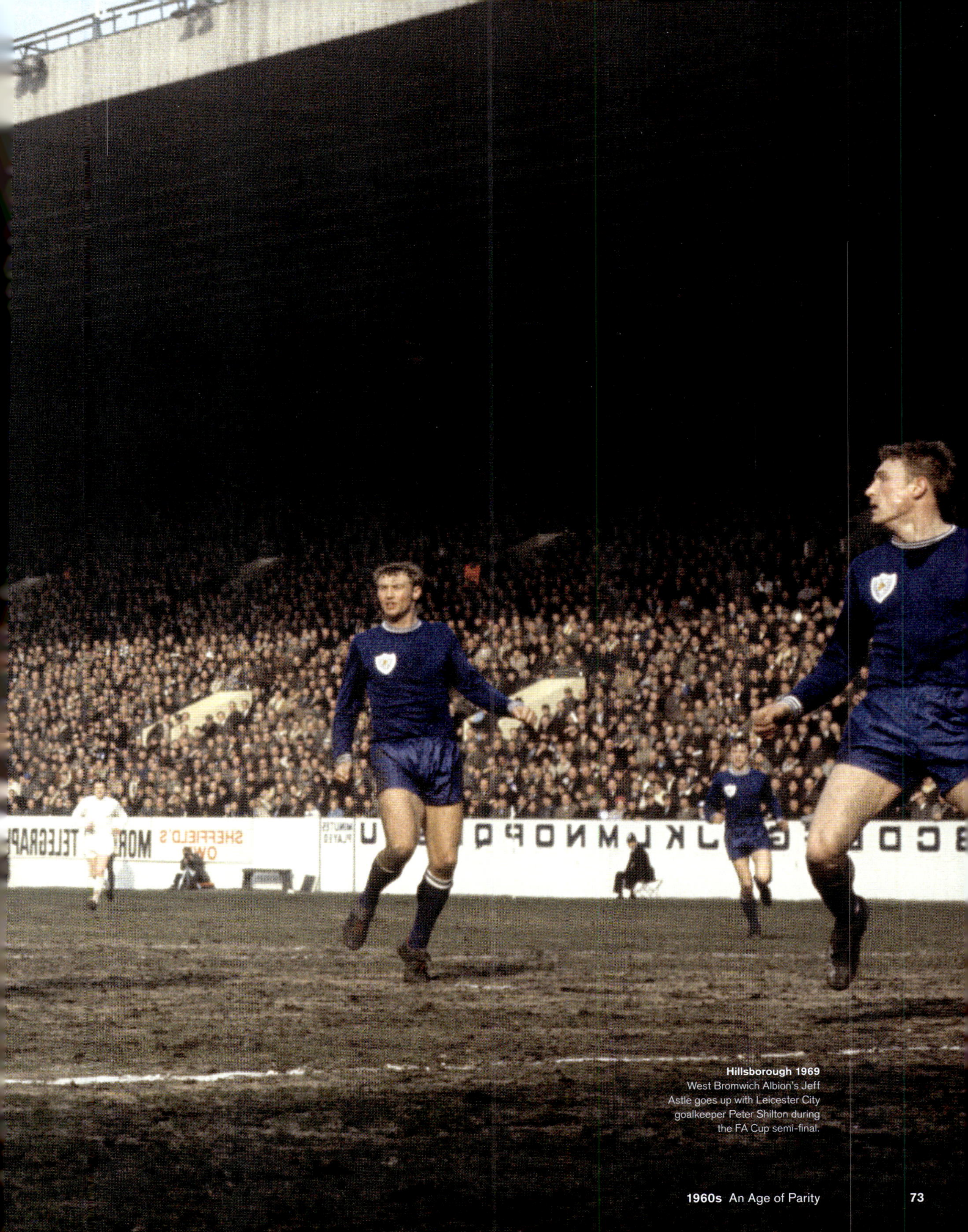

Hillsborough 1969
West Bromwich Albion's Jeff Astle goes up with Leicester City goalkeeper Peter Shilton during the FA Cup semi-final.

1960s: An Age of Parity

One of the most common words used in NFL is parity, and refers to the competitive nature of the league. Teams can have a terrible year, or even a bad ten years, then go on to be Super Bowl winners. One of the reasons for this 'parity' is the league's salary cap. No individual player has wage restrictions, and some of the salaries are eye-watering, but a squad does have restrictions and budgets are not allowed to breach the limit, which at the time of writing is $198m per team (the cap doesn't factor transfers, but NFL doesn't really have a transfer market. Instead, players are traded for better picks when the best young players get drafted from college). This salary cap prevents all the best talent from being monopolised by just a handful of clubs. Our football had individual wage restrictions up until 1961, but the end of the cap didn't result in a lack of healthy competition. Sixties football reflected the decade; it was a time when working-class people felt they could gain a stronger foothold in society; and being in an unfashionable club didn't mean you couldn't win the big prizes. There were big clubs and smaller clubs, but the financial disparity wasn't extreme enough to prevent an age of parity that is so missing from football in today's era both in England and the major European leagues.

In 1995 the European Court of Justice ruled in favour of footballer Jean-Marc Bosman in his lawsuit which argued that he should have been free to leave his club RFC Liege, after his contract had expired. Perhaps the most surprising thing about this case was that this ruling had not successfully transpired years earlier, such was the unfairness of trading someone for a fee when you have no contract with them. The most notable previous attempt at challenging this was when George Eastham brought forward a legal case against Newcastle United in 1963. In the 1959/60 season his contract was winding down and Eastham desired a move. Newcastle couldn't make him play or train for them, but they did have the right to 'retain and transfer' and he was sold to Arsenal for £47,000 in 1960. Eastham got his move but felt strongly enough about the issue to take it to the High Court with his expenses paid for by the Professional Footballers' Association (PFA). The judge ruled that 'retain and transfer' was unreasonable but ultimately clubs still had the right to make money from a transfer. Two years earlier the PFA had already won a major case for players in 1961 when its chairman Jimmy Hill famously campaigned to scrap the maximum wage which stood at £20 a week. The issue had dogged football for years. As lavishly as players are paid today, the pendulum was very much in the other direction in decades past. In the 50s and 60s, university-educated, high-earning professional people would aspire to earn around £20 a week, so footballers on this wage were far better paid than the average person on the street, but still massively underpaid in relation to club revenue.

Outside Craven Cottage stands the statue of Johnny Haynes, who was the immediate big winner of a game that no longer had wage restrictions. Fulham made him the first £100-a-week footballer, and were happy to do so with the chairman stating that he wanted to pay Haynes what he was worth. That was big money in 1961 where the average yearly wage was £700. Forward the clock to today, and Haynes's £100 a week is earned by Gareth Bale in under two minutes, meaning inflation is not very relevant when comparing footballer wages of different eras. Fifties and 60s footballers were not getting their fair share of the income, whereas

> **'Pressure is working down the pit. Pressure is having no work at all. Pressure is trying to escape relegation on 50 shillings a week. Pressure is not the European Cup or the championship or the cup final. That's the reward.'**
>
> Bill Shankly

post-millennium wages would make up the vast bulk of club outgoings. The end of the maximum wage didn't change football culturally in the 1960s. Ticket prices remained affordable, and players were better off but not to the point where they could retire after a month's earnings. The maximum wage ended, and the People's Game carried on the same as before.

In the 1960s, white balls became standardised alongside the traditional brown ones. The 1958 World Cup used white footballs and the new colour was more compatible with floodlit night games. Muddy pitches may have also played a part and when Burnley won the title at Maine Road in 1960 the ball was so hard to spot in the mud that the fans chanted 'white ball, white ball'.

One of the most fundamental rule changes to English football came in the 1965/66 season. Bolton Wanderers were hosting Charlton Athletic, and in the 11th minute, the away goalkeeper Mike Rose went down injured. Charlton then brought on Keith Peacock who became the first ever substitute to be used in the Football League. Each team was now allocated the use of one sub, but that was only allowed if a player was injured. The chances of the goalkeeper being injured in a team is one in 11 so the sub would always be an outfield player, like Peacock who was a midfielder. Even decades later when two subs were allowed, they would always be outfield players, with the two subs having to be designated before the match instead of being chosen during it from a range of options. By 1966/67, subs were allowed to be used for tactical reasons and could be brought on at any time. The rule change of 1965 didn't apply to the World Cup, and if it did then perhaps Jimmy Greaves would have played a part in the 1966 World Cup Final. Greaves, it sometimes seems, is remembered more for being England's star player who got left out of the final, as opposed to the most prolific goalscorer of the time. To this day Greaves holds the record for top-flight goals in English football, with his 364 strikes coming in 516 matches for Chelsea, Spurs and West Ham. He is fourth on the all-time England international top scorers' list behind Wayne Rooney, Bobby Charlton and Gary Lineker, but it's worth noting that his ratio is a lot higher, with his 44 goals for his country coming in just 57 appearances. When Spurs beat Burnley in the 1962 FA Cup Final, it only took Greaves three minutes to score the opening goal. However, he never made it on to the scoresheet against his former team Chelsea in the 1967 'Cockney Cup Final' which was the first time in the cup's 95-year history that two London teams had met in the final, as Spurs won their fifth and final trophy of the decade.

The goals per game ratio in professional football would decrease, decade by decade, as tactics evolved. In 1890 it was 4.5 goals per game, and 100 years later in 1990, the ratio was 2. Defences got better, but that certainly wasn't the case in Division One on Boxing Day 1963 in one of the most wonderful, insane and defensively dreadful days in English football history:

26 December 1963 – Division One

Blackpool	1-5	Chelsea		Nottingham Forest	3-3	Sheffield United
Burnley	6-1	Manchester United		Sheffield Wednesday	3-0	Bolton Wanderers
Fulham	10-1	Ipswich Town		West Bromwich Albion	4-4	Tottenham Hotspur
Leicester	2-0	Everton		West Ham United	2-8	Blackburn Rovers
Liverpool	6-1	Stoke		Wolves	3-3	Aston Villa

In just one day's fixtures in the top flight, 66 goals were scored, and it would have been more had Arsenal's tie with Birmingham not been postponed. On the same day, in Division Two, Manchester City beat Scunthorpe 8-1 indicating that in 1963 a lot of players overindulged on Christmas Day. The parity of football in that time was very much highlighted a couple of days later, when the same fixtures were repeated. Ipswich avenged their 10-1 defeat by Fulham and beat the Londoners 4-2 at Portman Road. Manchester United reversed the 6-1 thrashing by Burnley and gave the Clarets a taste of their own medicine with a 5-1 win at Old Trafford. West Ham got smashed 8-2 by Blackburn at Upton Park, but as the away team at Ewood Park they won 3-1. It's quite incredible that three of the teams on the end of such huge defeats beat the same opposition just two days later.

Haynes being the first player to be offered £100 a week is surprising when viewed with modern eyes, in that his Fulham team fluctuated between the top two divisions. Certainly not one to be muttered among the big clubs of the day, and in today's era it would be the same as a yo-yo club like West Brom (or come to think of it, Fulham) having the country's best-paid player. The concentration of the best players was more evenly spread out; for example in England's 1966 World Cup squad of 22 players, two of them, Terry Paine (striker) and Ron Flowers (midfield), were with clubs in Division Two. The 60s was still an era where distribution of the top playing talent hadn't yet been concentrated to a small handful of elite clubs.

The diversity of competition in 1960s football would result in a decade that produced eight different winners of the league, and the same figure for the FA Cup. Traditionally, English football has had a good share of honours spread out over the teams if you take into account the whole history instead of the last 30 years. There have been 24 different winners of the league, and 43 teams who have won at least one FA Cup. The number of first-time winners of the top division would then became a rarity as we had no new club become champions between Nottingham Forest's triumph in 1979 to Leicester's remarkable title win in 2016. A similar fate happened to the FA Cup, where first-time winners Wimbledon and Wigan were separated between 1988 and 2013. The 1960s saw the opposite to this. Spurs and Manchester United were the glamour clubs of the decade, but title winners included Burnley, and an Ipswich side managed by Alf Ramsey. The traditional big clubs of the north-west – Liverpool, Manchester United, Everton and Manchester City – all won the title at least once during the 60s, and so did another team in the region who no one really liked! Leeds United were a young club by English football standards, founded only in 1919, their life span in the 1960s making them an infant in comparison. From the start of the 60s to the decade's end, Leeds had gone from an unremarkable Division Two club with no history of success to champions of England, though many people would refer to them as 'Dirty Leeds'. They were led by Don Revie, who is one of four title-winning managers of the 60s who now have statues outside a stadium along with Alf Ramsey (Portman Road), Bill Shankly (Anfield) and Matt Busby (Old Trafford).

The decade saw the end of one legendary career, and the beginning of another as Stanley Matthews retired in 1965, nearly 33 years after making his debut for Stoke City at the age of 17. Two years earlier Northern Ireland's George Best made his debut for Manchester United. A total paradox when comparing the longevity and dedication of the two, but both men were arguably the greatest players to have come out of the British Isles.

'I had no plan for Ipswich when I went there.'

Alf Ramsey – title-winning manager of Ipswich Town's 1961/62 team

'He was able to use either foot. Sometimes he seemed to have six.'

Matt Busby on George Best

Matthews was denied the chance to play in a World Cup during his 1930s and 1940s prime, as England had disputes with FIFA, to be followed by World War II. Even in the 1950s, Matthews was known as the 'grand old man' of English football and still represented his country at the age of 40. A humble man, who would walk to the stadium with the fans and talk to anyone who approached him, his outlook on life was, 'You can be the best surgeon in the world, the best hairdresser in the world, or the best at anything you do. But if you're not warm with people, then you're not going to have a successful and happy life.' His domestic career ended after his 50th birthday, when Stoke City beat Fulham 3-1 in a Division One game, not long after Matthews had been knighted. Going down in history as the oldest player to have played in the top flight, and to be capped by England, he contradicted the Chinese philosopher Laozi's idea that the candle that burns twice as bright, burns half as long. George Best on the other hand made Laozi right! The Belfast Beatle was an icon of the 1960s, let alone football. His fame, on a level with the Fab Four, hit a height when he led Manchester United to a European Cup win in 1968, the first English club to bring home the trophy. A year earlier Best was ever present as United won the league for a seventh time. What no one could have predicted was that win in the 1966/67 season was the start of a long title drought. A full 27 years would go by before Alex Ferguson managed the club to league glory in 1993, and buried the ghost of 1967. Manchester City's championship win in 1968 carried a similar story to United's; it would be the last time for many years where they could call themselves champions. The blue half of Manchester would face a 44-year wait until title win number three, when Sergio Aguero fired home a last-second winner against QPR in 2012.

'The man who taught us the way football should be played.'

Pele on Stanley Matthews

Reputations of clubs can change. A club's status can change, its rivalries unequal. In the 1960s, the prestige of the two big Merseyside clubs Everton and Liverpool didn't carry the same wide berth as it does today in regards to success. Everton are still a big club, and still in the elite of English football, but not on the same scale as their neighbours who went on to dominate in a way that no one else had done in the English game's history. However, by 1965 it was Everton who could lay claim to being the more successful club in the city; not to mention that Liverpool had spent time in Division Two at the start of the decade. Both teams had won six league titles, but Everton had the joker in the pack to their local rivals, having won the FA Cup twice, whilst Liverpool incredibly had yet to win the famous old trophy; probably the biggest team never to do so. The Bill Shankly era had begun and top of priorities was to deliver the cup to Anfield which they did by beating an up-and-coming Leeds United in the 1965 final. It was as big a moment for the Reds as any trophy they would go on to win at home or abroad, as not winning the FA Cup up to that point had been a tremendous stigma.

Everton themselves won the FA Cup the following year, coming back from two goals down to win the 1966 final 3-2 against Sheffield Wednesday in front of 100,000 fans who included Lennon and McCartney. The commentator for that final, Kenneth Wolstenholme, would make history later that summer with his 'they think it's all over' line as Geoff Hurst scored a hat-trick against West Germany, but his calling of the 66 FA Cup Final also carries a classic as well as funny moment upon Everton's equalising goal. Today a pitch invasion/celebration would come with condemnation and disgust from the commentator. In contrast, Wolstenholme simply called the action in front of him as an overjoyed Everton fan, Eddie Cavanagh, dressed in a suit, ran the length of the pitch whilst the police chased after him in Keystone Cops fashion. One officer grabbed hold of him by the jacket whilst still in motion, only for Eddie to remove his jacket as the policeman went tumbling to the ground, to the crowd's delight. Cavanagh thought he had eluded capture, but out of nowhere another policeman, with the speed of Jesse Owens, caught up with him and rugby tackled him to the ground on the edge of the area as the crowd roared. The floored fan lay on the turf with his arms out in celebration as Wolstenholme commentated, 'And a great tackle, almost on the line.' He didn't condemn the scene, he just simply called the action. It does point to a game and an era where things were more relaxed and forgivable. A year later, in the League Cup Final, the reporter casually noted that getting on the pitch and celebrating, 'For some supporters it was well worth a brush with the police.' No one condoned such behaviour, but nor did it make someone 'scum' or a 'mindless idiot'. Years later such an act would be met with court action and a ban from attending matches.

Leicester City will look back at the 1960s and ask themselves, how on earth did we not win an FA Cup? The Foxes made it to three finals and lost all of them, gaining an unenvied record of the most FA Cup Final appearances for a club without ever winning it (four), finally breaking that duck in 2021 by beating Chelsea 1-0 in what felt like an old-fashioned cup final, such was the joy it brought to Leicester. Other clubs got success quicker, but are starved of glory today. In the 1968 final, West Bromwich Albion had beaten Everton 1-0 with a goal from Jeff Astle. This was the tenth FA Cup Final they had competed in and the fifth time they had won, giving them one of the best records in the competition. Given the prestige the FA Cup still carried, West Brom at this point in time had every right to consider themselves as one of the most successful teams in English football history, given that they also had a league title to their name as well as a League Cup. Again, reputations change; the 1968 final was their last to date and slowly over time West Brom have become viewed as a club that achieves very little.

Not only did the 1960s provide diversity in winners for the league and FA Cup, but there were now more things to win. The decade saw the introduction of two new competitions: the League Cup, and the European Cup Winners' Cup. The UEFA Inter-Cities Fairs Cup had been in place since the late 1950s, and was the pre-curser for the UEFA Cup. That trophy, over time, would become the second most prestigious European prize, but it struggled to gain status in its infancy and throughout the 60s the newly formed Cup Winners' Cup was a bigger competition. Consisting of teams who had won their country's domestic cup, the importance that a trophy like the FA Cup had meant the Cup Winners' Cup had credibility. In contrast, the Inter-Cities Fairs Cup was convoluted, scheduled around trade fairs and could only include one team per city. In 1963 Spurs became the first ever British club to win a European trophy when they beat Atletico Madrid in the Cup Winners' Cup Final. West Ham, led by Bobby Moore, also won the trophy in 1965. As the decade wore on, the Fairs Cup gained status. The first final in the 1950s was London XI v Barcelona XI, but by the late 60s, big English clubs were now heavily involved and Leeds won the trophy in 1968 followed by Newcastle United in 1969.

The parity of success in the 60s was more than evident in the newly formed League Cup. Its introduction came as a power move by the Football League towards the rise of European football as well as a note to the

FA that the Football League could run their own domestic cup competition. In 1961 Aston Villa, the most successful team up to that point in English football, won the first League Cup suggesting more status quo than parity. However, their opponent was Rotherham which showed that perhaps this 'People's Cup' could be won by the smaller clubs. The following year, Division Three Rochdale got to the final, losing to Norwich City. In 1967, QPR, also from the third tier, did prove that anyone can win this trophy when they beat West Brom 3-2 to win the club's first and only major trophy. Third Division Swindon Town repeated this feat in 1969, beating Arsenal 3-1 in extra time, in what could go down as the worst the pitch at Wembley had ever looked; better suited to a farm than a football stadium. This capped off a horrendous 1960s for the Gunners who had lost the League Cup Final a year earlier to Leeds, and didn't even make it to an FA Cup Final. Whilst Spurs had the best decade of their history, Arsenal had their worst, in what was the one decade between the club's first trophy in 1930 to the present day where they would win nothing.

England fans remember the 1960s, of course, because their national team won the biggest prize in world football. For the one and only time in history, England fans sung with joy the chant of the 1960s, 'We won the cup, we won the cup, ee aye addio, we won the cup.'

1960s Domestic Honours

Division One Champions

1960: Burnley (overall title wins 2)
1961: Tottenham Hotspur (overall wins 2)
1962: Ipswich Town (overall wins 1)
1963: Everton (overall wins 6)
1964: Liverpool (overall wins 6)
1965: Manchester United (overall wins 6)
1966: Liverpool (overall wins 7)
1967: Manchester United (overall wins 7)
1968: Manchester City (overall wins 2)
1969: Leeds United (overall wins 1)

League Cup Winners

1961: Aston Villa (overall wins 1)
1962: Norwich City (overall wins 1)
1963: Birmingham City (overall wins 1)
1964: Leicester City (overall wins 1)
1965: Chelsea (overall wins 1)
1966: West Bromwich Albion (overall wins 1)
1967: Queens Park Rangers (overall wins 1)
1968: Leeds United (overall wins 1)
1969: Swindon Town (overall wins 1)

FA Cup Winners

1960: Wolverhampton Wanderers (overall wins 4)
1961: Tottenham Hotspur (overall wins 3)
1962: Tottenham Hotspur (overall wins 4)
1963: Manchester United (overall wins 3)
1964: West Ham United (overall wins 1)
1965: Liverpool (overall wins 1)
1966: Everton (overall wins 3)
1967: Tottenham Hotspur (overall wins 5)
1968: West Bromwich Albion (overall wins 5)
1969: Manchester City (overall wins 4)

European Honours for English Clubs

1963: Tottenham Hotspur, Cup Winners' Cup
1965: West Ham United, Cup Winners' Cup
1967: Manchester United, European Cup
1968: Leeds United, Fairs Cup
1969: Newcastle United, Fairs Cup

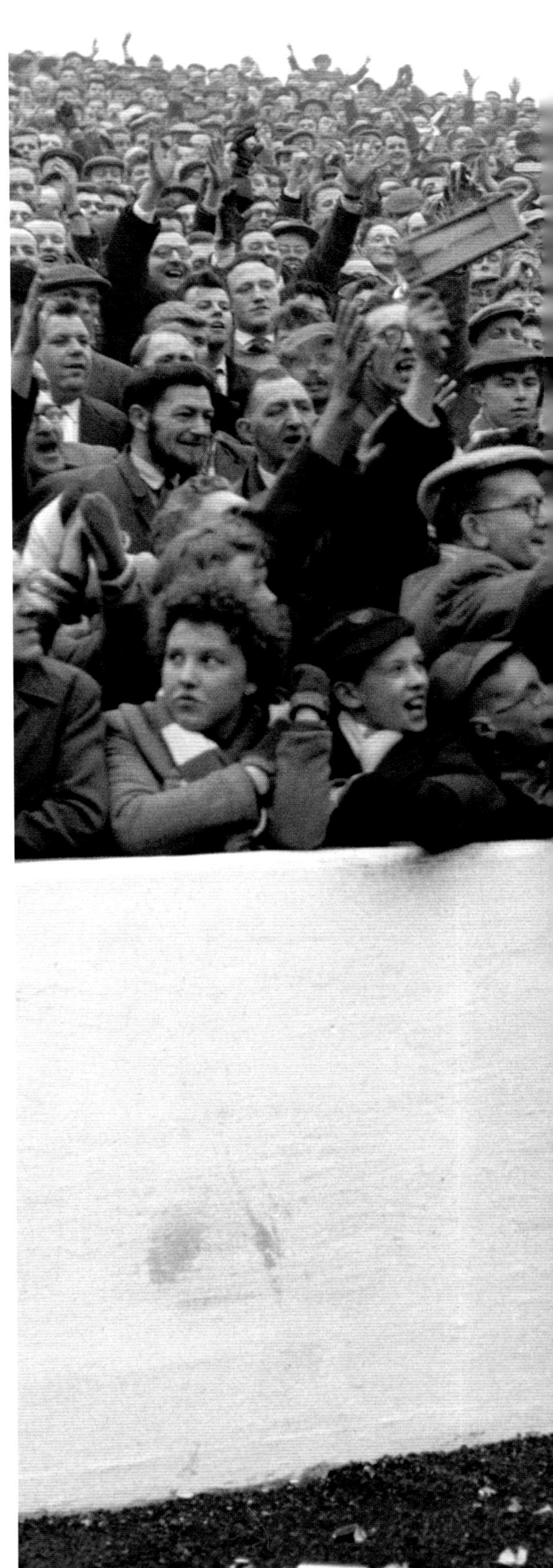

Maine Road 1960
Blackburn's Derek Dougan celebrates
scoring one of his two goals against
Sheffield Wednesday in the 1960 FA Cup
semi-final. Rovers went on to lose in the
final to Wolves.

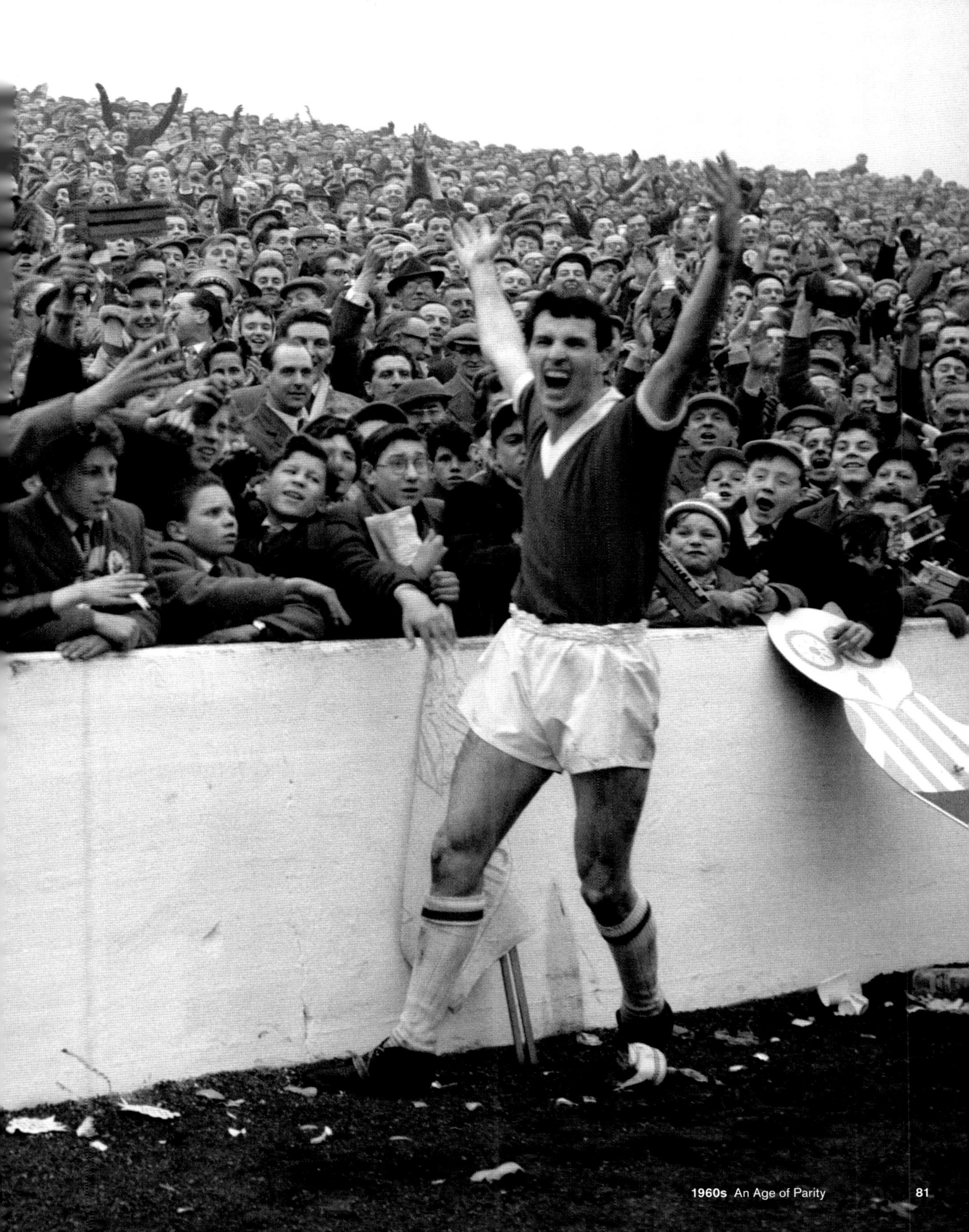

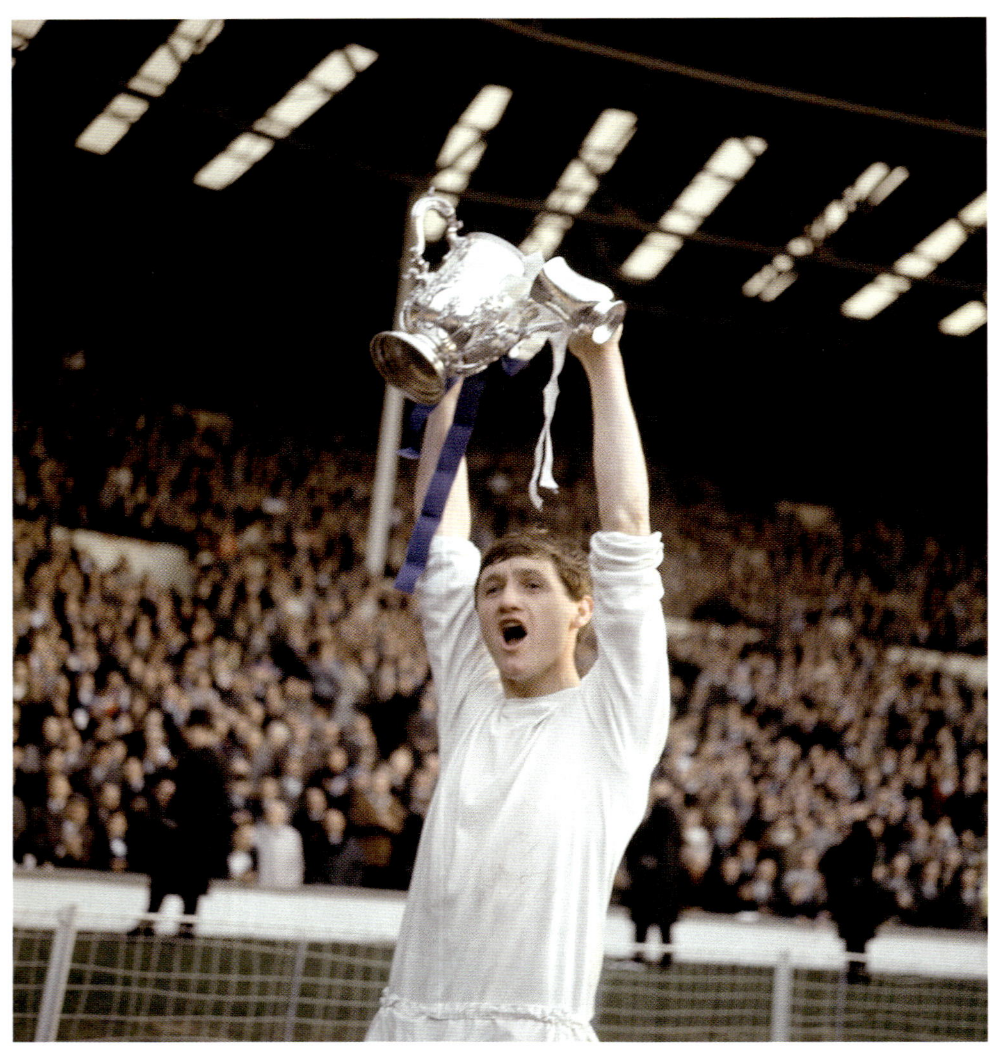

Wembley 1967
QPR captain Mike Keen lifts up the League
Cup after a 3-2 thriller against West Brom.
QPR were the first team from Division Three
to play for a cup at Wembley and won the
game in the closing moments.

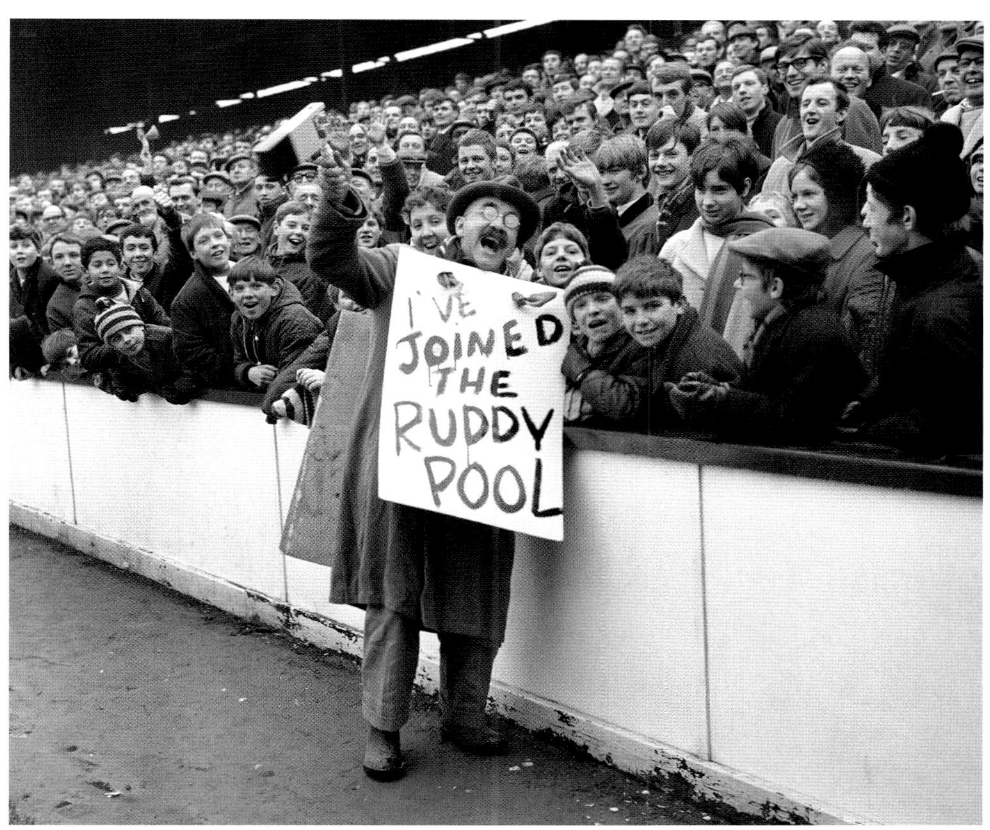

Upton Park 1968
'Up the Hammers!' West Ham fan Alf
Garnett, played by actor Warren Mitchell
(a Spurs fan in real life), drums up
support for a Pools enterprise.

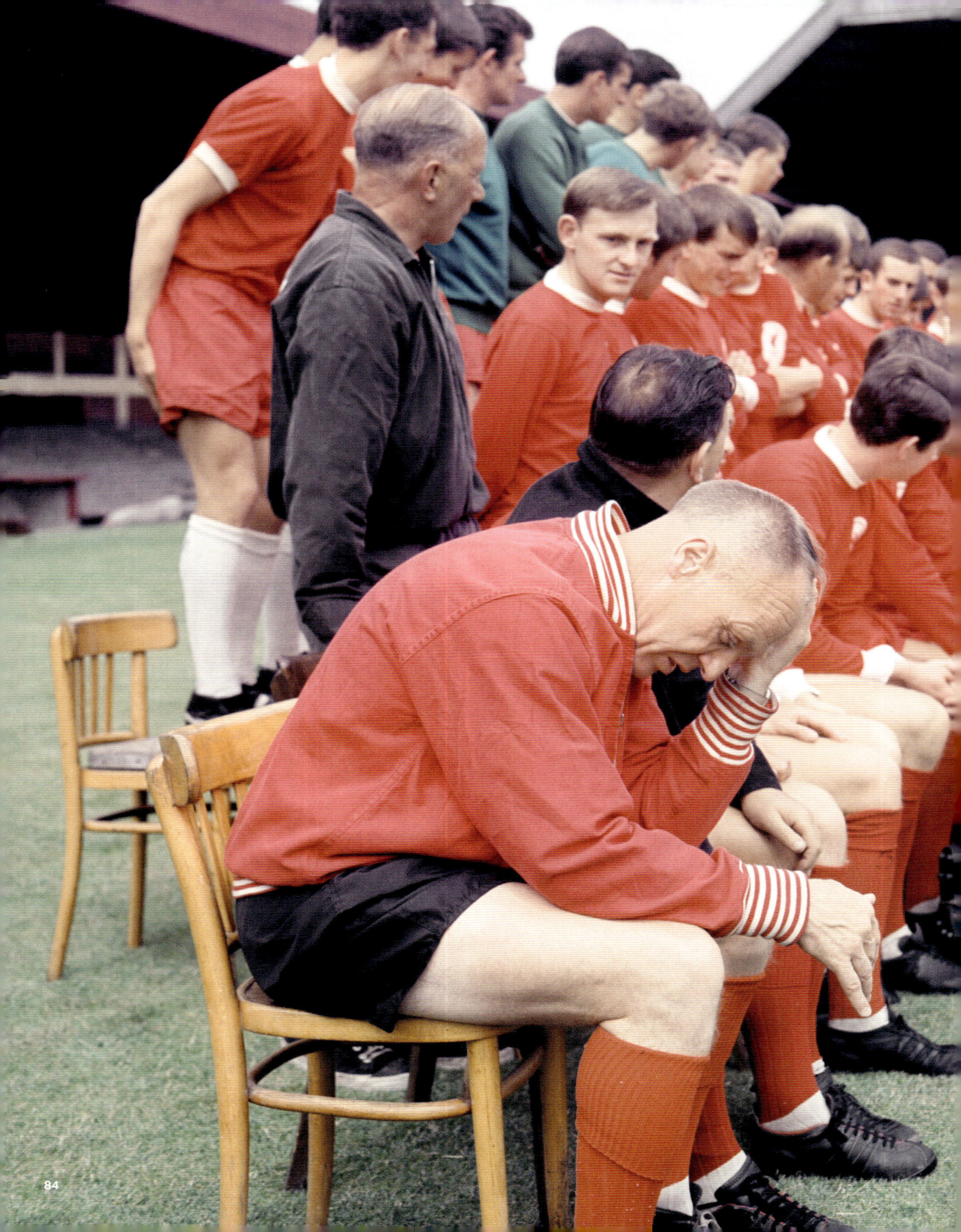

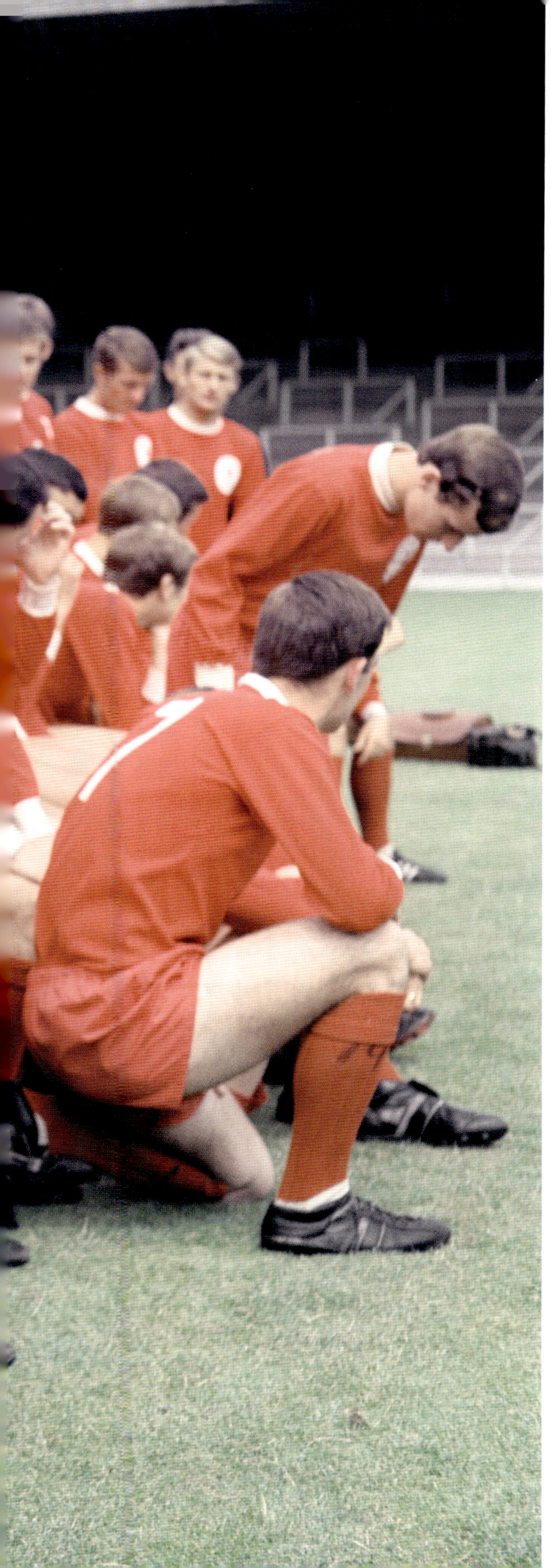

Anfield 1967
Before the 1967/68 team photo,
Liverpool manager Bill Shankly looks
tired and in deep thought.

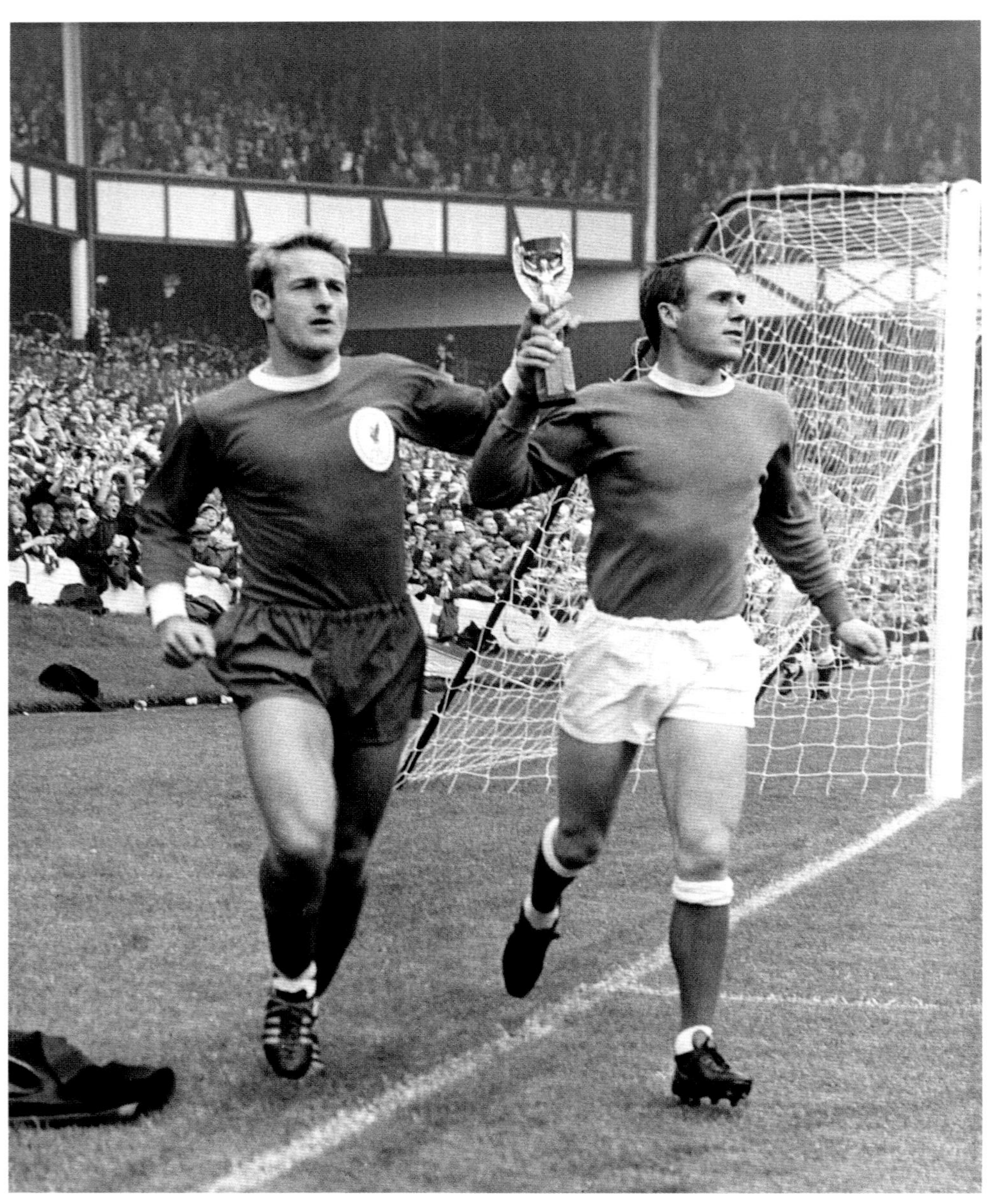

Goodison Park 1966
Before the Charity Shield between
champions Liverpool and FA Cup winners
Everton, Roger Hunt (l) and Ray Wilson (r)
parade the World Cup they had won with
England a month earlier.

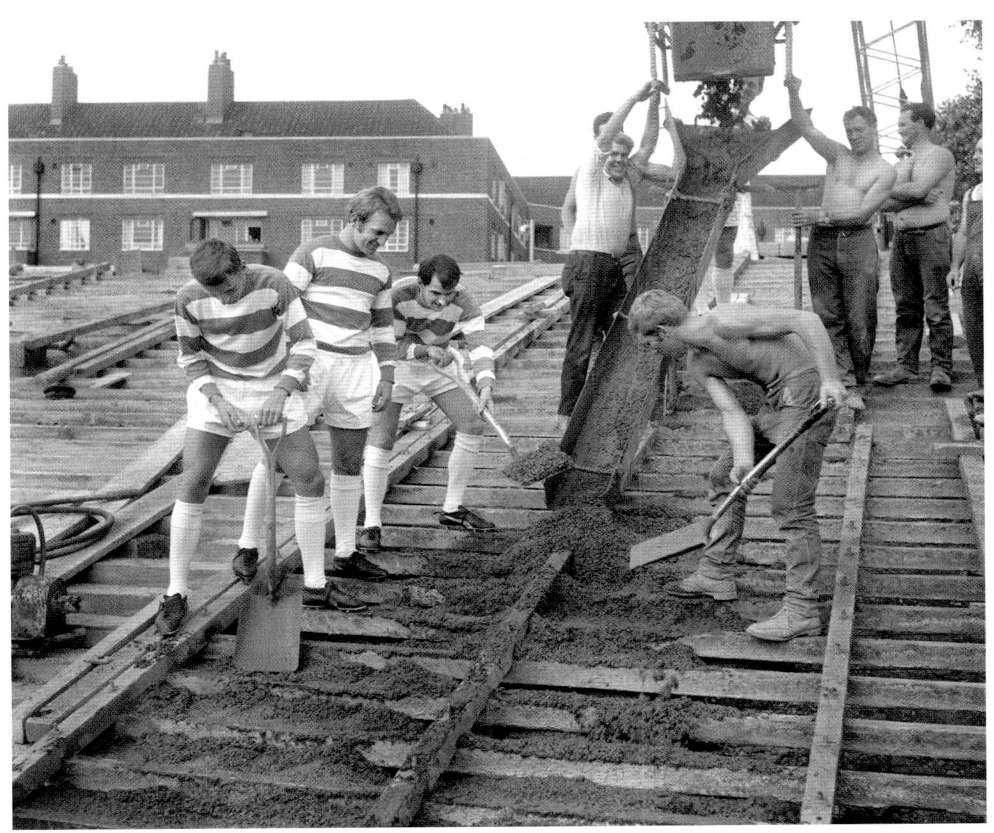

Loftus Road 1969
QPR players give a hand
to the builders as they
construct a new stand.

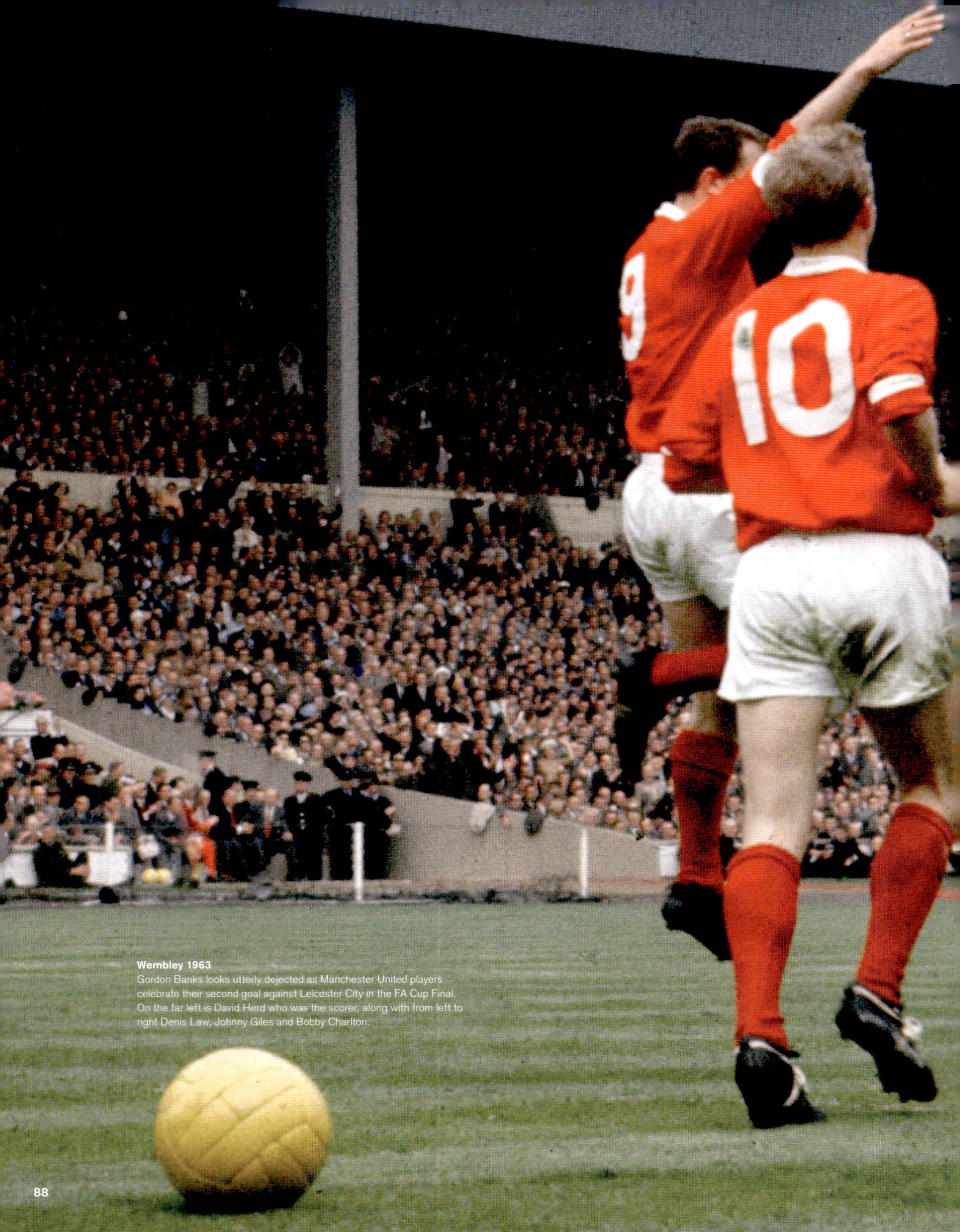

Wembley 1963
Gordon Banks looks utterly dejected as Manchester United players celebrate their second goal against Leicester City in the FA Cup Final. On the far left is David Herd who was the scorer, along with from left to right Denis Law, Johnny Giles and Bobby Charlton.

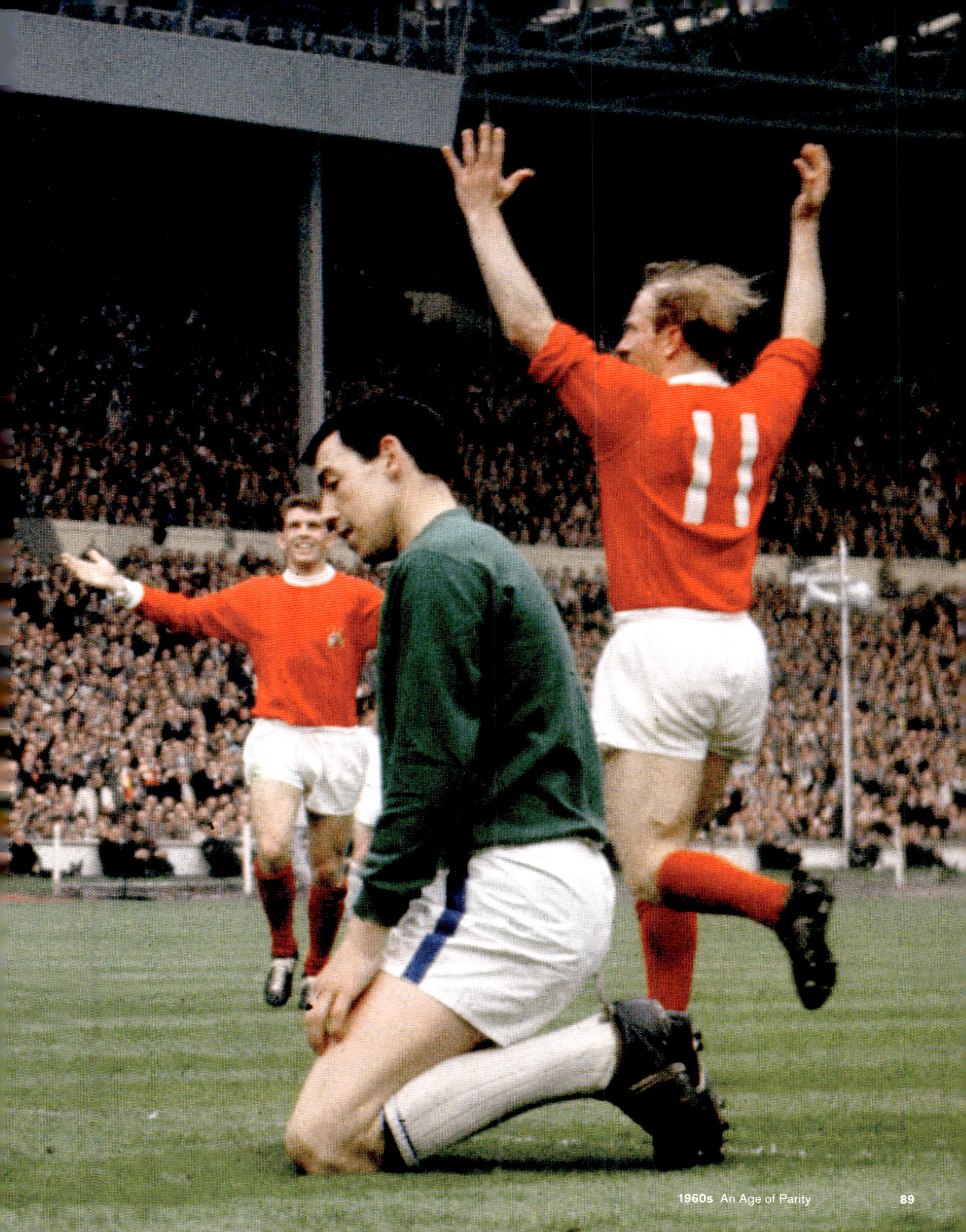

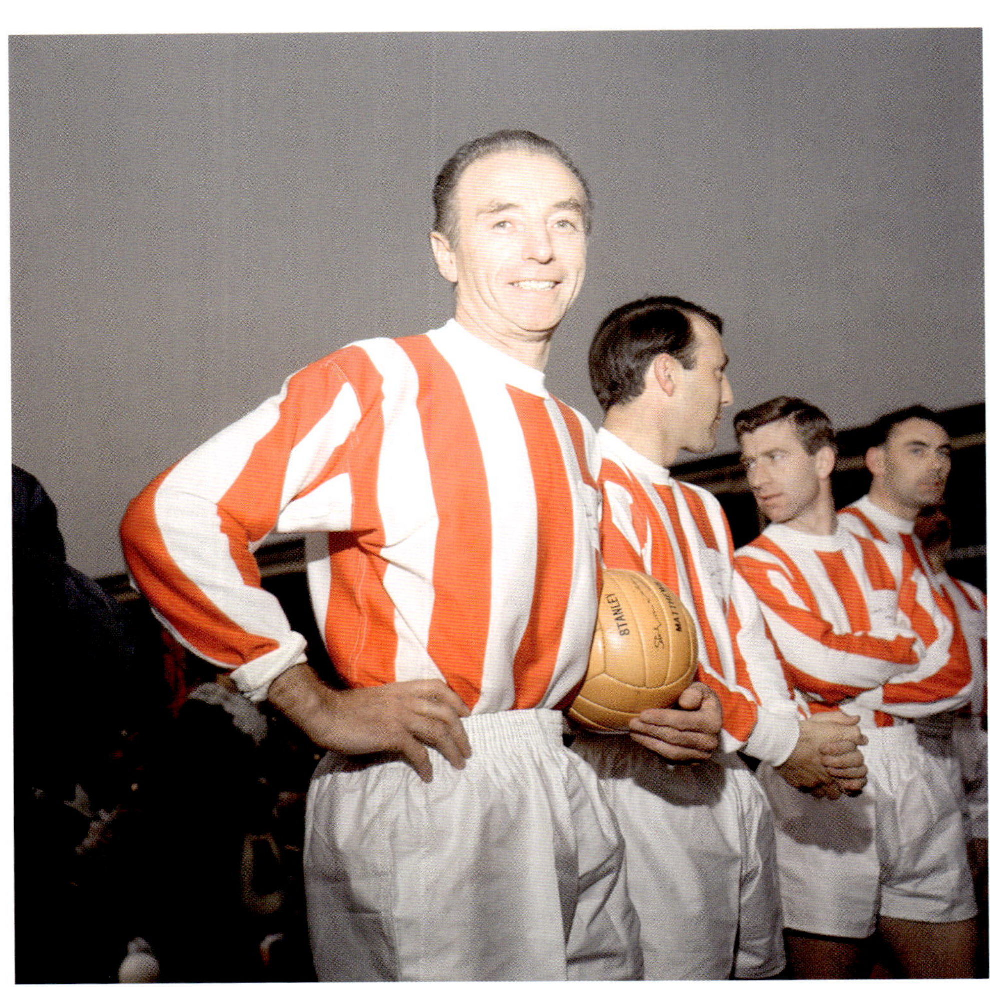

Victoria Ground 1965
Stanley Matthews, aged 50, is all smiles
before his testimonial match against a team
of international superstars. From left to right
are Jimmy Greaves, Bryan Douglas, and
Alan Gilzean.

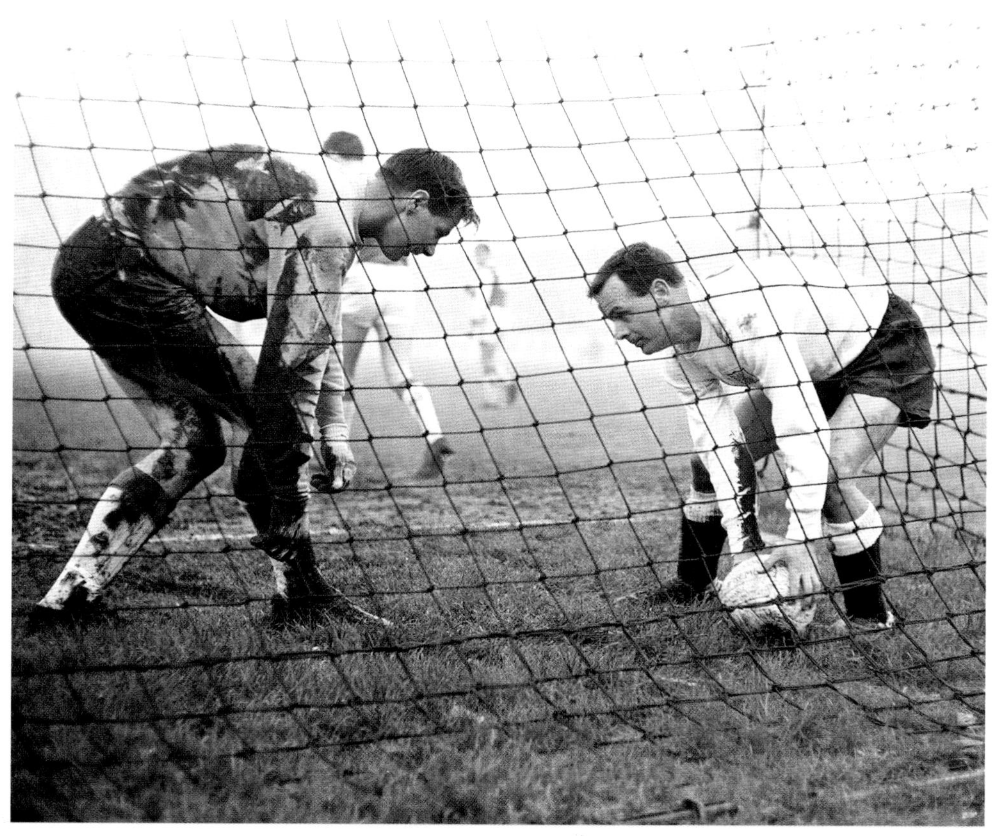

Craven Cottage 1963
Fulham's Graham Leggat picks the
ball out of the Ipswich goal in a terrible
Boxing Day for goalkeeper Roy Bailey.
Leggat scored four in a 10-1 massacre.

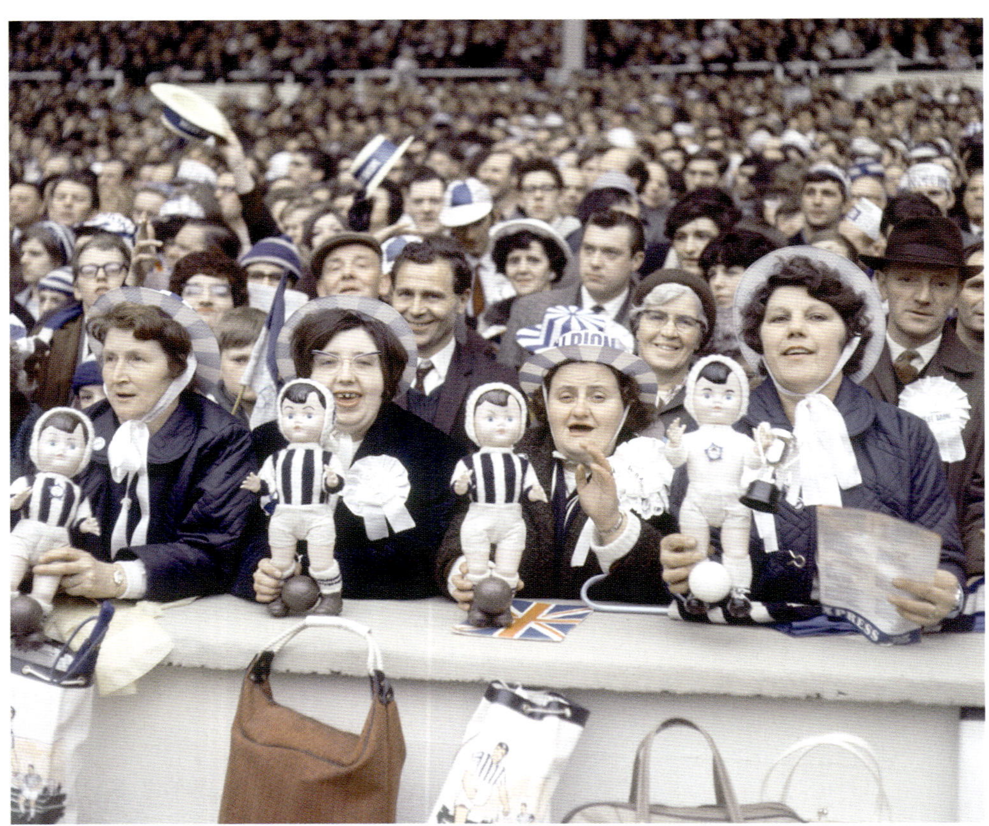

Wembley 1969
West Brom fans hold up club style
dolls, as the Baggies beat Everton
1-0 in the FA Cup Final with a goal
from Jeff Astle.

Wembley 1967
Up in the Royal Box, Spurs lift up the FA Cup as
Chelsea players watch on from below. Dubbed
the 'Cockney Cup Final', it was the first time two
London teams had met in the final.

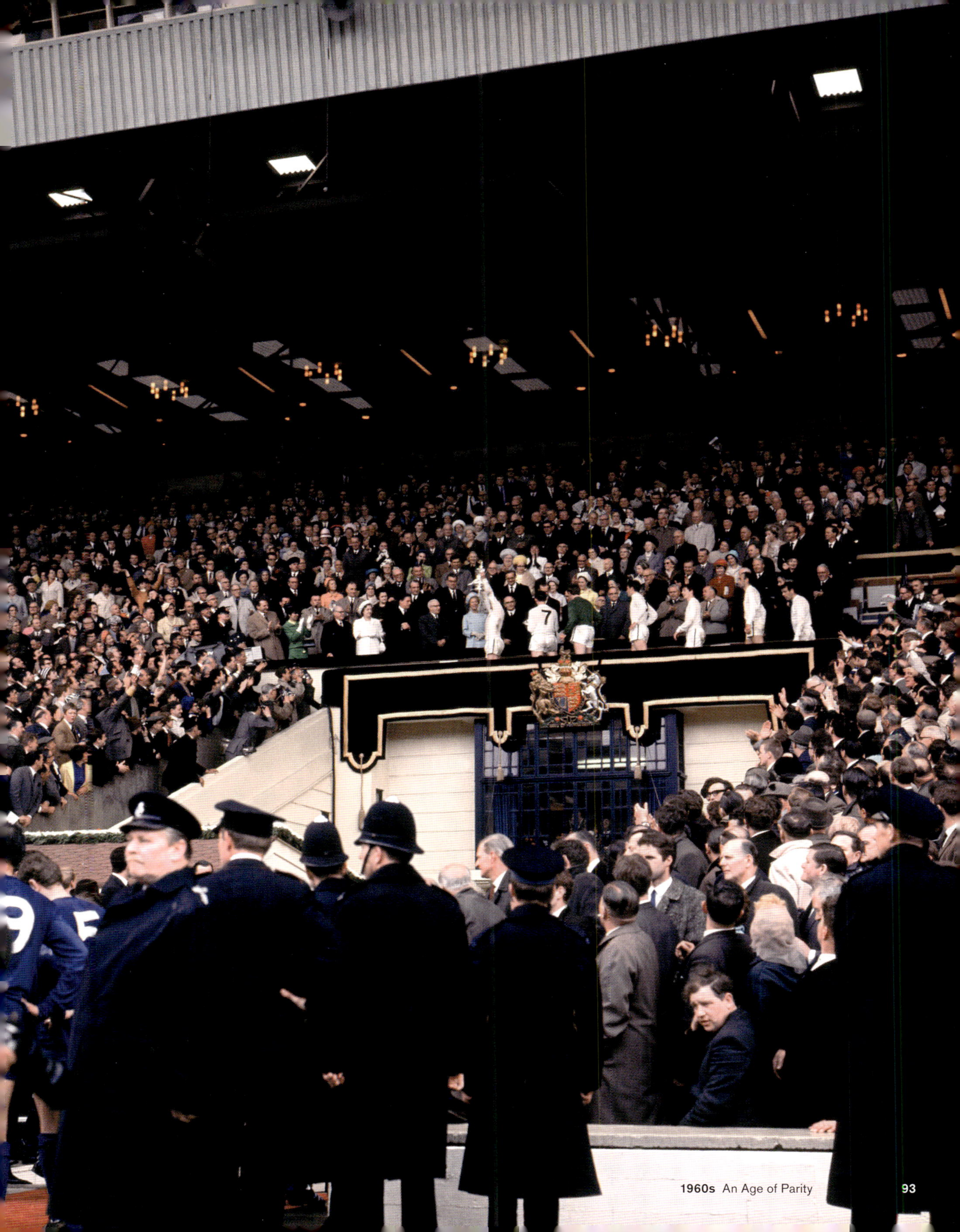

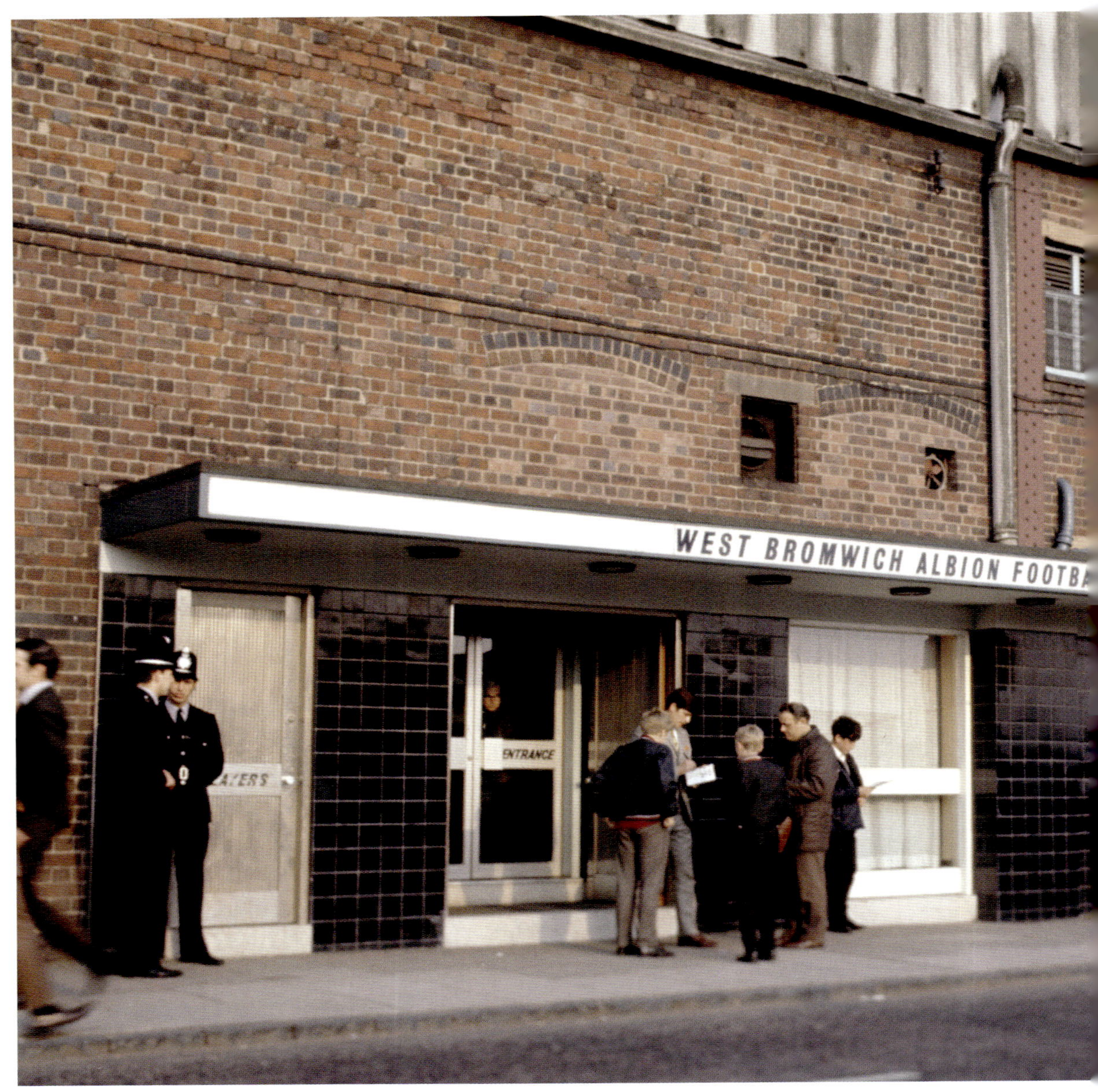

The Hawthorns 1968
The old entrance to West Bromwich Albion's
ground, which had the appearance of a cinema.

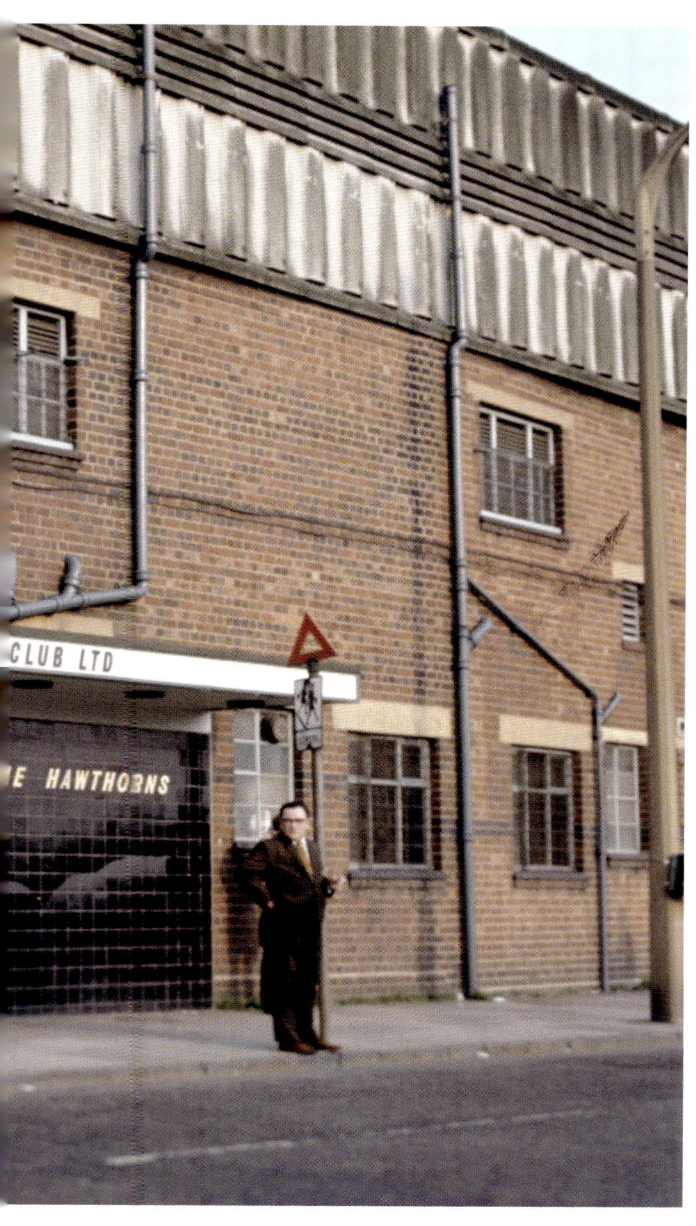

CLUB LTD
E HAWTHORNS

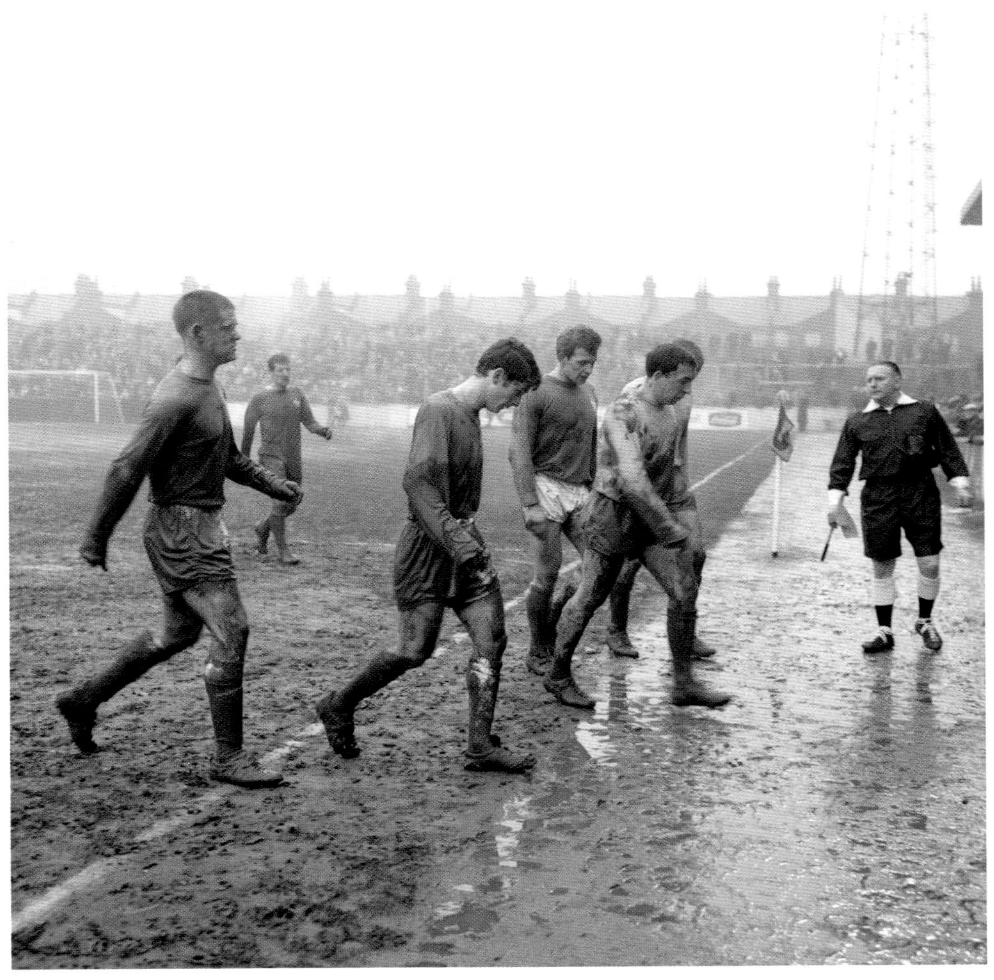

Brisbane Road 1966
A cold and muddy day in east London
as Leyton Orient host Norwich City in
an FA Cup tie.

Ewood Park 1965
At half-time, with the score 0-0 against
Manchester United, fans of Blackburn Rovers
swap ends so they can be at the end their team
is attacking. United ended up winning 5-0.

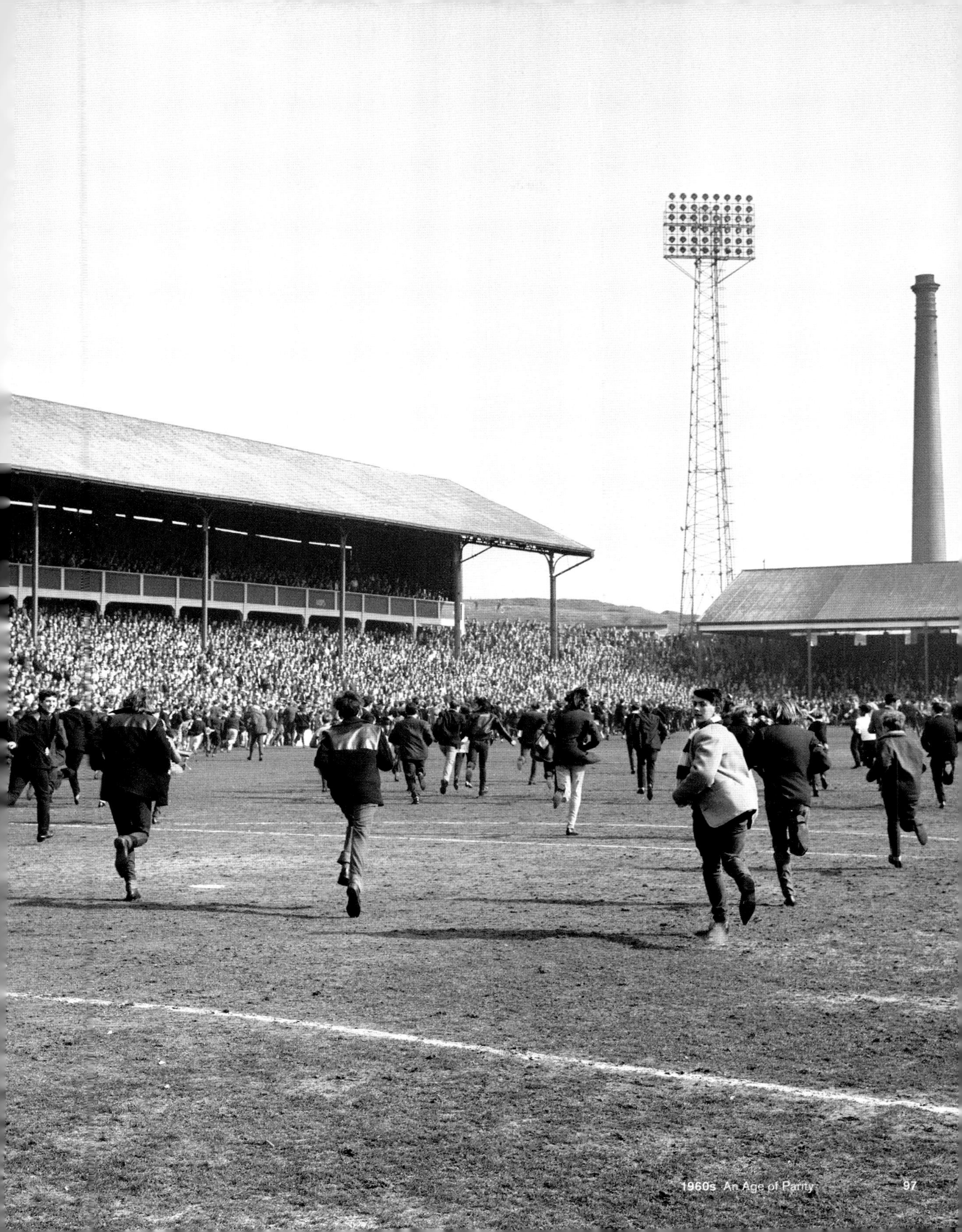

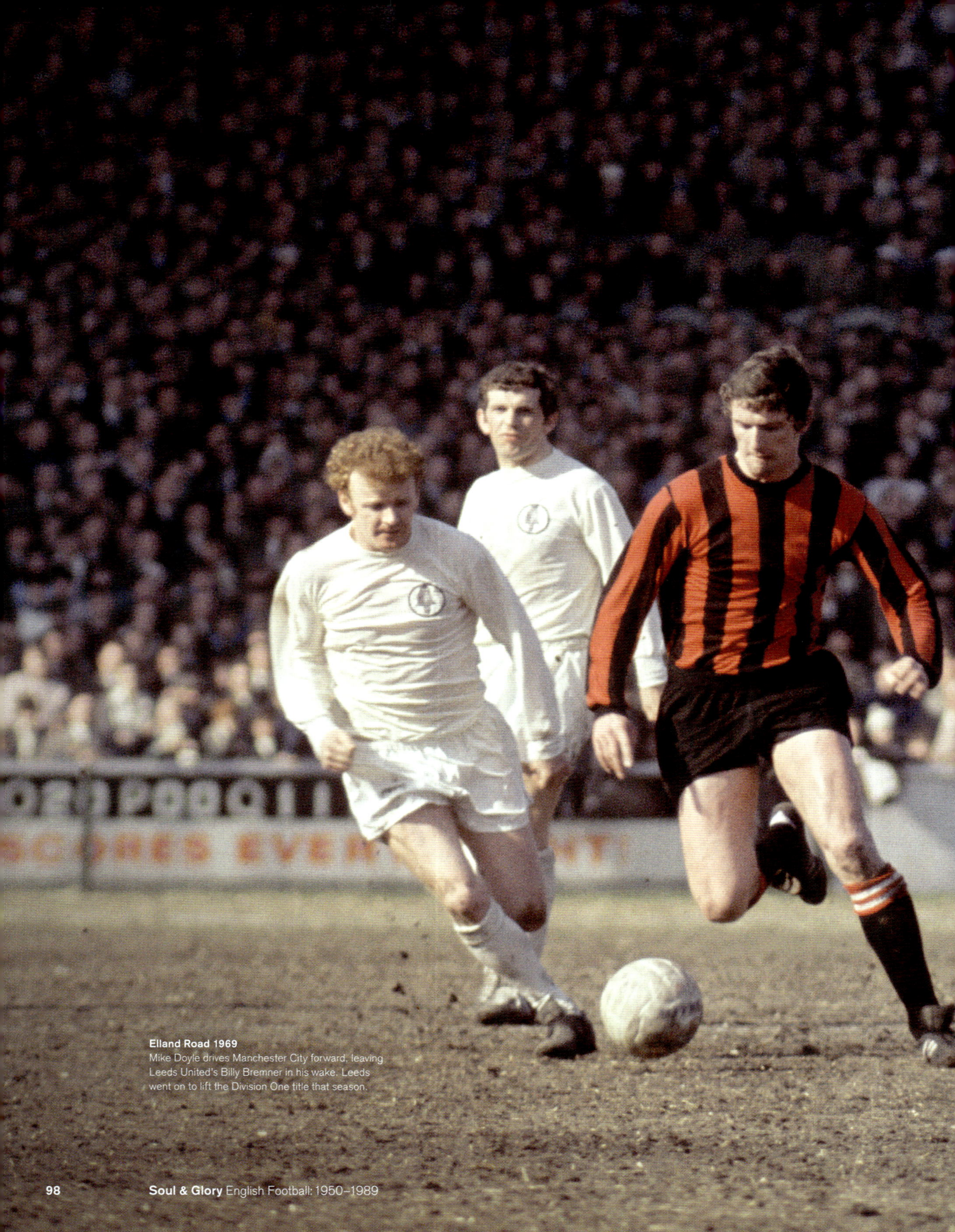

Elland Road 1969
Mike Doyle drives Manchester City forward, leaving
Leeds United's Billy Bremner in his wake. Leeds
went on to lift the Division One title that season.

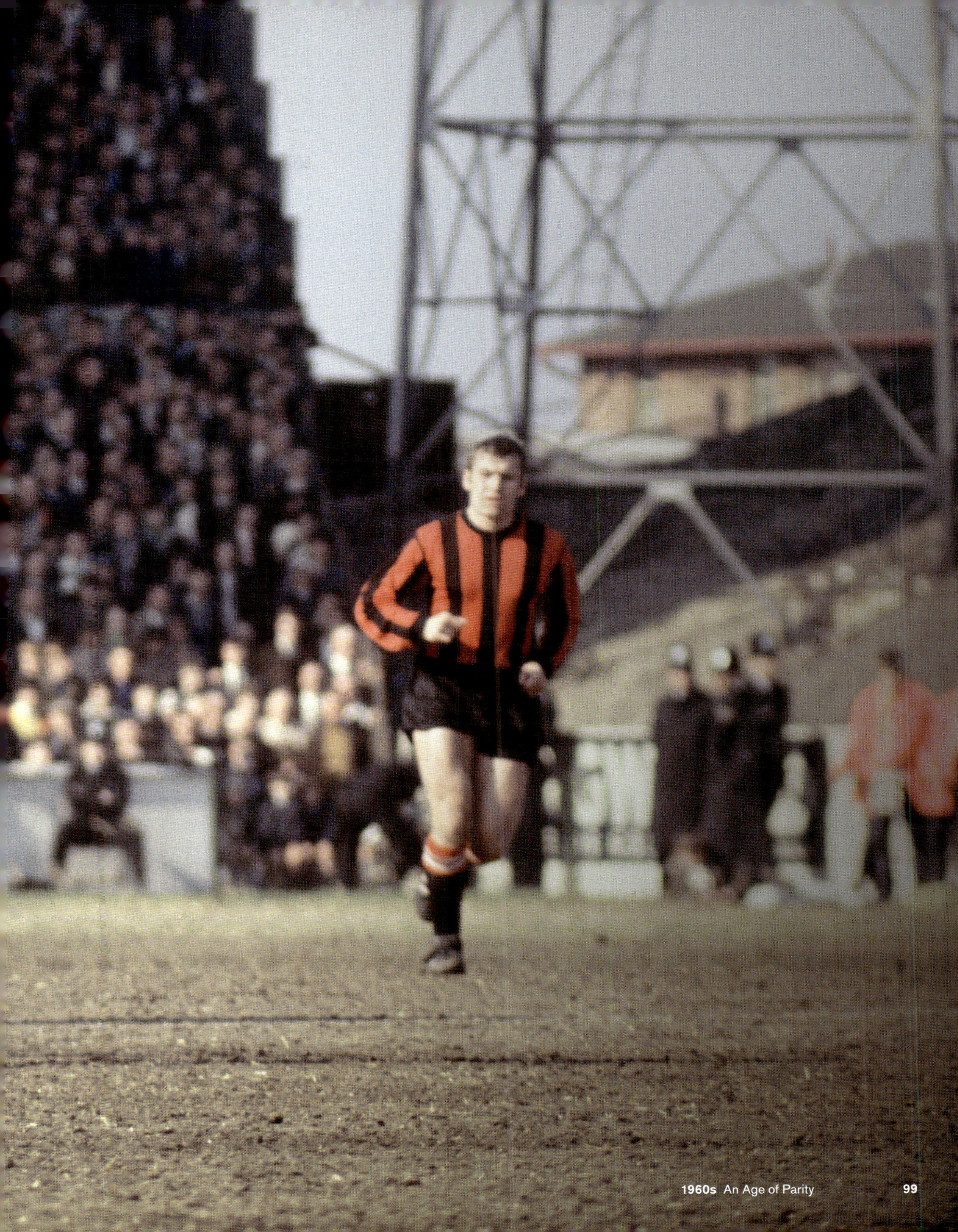

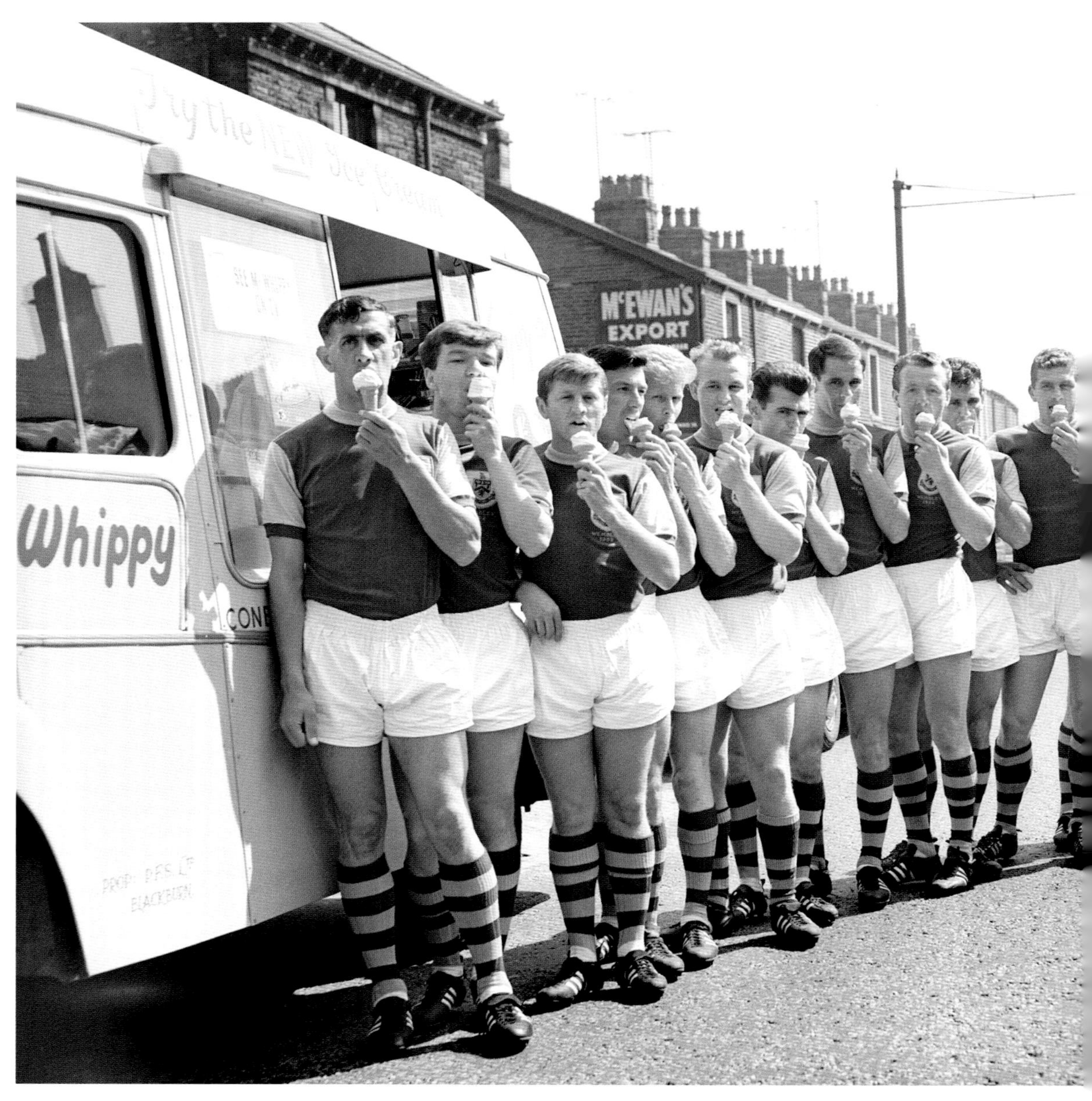

Burnley 1962
The Burnley team get some respite
from training as they prepare to face
Tottenham Hotspur in the FA Cup Final.

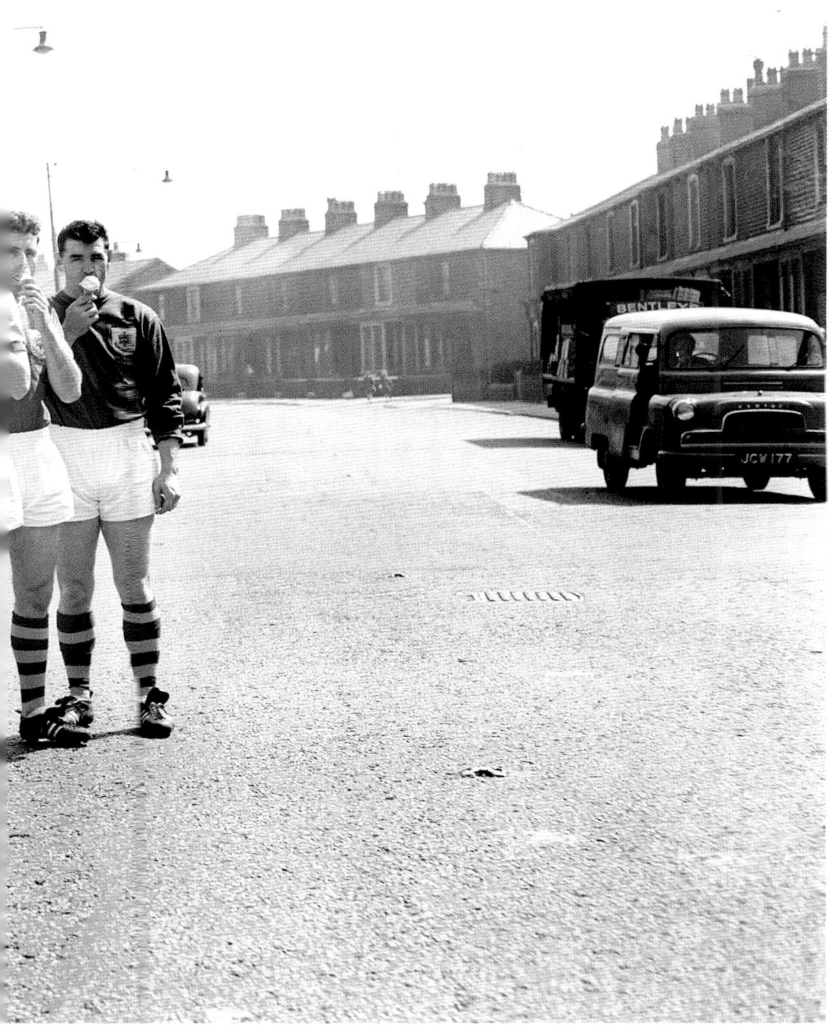

JCW 177

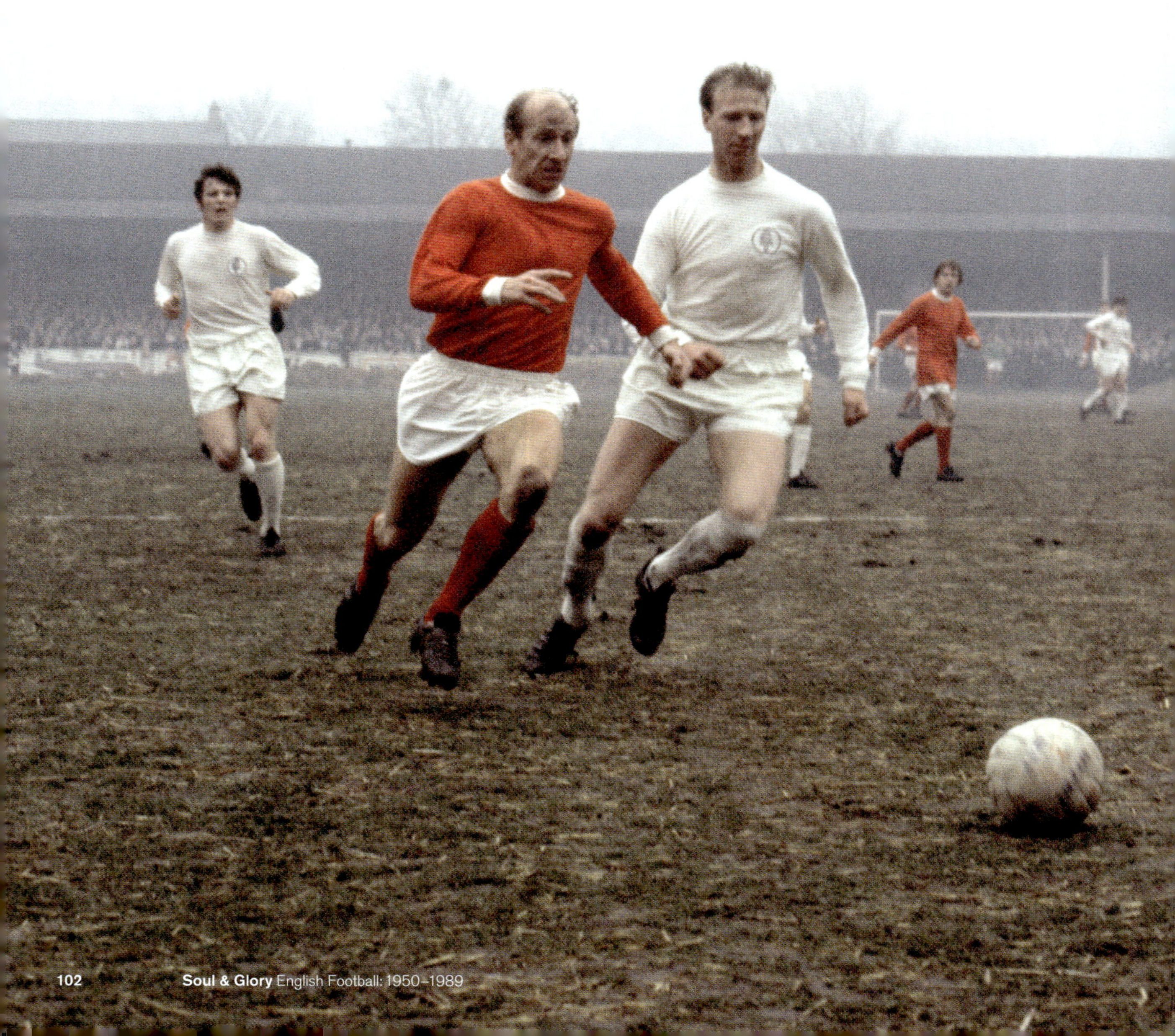

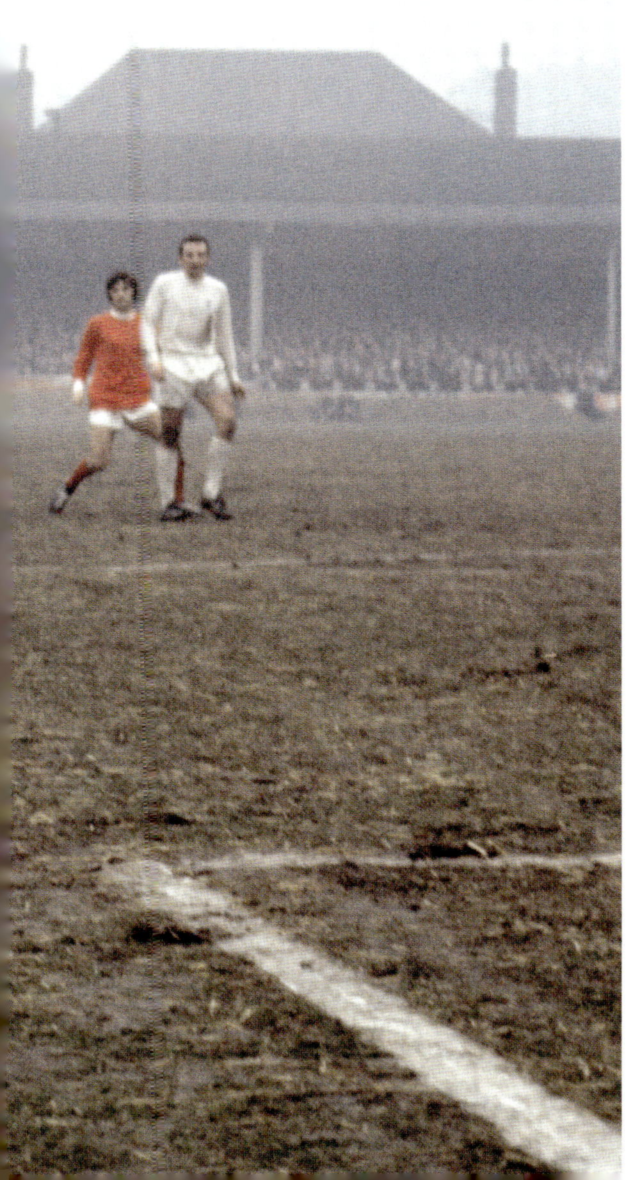

Elland Road 1969
Bobby Charlton takes on brother
Jackie Charlton. Bobby scored
that day, but Jackie's Leeds beat
Manchester United 2-1.

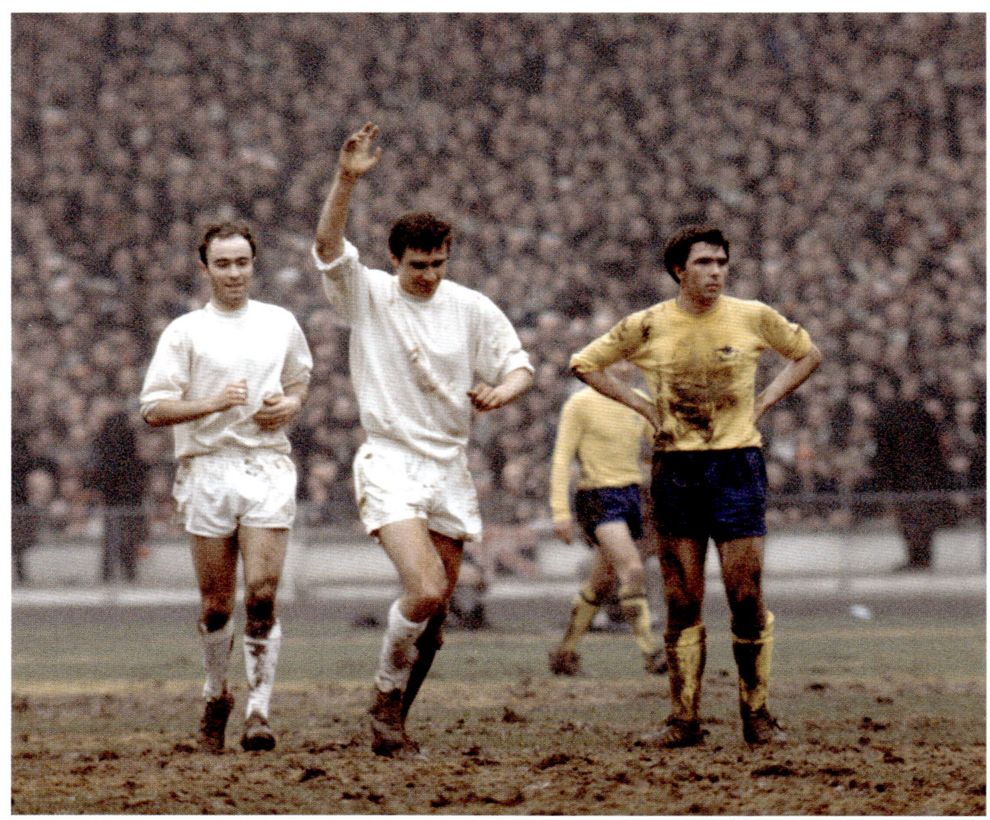

Wembley 1969
On a cut-up Wembley turf, Roger Smart celebrates as Division Three Swindon Town cause a massive upset, by beating Arsenal 3-1 in the League Cup Final.

Vicarage Road 1962
Carlisle United's Peter McConnell puts a penalty into the net, despite a desperate stretch from Watford goalkeeper Dave Underwood.

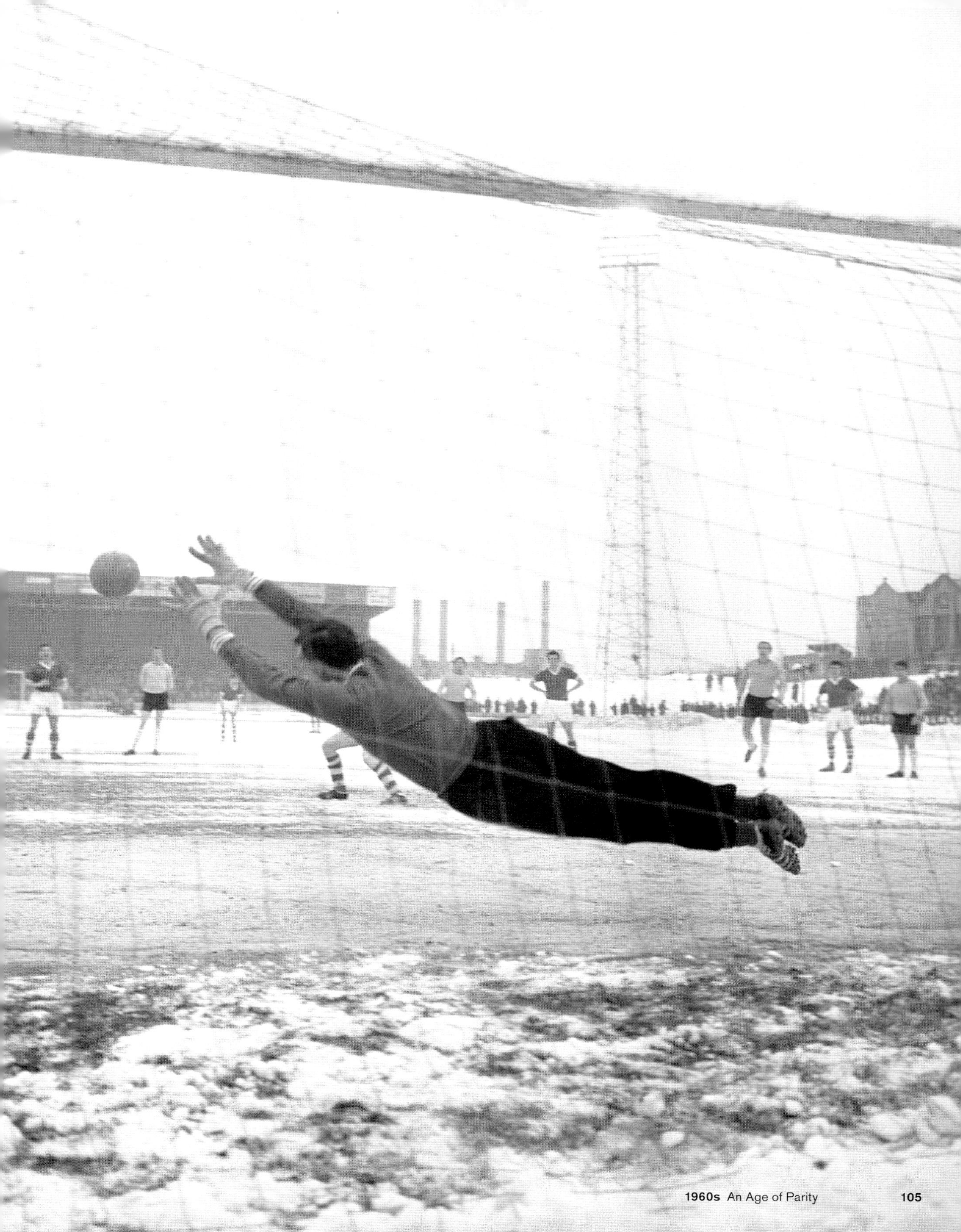

The Dell 1966
Southampton celebrate beating
Charlton 1-0 and gaining
promotion to Division One.

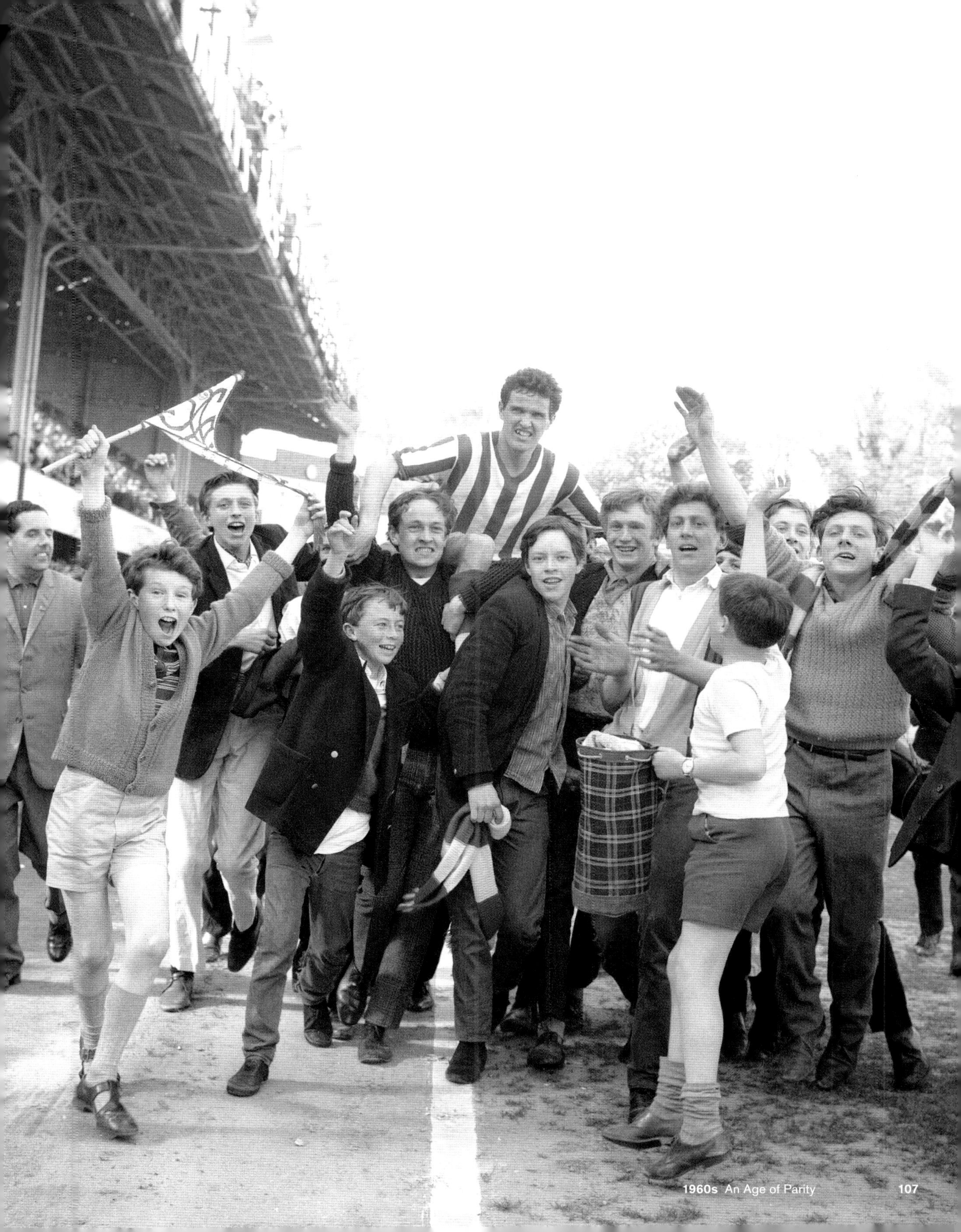

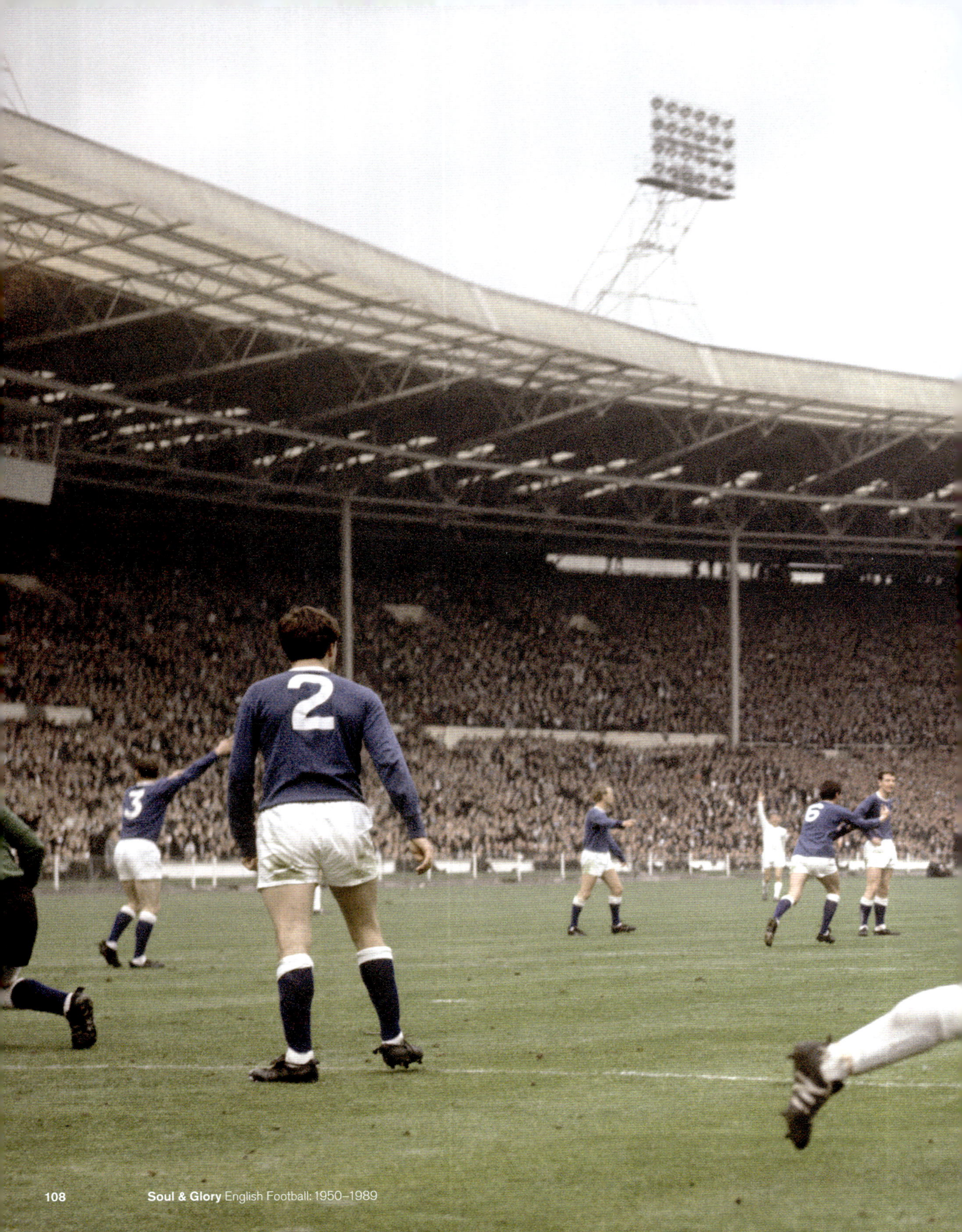

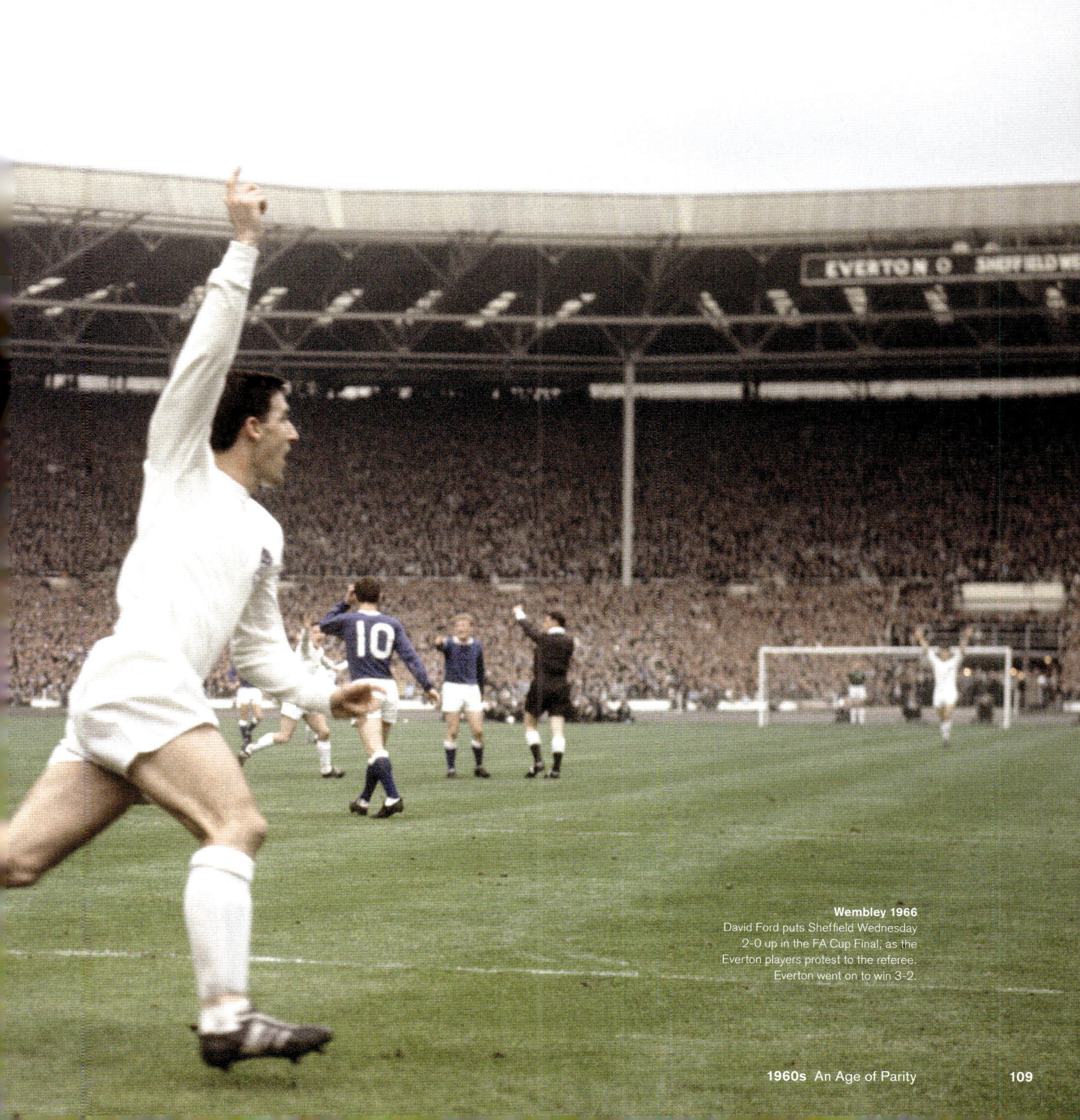

Wembley 1966
David Ford puts Sheffield Wednesday
2-0 up in the FA Cup Final, as the
Everton players protest to the referee.
Everton went on to win 3-2.

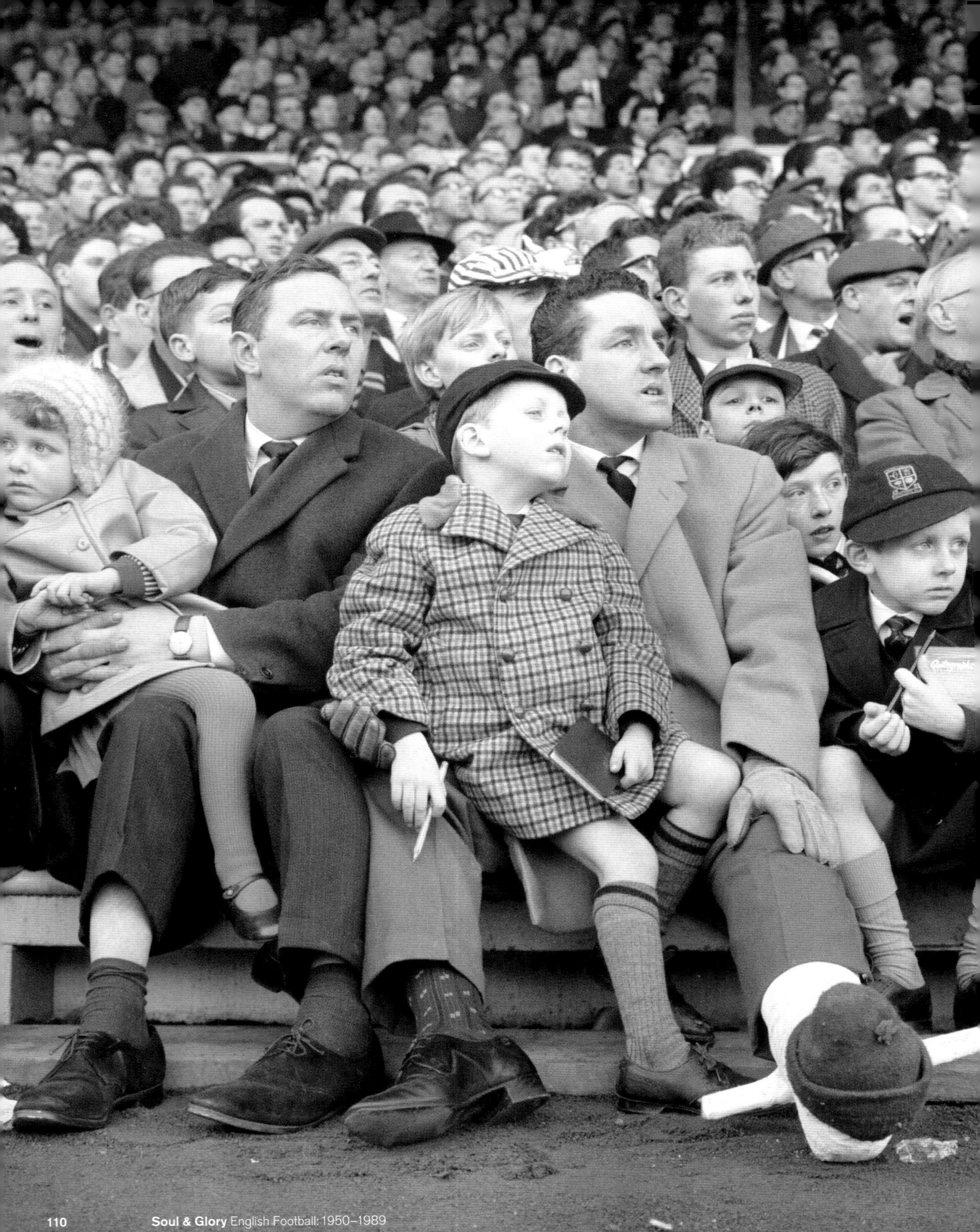

Tottenham's Dave Mackay, injured with a
broken leg, watches his team play Chelsea
in close proximity to the fans. His children
Derek and David are by his side.

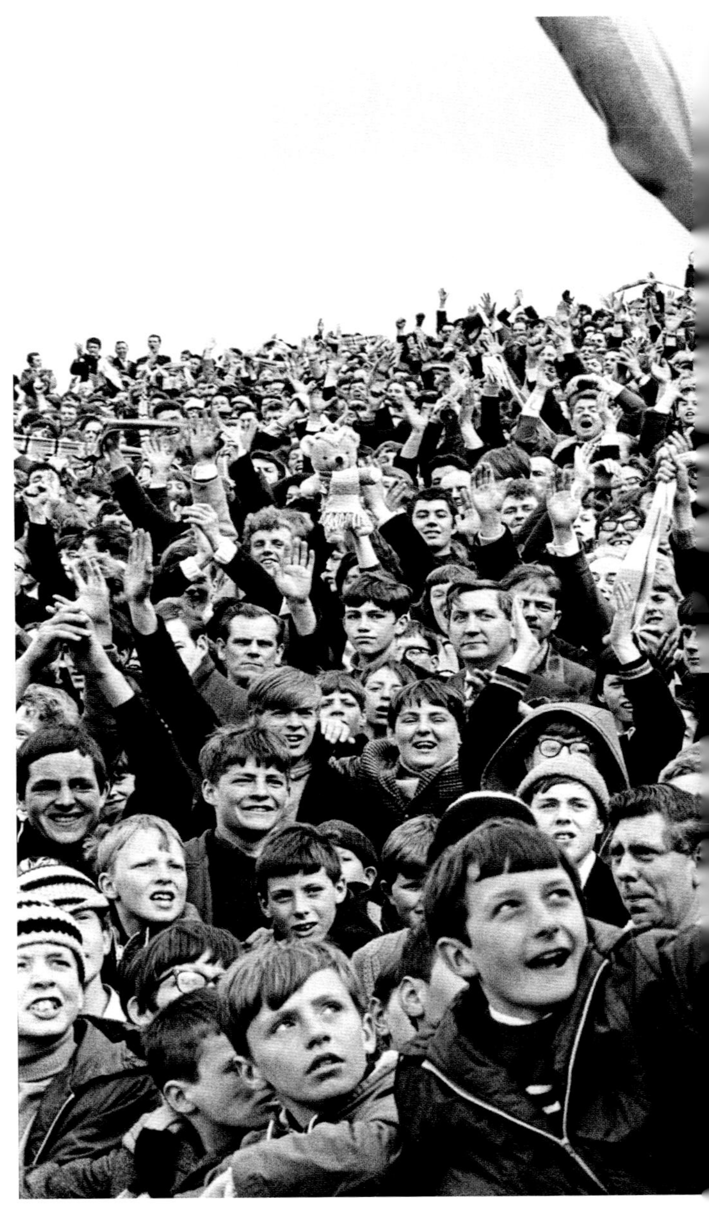

St James' Park 1968
Francis Lee celebrates in front of
delirious Manchester City fans, as they
beat Newcastle 4-3 in a thrilling game
which confirmed City as champions.

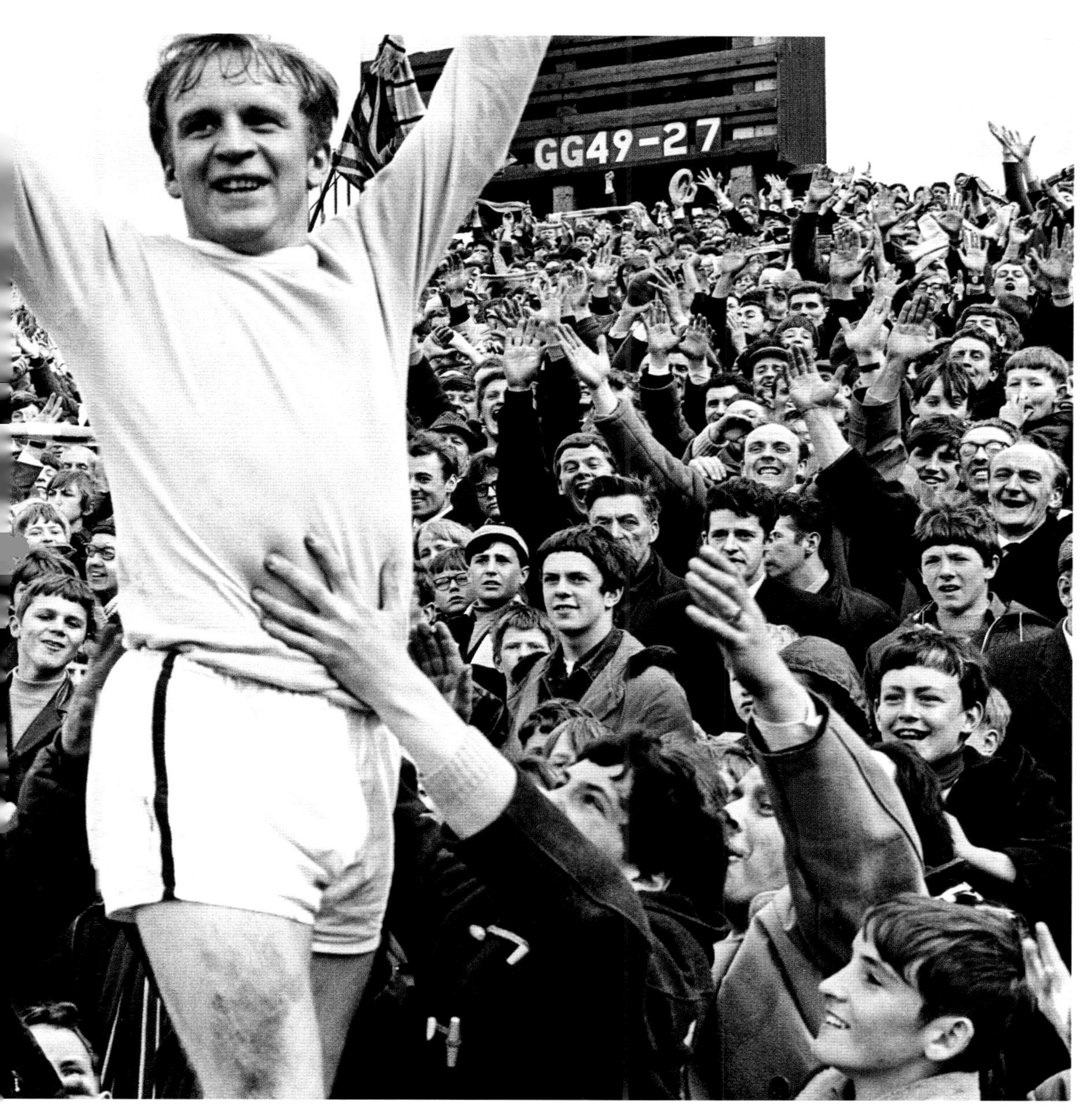

GG49-27

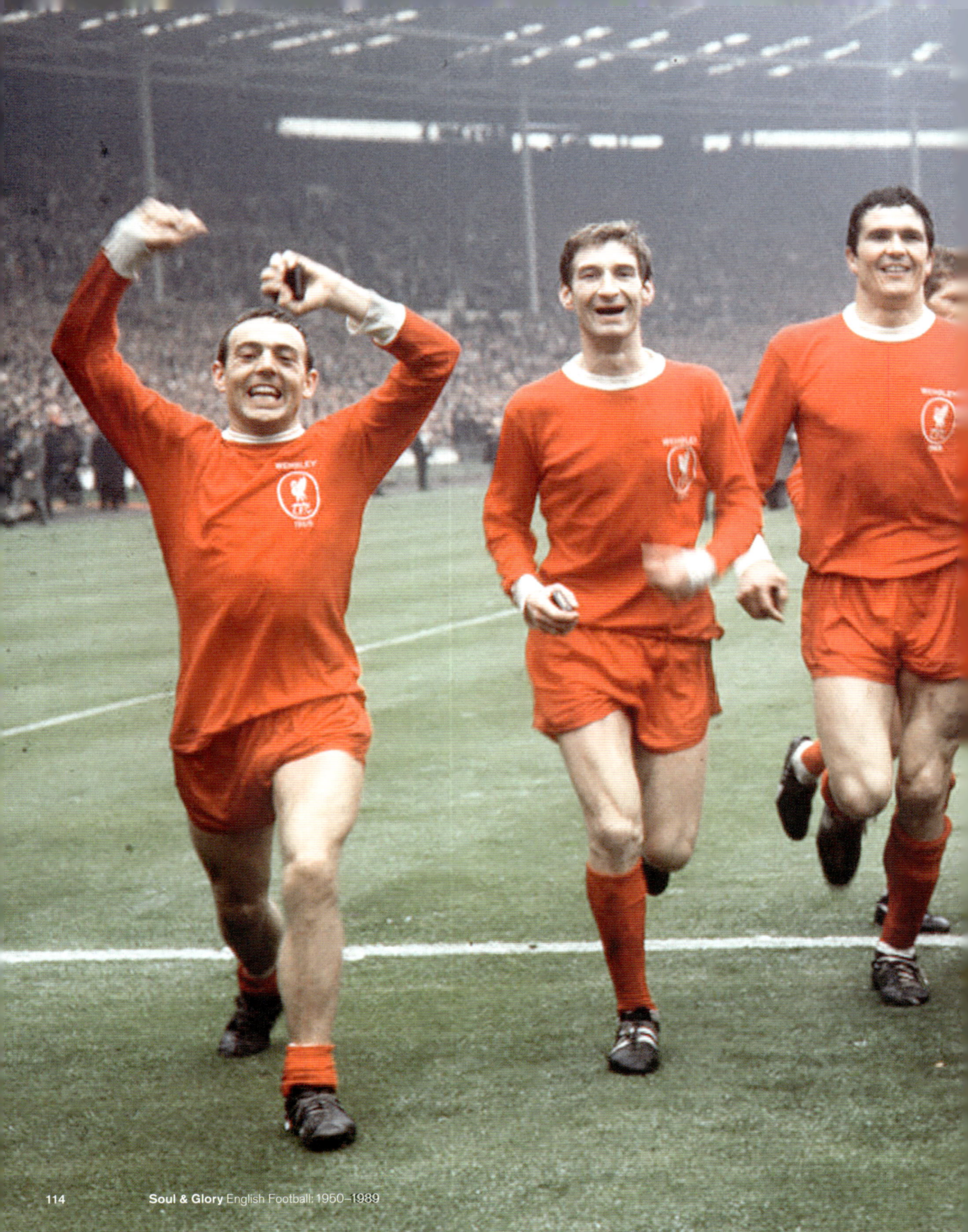

 Soul & Glory English Football: 1950–1989

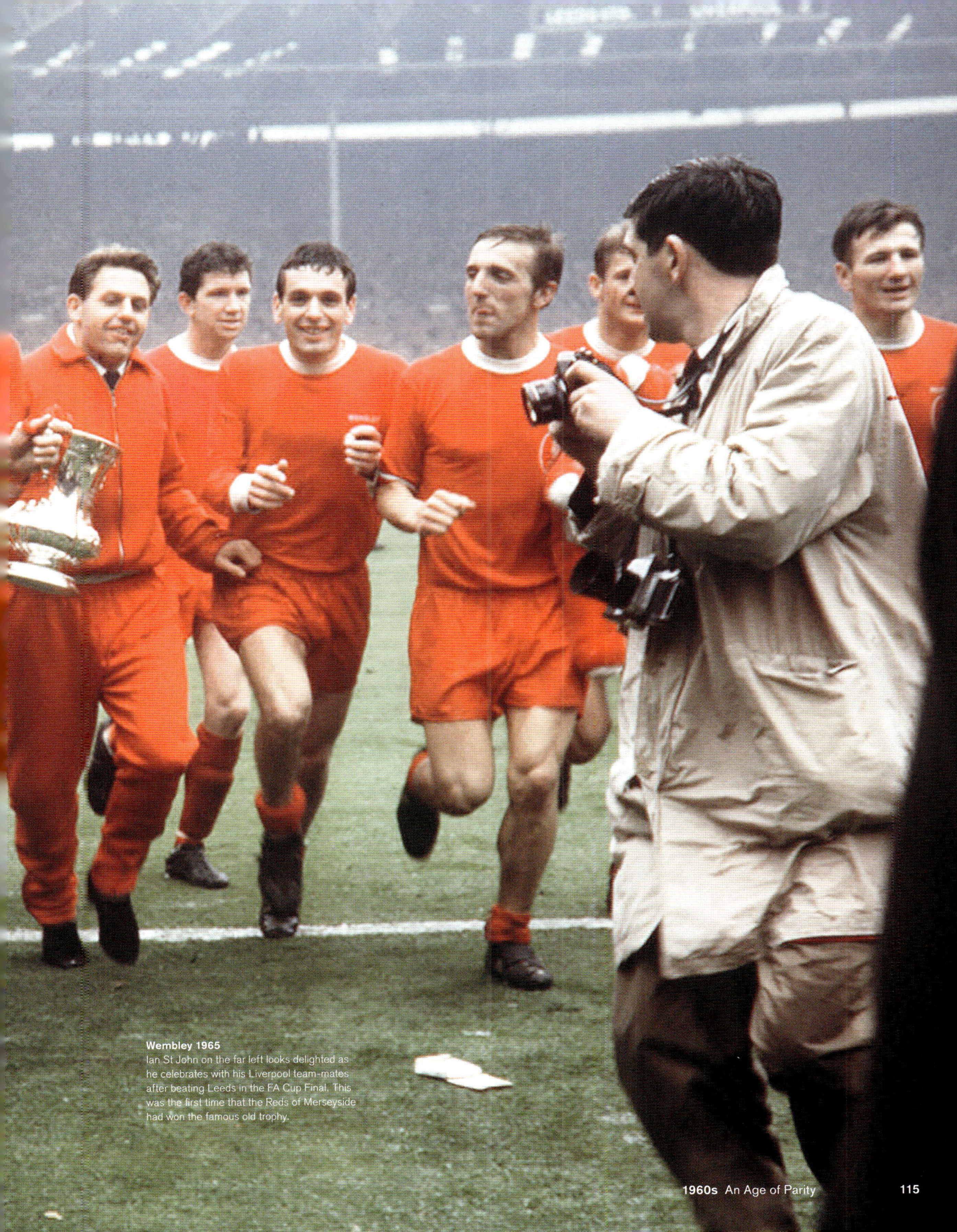

Wembley 1965
Ian St John on the far left looks delighted as
he celebrates with his Liverpool team-mates
after beating Leeds in the FA Cup Final. This
was the first time that the Reds of Merseyside
had won the famous old trophy.

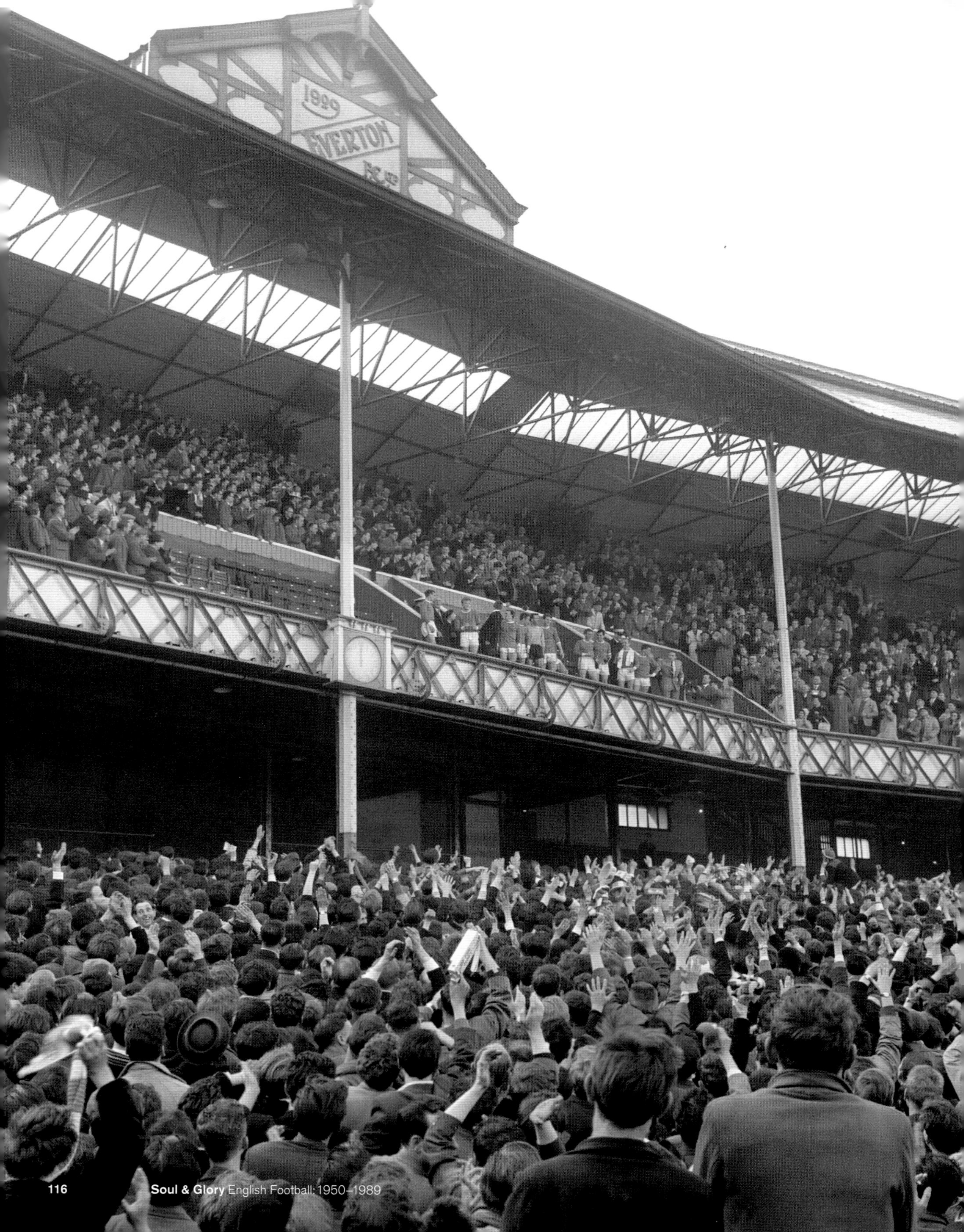

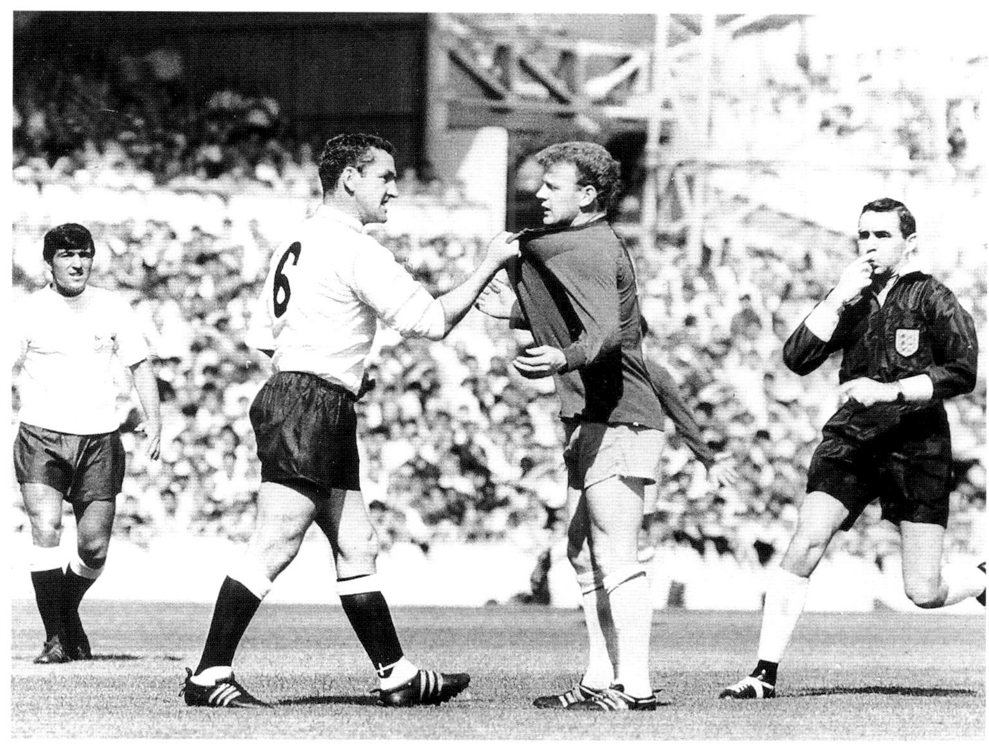

Goodison Park 1963
Everton are crowned champions of
England for the sixth time in their history,
as the team stand on parade in the upper
tier of the Goodison Road Stand.

White Hart Lane 1966
Tottenham's Dave Mackay looks furious at his fellow Scottish international Billy Bremner
who he claims was kicking him in the same leg that he had previously broken twice.
Mackay later said that he didn't like the photograph as it made him look like a bully
considering he was bigger than Bremner. In the background, Terry Venables looks on.

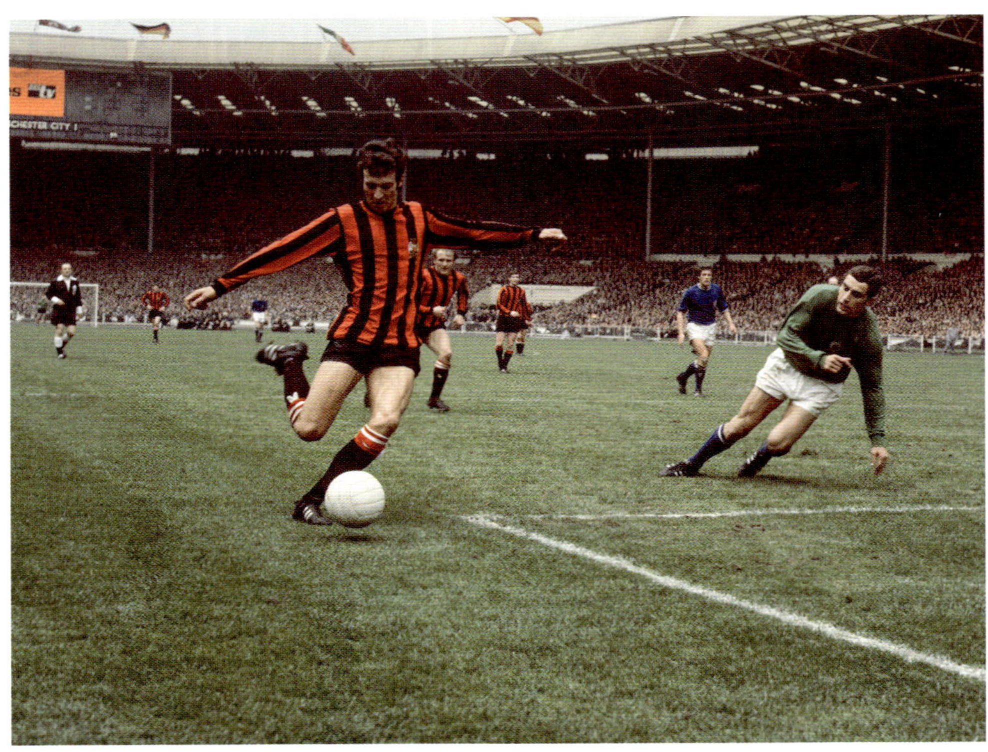

Wembley 1969
Peter Shilton is beaten by
Manchester City's Neil Young,
as Leicester lose their fourth
consecutive FA Cup Final.

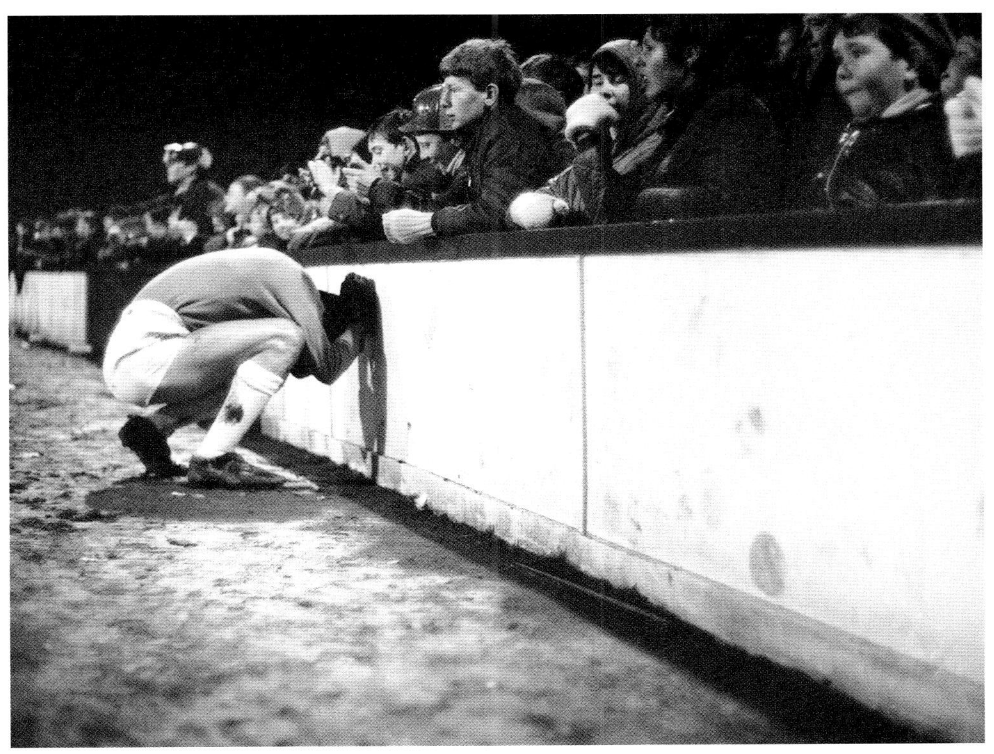

Upton Park 1967
West Brom goalkeeper John Osbourne
can't bear to watch as his side gets a late
penalty against West Ham in a 3-2 win.

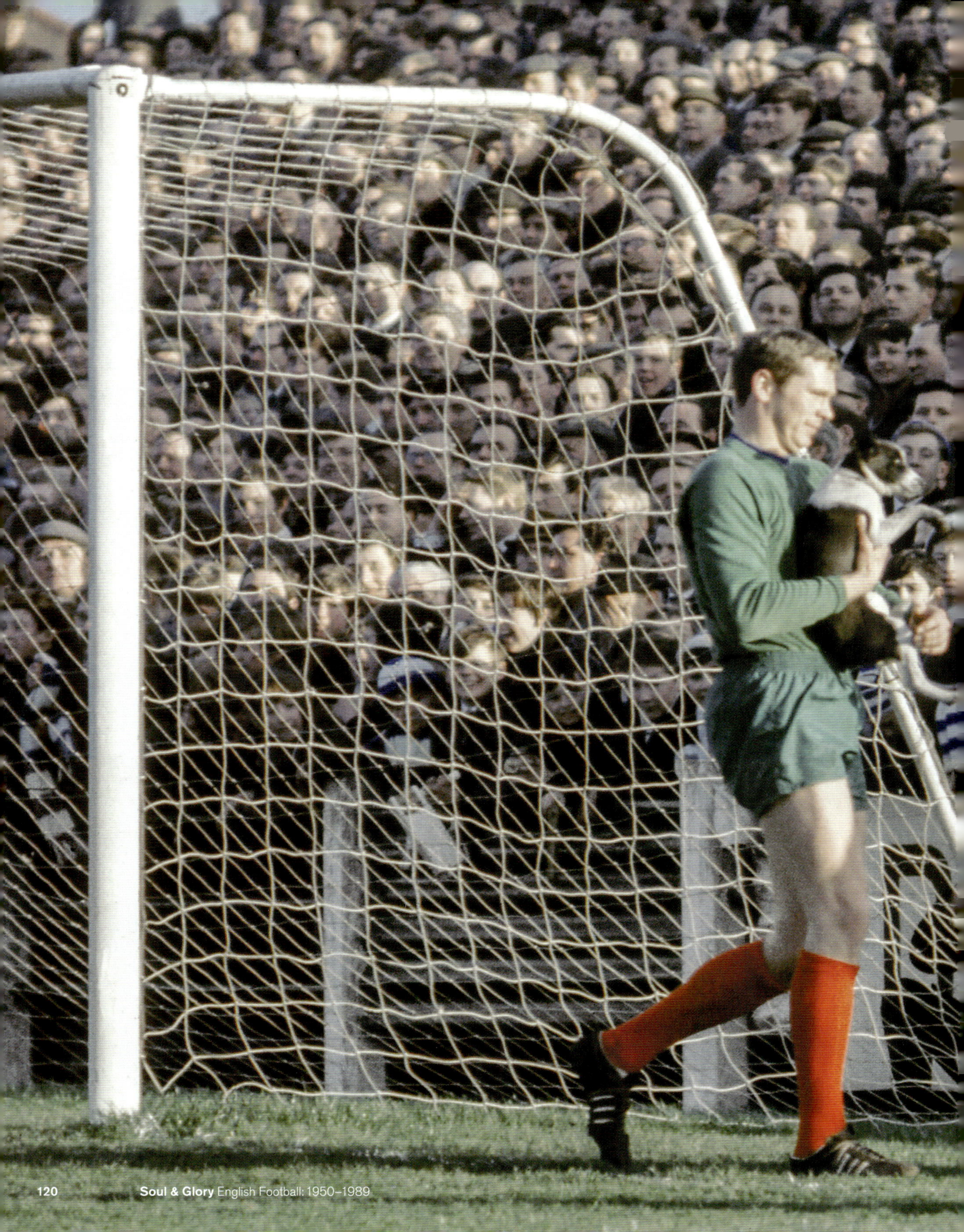

  Soul & Glory English Football: 1950–1989

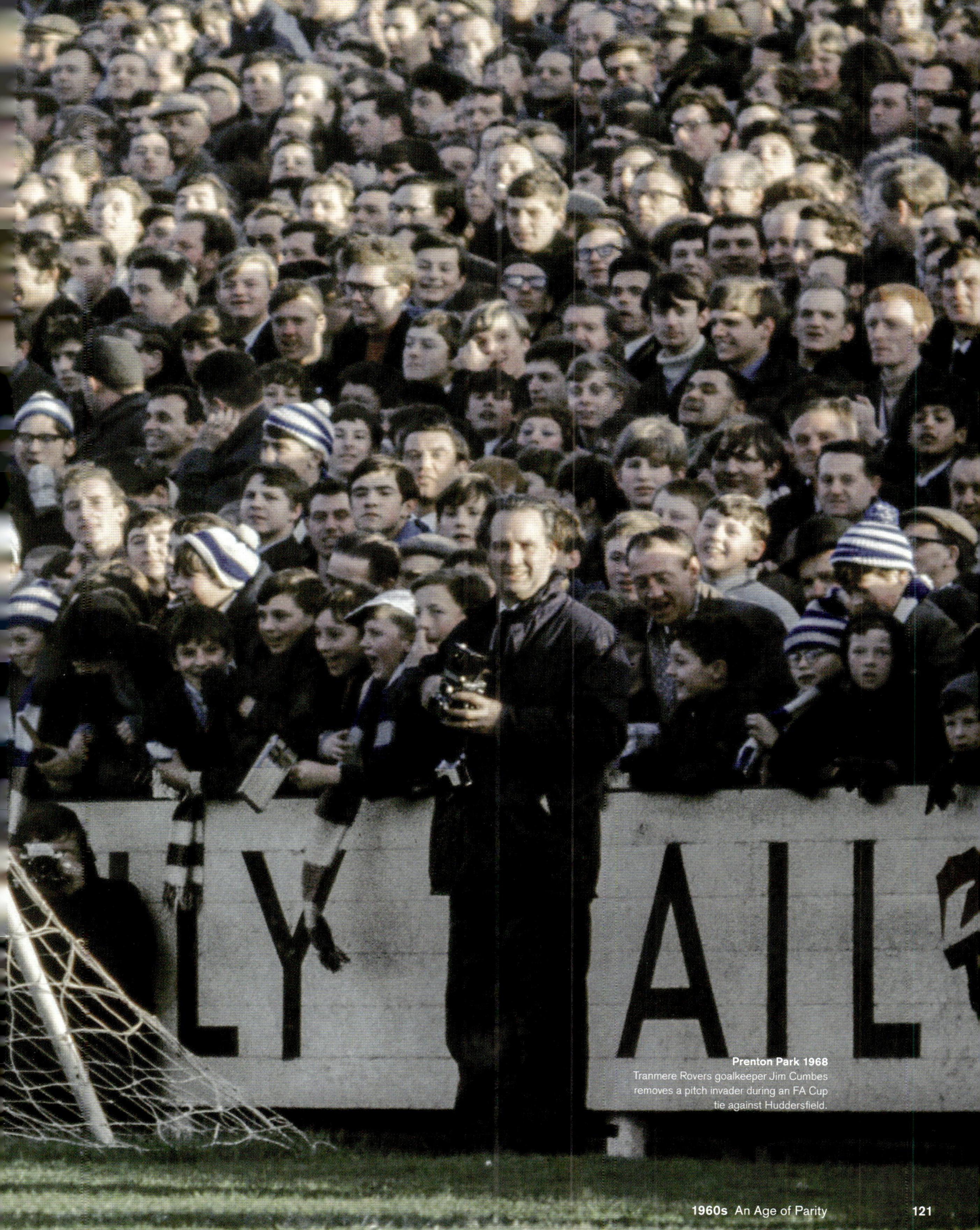

Prenton Park 1968
Tranmere Rovers goalkeeper Jim Cumbes
removes a pitch invader during an FA Cup
tie against Huddersfield.

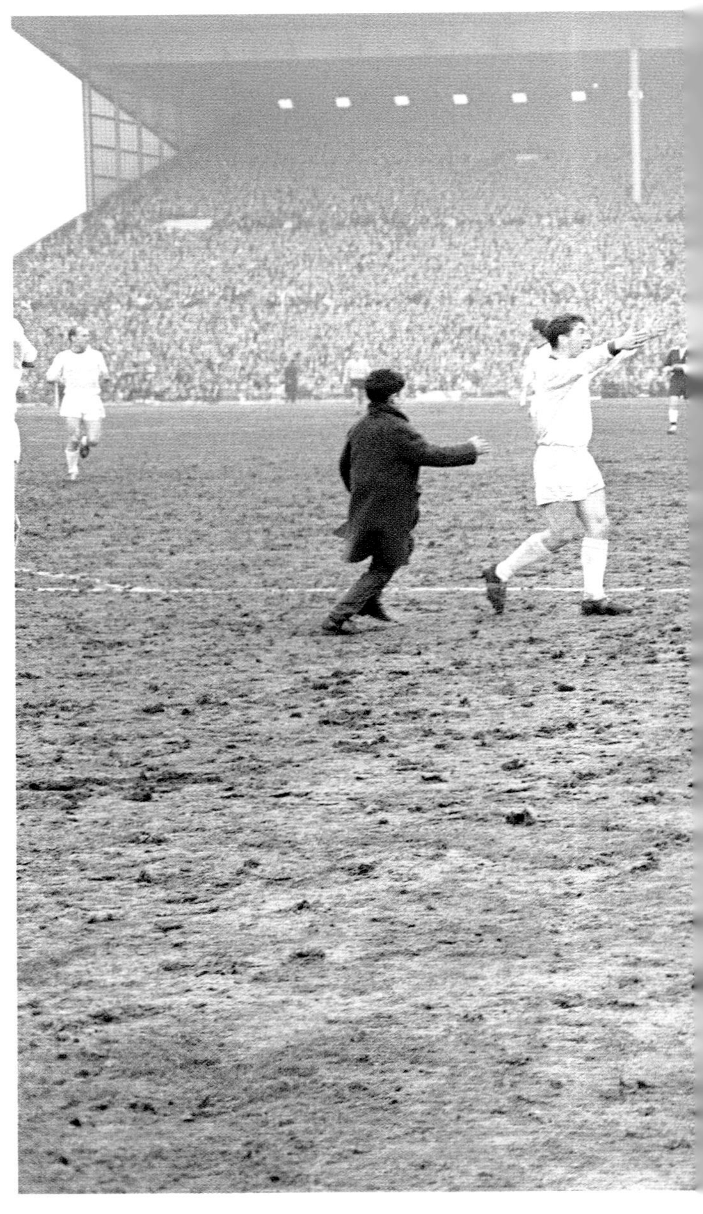

Villa Park 1963
Nobby Stiles celebrates with
Manchester United fans after a
1-0 win against Southampton in
the FA Cup semi-final.

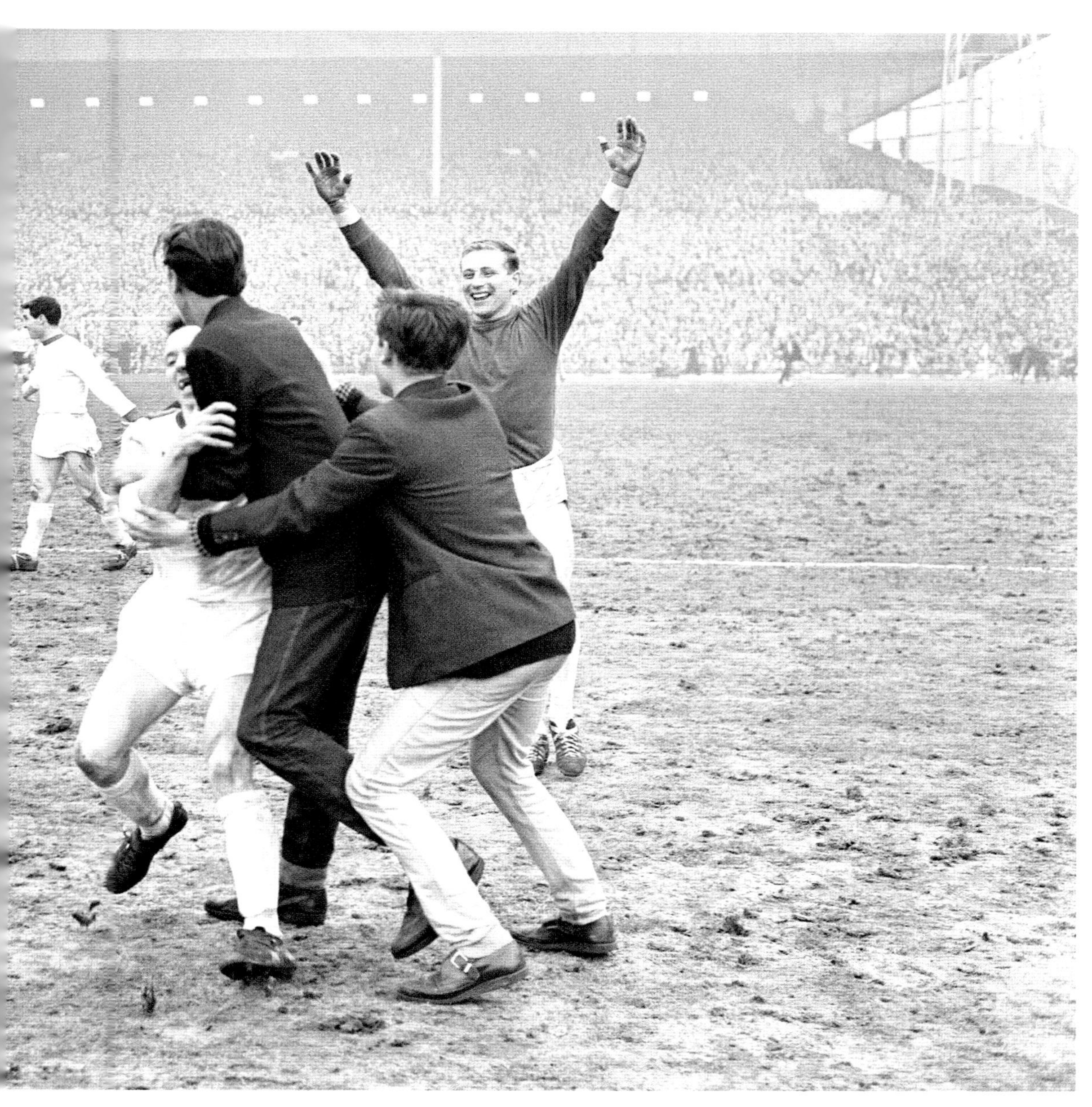

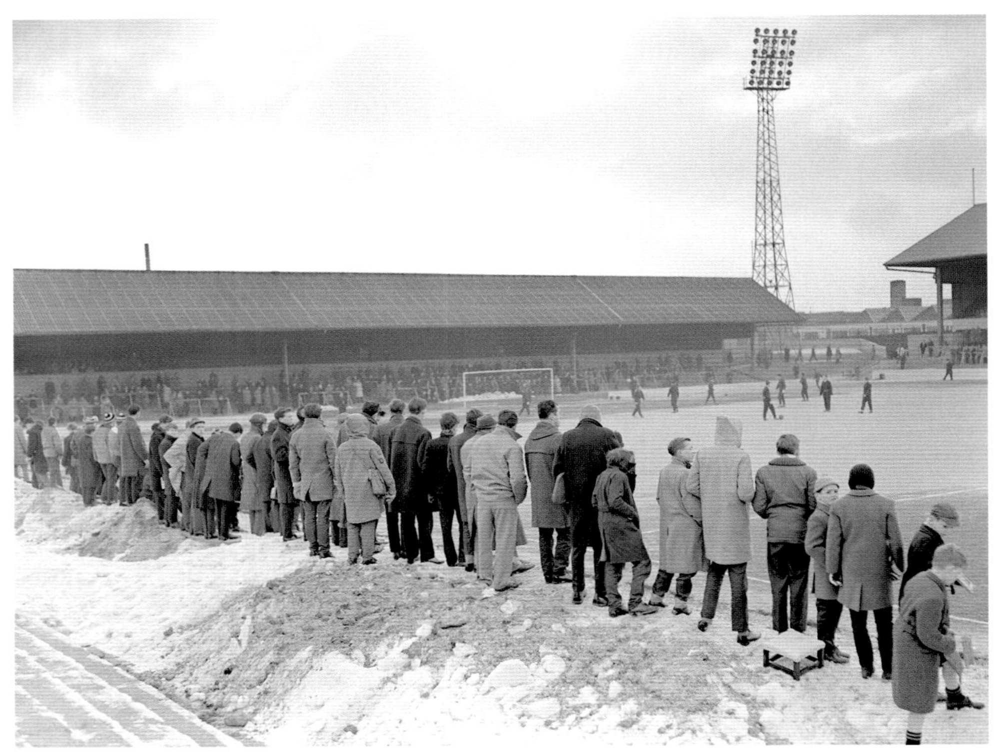

Goldstone Ground 1963
A case of getting in early to get the best view.
Brighton fans stand on the piled-up snow,
as they watch their team warm up before a
Division Three match with Crystal Palace.

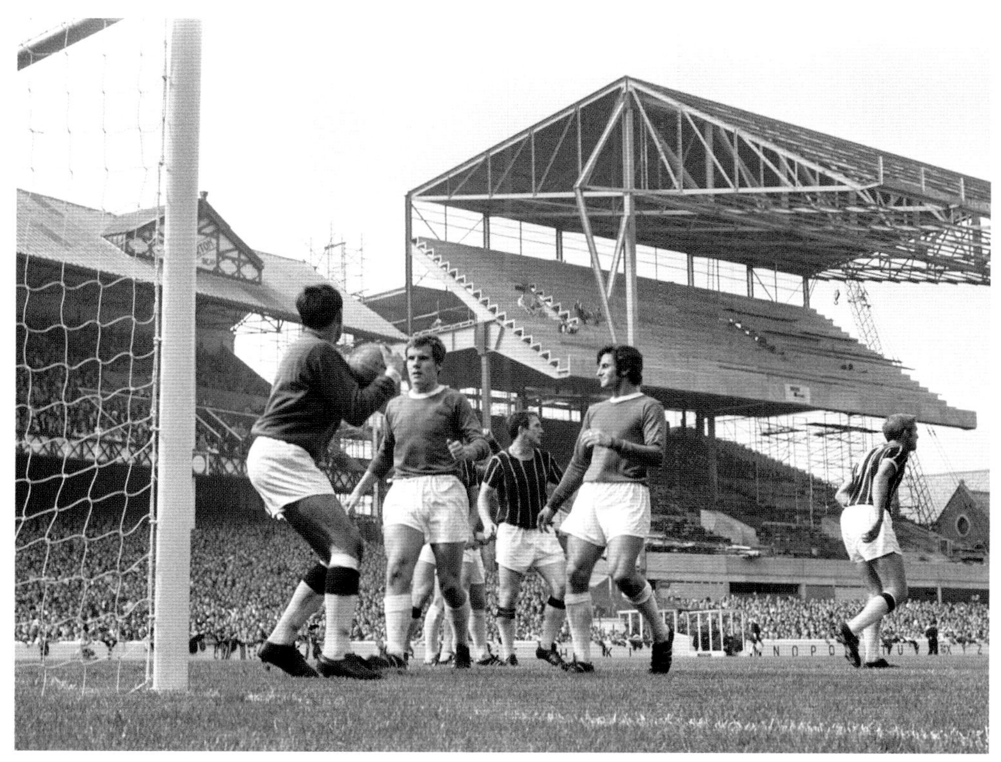

Goodison Park 1969
Everton play host to Crystal Palace
as construction takes place in the
background for a new three-tiered stand.

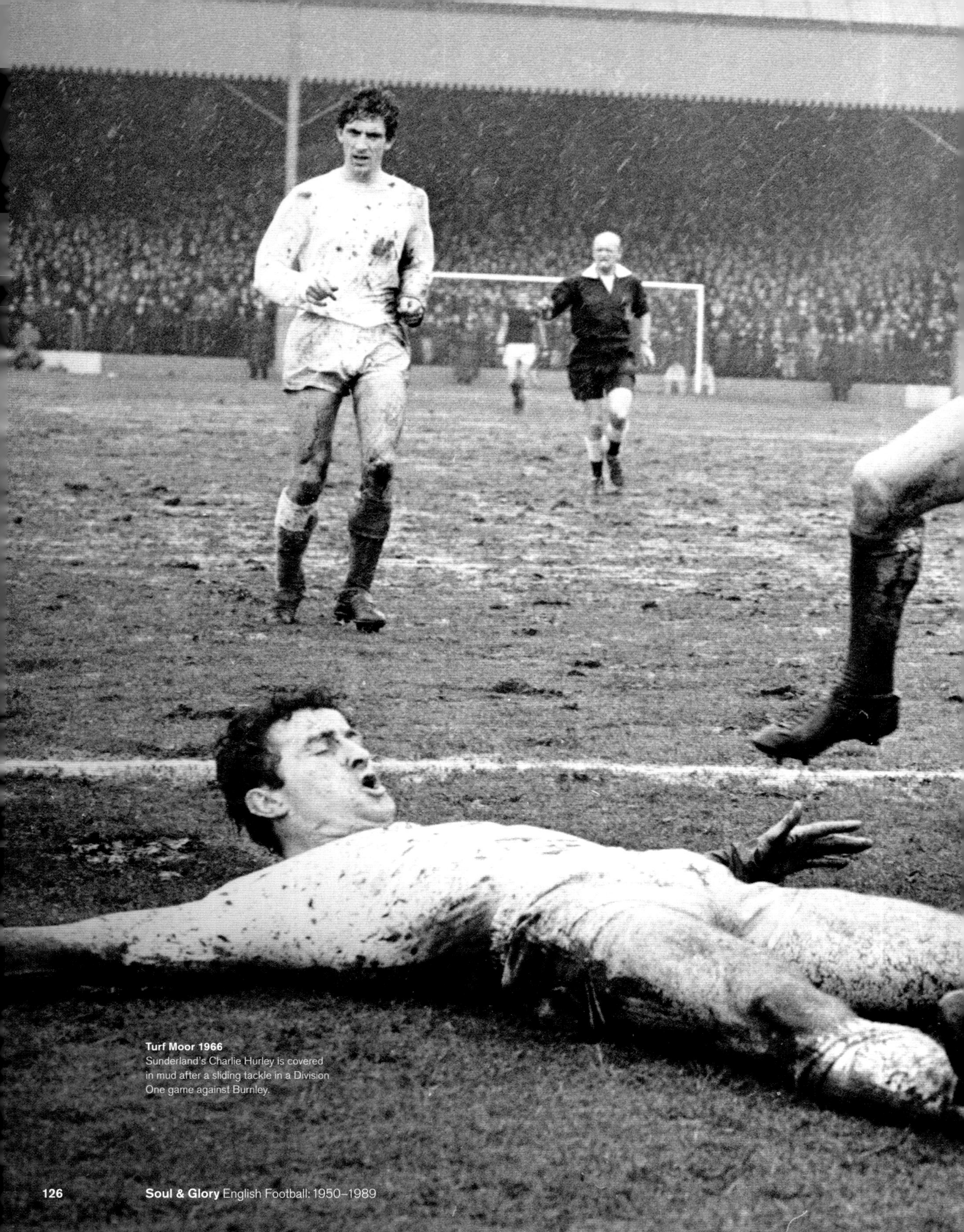

Turf Moor 1966
Sunderland's Charlie Hurley is covered in mud after a sliding tackle in a Division One game against Burnley.

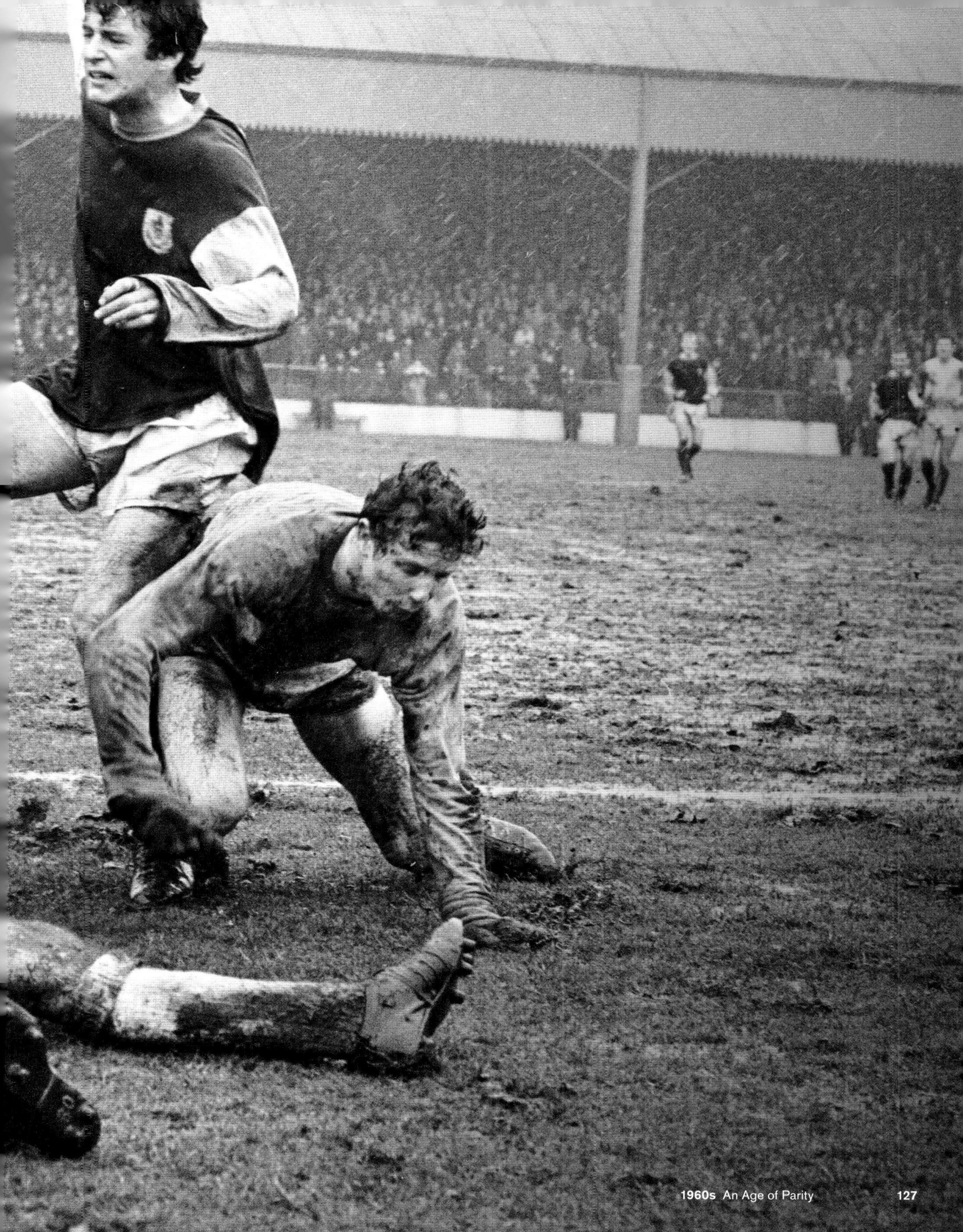

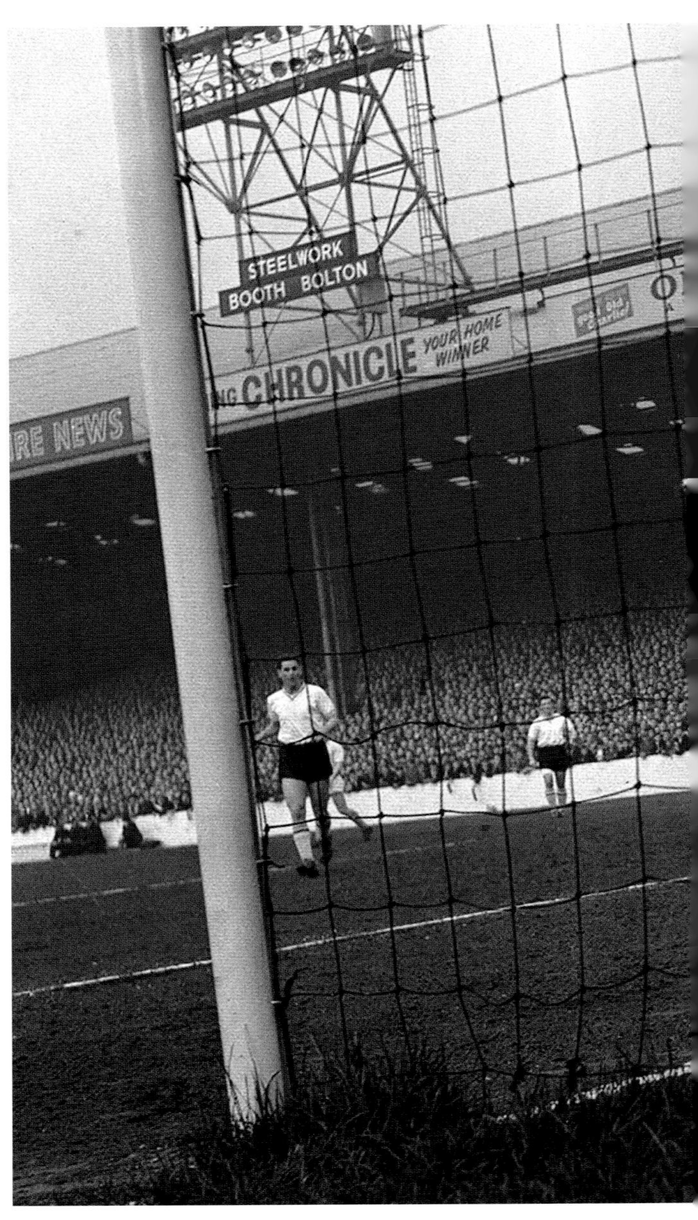

Maine Road 1960
Burnley go 1-0 up as Manchester City
goalkeeper Bert Trautmann makes an
error. An historic day for the Clarets
as the 2-1 win confirmed them as
champions of England.

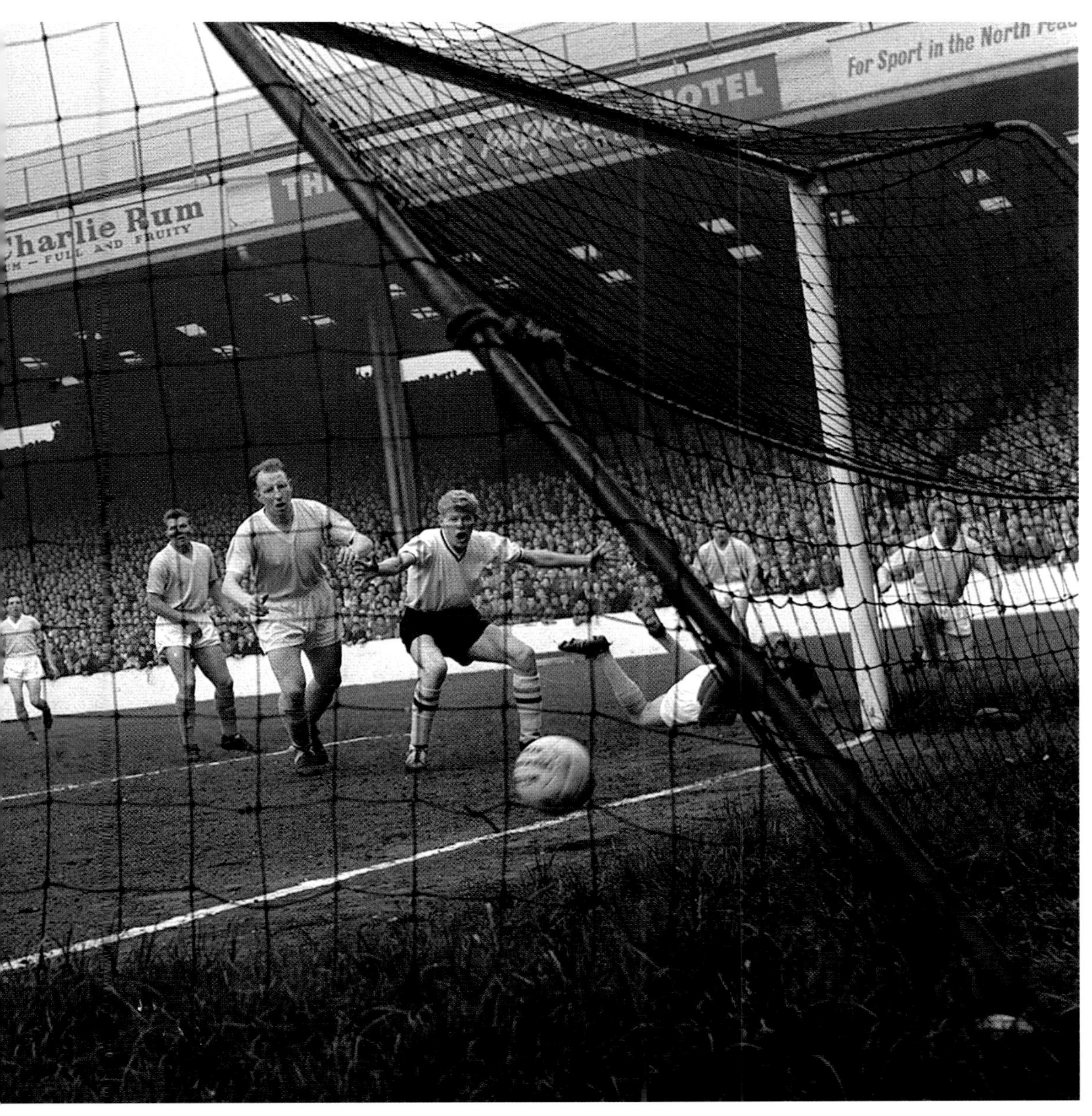
Charlie Rum
UM — FULL AND FRUITY
NOTEL
For Sport in the North read

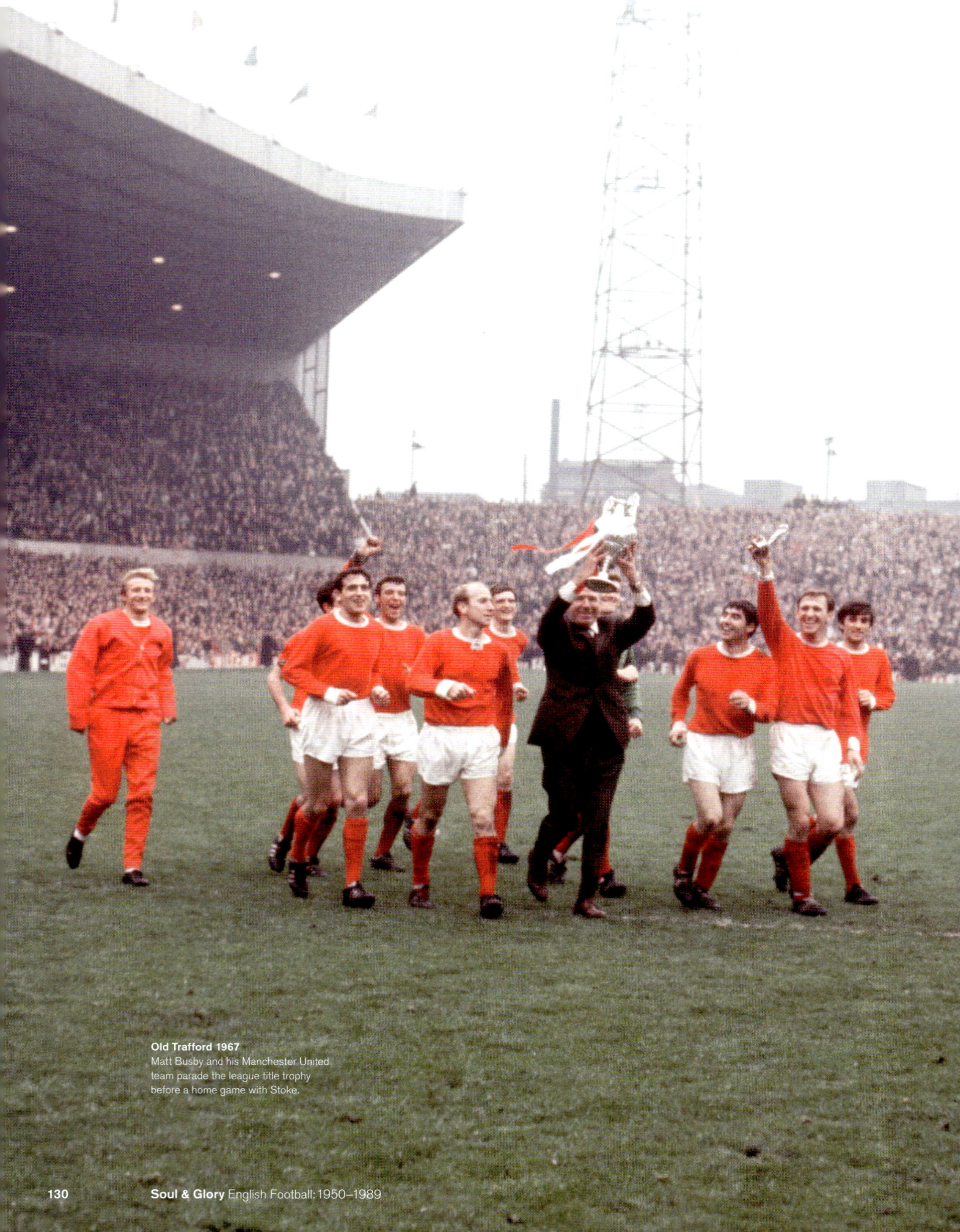

Old Trafford 1967
Matt Busby and his Manchester United
team parade the league title trophy
before a home game with Stoke.

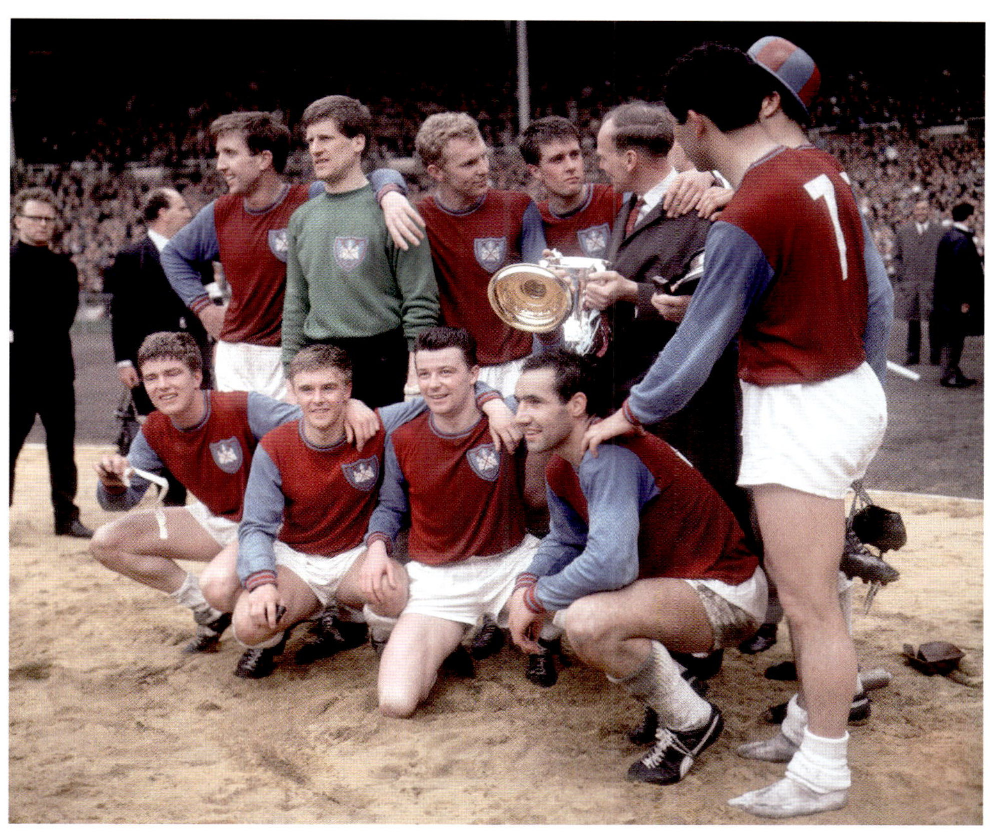

Wembley 1964
Bobby Moore and Geoff Hurst in the
centre of the photo, celebrate with their
West Ham team-mates, after beating
Preston North End 3-2 in the FA Cup
Final, the club's first major honour.

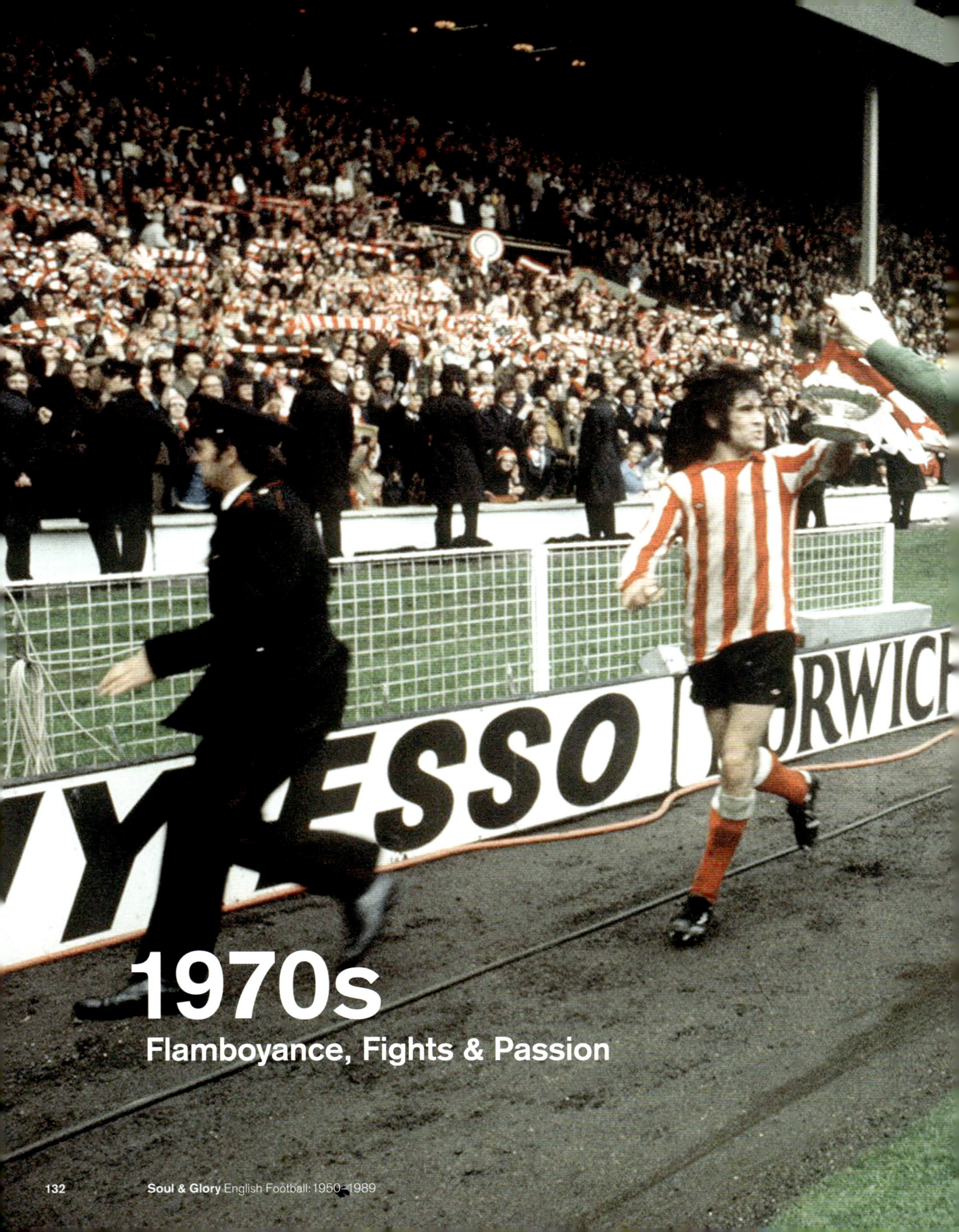

1970s
Flamboyance, Fights & Passion

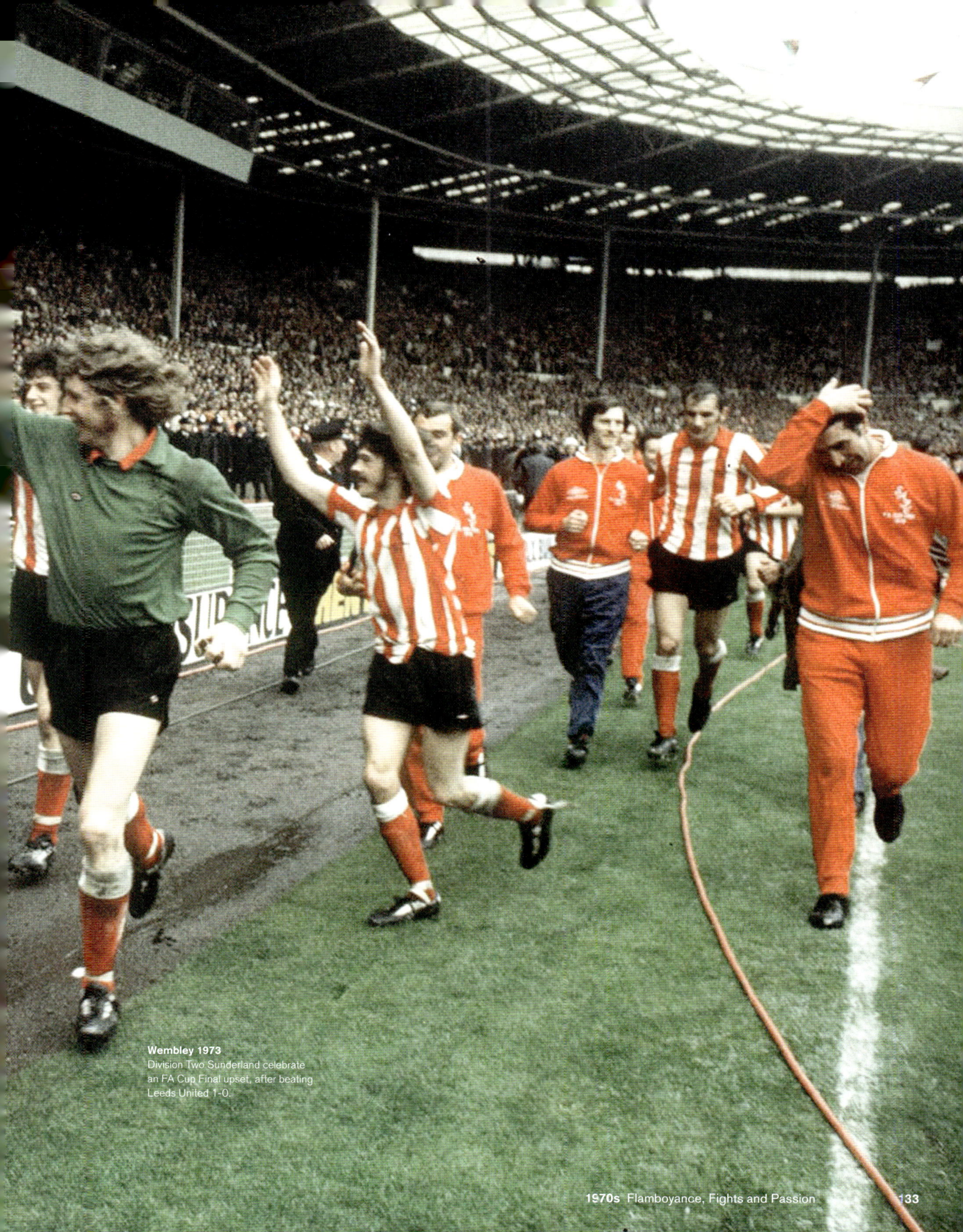

Wembley 1973
Division Two Sunderland celebrate
an FA Cup Final upset, after beating
Leeds United 1-0.

1970s: Flamboyance, Fights and Passion

'There's some fella in London, England named Brian, er Brian Clough. Some soccer player or something. Anyway, I heard all the way in America, heard all the way in Indonesia, that this fella talks too much, they say he's another Muhammad Ali, [but] there's just one Muhammad Ali…you're not a fighter, and you don't take my job. I'm the talker. Now Clough – I've had enough. Stop it!'

Muhammad Ali

A handful of Leeds United games in the early 70s nicely summed up the flamboyance and heated intensity of this era. In the 1970/71 season chaos erupted at Elland Road when the linesman put his flag up and everyone stopped, only for the referee to wave 'play on' and West Brom went to score what turned out to be the winning goal. So incensed were the Leeds players and crowd that there were more police on the pitch than anyone else, in order to protect the referee. The TV coverage was passionate as Barry Davies remarked, 'And Leeds will go mad, and they've every right to go mad…Leeds have every justification in going mad.' It was a classic piece of commentary in which Davies described the distraught Don Revie as 'a sickened man, look at him looking up to the heavens in disgust.' As furious Leeds fans were dragged off the pitch by policemen, Davies continued, 'And the Yorkshire spirit really coming to the fore.' The following season, Leeds demolished Southampton 7-0 in one of the most brilliant and flamboyant one-sided displays in English football. As Leeds passed the ball around the pitch in exhibition style, Davies said, 'To say that Leeds are playing with Southampton is the understatement of the season. Poor Southampton just don't know what day it is. It's almost cruel.' Leeds, like the 1970s, were a paradox; they were beautiful and ugly at the same time. Passionate and exciting but violent. One of the most classic examples of 'Dirty Leeds' was their match at Derby in 1975. Norman Hunter had punched Derby's Francis Lee in the face after an exchange between the two players which commentator John Motson observed 'has been brewing for some time'. A sending off was made, though there was confusion as to if it were just Hunter or both men who had been sent walking. Lee walked off with Hunter before deciding to clear up any confusion on whether two dismissals had been issued. In the purest example of an actual genuine fight between players on an English football field, Lee started swinging a flurry of clean punches on to a stunned Hunter. As the little man steamed in with the windmill technique, Hunter crashed to the ground and the rest of the players ran in to break it up. Motson exclaimed, 'I'm sure they must have been sent off this time anyway.' A year earlier in the 1974 Charity Shield at Wembley, Liverpool's Kevin Keegan was punched to the ground by Leeds' Johnny Giles in full view of the referee, as Davies noted, 'That looked very much like a right hook from Johnny Giles.' For that sentence from the commentator to then be followed by a yellow card to the offending player shows just how lenient football could be at this time. Moments later Keegan was sent off after a tussle with Billy Bremner, who was also dismissed. 'Come on man I've not done fuck all, I've been hit twice,' protested Keegan as he removed his shirt and left the pitch in a rage. Football is a sport

'Well Brian, are you going to stop?'

Brian Moore

'No, I'm going to fight him.'

Brian Clough

that swung from one extreme to the other, culturally in the stands as well as matters on the pitch. No one likes today's diving and injury feigning. It ruins football; so far removed from the physical origins of the sport. The words 'there was contact' justify a foul being given even though fair contact is not illegal in football. Fans love to see a hard-fought game, not one where players fall over at every opportunity. The opposite end of that pendulum, however, would be thuggery and the example that tends to get used is Leeds v Chelsea in the 1970 FA Cup Final replay at Old Trafford, which resembled a karate dojo more than a football match. The consensus today is that there would be so many red cards that no one bar the goalkeepers and referee would be left on the pitch.

When Everton won the first title of the decade in 1970, it was the club's seventh overall league triumph, equalling the record of Liverpool, Arsenal and Manchester United. Four teams shared the honour of most title wins which is unlikely to happen again any time soon. Arsenal started the decade with a European triumph in 1970, in the Fairs Cup, ending the club's 17-year trophy drought. The following season would be the greatest in the club's history and a return to the glory years. Ten years after Spurs won the double, their north London rivals matched that achievement, with a bit of extra panache, as the league title was won at White Hart Lane, sparking a pitch invasion by celebrating Arsenal fans. Thousands of Gooners celebrating a league title on the pitch at White Hart Lane was the perfect tonic for the 1960s when Spurs had the upper hand. This made Arsenal the first club to win the title eight times, and along with four FA Cup wins and a European trophy, they could at this point in time lay claim to being the most successful English club.

'He wanted the yes-men. He didn't want the individuals, the characters, the rebels.'

Frank Worthington on England manager Don Revie

As great as the 1960s were for the England team, the 1970s went in the opposite direction. The decade started with England as favourites for the 1970 World Cup. The team was strong, some said stronger than in 66, but Alf Ramsey's boys went out to West Germany in the quarter-final, having given up a two-goal lead; and complacent to the point of taking off Bobby Charlton whilst the scoreline was 2-0. Failure to qualify for the 74 and 78 tournaments would indicate a lack of quality among English players, but that wasn't the case at all. Quite the opposite; England had several flamboyant and exciting players – but with one major drawback: England managers didn't think much of them. Charlie George, Peter Osgood, Rodney Marsh, Tony Currie, Frank Worthington, Alan Hudson and Stan Bowles are among a group of attacking players who would, in later years, be branded as the 'Mavericks'. Perhaps the most staggering and depressing statistic of 1970s English football was that between them they would earn 46 combined England caps: Hudson (2), George (1), Worthington (8), Marsh (9), Osgood (4), Bowles (5) and Currie (17). That is an astonishingly low number of international appearances for such an assortment of creative talent. The waste of playing talent was confounded by also ignoring the maverick manager of the 1970s, Brian Clough. 'Old Big Head' was interviewed for the vacant England job in 1977, but was the opposite of the 'yes man' that the FA establishment were looking for. As Clough would go on to say, 'I was not only ready for the job. I was perfect for it because I would have been good at it.'

Clough had already made his mark early in the decade. Derby County, a club with only one FA Cup to their name since their foundation in 1884, became champions of England in 1971/72, three years after gaining promotion. The parity of competition we saw in the 60s wasn't reversed in the 1970s. Overall there were six different winners of the league title and nine different winners of the FA Cup. Clough's second championship win, this time with Nottingham Forest, would be so similar to the first. He took a medium-sized Division Two club from the East Midlands up, and won them a title for the first time in their history. However, this time, he would take glory a step further, winning successive European Cups in the quintessential 'it will never happen again' scenario. A humble team gaining promotion, winning the top division, then becoming champions of Europe was a remarkable achievement. What Clough had done was unique, and is why the cities of Derby and Nottingham are linked by an A road named Brian Clough Way. Two clubs that hate one another united in respect for the best manager they ever had.

A wonderful example of 70s flamboyance led to the goal of the season in the 1970/71 season, followed by a change of the rules meaning it could never happen again. Coventry City hosted Everton at Highfield Road, and had a free kick near the edge of the area. Willie Carr stood over the dead ball, before gripping it with both feet, jumping in the air and flicking the ball upwards in a 'donkey kick'. As the ball dropped down Ernie Hunt blasted a volley into the top corner of the net. Some have described it as the best free kick of all time, but there was an issue over its legality, as the player taking the free kick can only touch the ball once before it is touched by another player. The wedging of the ball between both feet was viewed as multiple touch, so the routine was outlawed and will forever be unique to Carr and Hunt.

By the 1973/74 season the rules were changed so that now three teams instead of two would be relegated. This though wouldn't have affected the two most stand-out relegations of the decade. In the 1976/77 season Spurs finished bottom and were back in Division Two for the first time in 27 years. A few seasons earlier in 1973/74 saw the most famous relegation in English football history as Manchester United finished second-bottom. It wasn't the first time this had happened, as United had been relegated twice in the 1930s, but they weren't as famous back then. The 50s and 60s, through triumph and tragedy, had created the modern image of Manchester United. Not only had this huge club suffered the indignity of demotion in 74, but it was Manchester City who helped seal their fate with a 1-0 win at Old Trafford. To add even extra spice, United legend Denis Law was now in a City shirt and in typical 70s flamboyance back-heeled the ball into the net for the winning goal, sparking a series of pitch invasions from angry United fans, as the game was waved off four minutes from time. Law's 'celebration' was famous for being the least joyous in football history. Never has a man looked so devastated at scoring a winning goal (and a good one at that) as the Scot did; his head down, walking in a bereaved state, before being subbed off.

'I just felt depressed. I was inconsolable. I didn't want it to happen. They were pals. I didn't want them to go down. It's the last thing in the world I wanted.'

Denis Law

Team kits were about to become a lot more flamboyant. What today is a multibillion-pound industry was pioneered in the 70s by a small manufacturer in Leicester called Admiral. The company needed a big break to push forward their vision of football kits as merchandise that fans will want to buy, and they got that break when Leeds United agreed to a deal in 1973/74, the year they won their second league title. That was the start of a massive success story for the company during the 70s, peaking when they signed a £15,000-a-year deal with the England national team. Their kits became distinctive, as the Admiral logo went down the sleeves in the opposite to the minimalist style of previous decades. Like most kits, some were great, some were okay, some were terrible; the designs that were viewed as the worst are now the most expensive. A bit like *Star Wars* memorabilia (also manufactured in the Leicester region), the ones that no one liked are now huge collectors' items, because production was low due to lack of demand. Today that hot piece of memorabilia is Coventry City's 1978 brown Admiral kit, over 40 years old and still included in the conversation of worst kits ever (I have to confess to liking this kit. Brown is cool!) and there have been some bad ones over the years, not least Manchester City's 2020 away kit which looked like a Wall's ice lolly. On eBay, genuine Coventry brown kits from 1978 come with an eye-watering starting bid price of £700.

For years, football coverage was produced by the wonderful British Pathe whose old videos today are available to watch on YouTube. However, football coverage of this kind was in essence short highlight news reels intended for cinema audiences before the main feature, not dedicated football coverage in its own timeslot. BBC's new programme *Match of the Day* would change that in the 1960s, to be followed later that decade by ITV's *The Big Match*. Once into the 70s *The Big Match* would take coverage and analysis to another level. Colour TV was upon us, and *The Big Match* was new, exciting, detailed and Jimmy Hill's range of ties, extremely flamboyant. The pitches were not any muddier than before, but colour TV highlighted just how many games were played out on surfaces that resembled the Somme. To highlight just one of many examples, West Ham played away at Manchester City in 1970, and the Maine Road pitch was one slippery and wet mud pie, to the point where it looked like a chocolate cake with goals, with the only grass visible being in between the goal line and the net. That still didn't stop Jimmy Greaves scoring on his West Ham debut. Hill was joined on *The Big Match* by Brian Moore, in the opinion of many the greatest commentator in the history of the English game. Moore's tone had the elegance of a gentleman film star, but he also projected great passion and exuberance when something exciting happened; one moment such as a good save could be elevated to so much more by Moore's commentary. Football had been an English obsession, and now with *The Big Match* it was given the minimum coverage it warranted, though live matches were a rarity. Brian Clough was a regular face on the programme, and Hill's vision had brought detailed analysis and debate to football coverage. He used to answer letters from viewers, where in stark contrast to Twitter, the person's name and full address was read out on the show; certainly not allowing for anyone to hide under a pseudonym. A response to one letter (from J.R. Partlet, Parade Mansions, Hendon, NW4) shows us how much the game has changed with regards to physical contact. Chelsea were at home to Spurs and Mike England had hacked down Peter Osgood long after the Chelsea striker had passed the ball on (Osgood rolled around in agony, and when a 70s player did that you knew he was genuinely hurt). Hill had not condemned this foul in the way he did for a Ron Harris tackle in the same match, and the viewer's letter challenged him on this. Hill provided a slow-motion replay of the tackle, to which our modern eyes scream 'that makes it even worse, that's clearly a straight red card' as two feet crashed into a man standing four feet away from the ball, but Hill insisted, 'He does bring him down very heavily but one could argue that he was going for the ball.' It makes you wonder how bad the Ron Harris tackle was.

> '**We were the first ones to come up with the idea of a pundits panel. Although, since I was one of the pundits, it's debatable how good an idea that was.**'
>
> Jimmy Hill – pundit for ITV's groundbreaking football show, *The Big Match*

'Brilliant save…And Lorimer makes it one-each…NO…astonishing.'

David Coleman – BBC commentator

There was a time when Sunderland were known for glory and success. So far removed from the heartache and underachievement we see today in the painful-to-watch Netflix series *Sunderland 'Till I Die*. By the late 1930s the Black Cats had racked up six league titles and an FA Cup. Even up to recent years, those multiple successes from so long ago were enough to place the club in sixth overall place for most championship wins of all time; only recently being caught up by Manchester City and Chelsea. By 1973, the glory days were seemingly behind the old club who were in Division Two, but in a shock, they beat Arsenal in the FA Cup semi-final. Meanwhile their opponents for the final, the young and successful Leeds United, were regular challengers for all the major trophies and nobody outside of Wearside expected anything but a Leeds win. The 1973 FA Cup Final still goes down as one of the biggest upsets in the competition's history, and the first time that a team outside Division One had won the cup since West Brom in 1931. A half volley from Ian Porterfield brought the cup home to Sunderland as the hat-and-mack-wearing manager Bob Stokoe ran on to the pitch in flamboyant fashion at the end of the game, in a moment that inspired a statue outside the Stadium of Light. Even more flamboyant was the double save from goalkeeper Jimmy Montgomery that denied Leeds an equaliser. Before saving the rebound, the commentator David Coleman had already proclaimed that Lorimer had scored, before taking a few seconds to realise that the keeper had somehow got a hand to it and pushed it on to the bar. There were two other noticeable cup upsets in the decade, as two clubs won the FA Cup for the first time in their history. In 1976, Southampton beat Manchester United 1-0 in what to date is their only trophy. Two years later, the same score was repeated as Ipswich Town beat Arsenal with a Roger Osborne goal. Led by manager Bobby Robson, Ipswich had dominated Arsenal throughout the game and deserved the victory. Arsenal were trophy-free since the start of the decade, but the following year the Gunners would beat Manchester United in the famous 'Three-Minute Final'. By the 86th minute Arsenal were ahead 2-0 and cruising. By the 88th minute it was 2-2 amid wild scenes of celebration in the United end. In the 89th minute Alan Sunderland scored one of the most celebrated winners in cup history, and Arsenal were five-time winners.

The League Cup continued to be a competition that offered hope for teams that had been starved of success. Stoke City today have the honour that comes without a piece of silverware – that of being the oldest club in league football (since Nott County got relegated in 2019), having been founded in 1863, but they would be 109 years old before getting their hands on an actual trophy. Chelsea were strong favourites to beat the Potters in the 1972 final but Gordon Banks and co. would win 2-1 in front of 97,852 fans, with a winning goal from none other than 50s and 60s star George Eastham, aged 35, making him the oldest player at that time to receive a League Cup winners' medal.

Derby won another title in 1974/75, under the management of Dave Mackay, also suggesting that the parity English football was used to would be as strong as ever. Instead, the following year saw the start of a trend that would continue in the majority of seasons for the next 15 years. Between seasons 1975/76 and 1989/90 Liverpool would win ten titles in the biggest show of dominance in Division One history. English football never regained that parity of competition, as in the 1990s and beyond Manchester United would carry on where Liverpool left off. Other clubs also won the title, but they were part of a new financial elite. The exception (not Blackburn in 1995 as they outspent everyone else) being Leicester's 2016 title win, which was against the trend and truly remarkable. What with unexpected title wins in the 70s for Derby and Nottingham Forest, Leicester completed the trinity of East Midlands clubs who won the league for the first time in their history and against all expectation.

From the era at the start of this book to where we are now, two notable changes would happen to English football that were related and led to disaster. Firstly, European competition had cemented its place in the football calendar and English teams were thriving. Trophies came in abundance and there was the first all-English final in 1972 when Spurs beat Wolves to win the UEFA Cup. Success in all major European competitions peaked in the 70s, because in the 80s it wasn't allowed to go beyond the first half of the decade. Hooliganism caused deaths at Heysel in 1985 and the ban of all English clubs until 1990. Football fan violence started in the late 60s, peaked in the 70s, and continued in the 80s. Older fans would talk about how football was better when there was no segregation, and opposing fans could stand together, which meant football before the 1970s. The decade without question had a dark and violent side. The paradox is that it was also a wonderful, fun, heated, flamboyant, passionate and exciting era and the photos in this chapter celebrate that part of it.

1970s Domestic Honours

Division One Champions

1970: Everton (overall title wins 7)
1971: Arsenal (overall wins 8)
1972: Derby County (overall wins 1)
1973: Liverpool (overall wins 8)
1974: Leeds United (overall wins 2)
1975: Derby County (overall wins 2)
1976: Liverpool (overall wins 9)
1977: Liverpool (overall wins 10)
1978: Nottingham Forest (overall wins 1)
1979: Liverpool (overall wins 11)

FA Cup Winners

1970: Chelsea (overall wins 1)
1971: Arsenal (overall wins 4)
1972: Leeds United (overall wins 1)
1973: Sunderland (overall wins 2)
1974: Liverpool (overall wins 2)
1975: West Ham United (overall wins 2)
1976: Southampton (overall wins 1)
1977: Manchester United (overall wins 4)
1978: Ipswich Town (overall wins 1)
1979: Arsenal (overall wins 5)

League Cup Winners

1970: Manchester City (overall wins 1)
1971: Tottenham Hotspur (overall wins 1)
1972: Stoke City (overall wins 1)
1973: Tottenham Hotspur (overall wins 2)
1974: Wolverhampton Wanderers (overall wins 1)
1975: Aston Villa (overall wins 2)
1976: Manchester City (overall wins 2)
1977: Aston Villa (overall wins 3)
1978: Nottingham Forest (overall wins 1)
1979: Nottingham Forest (overall wins 2)

Major European Honours for English Clubs

1970: Arsenal, Fairs Cup
1970: Manchester City, Cup Winners' Cup
1971: Leeds United, Fairs Cup
1971: Chelsea, Cup Winners' Cup
1972: Tottenham Hotspur, UEFA Cup
1973: Liverpool, UEFA Cup
1976: Liverpool, UEFA Cup
1977: Liverpool, European Cup
1978: Liverpool, European Cup
1979: Nottingham Forest, European Cup

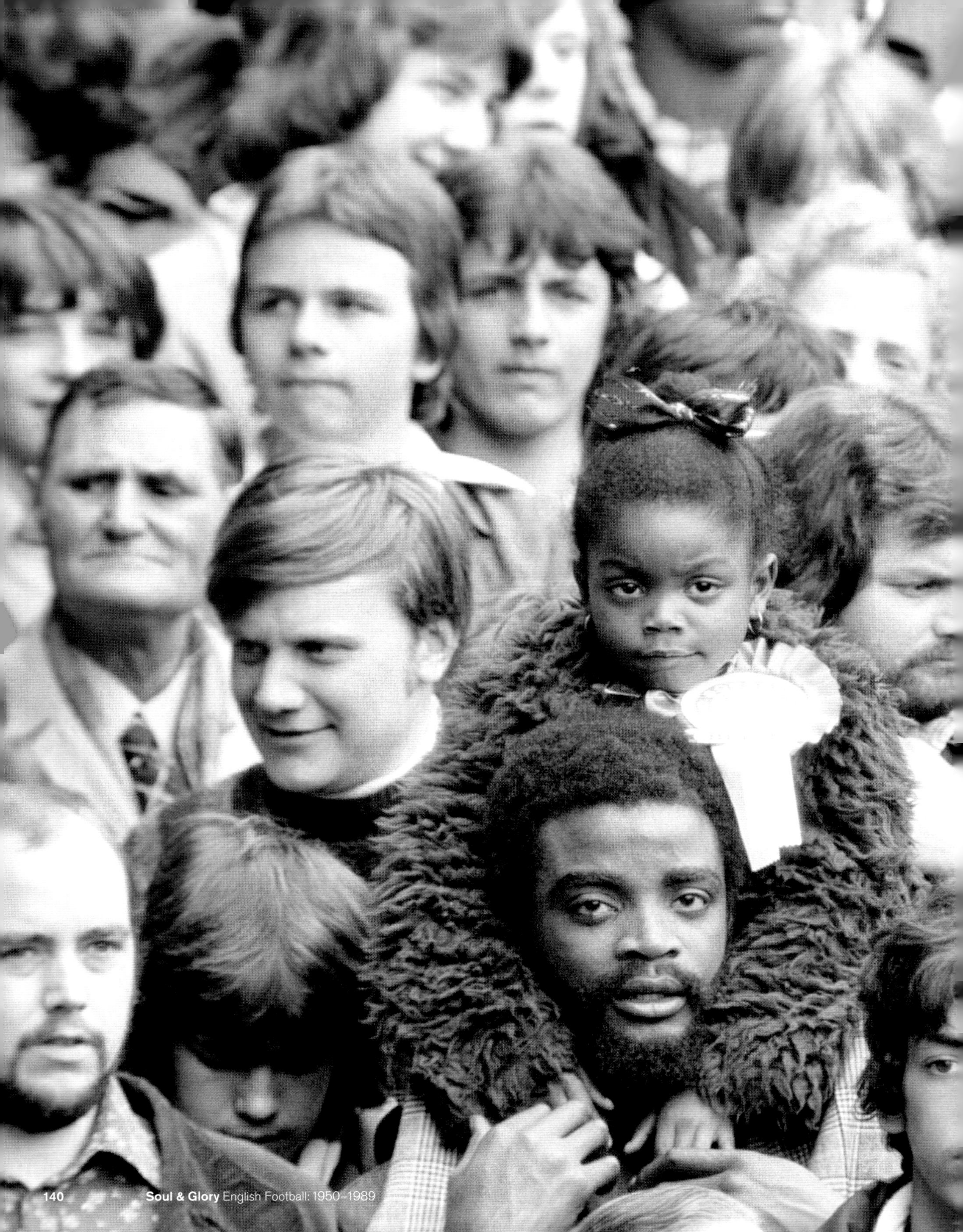

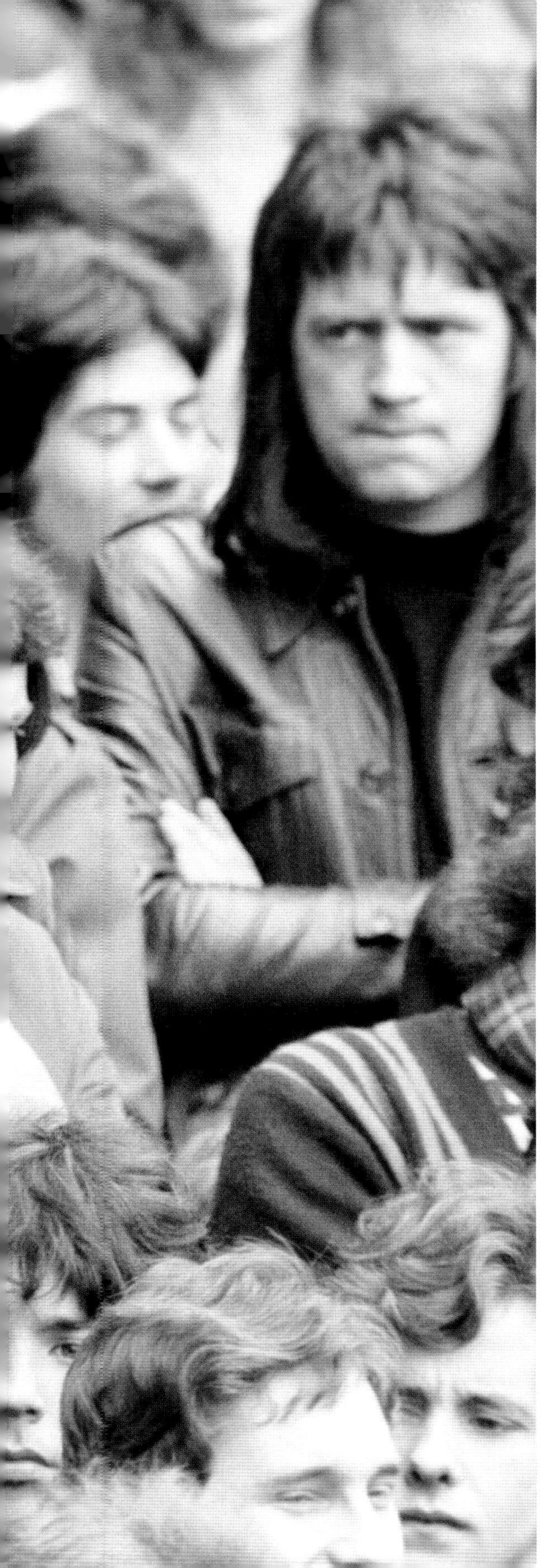

White Hart Lane 1975
A young Spurs fan doesn't look too
impressed about something, but her
team beat Chelsea 2-0.

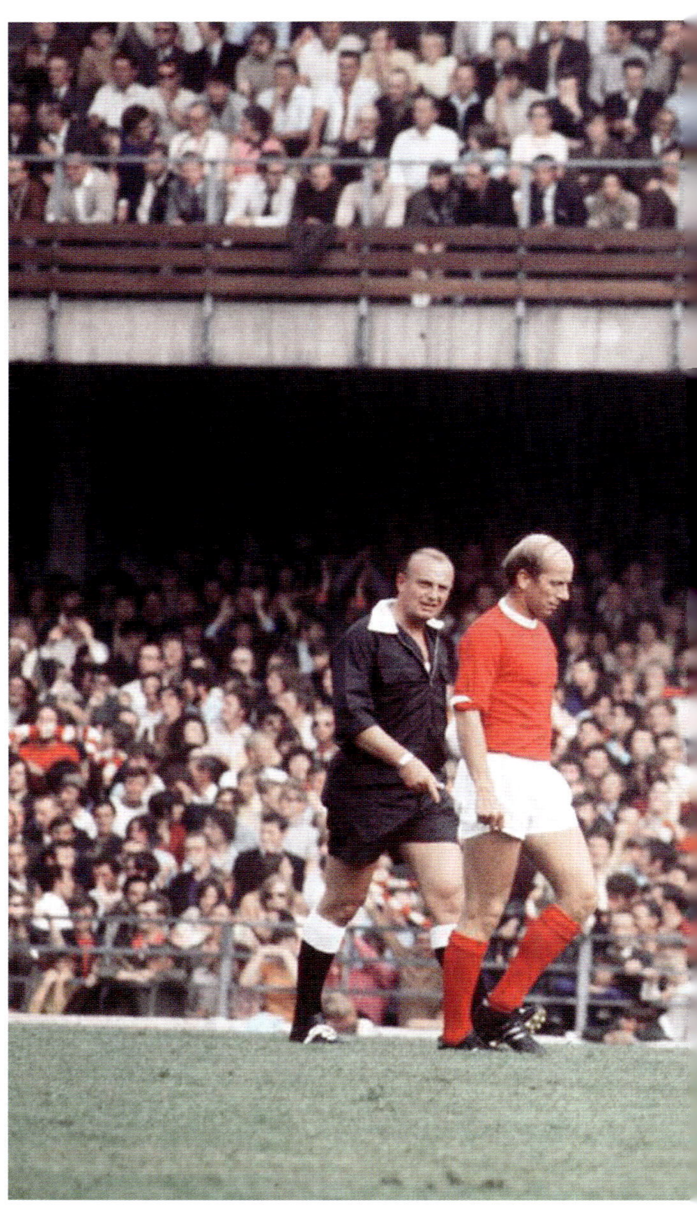

Baseball Ground 1970
Ian Ure congratulates George Best.

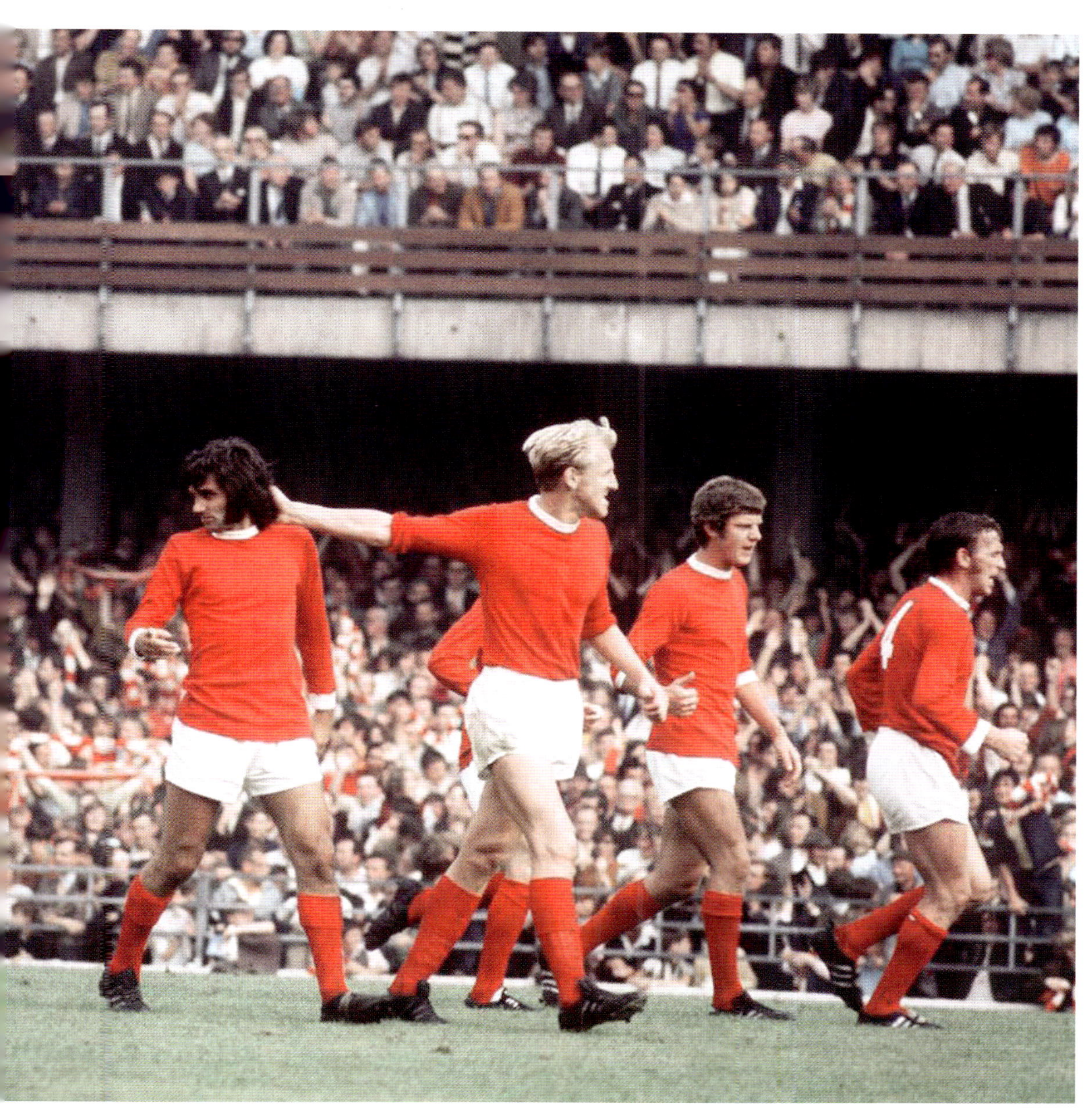

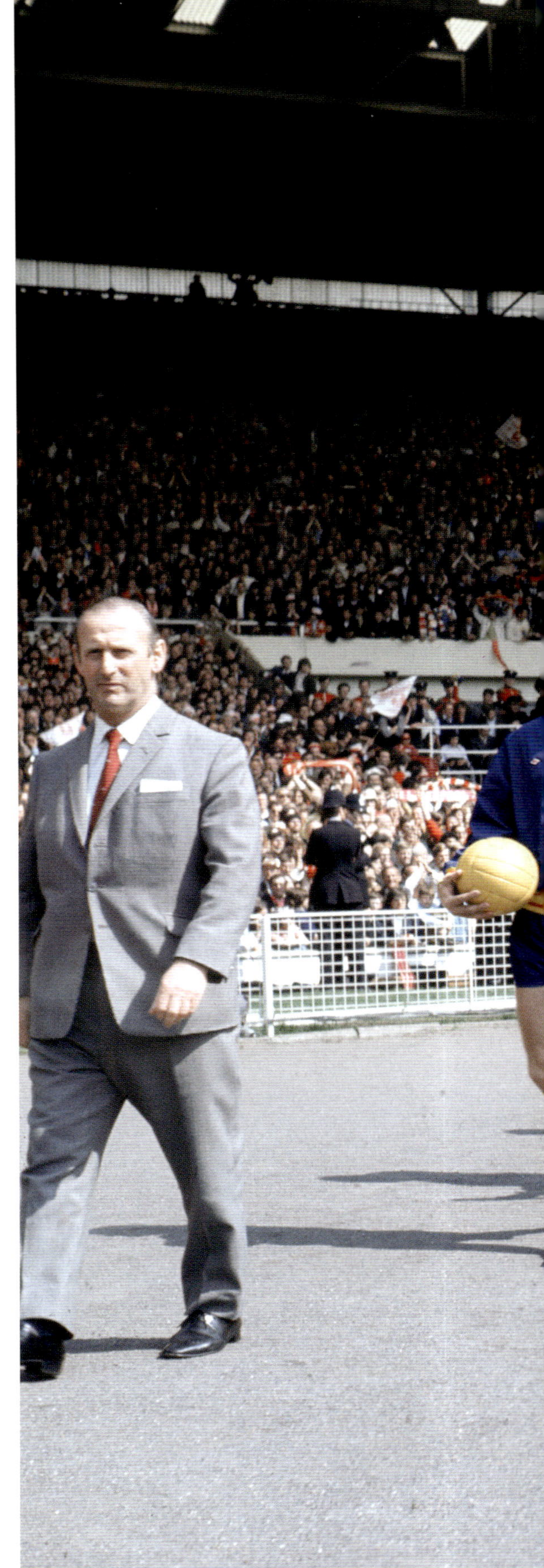

Wembley 1971
Arsenal are one win away from a league and cup
double as they face Liverpool in the FA Cup Final.
Charlie George doesn't seem too nervous as he
balances a ball on his head.

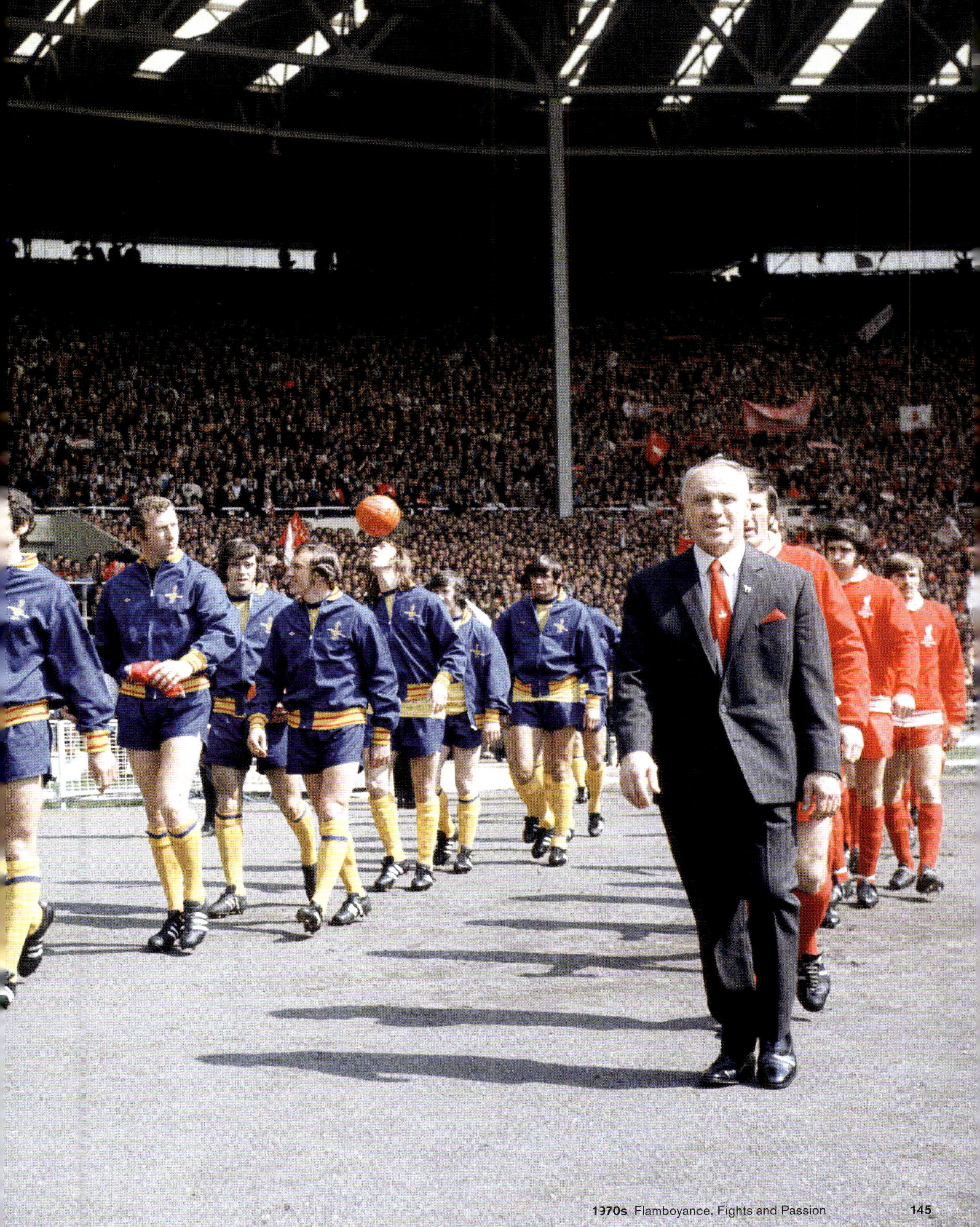

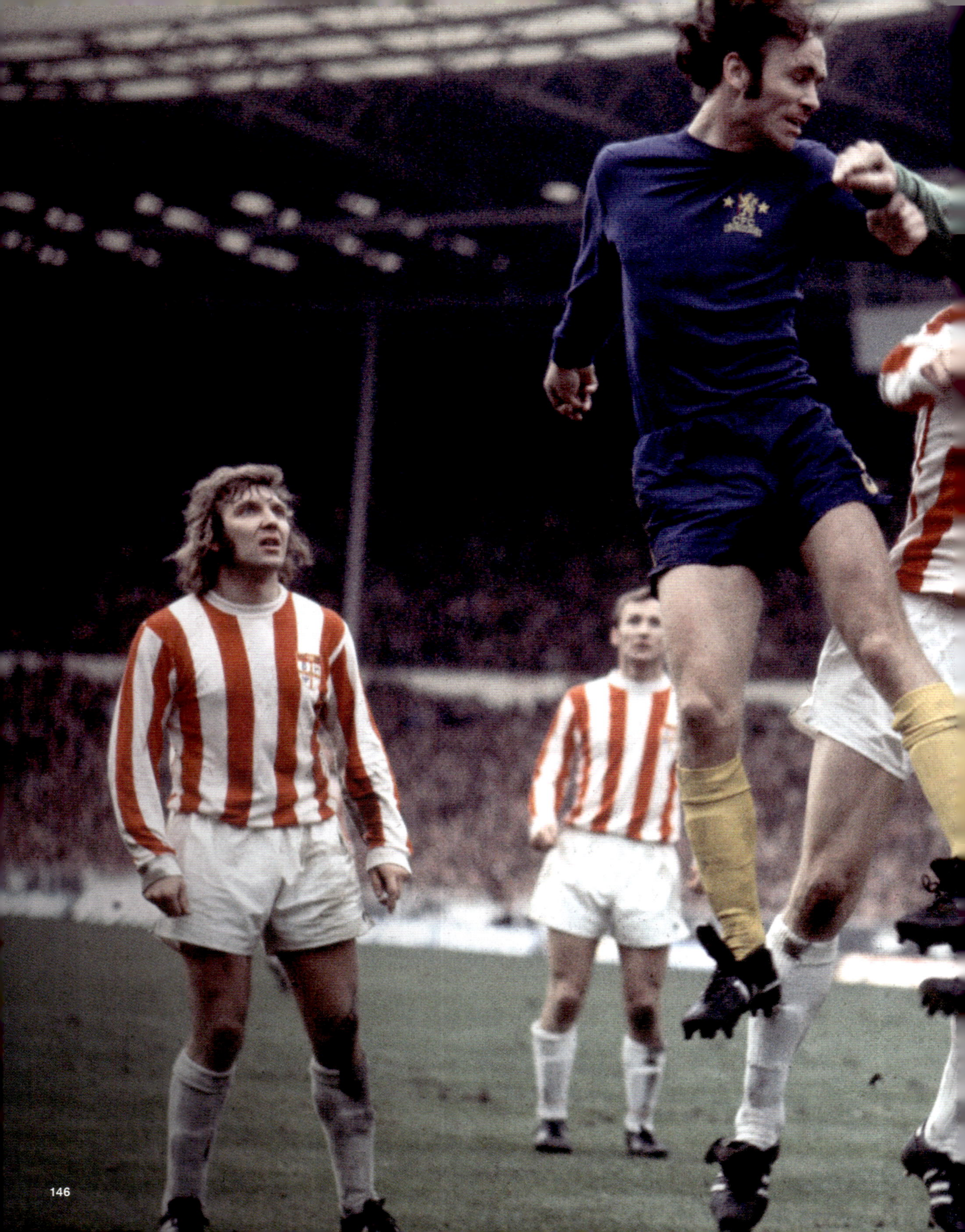

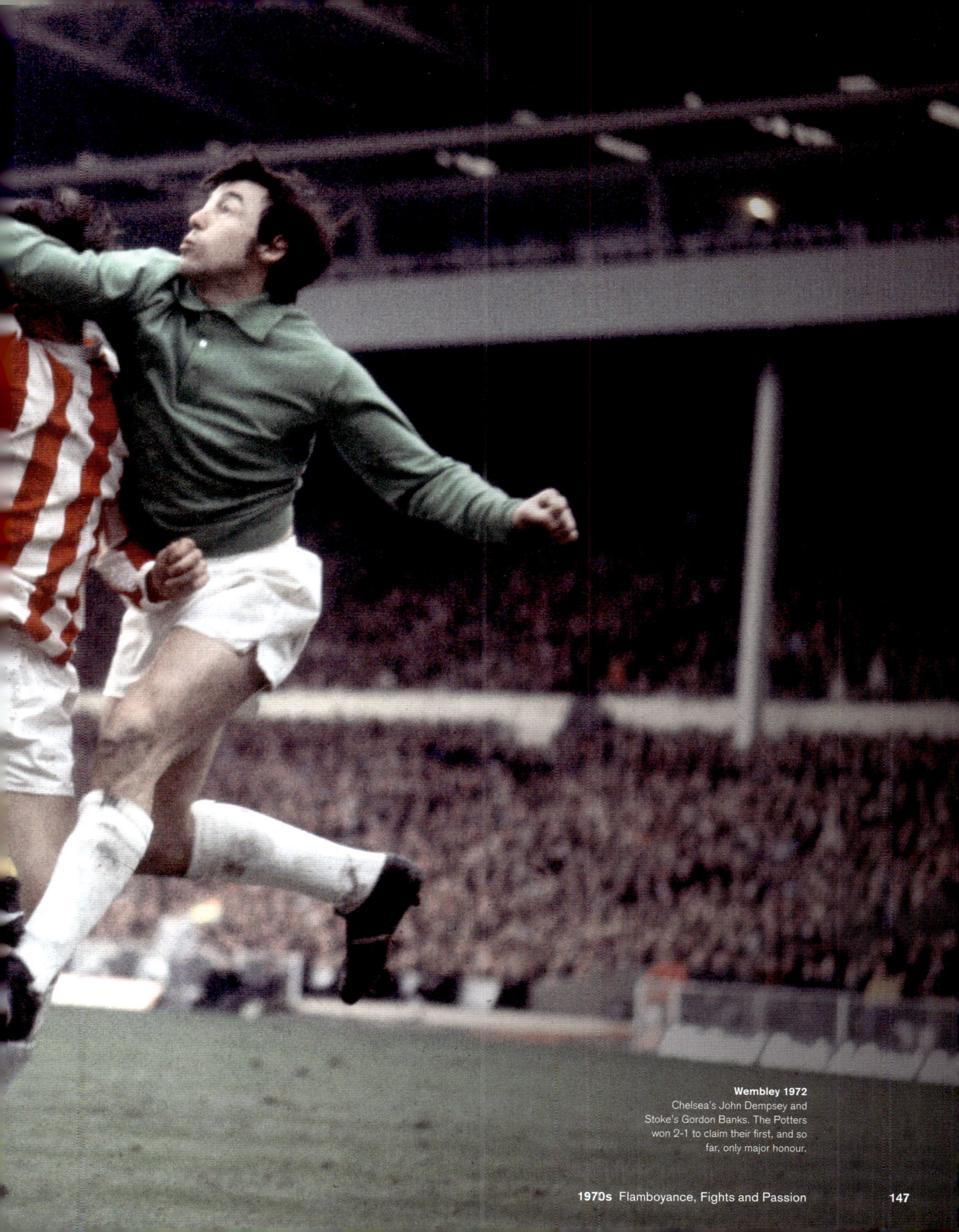

Wembley 1972
Chelsea's John Dempsey and Stoke's Gordon Banks. The Potters won 2-1 to claim their first, and so far, only major honour.

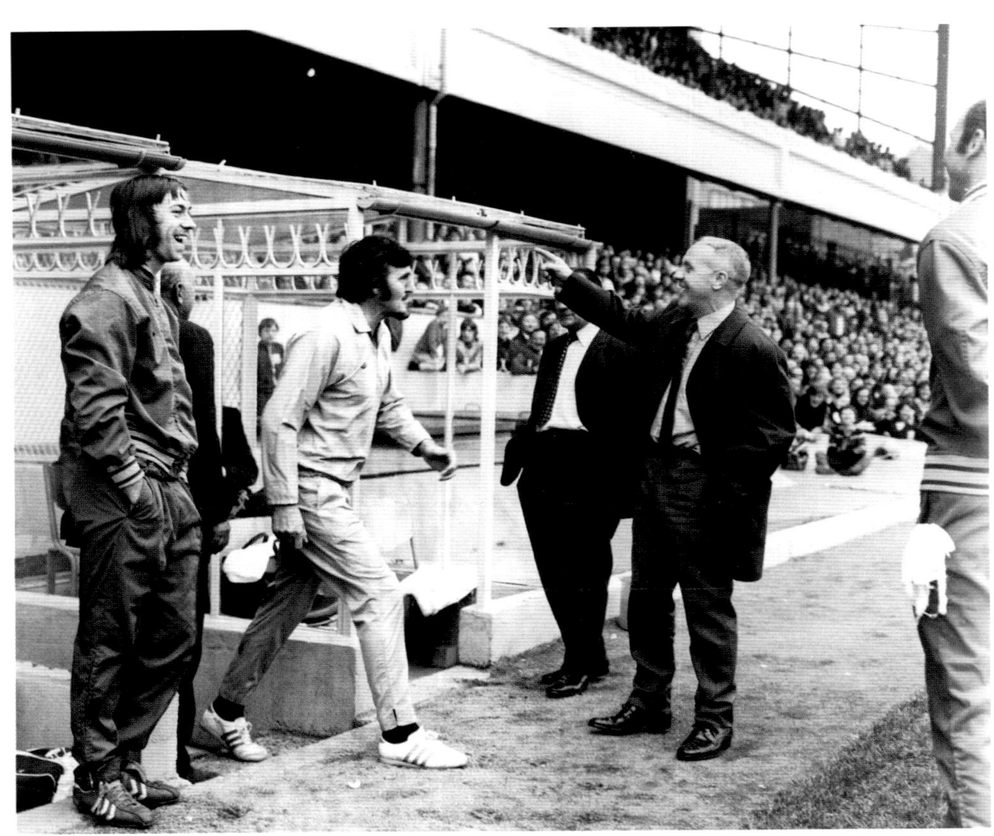

Highbury 1972

An announcement from the PA system asks if
anyone in the stadium is a qualified referee, after
the linesman hobbled off injured. Jimmy Hill in the
TV studio answers the call to the amusement of
Charlie George (l) and Bill Shankly (r).

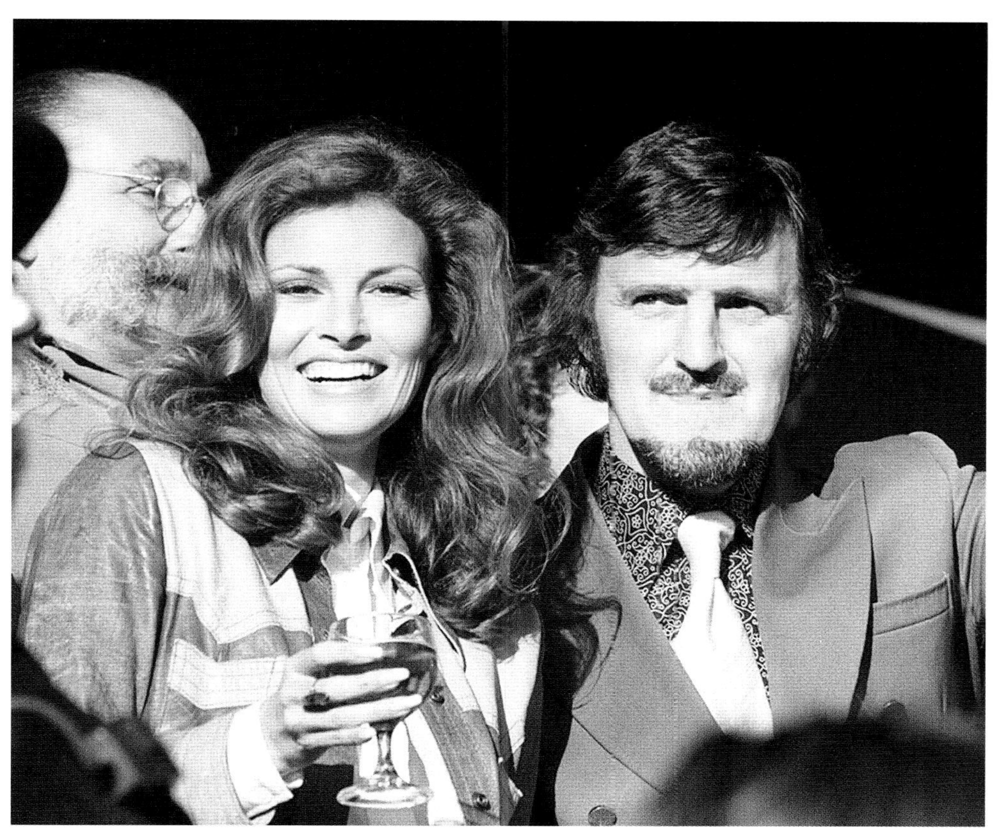

Stamford Bridge 1972
Jimmy Hill has good reason to smile, as he
entertains Raquel Welch during Chelsea v
Leicester. Two people you wouldn't normally
expect to see in the same photo!

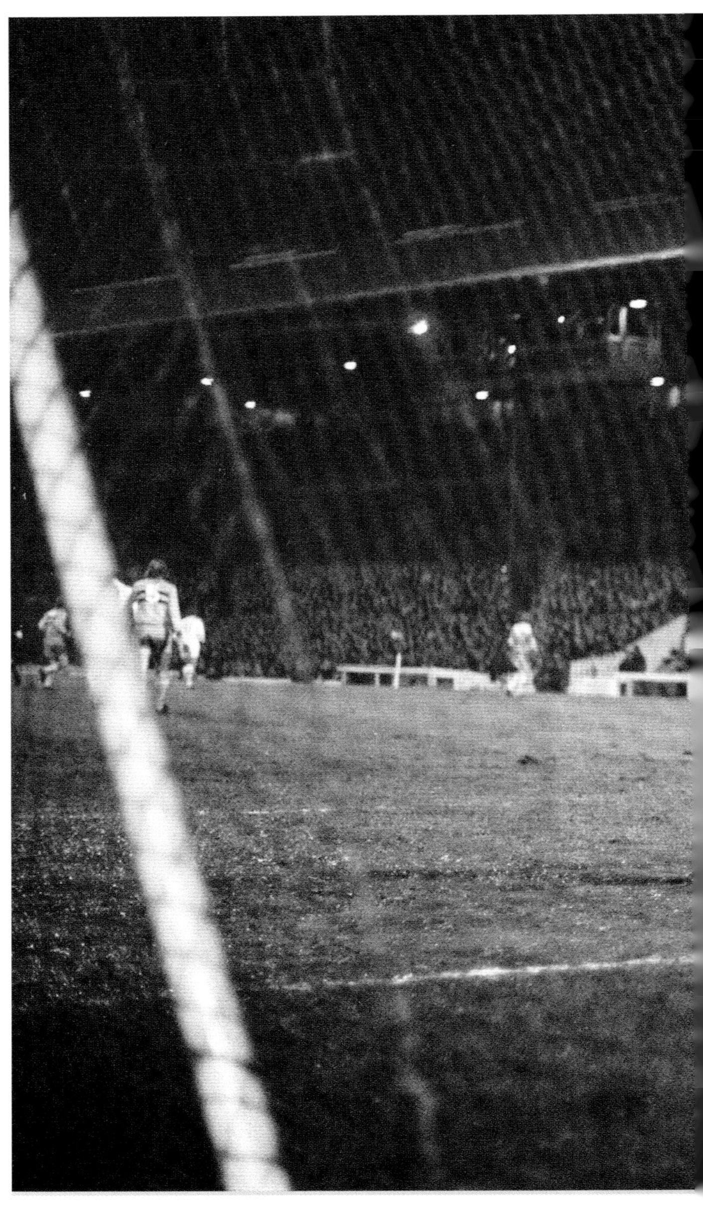

Victoria Ground 1972
A grim night for Bobby Moore. His West Ham team lost 3-2 and he had to play in goal for most of the game after Bobby Ferguson got injured in the 13th minute. His first task was to save a penalty, but the rebound was then scored.

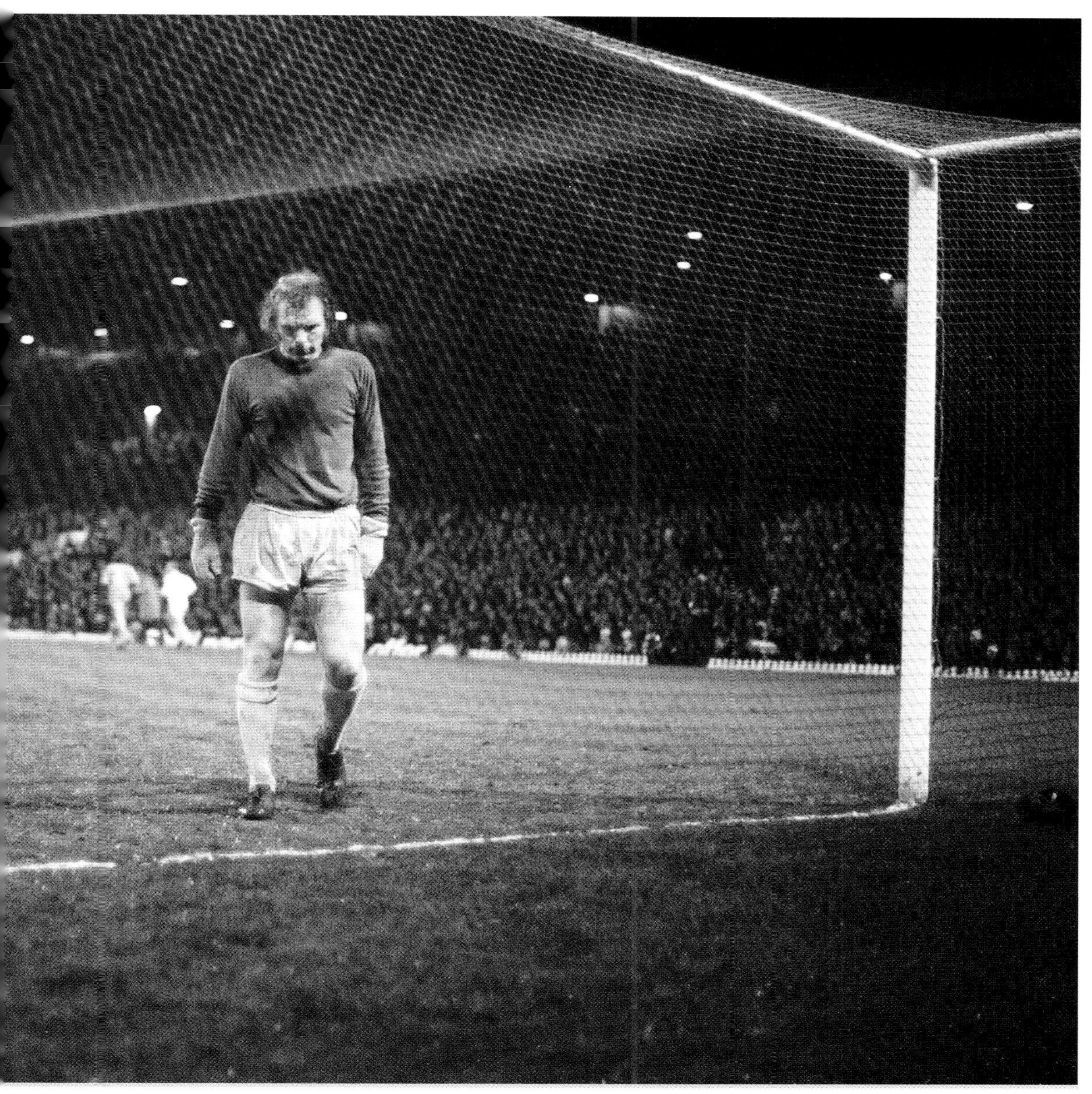

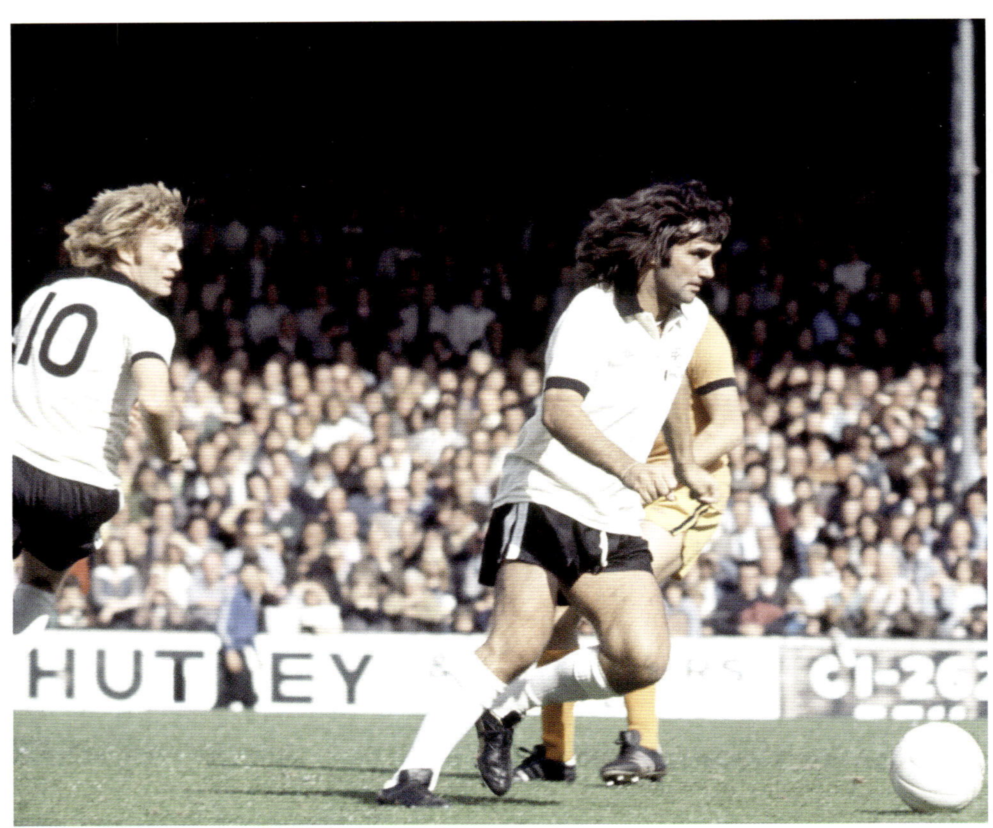

Craven Cottage 1976
George Best and Rodney Marsh bring flair and flamboyance to Fulham as the home team take on Wolves.

 Soul & Glory English Football: 1950–1989

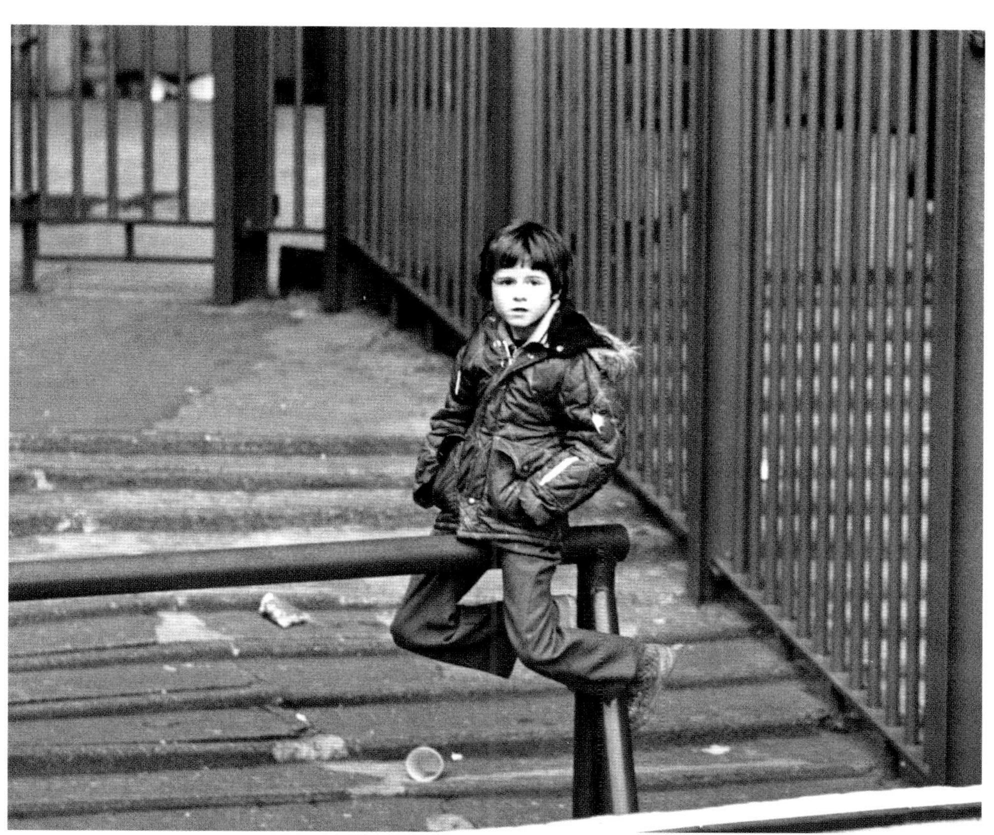

Goodison Park 1976
A disappointing attendance means this
young Everton fan has plenty of room to
himself on the Paddock terrace.

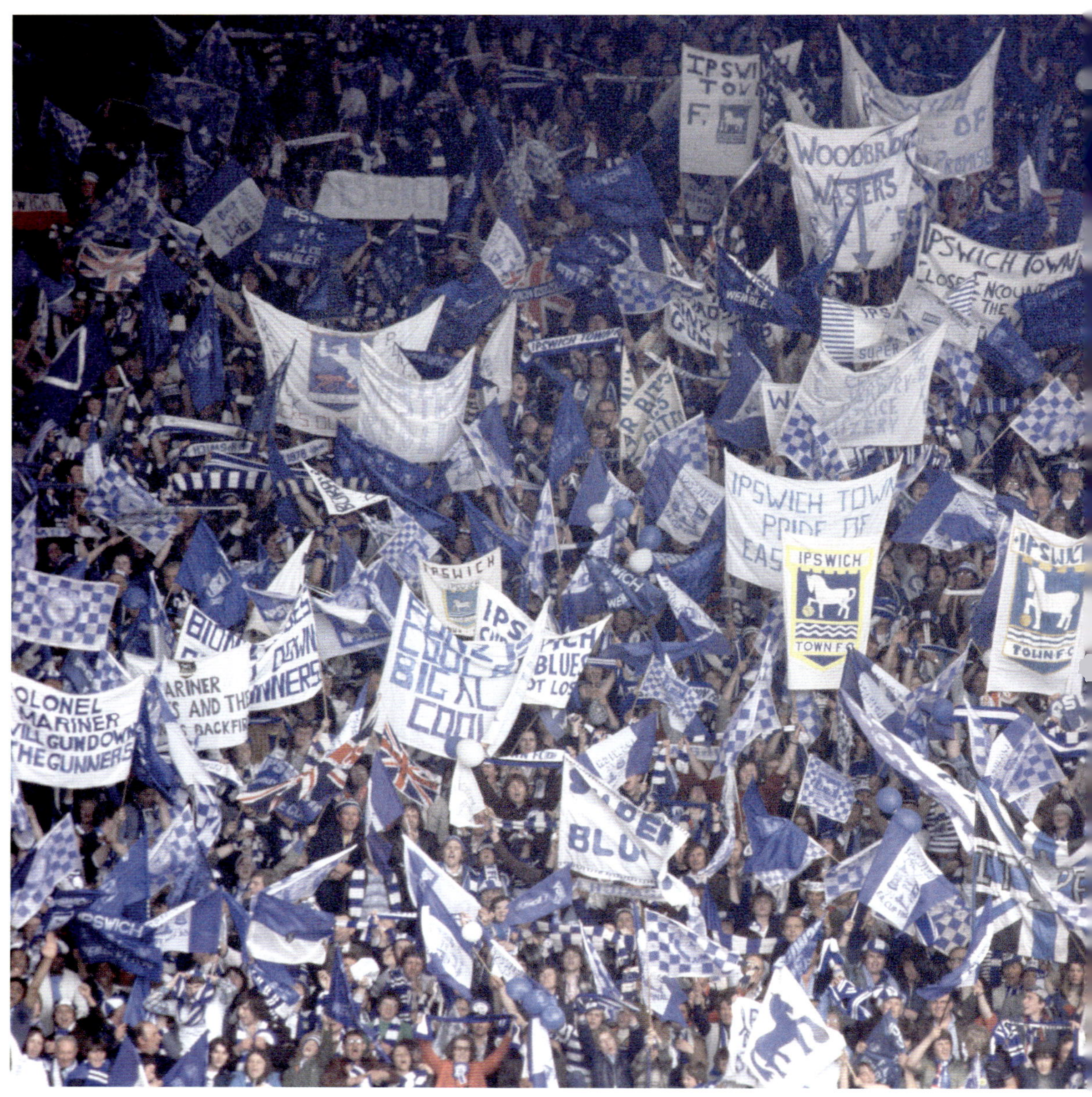

Wembley 1978
Fans of Ipswich Town parade home-made
banners and flags for the FA Cup Final,
which they won 1-0 against Arsenal.

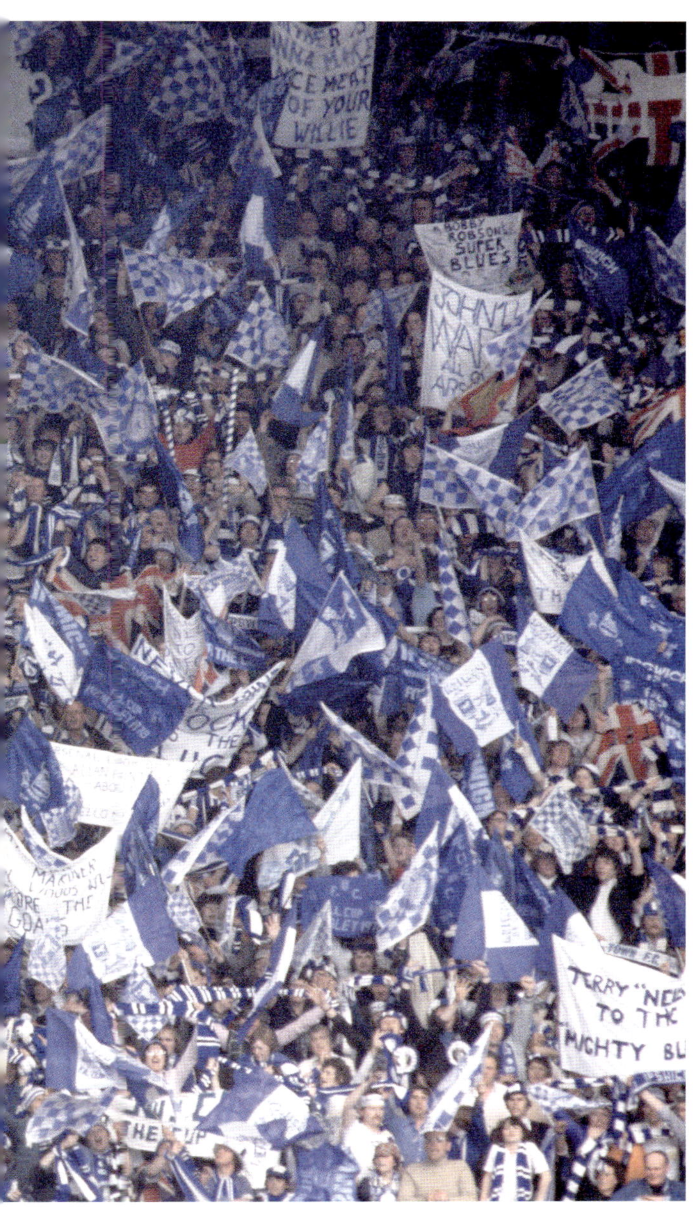
ICE MEAT
OF YOUR
WILLIE
BOBBY
ROBSON
SUPER
BLUES
JOHN
WAR
TERRY "NEE
TO THE
MIGHTY BLU
THE CUP

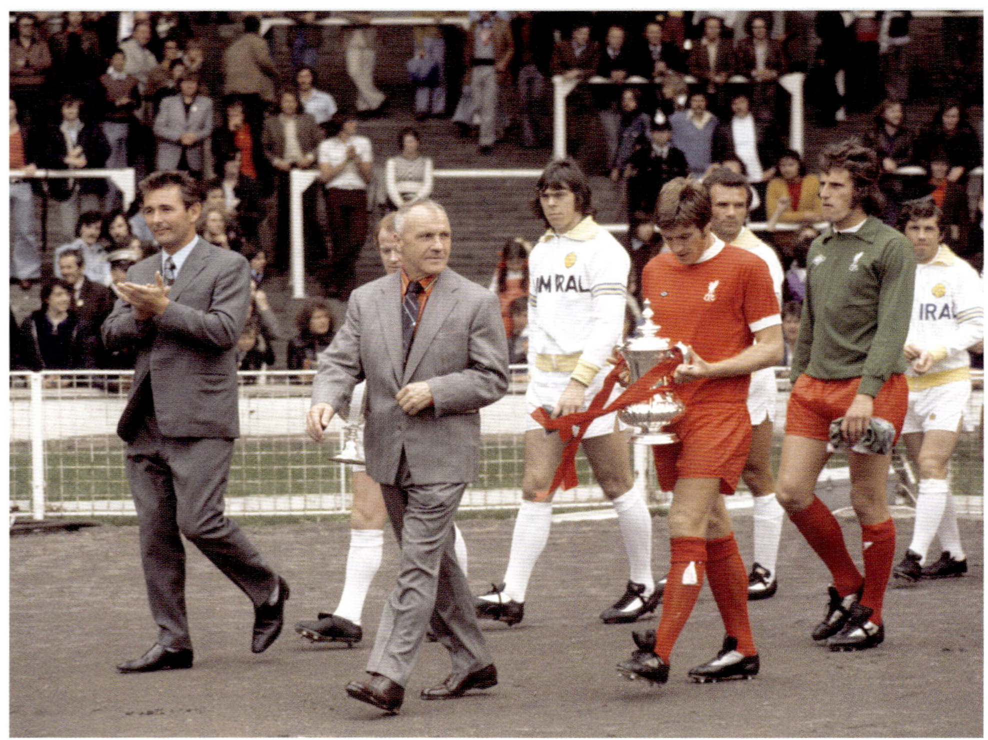

Wembley 1974
Brian Clough and Bill Shankly lead their teams
out in the Charity Shield between Leeds and
Liverpool. The team captains Billy Bremner and
Emlyn Hughes carry the trophies won from the
previous season. Clough would only manage
Leeds for a total of 44 days.

Baseball Ground 1975
For the second time in three years Derby
County are champions of England. After
their Division One match with Carlisle
United, David Nish (l) and Kevin Hector
parade the trophy.

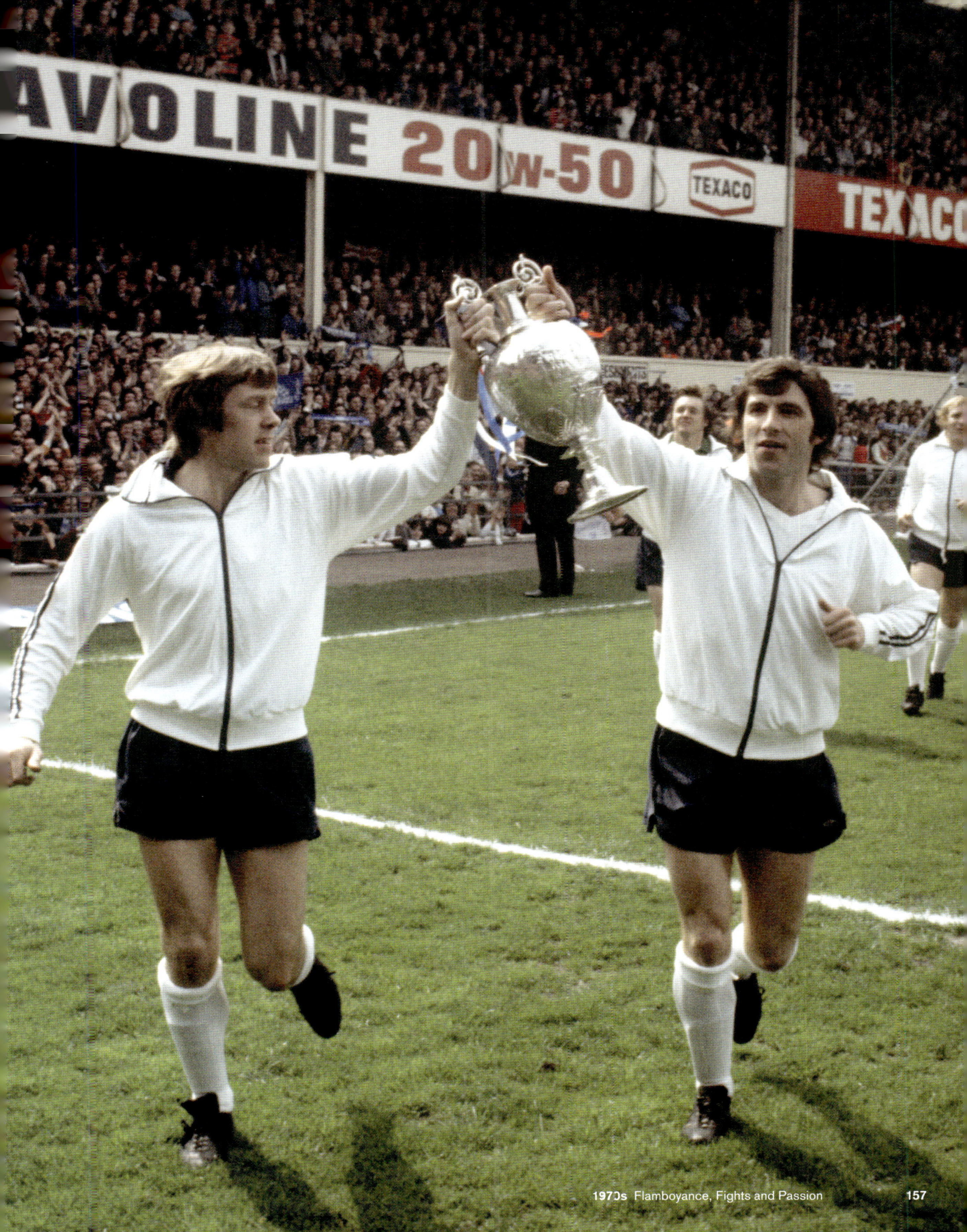
AVOLINE 20 W-50
TEXACO
TEXACO

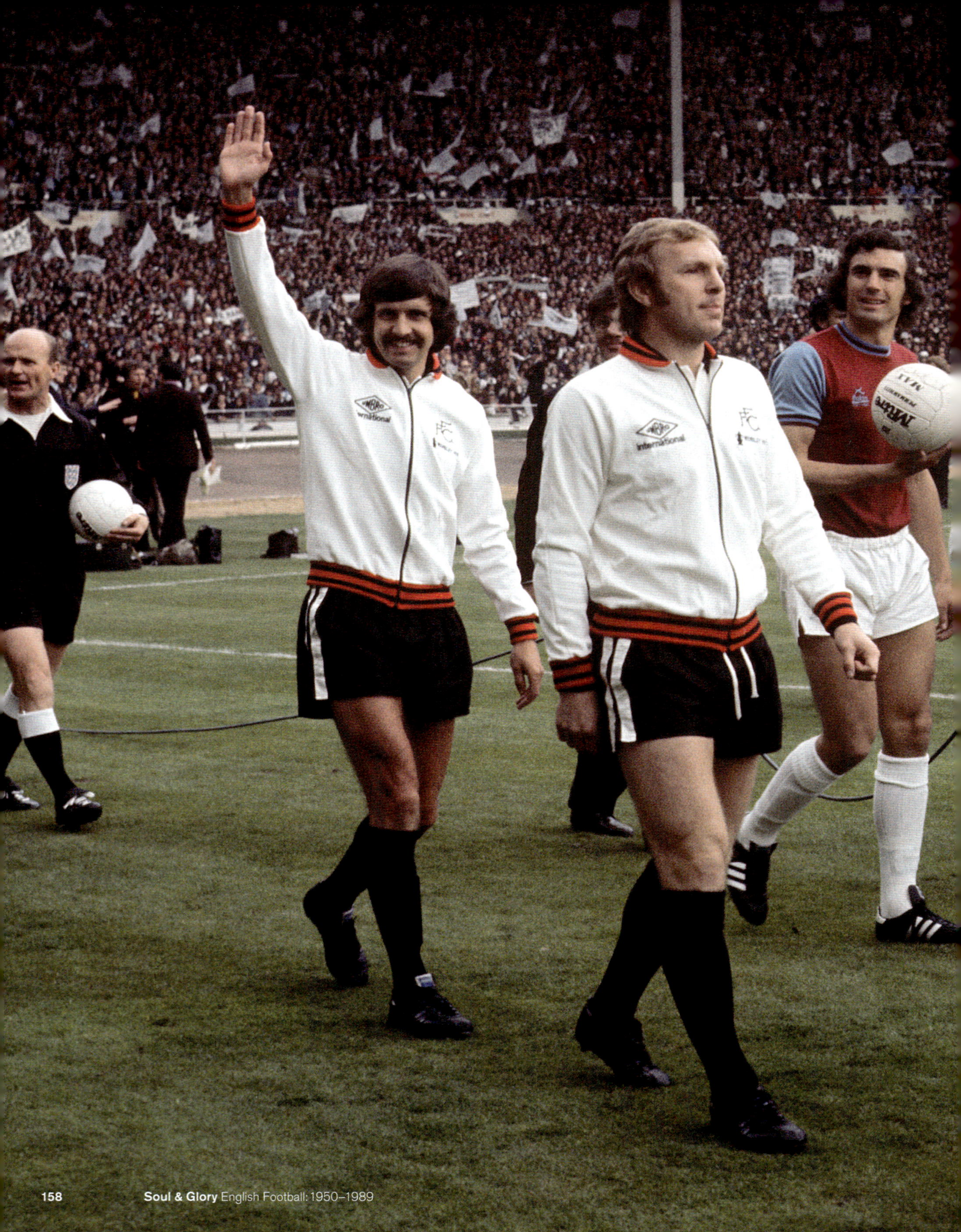

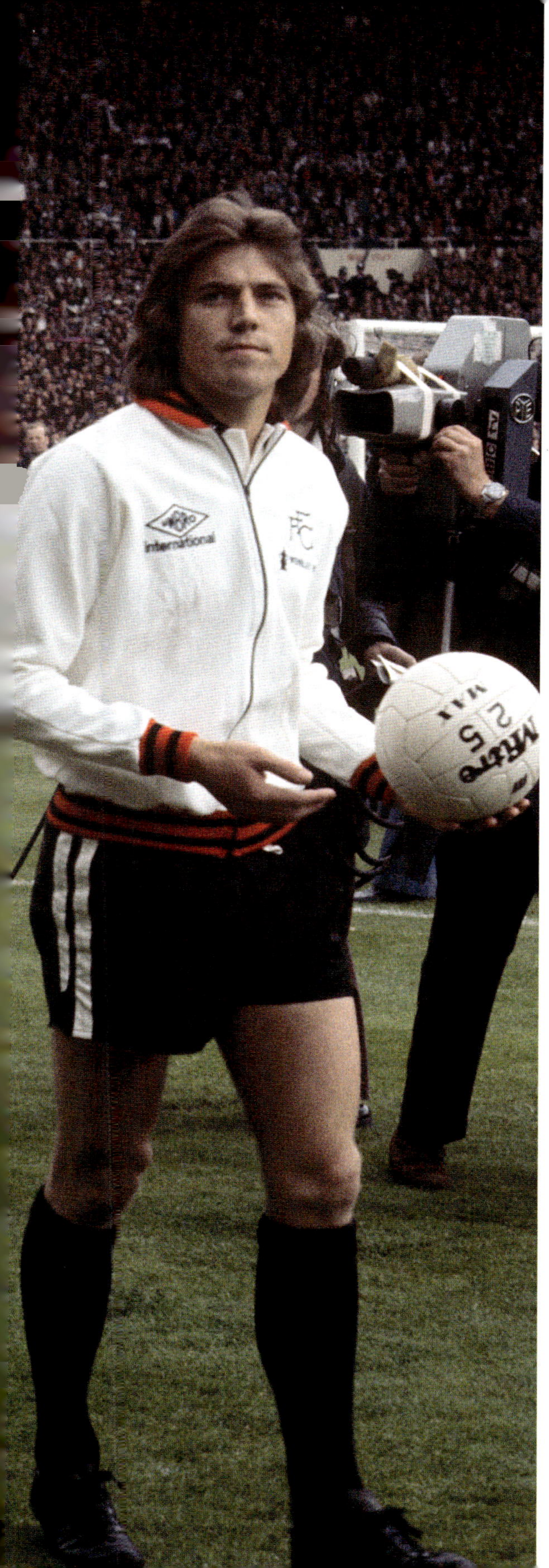

Wembley 1975
Fulham's Bobby Moore walks out for the
FA Cup Final against – of all teams – West
Ham. To the left is Alan Slough and to the
right John Mitchell. To Moore's left, Trevor
Brooking savours the moment.

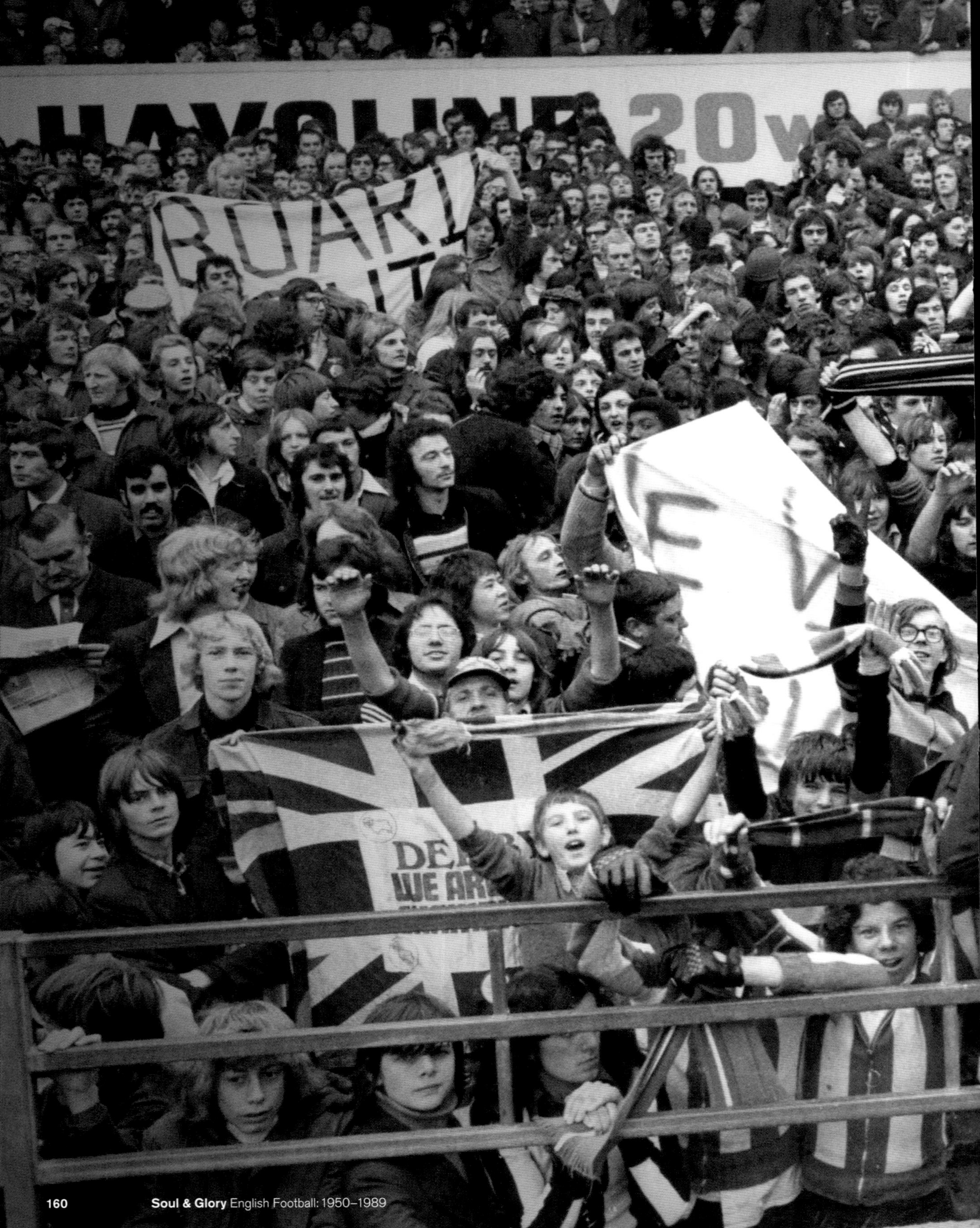

HAVOLINE 20w
ROAR
E V
DE
WE AR

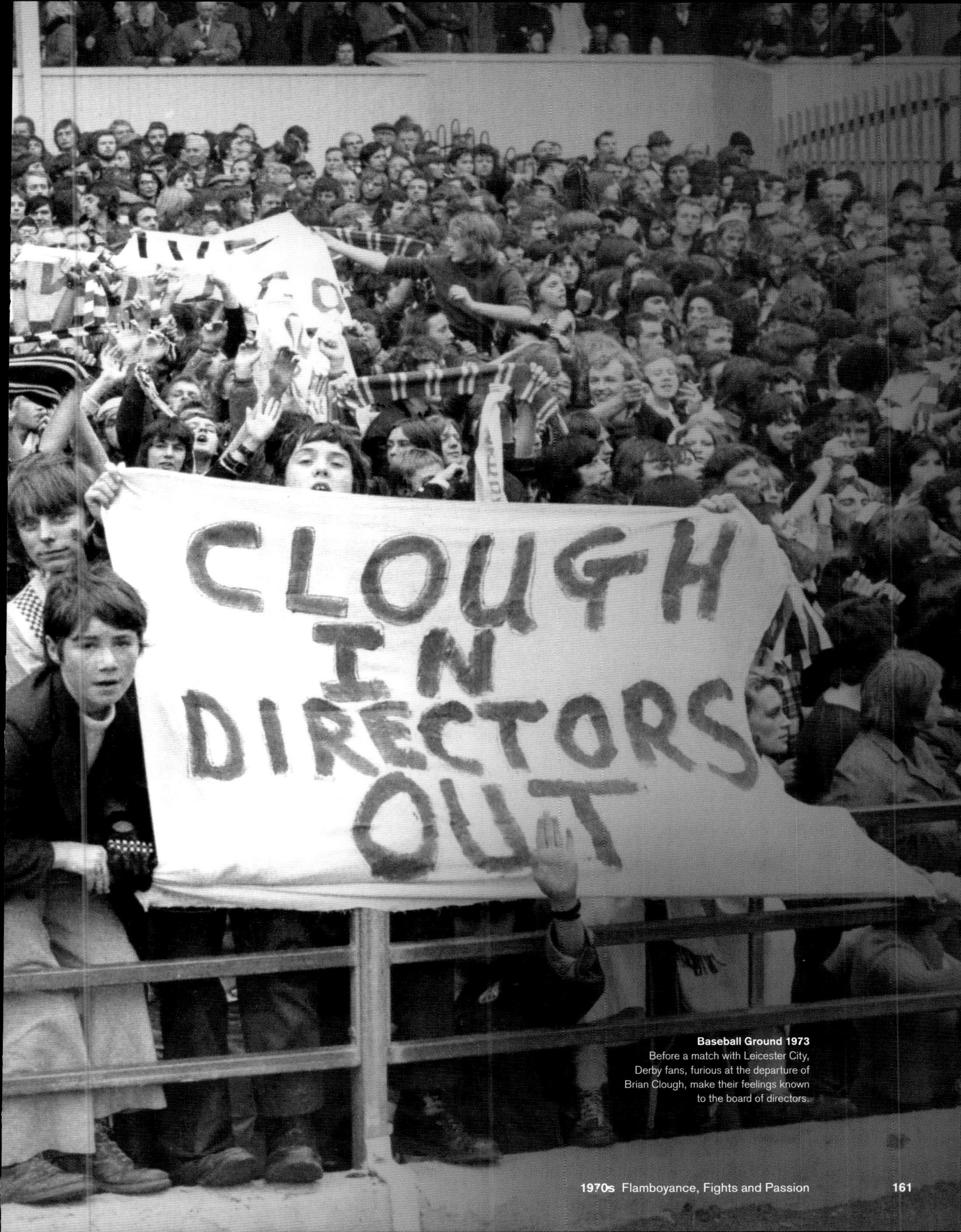

Baseball Ground 1973
Before a match with Leicester City, Derby fans, furious at the departure of Brian Clough, make their feelings known to the board of directors.

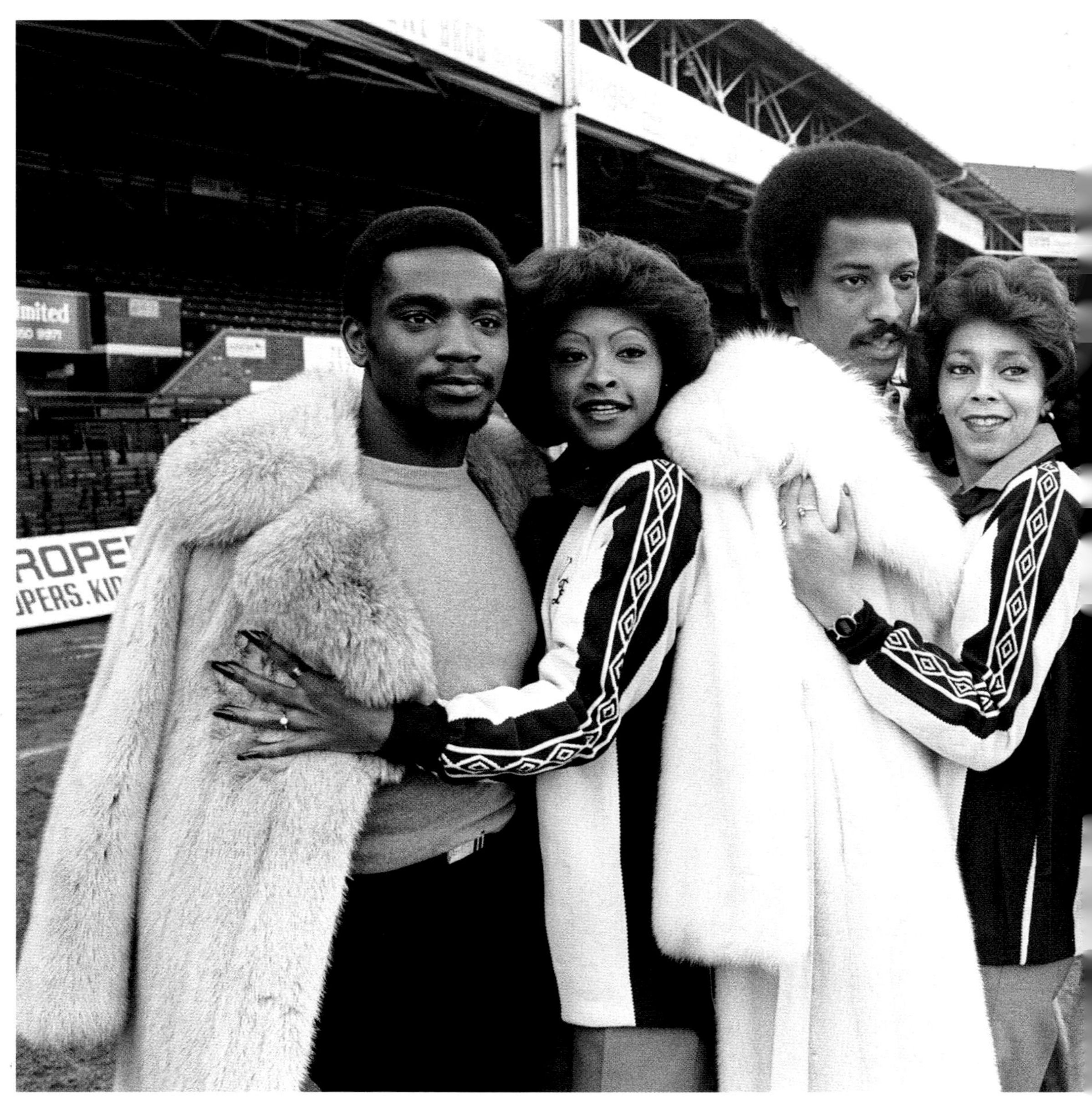

The Hawthorns 1979
The Three Degrees meet the Three
Degrees. West Brom's Laurie Cunningham,
Brendon Batson and Cyrille Regis, are
looking slick as they pose with pop's Valerie
Holiday, Helen Scott and Sheila Ferguson.

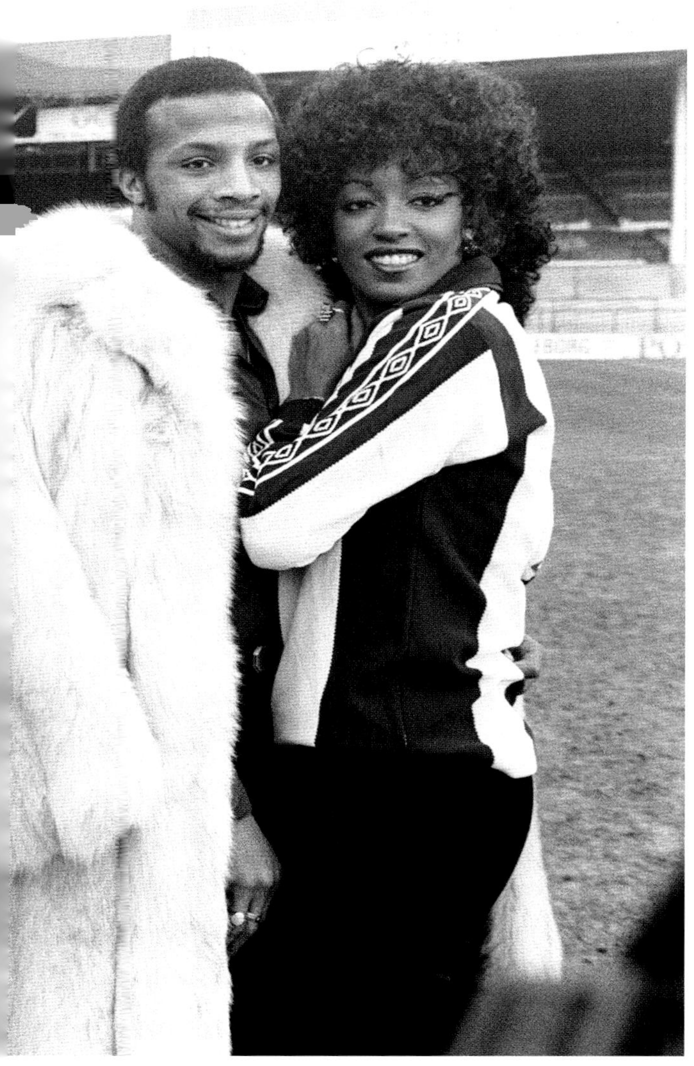

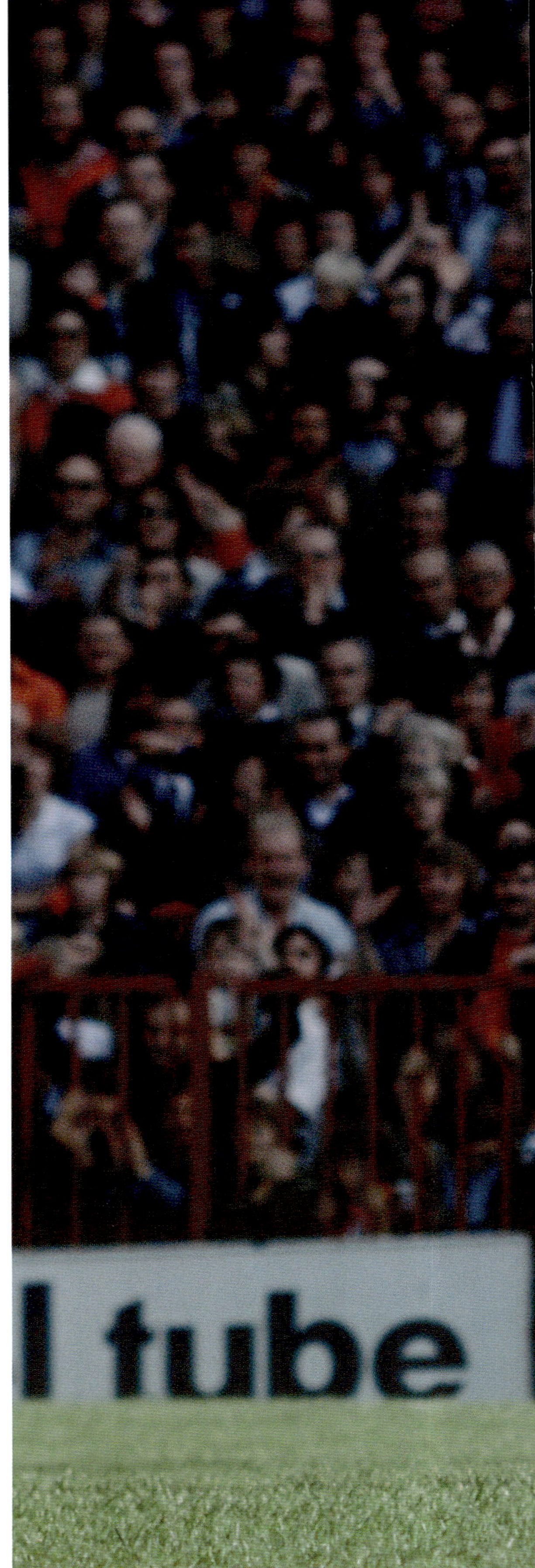

The Hawthorns 1978
Despair for Liverpool goalkeeper Ray
Clemence. Cyrille Regis celebrates as
his team-mate Laurie Cunningham
(out of shot) puts West Brom 1-0 up.

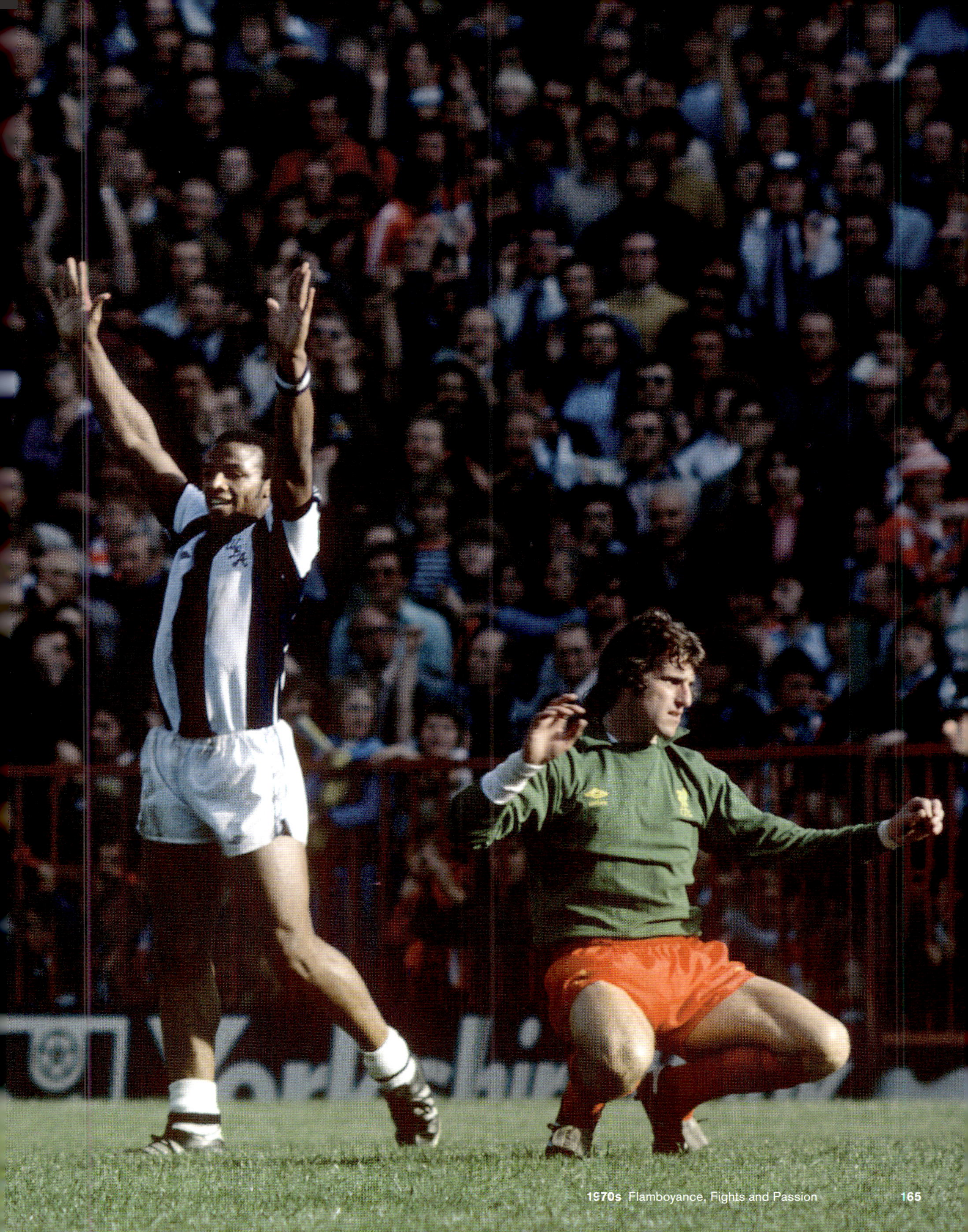

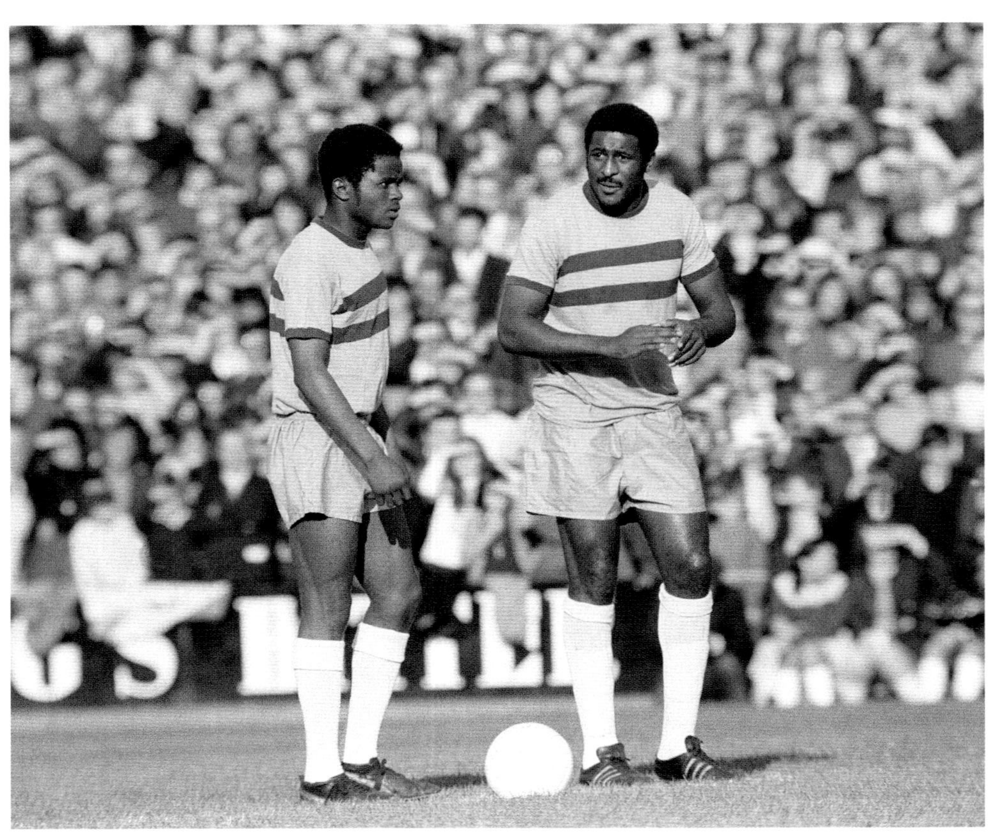

Selhurst Park 1971
West Ham's Clyde Best (r) and Ade
Coker (l) get ready for kick-off against
Palace. The Hammers won 3-0.

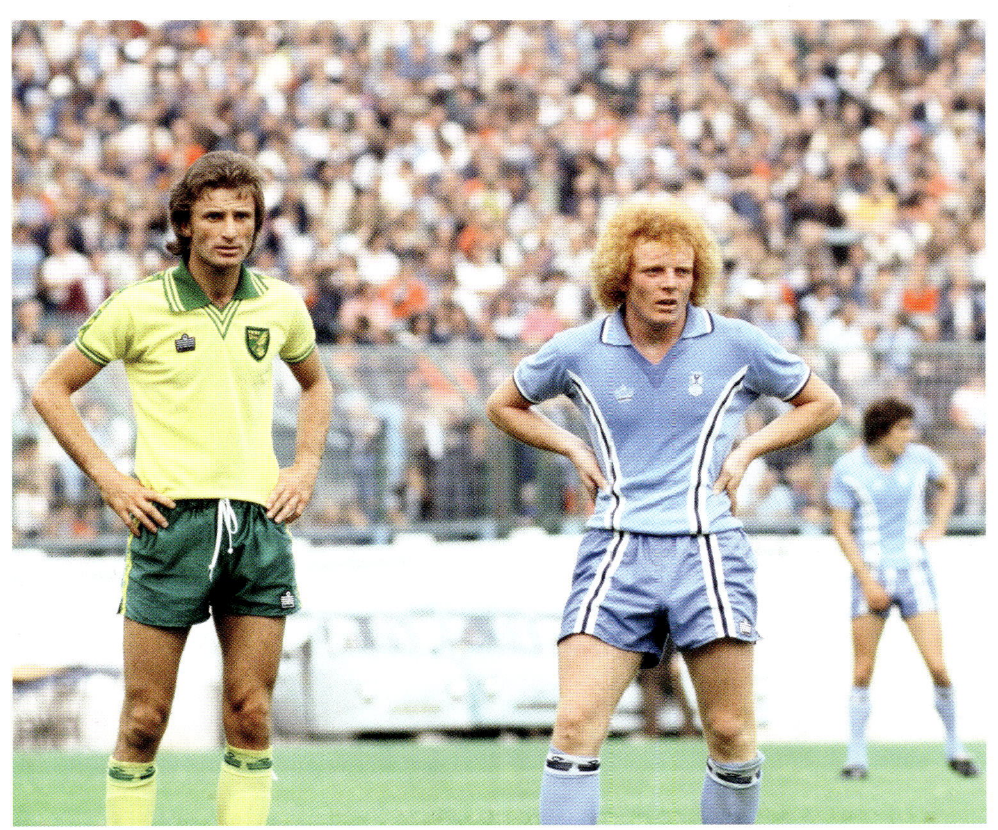

Highfield Road 1978

Tony Powell of Norwich, and Ian Wallace
of Coventry both in Admiral wear, the
dominant kit manufacturer of the 70s.

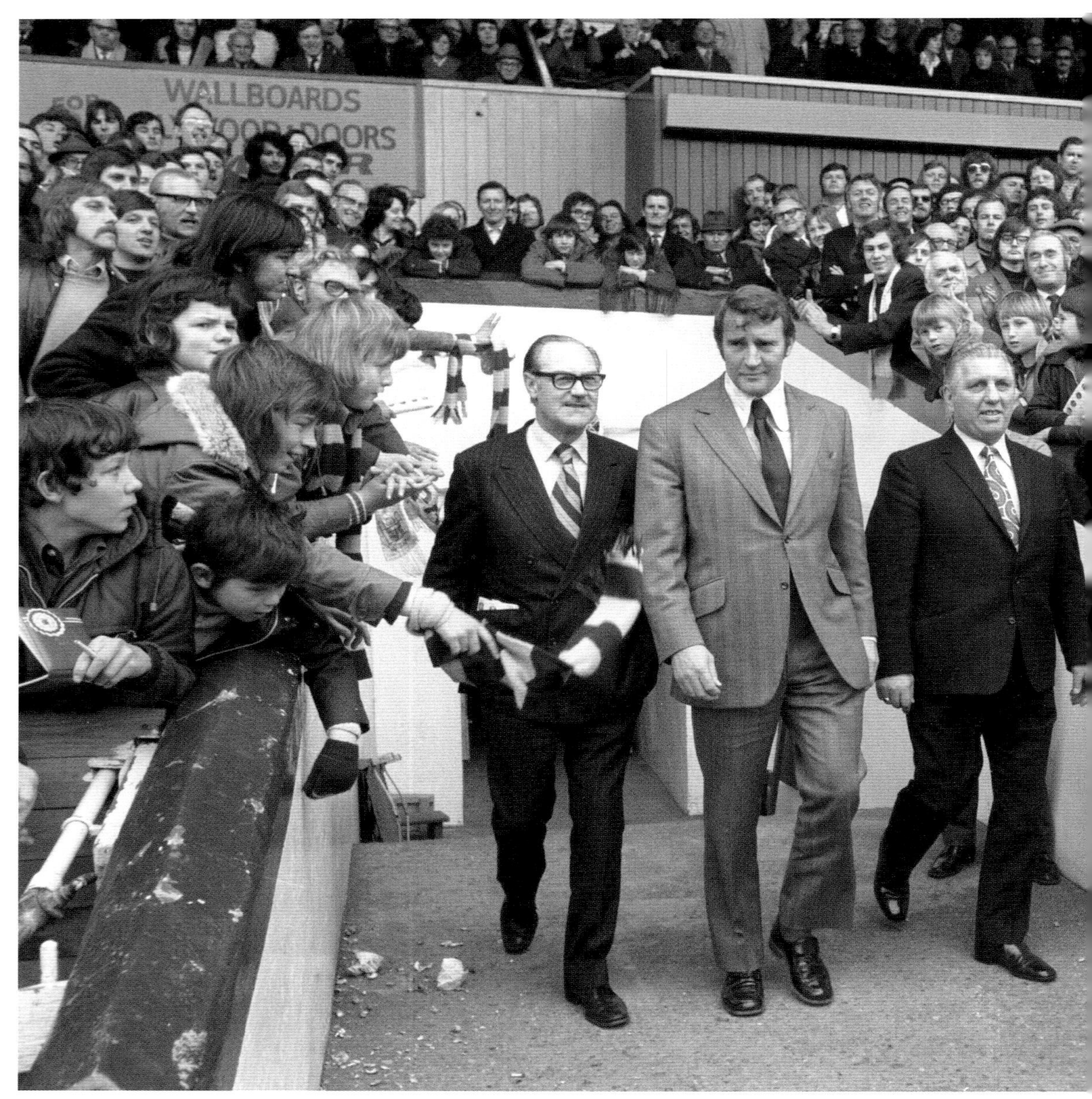

Selhurst Park 1973
Malcom Allison, looking very self-assured, walks out to a warm reception for his first home game as manager of Crystal Palace. To his left is chairman Ray Bloye, and to his right general manager Bert Head.

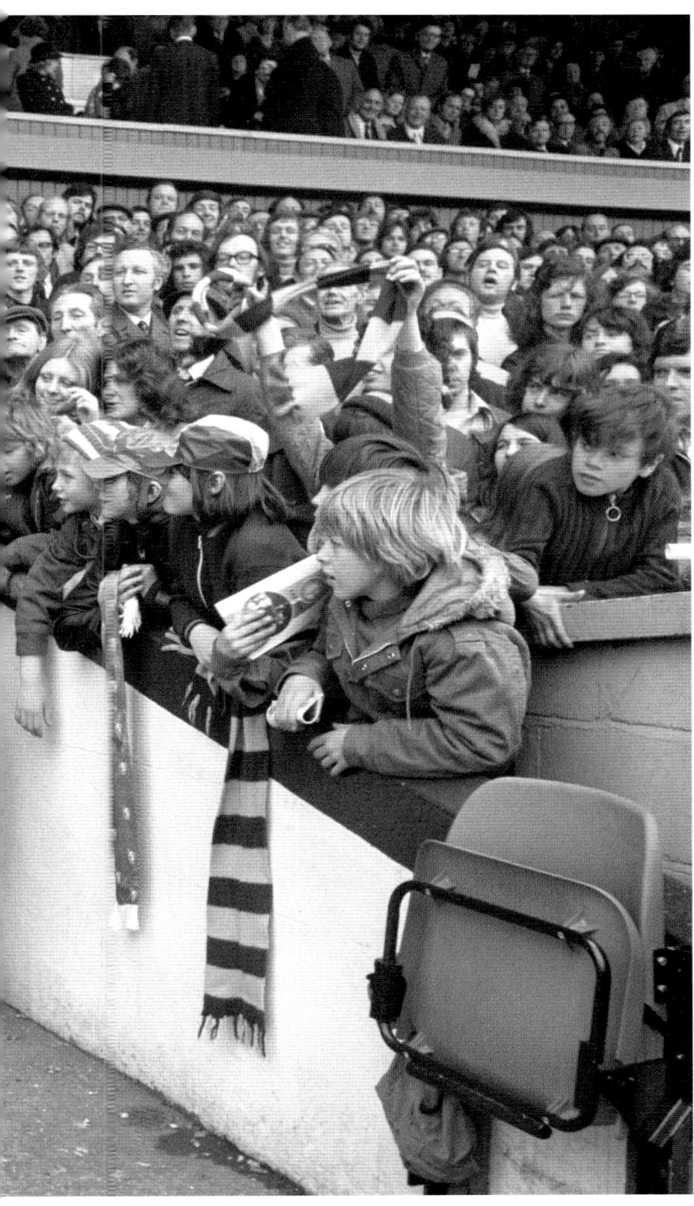

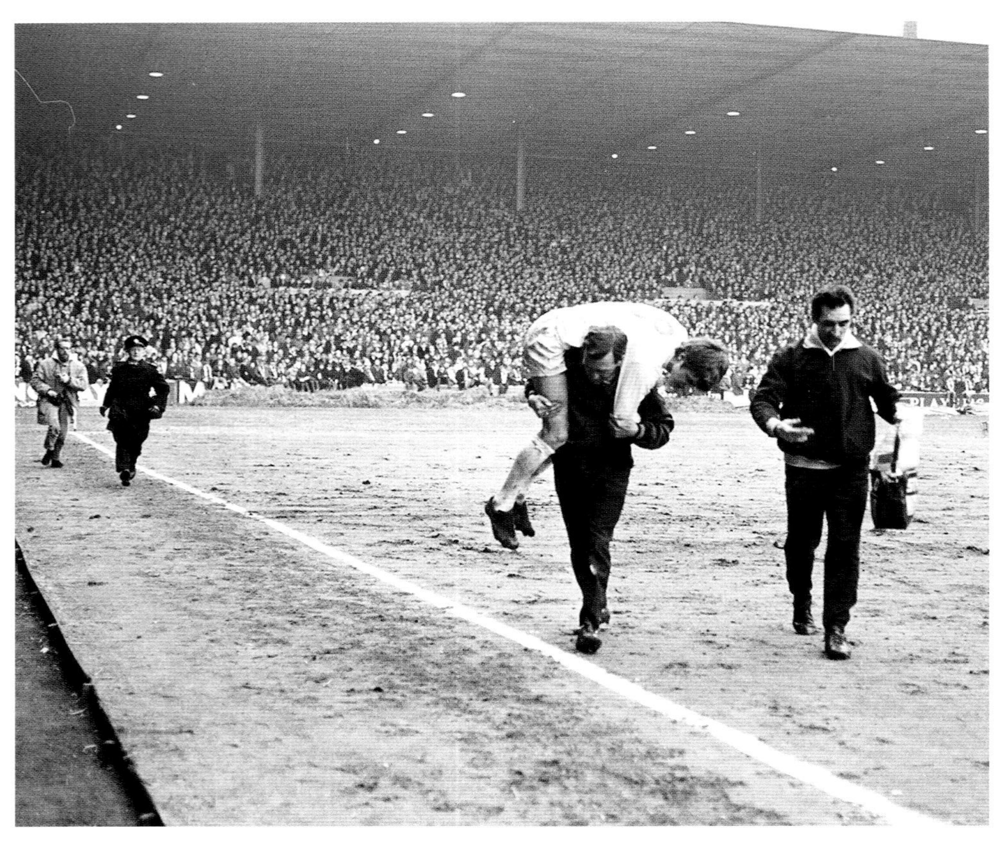

Elland Road 1970
Leeds at home to Crystal Palace. A day
when the stretcher was misplaced. Allan
Clarke is given a fireman's carry.

     Soul & Glory English Football: 1950–1989

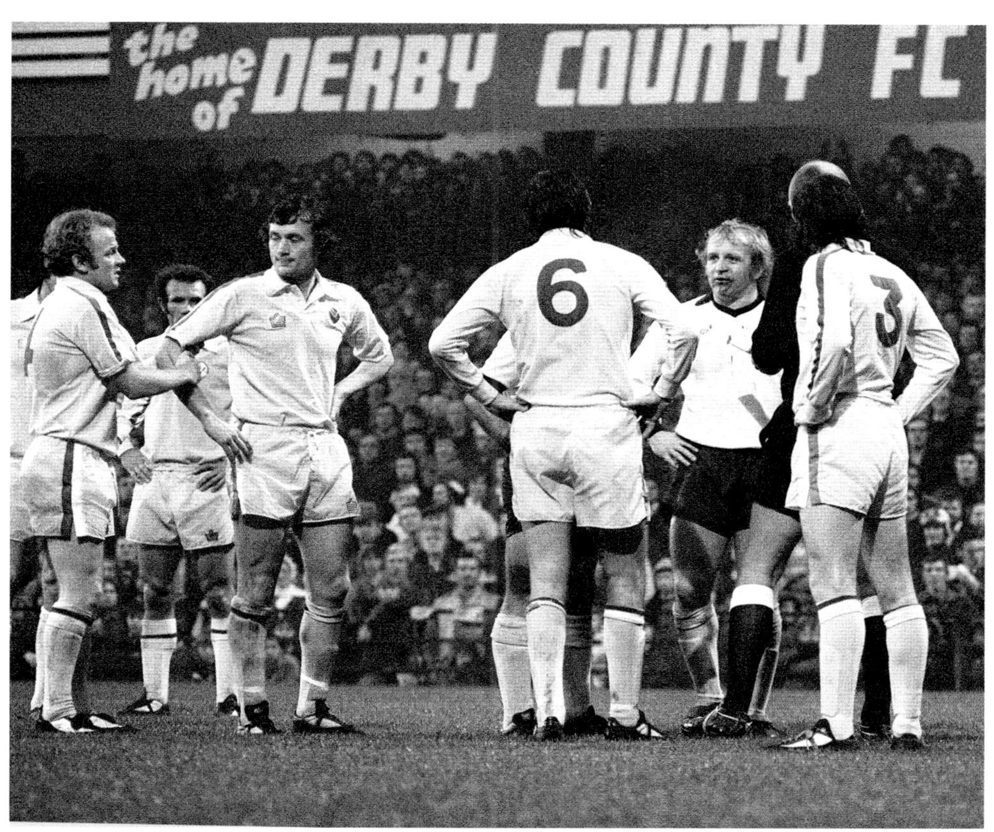

Baseball Ground 1975
A famous incident. Derby's Francis
Lee might have a bloody lip courtesy
of Norman Hunter (number 6) but he
also responded by throwing a flurry of
punches upon the Leeds man.

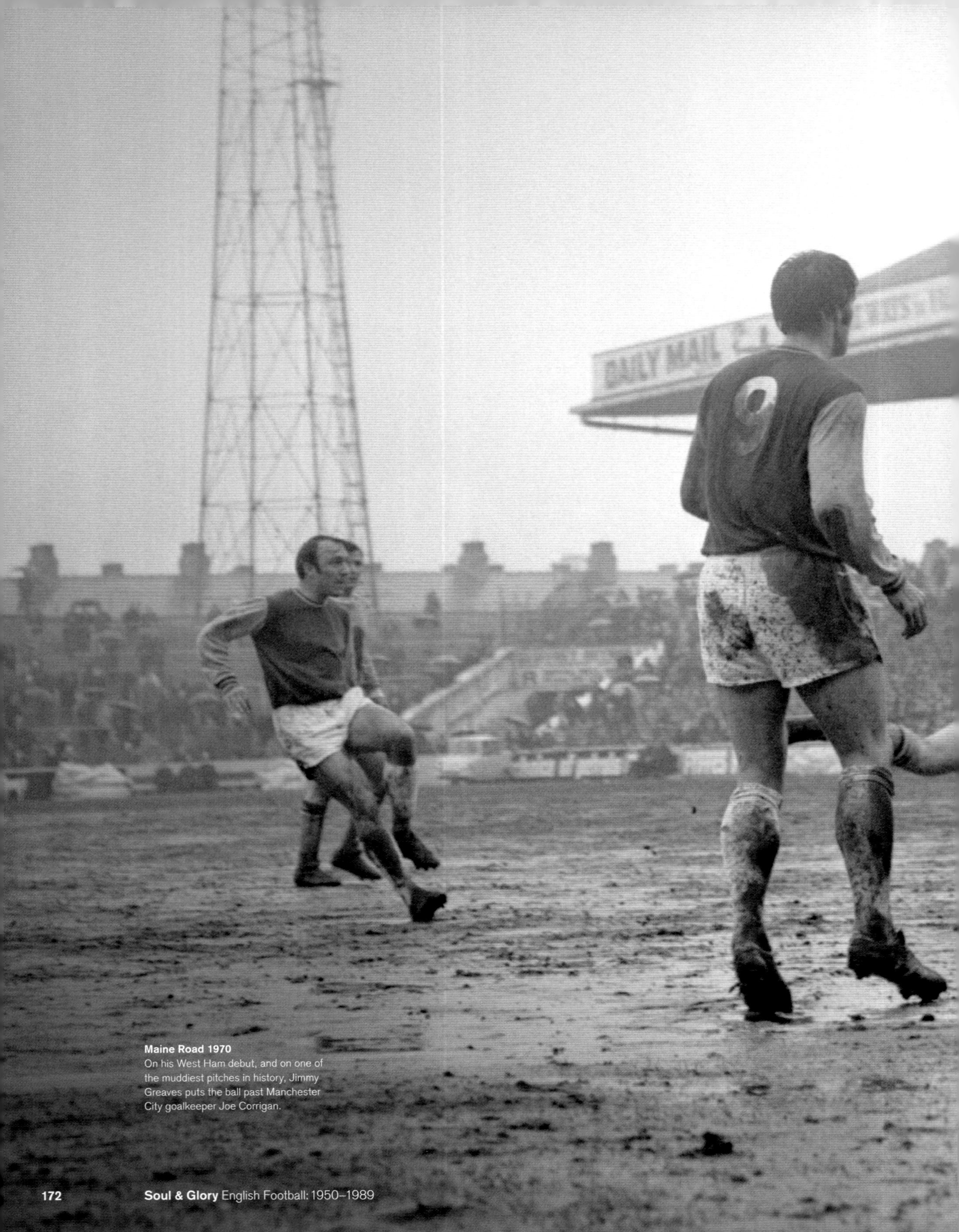

Maine Road 1970
On his West Ham debut, and on one of the muddiest pitches in history, Jimmy Greaves puts the ball past Manchester City goalkeeper Joe Corrigan.

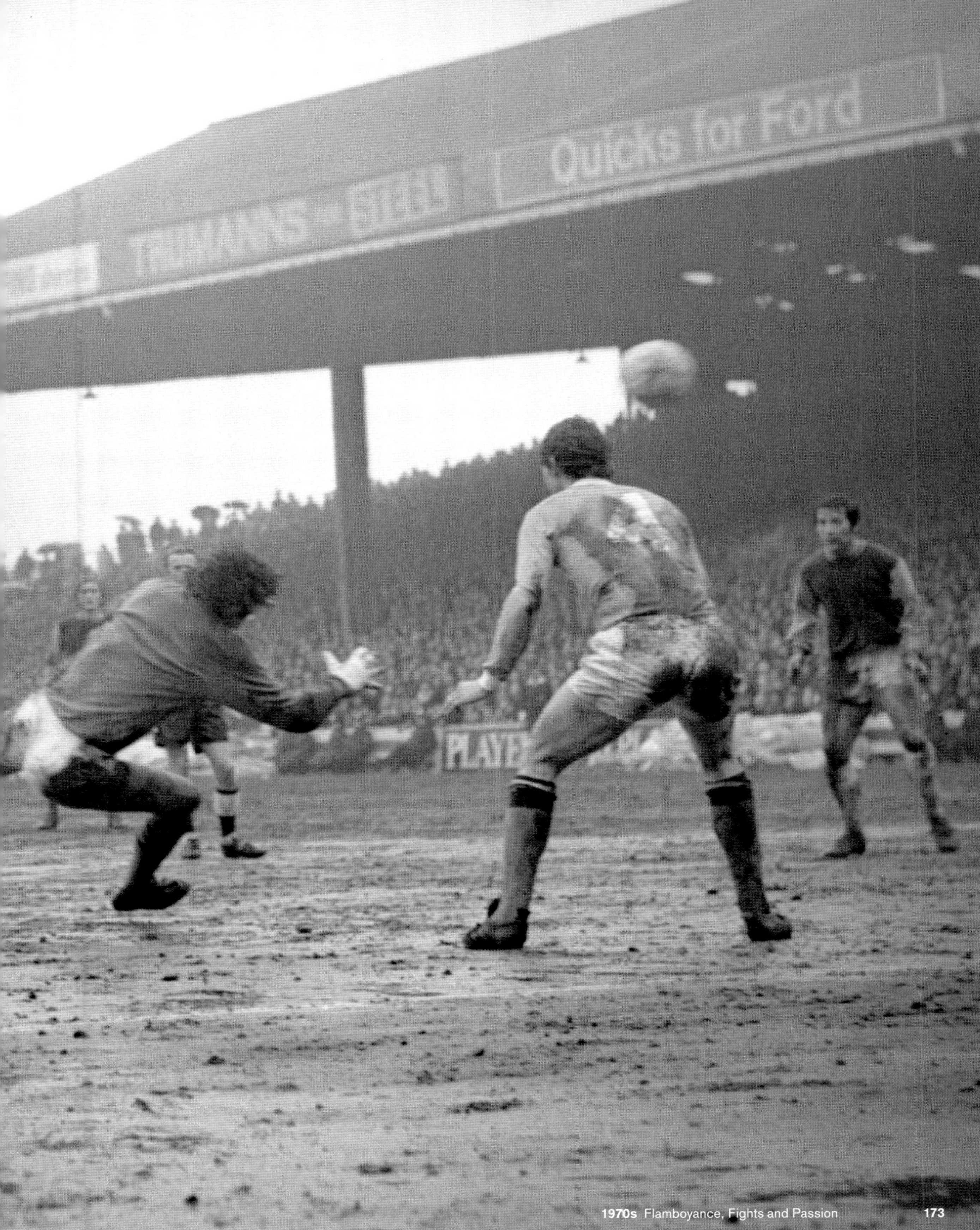

Quicks for Ford
TRUMANNS STEEL
PLAYER

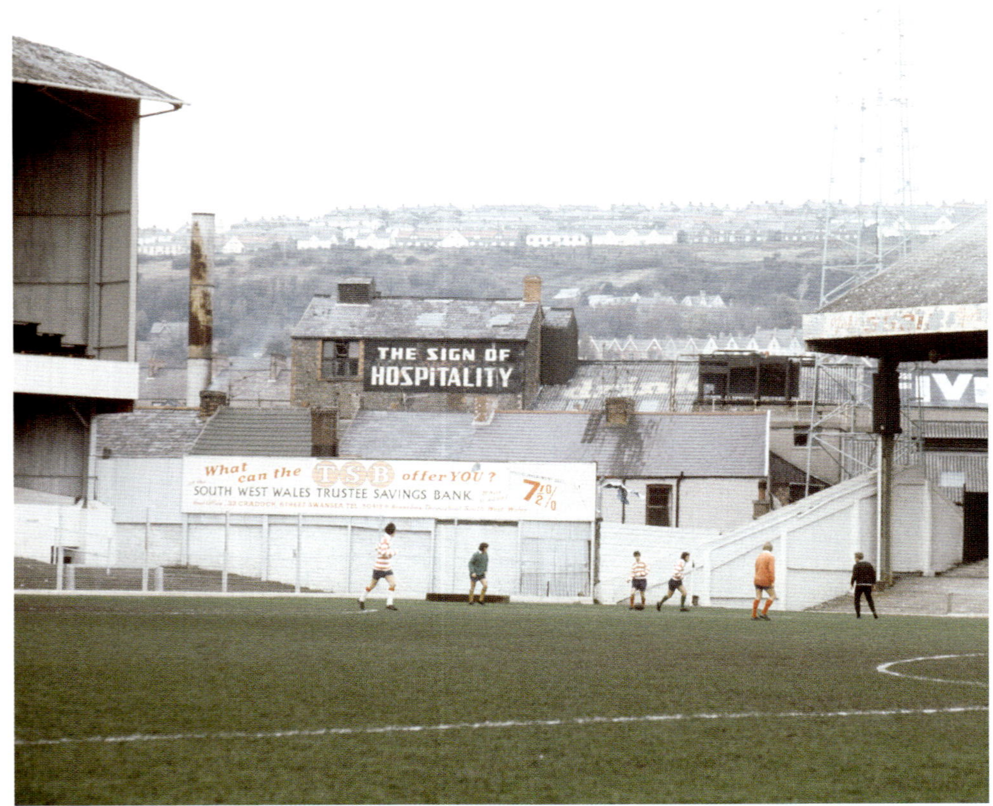

Vetch Field 1971
Swansea City players train with
the hills in the background.

Vetch Field 1971
The terrace at Swansea
is comprised of wooden
railway sleepers.

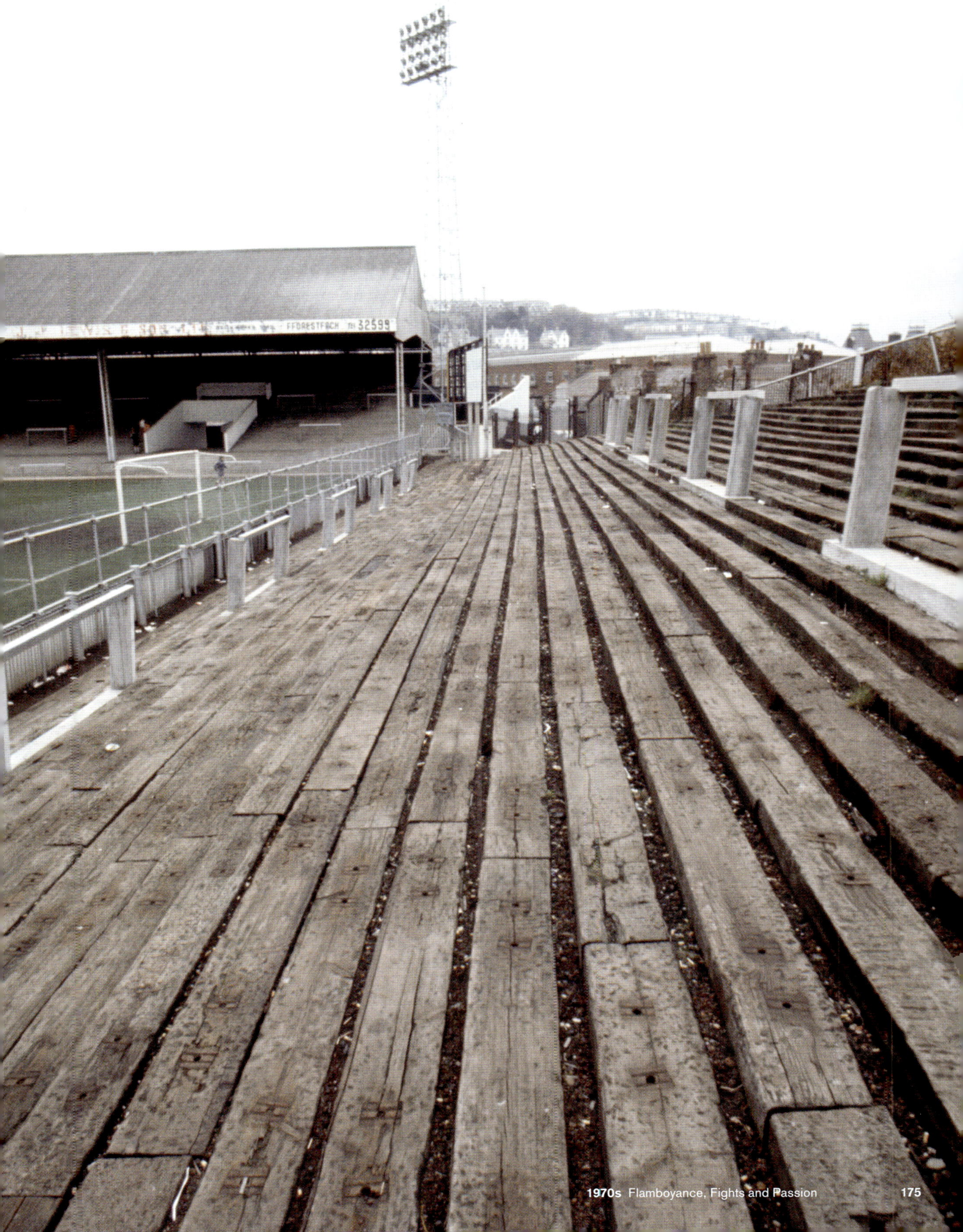

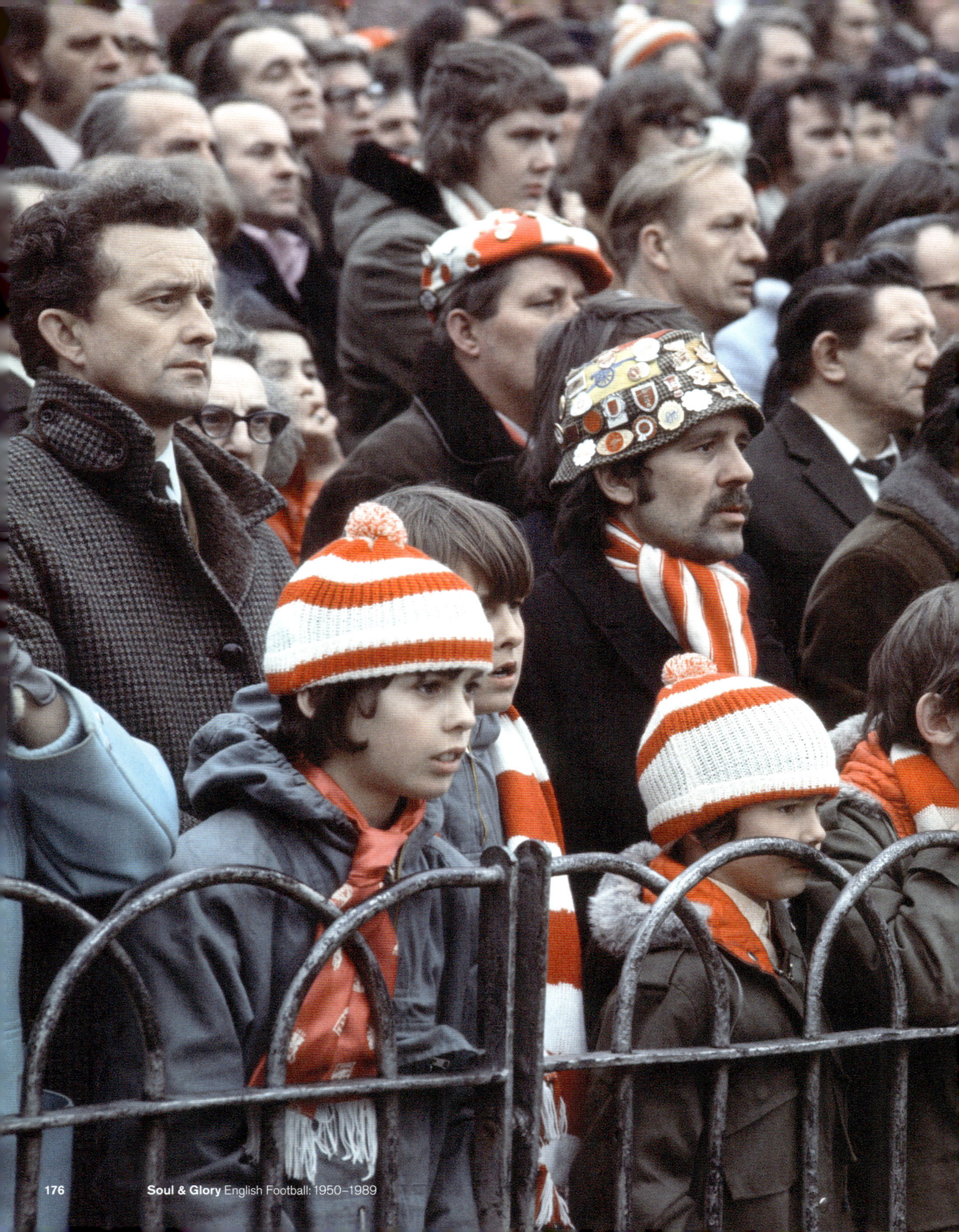

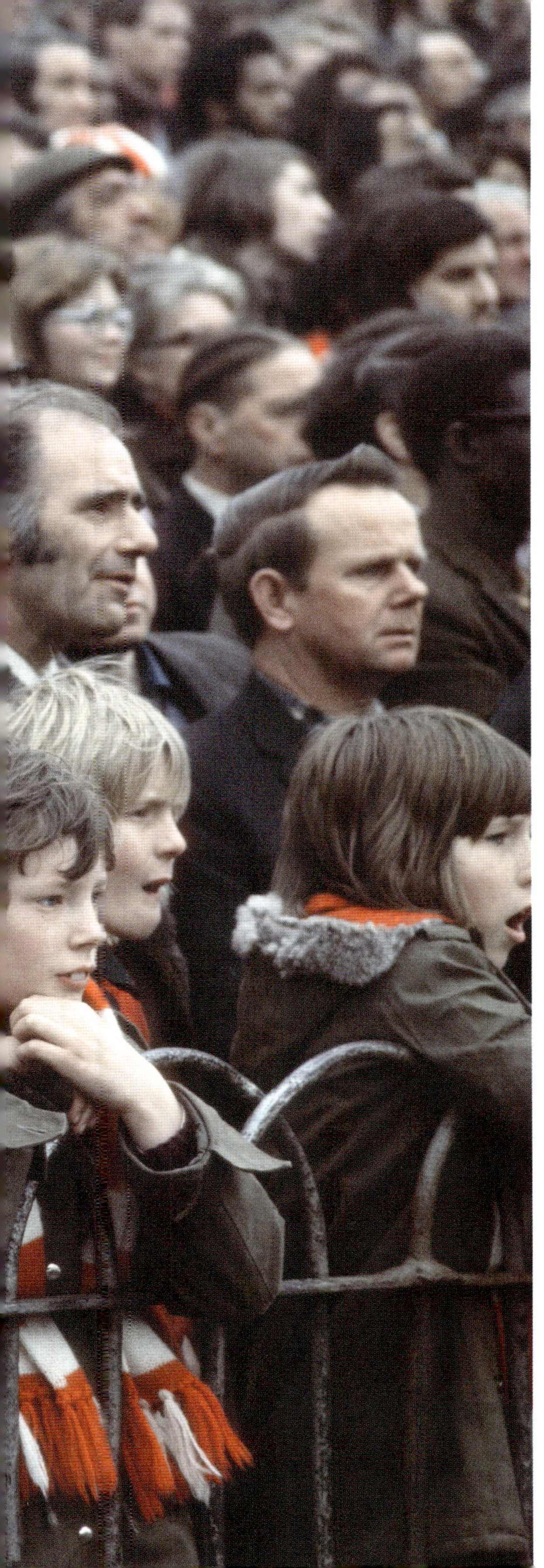

Highbury 1973
Arsenal fans young and old
watch their team in action
against Derby County.

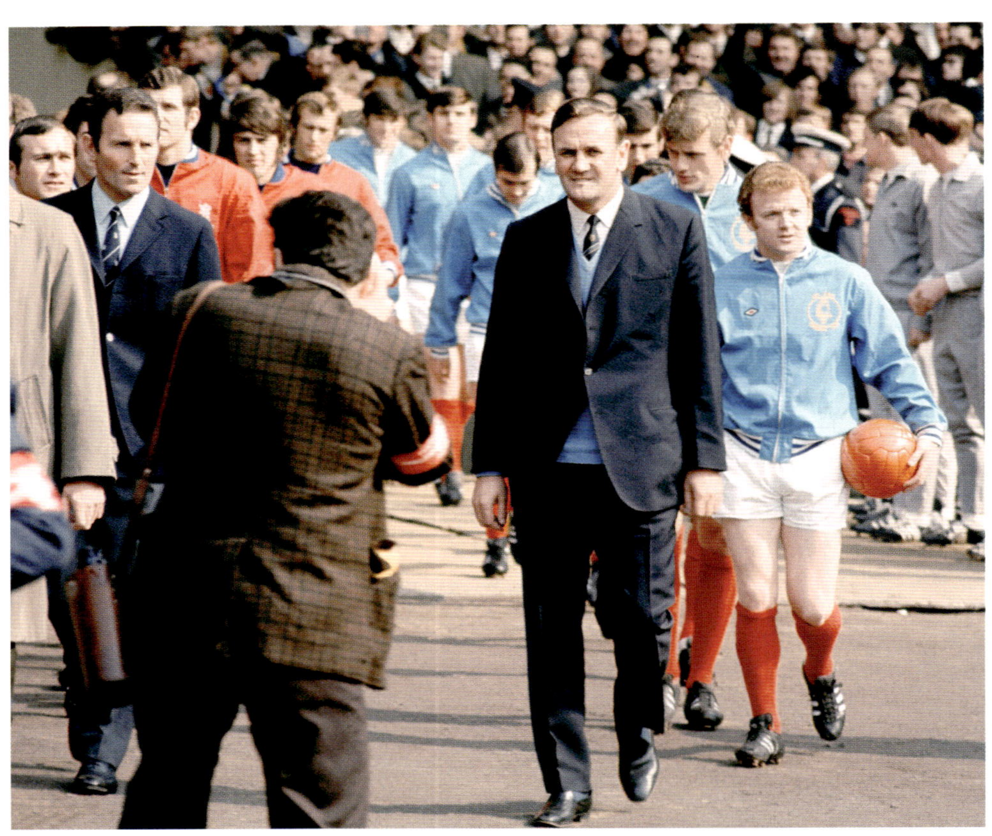

Wembley 1970
Managers Dave Sexton and Don Revie lead out
Chelsea and Leeds for the FA Cup Final, a game
which finished 2-2, and was the first final since
1912 to require a replay.

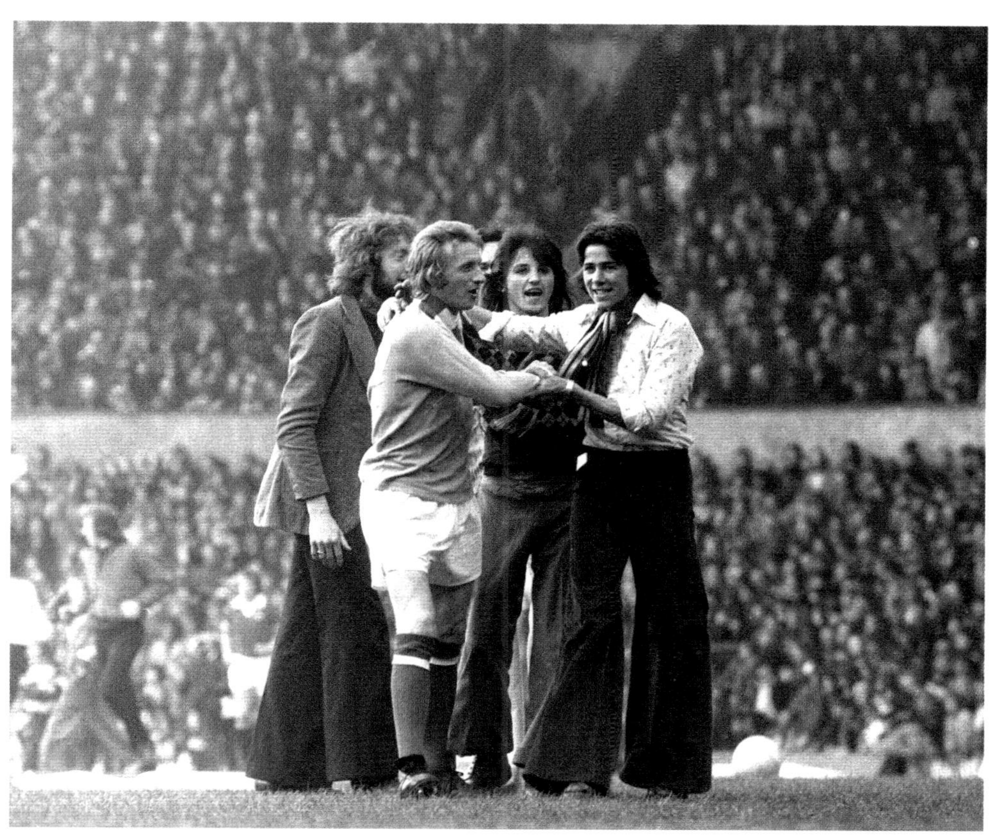

Old Trafford 1974
Manchester City's Denis Law is surrounded by
Manchester United fans moments after scoring
against his former club in a 1-0 win that helped
condemn United to relegation. The game was
abandoned due to the pitch invasion.

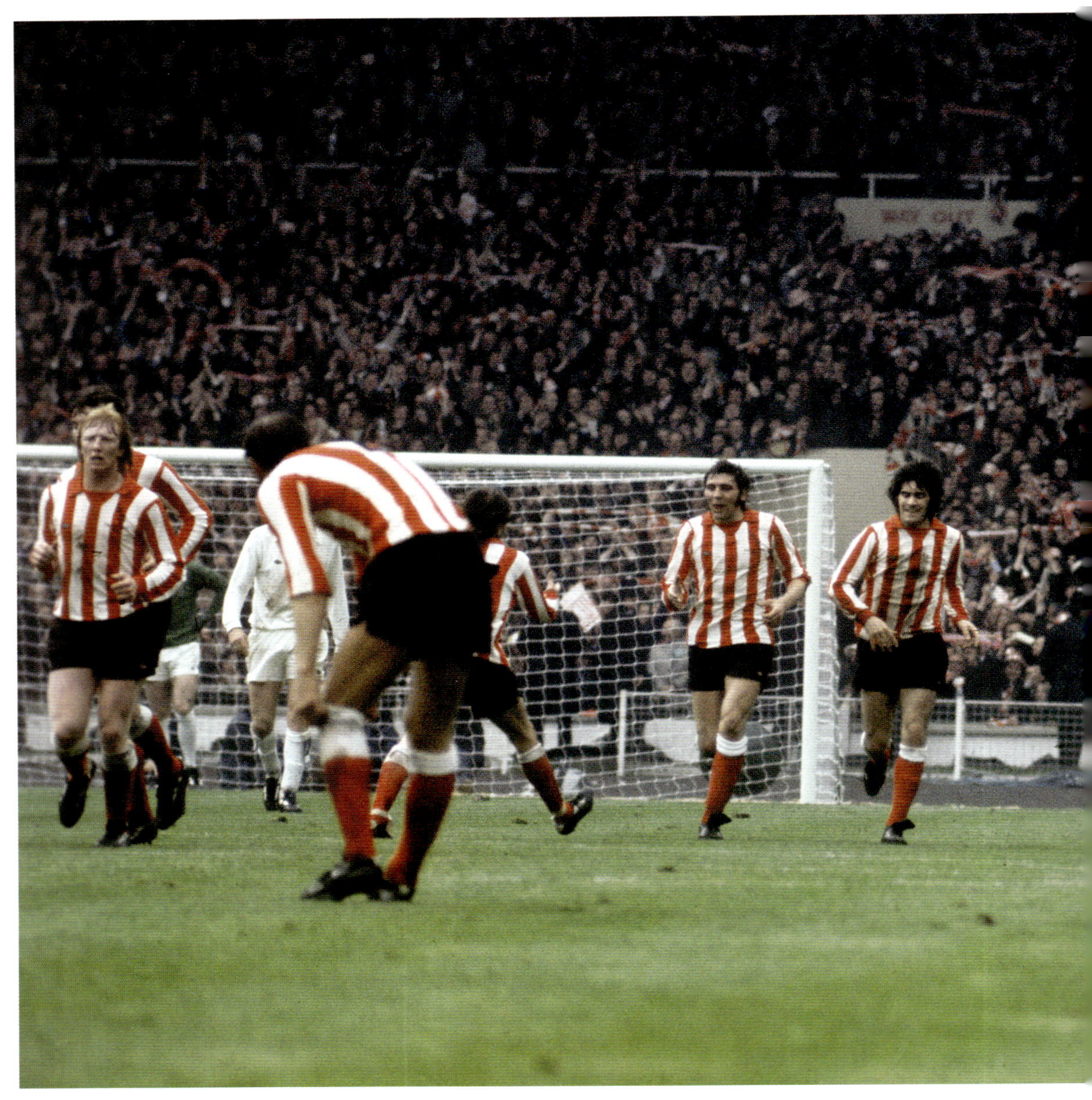

Wembley 1973
Ian Porterfield (third from right)
celebrates as his goal puts Sunderland
1-0 up in the FA Cup Final.

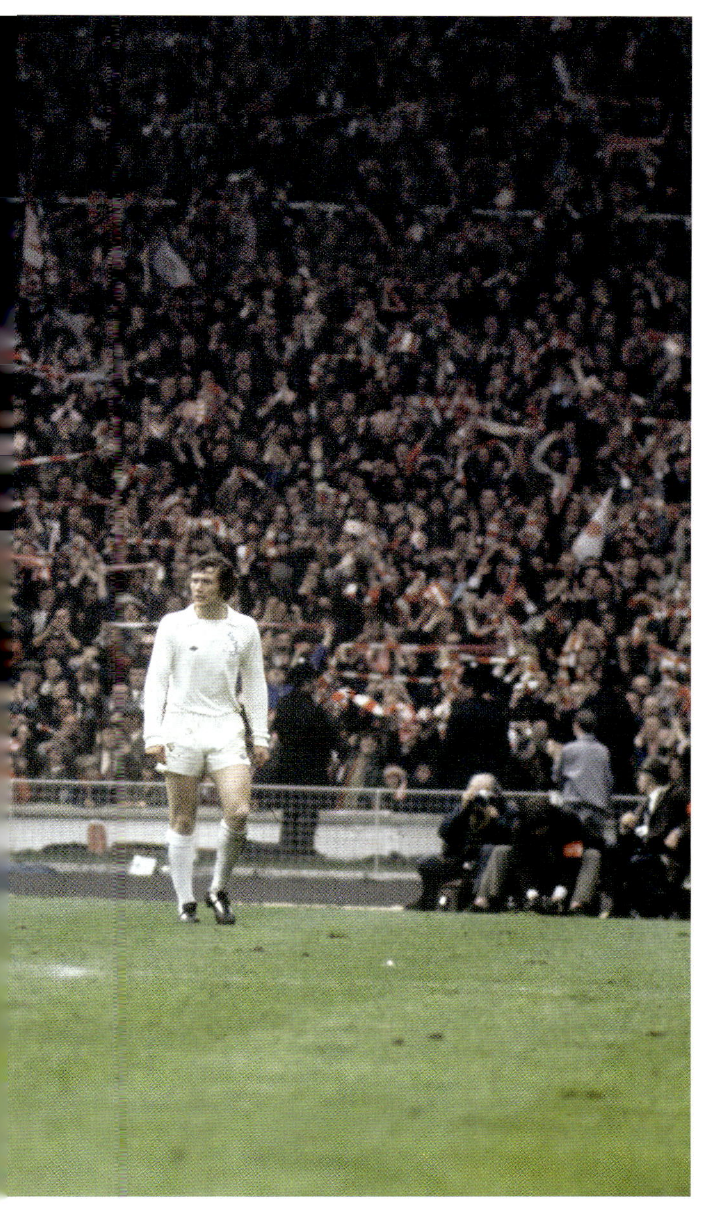

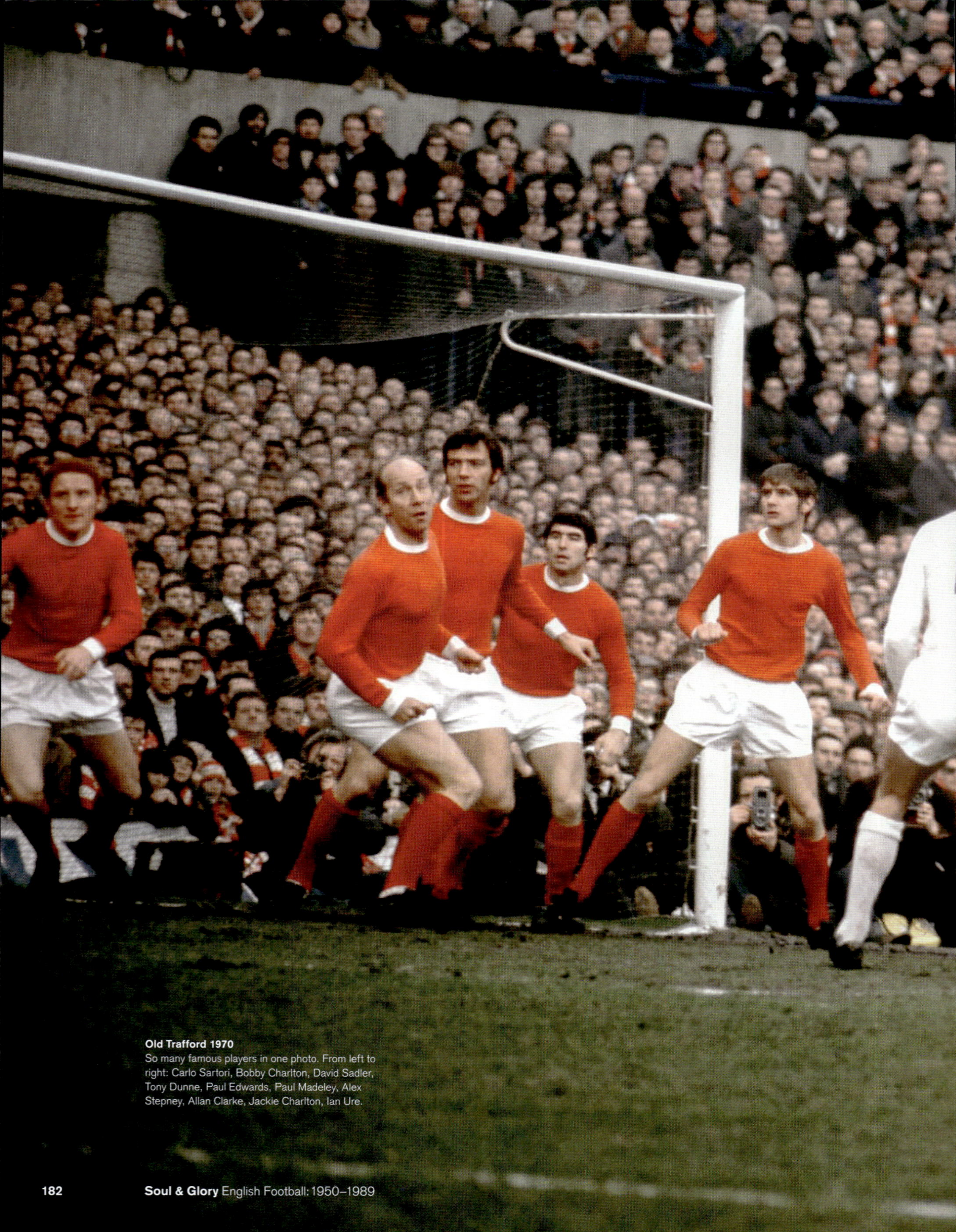

Old Trafford 1970

So many famous players in one photo. From left to right: Carlo Sartori, Bobby Charlton, David Sadler, Tony Dunne, Paul Edwards, Paul Madeley, Alex Stepney, Allan Clarke, Jackie Charlton, Ian Ure.

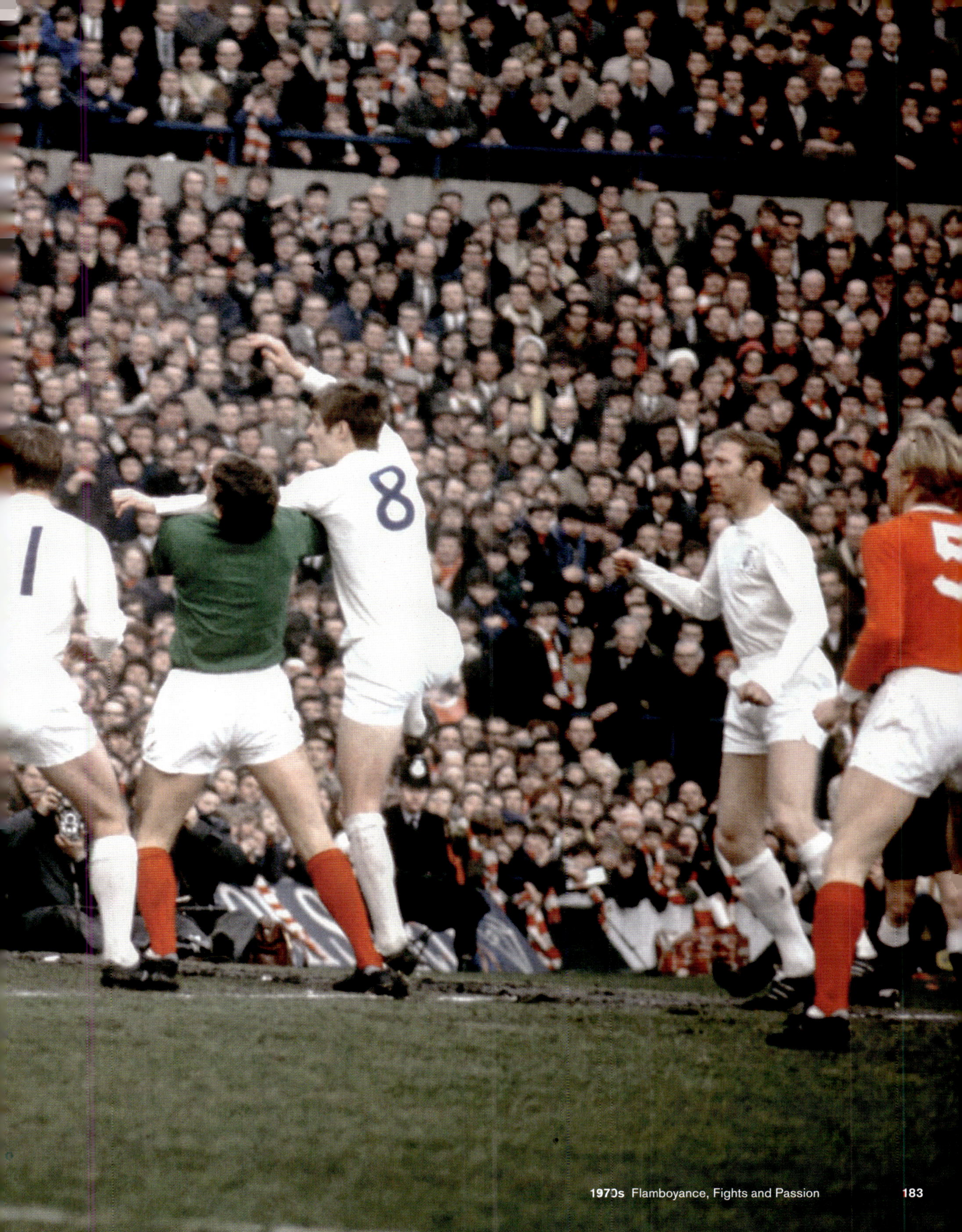

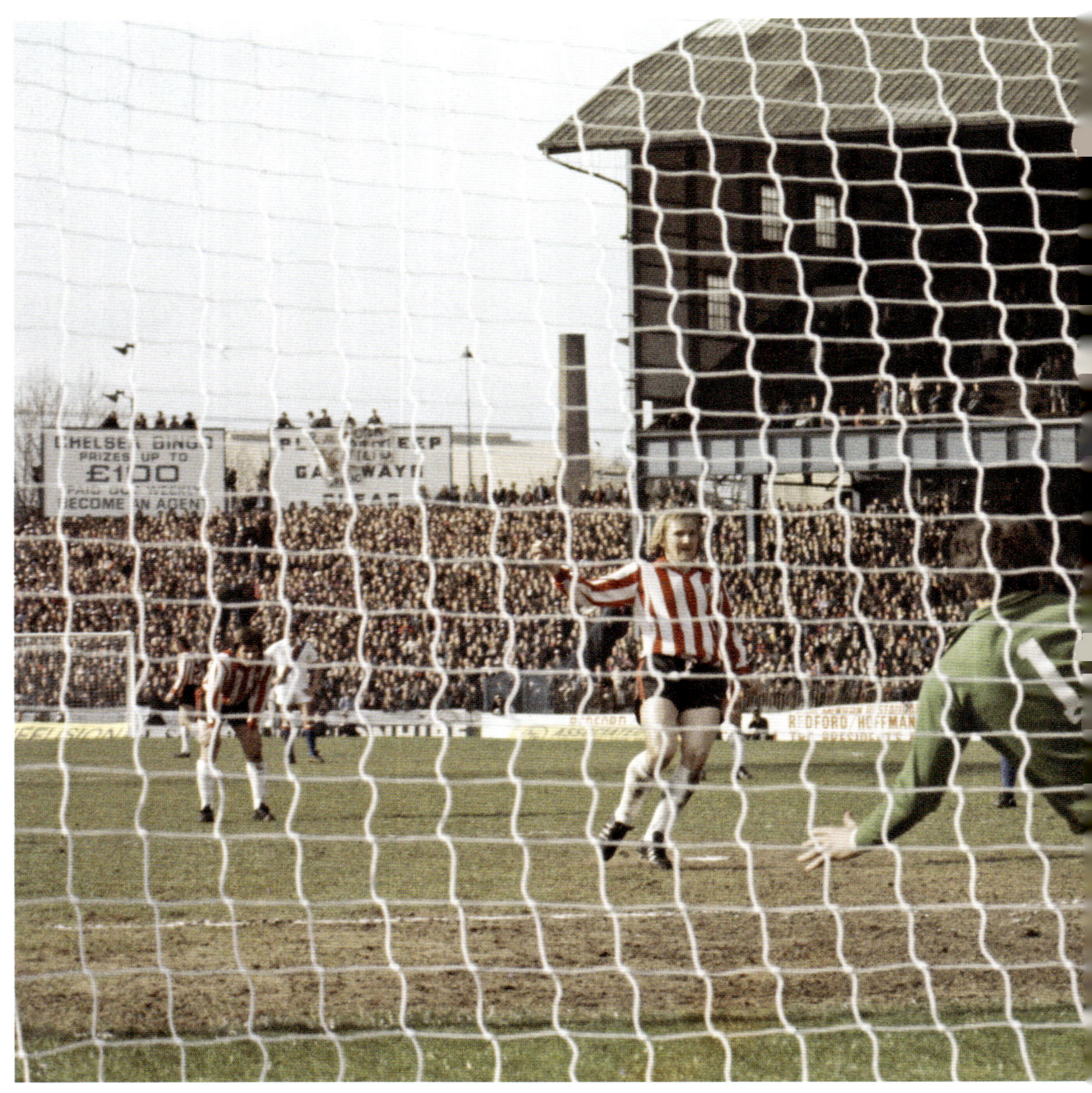

Stamford Bridge 1976
David Peach puts Southampton
2-0 up against Crystal Palace
in the FA Cup semi-final.

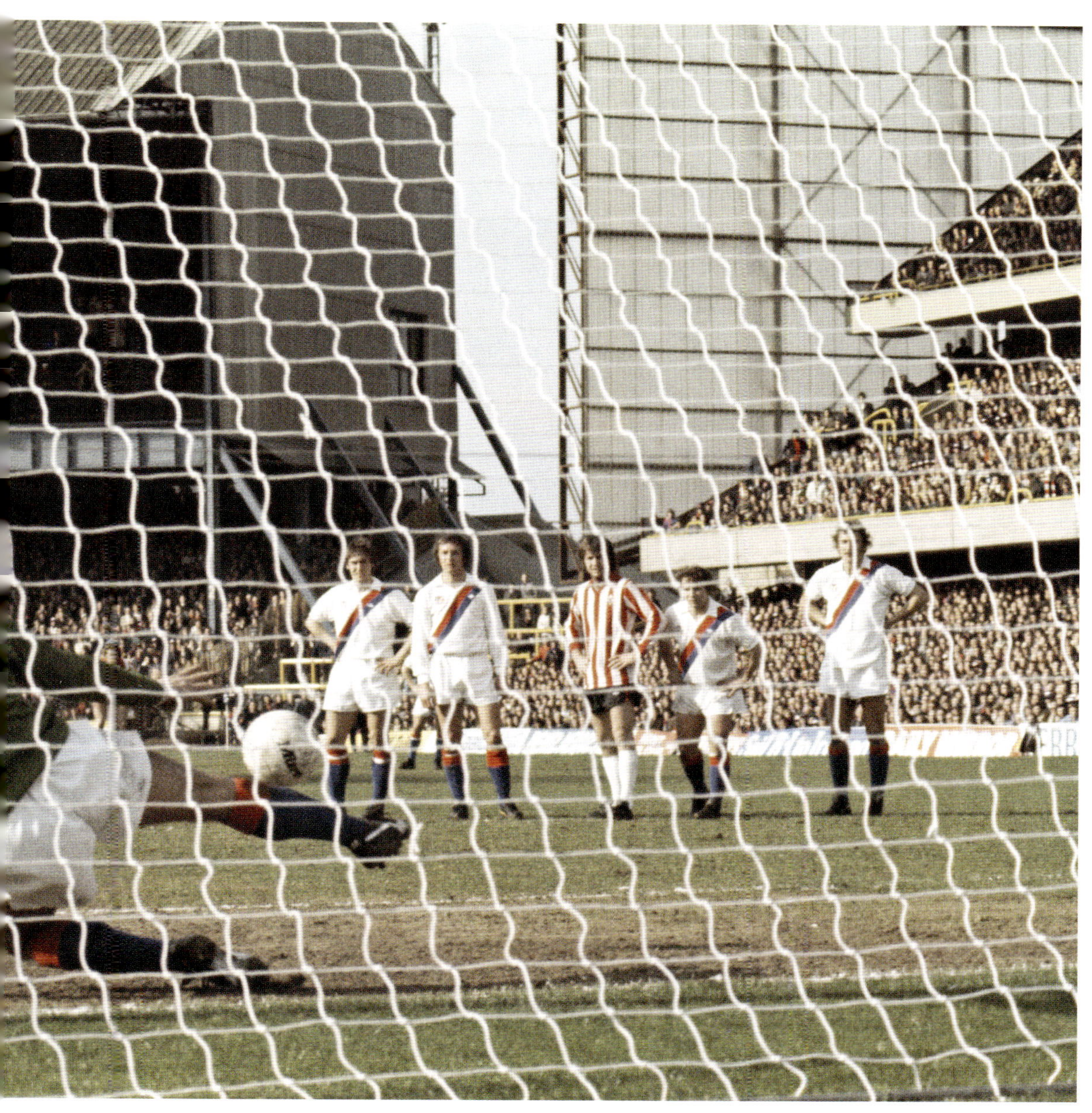

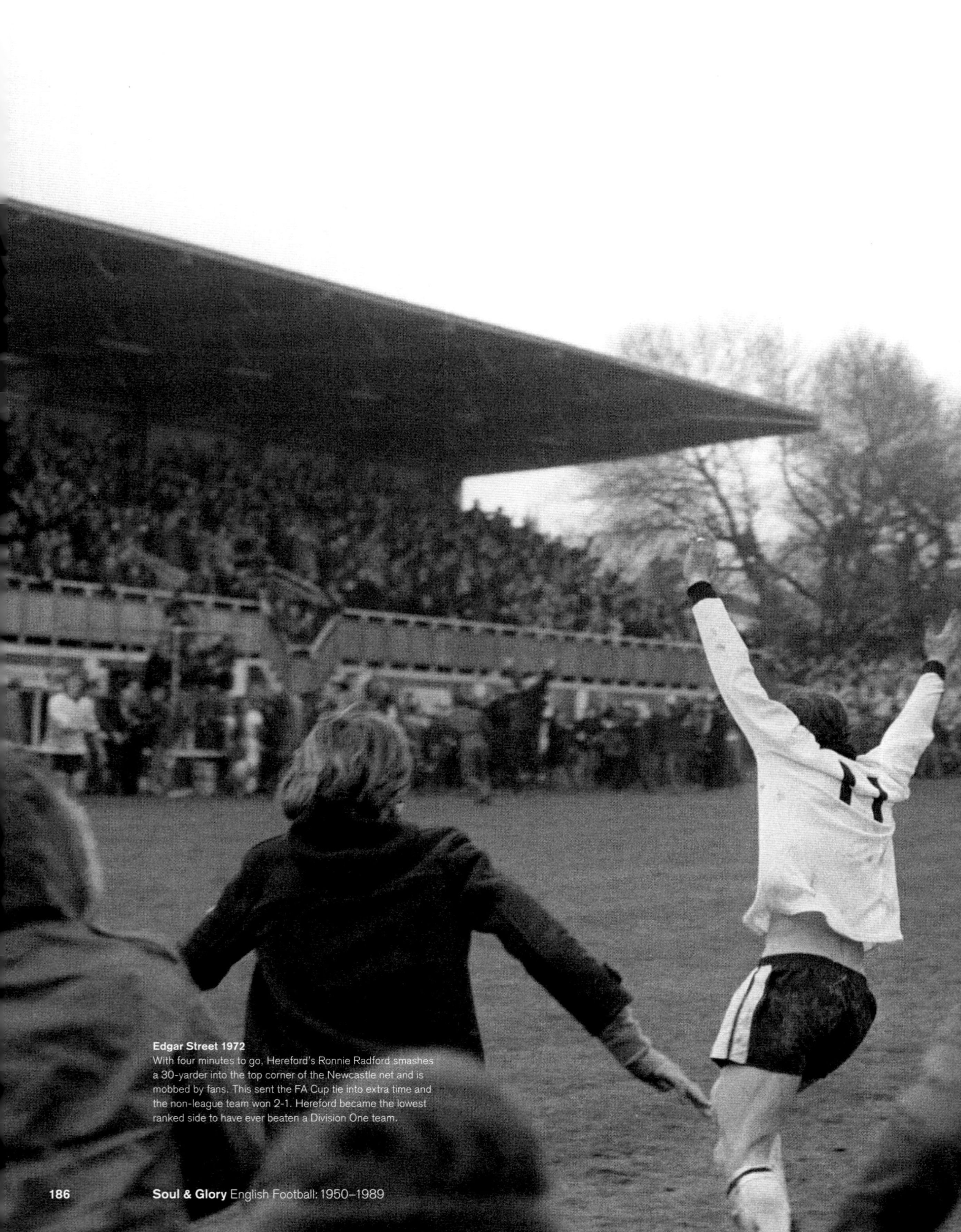

Edgar Street 1972
With four minutes to go, Hereford's Ronnie Radford smashes a 30-yarder into the top corner of the Newcastle net and is mobbed by fans. This sent the FA Cup tie into extra time and the non-league team won 2-1. Hereford became the lowest ranked side to have ever beaten a Division One team.

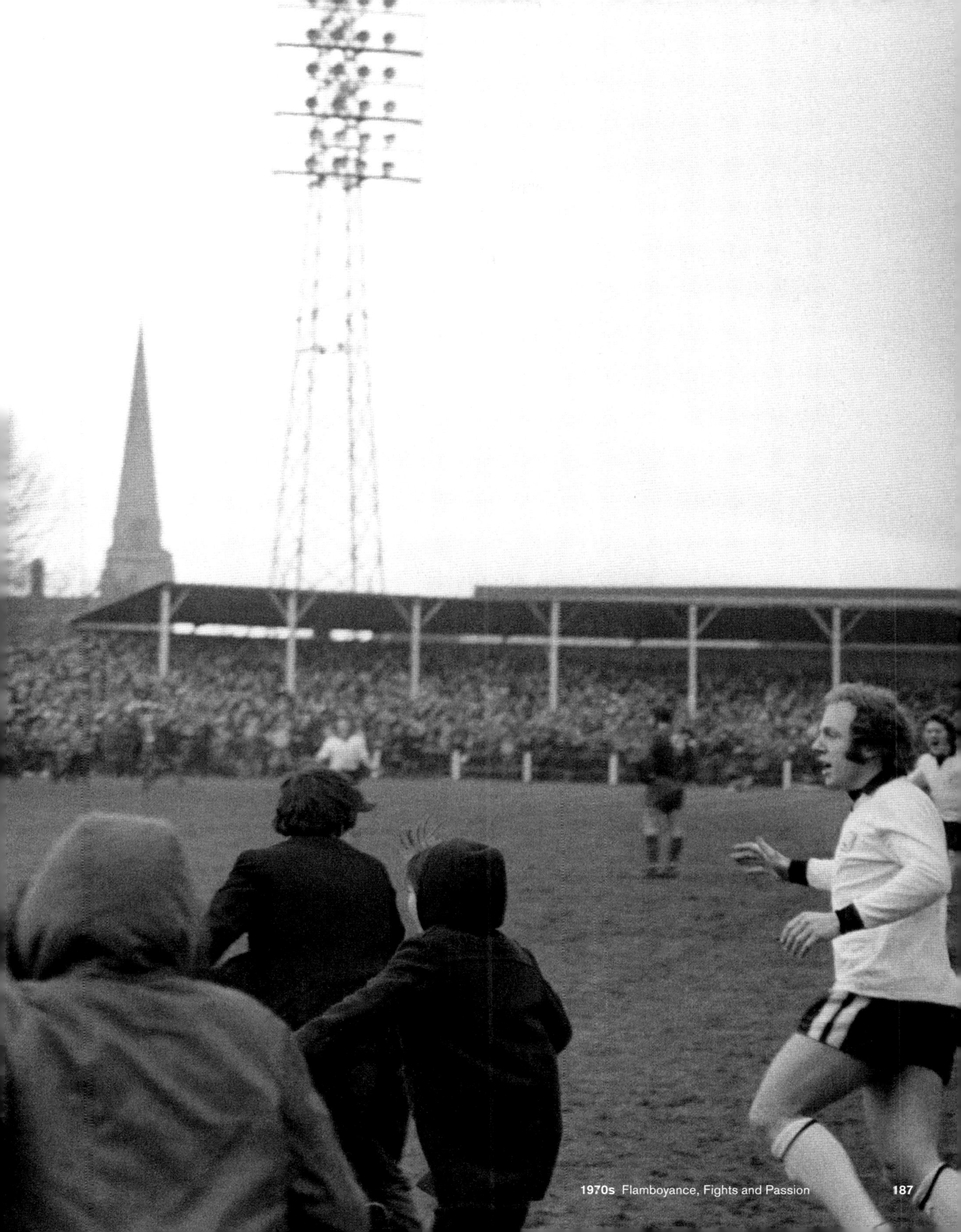

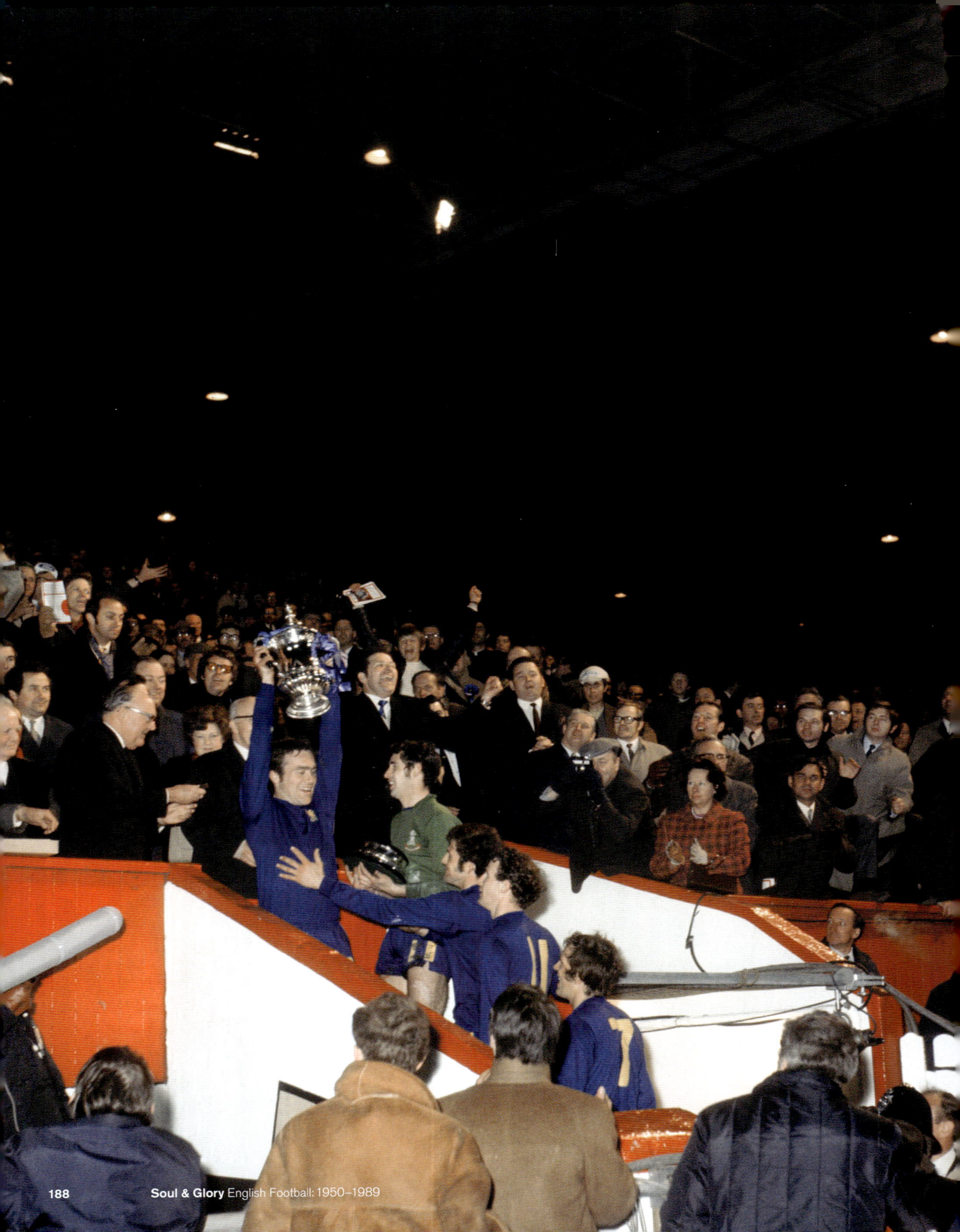

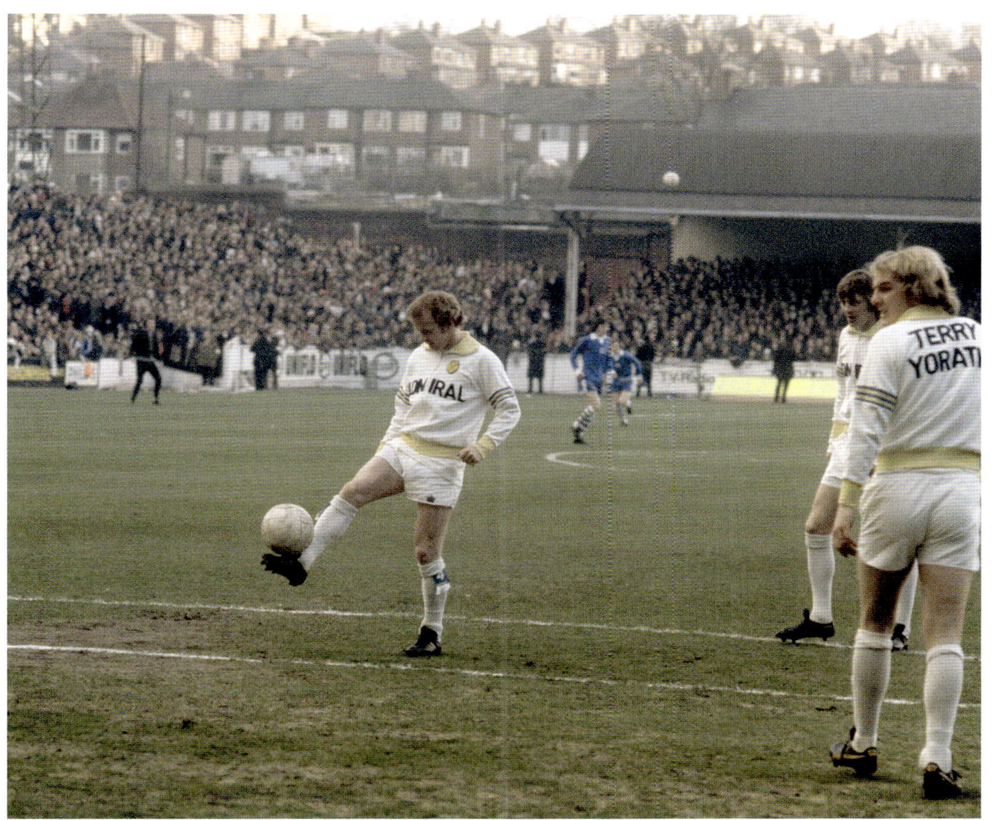

Old Trafford 1970

Chelsea captain Ron Harris lifts up the FA Cup
after the Blues beat Leeds United 2-1 in one
of the most physical games of football ever
played. Old Trafford was chosen as the venue
for the replay, due to the poor condition of the
Wembley turf.

Elland Road 1974

Leeds United players warm up before
a game against Newcastle United.
Their Admiral-branded kits were the
beginning of a 70s success story for
the manufacturer.

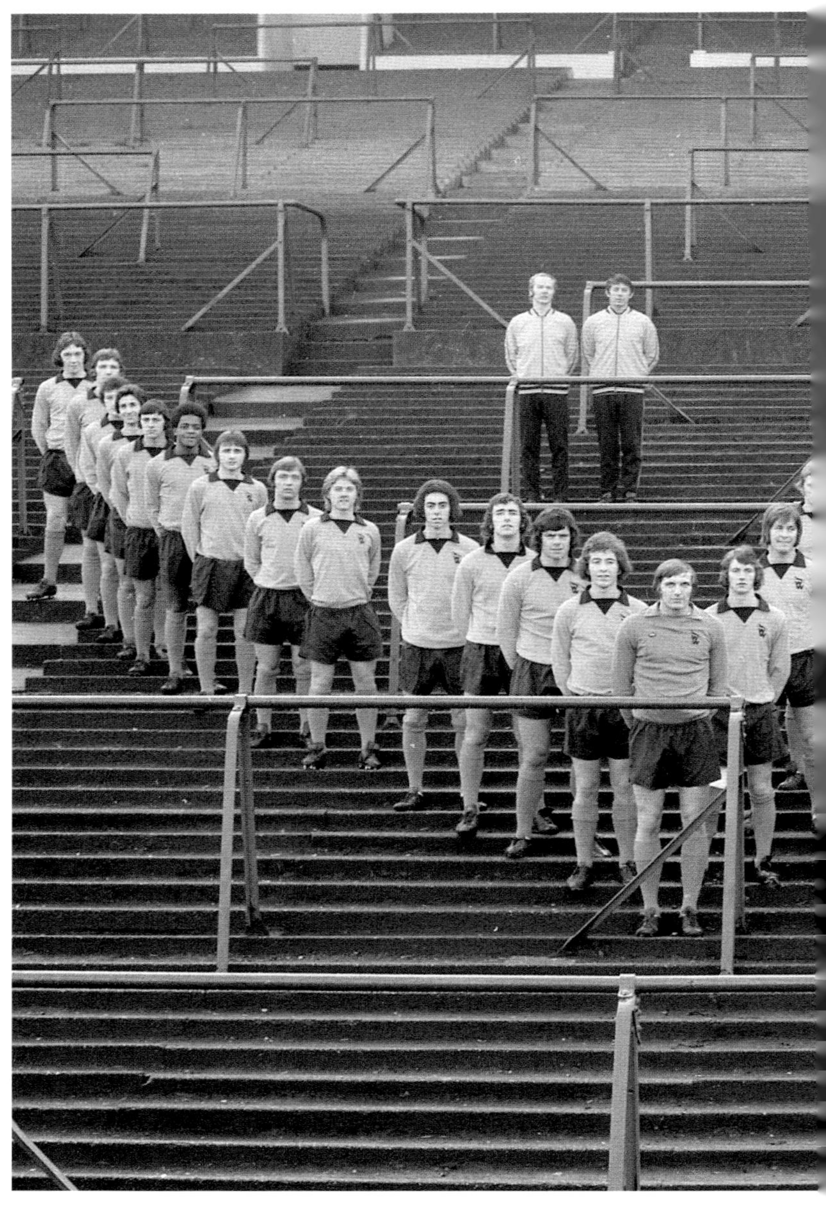

Molineux 1974
The Wolves squad form a W shape on
the South Bank terrace.

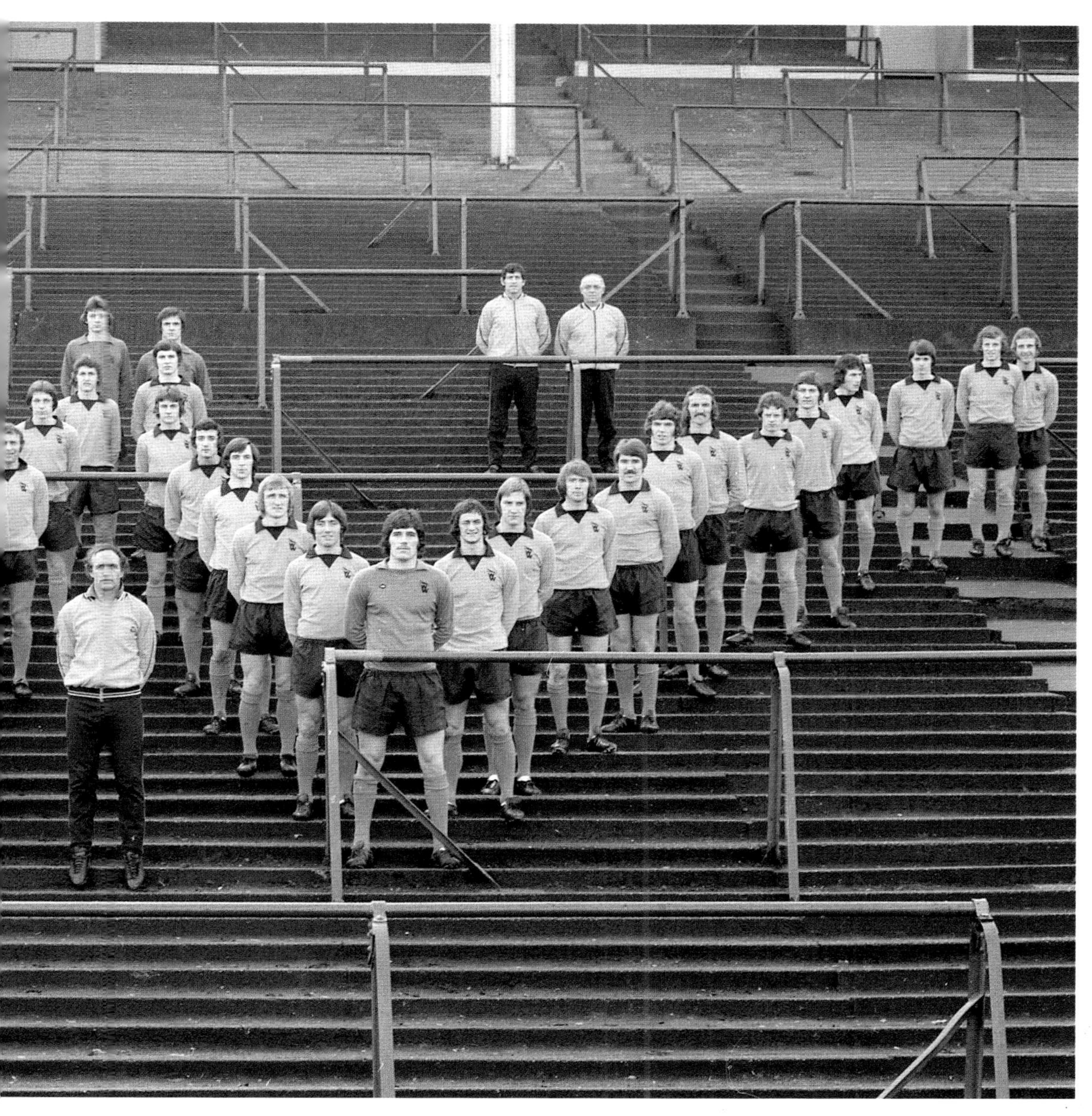

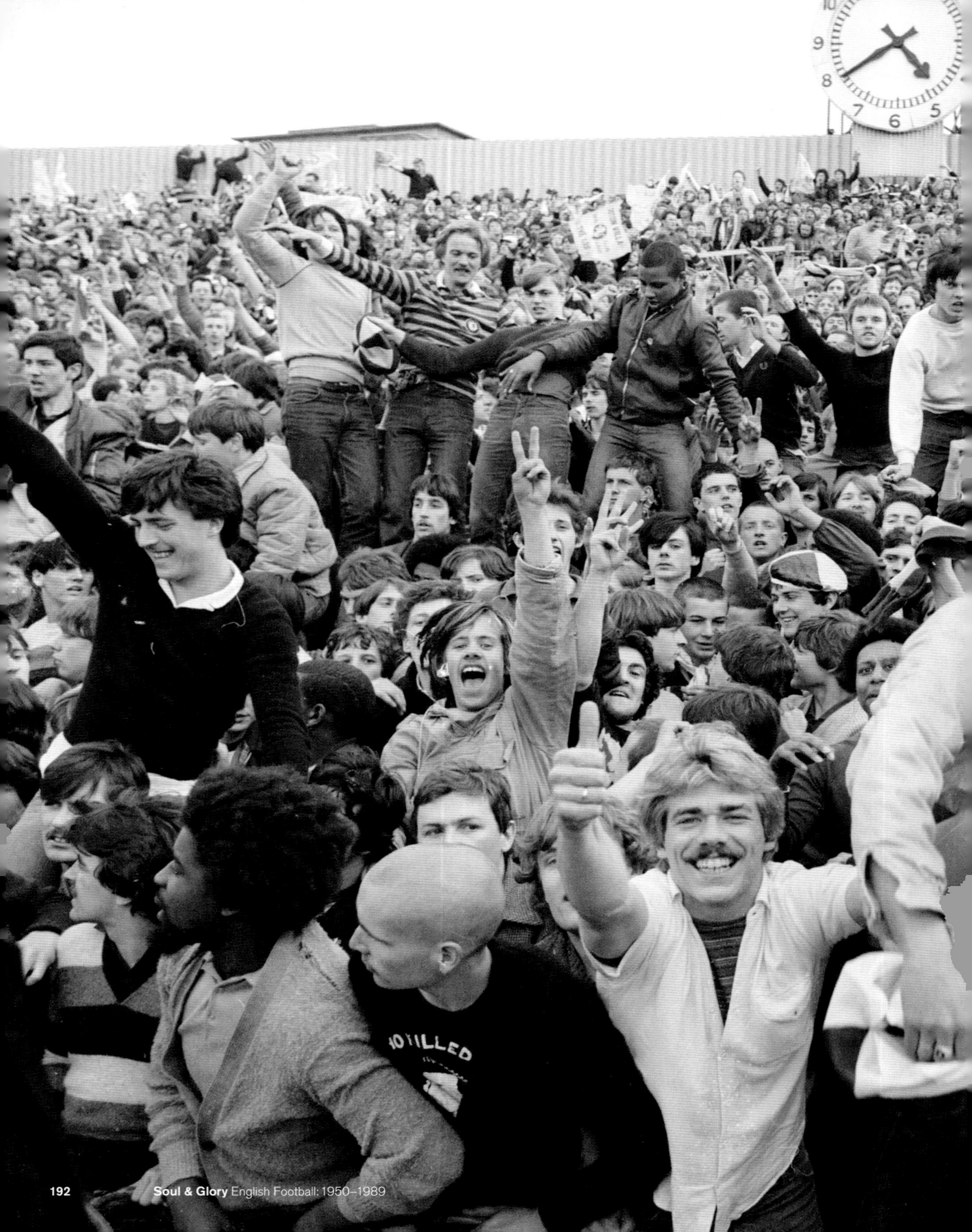

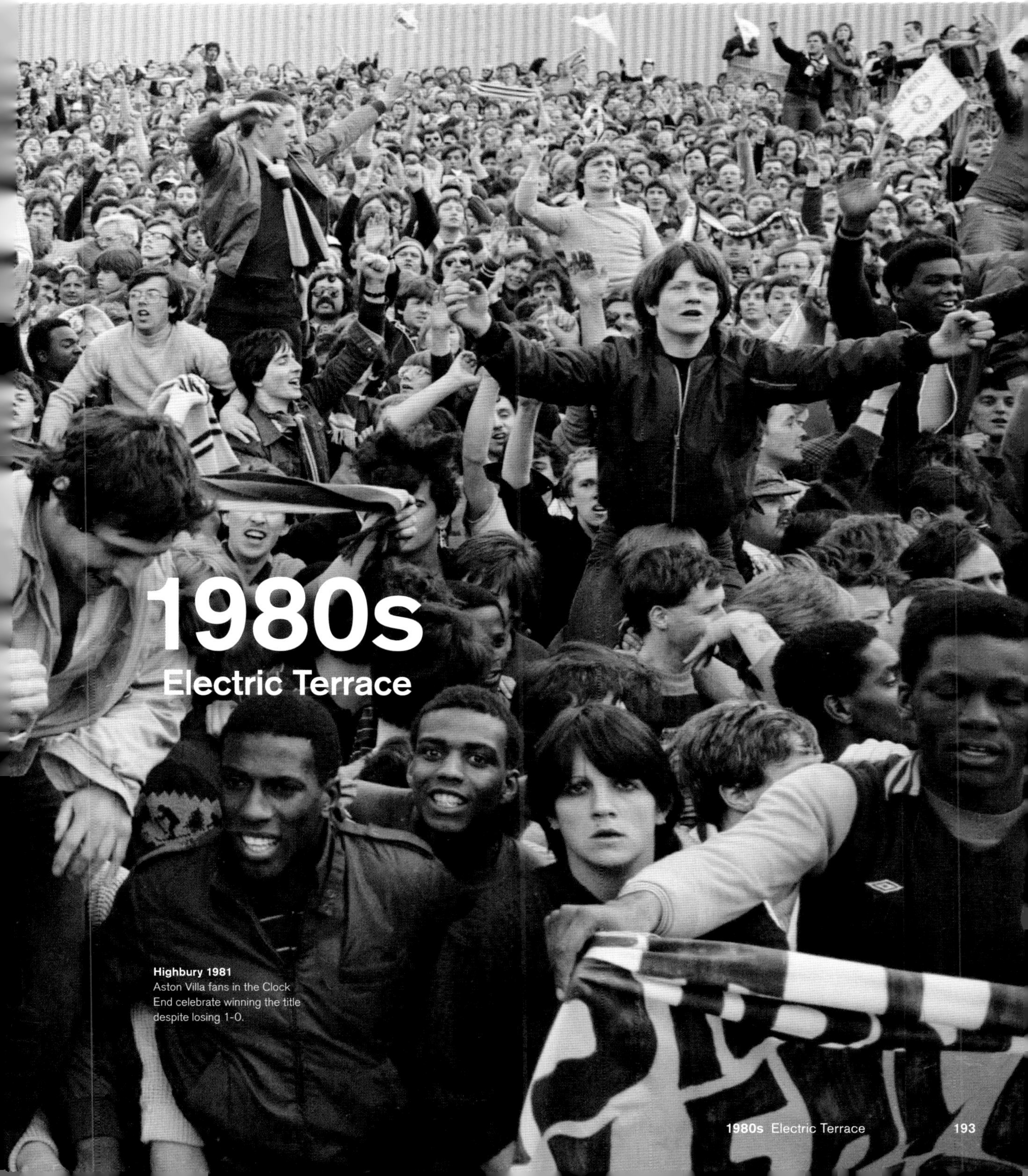

1980s
Electric Terrace

Highbury 1981
Aston Villa fans in the Clock
End celebrate winning the title
despite losing 1-0.

1980s: Electric Terrace

The 80s is when football began to look a bit more like it does today: more live games were on the TV. Sponsors on the team shirts was more widespread. The first executive boxes were installed. There were a lot more black players. More players from overseas. The game was becoming faster. Commercialism had crept in to the point where the very competitions were being named after brands. In 1983 the entire Football League got sponsored by Canon. A year earlier the League Cup became the Milk Cup, and has been named after by a brand ever since (milk as in milk, not a media company called milk, just good old milk in general). The 80s was a long way off the overt commercialisation of today, but it was certainly the precursor.

Bob Paisley, who won 13 major honours as Liverpool manager between 1976 and 1983

The influence of more widespread television coverage made a debate of things which today are not even an issue. In 1983 Jimmy Greaves had a heated argument with presenter Gary Newbon about television footage being used for retrospective punishment. Greaves argued, 'It's up to the people in charge of the game to report it. Not television cameras who are only there as guests of the club,' before comparing such practice to Big Brother in the book *1984*. Newbon corrected him that it was actually 1983, to which Greaves replied, 'There's only a few months to go.' In 1989, the last terrestrial TV deal was signed to show top-flight football. ITV paid £11m to the Football League to broadcast games until 1992, the year the Premier League formed and took away free-to-air top-division matches.

Electric terrace is not a reference to Chelsea chairman Ken Bates's shocking idea to electrify the steel fences to prevent pitch invasions, but rather because the energy from the terraces was at its most fevered during this decade. Goal celebrations were wild, electrifying and comparable to a mosh pit at a rock gig. This was a change from the previous decades. Fans were always passionate, and would always cheer a goal wildly with joy, but the sheer explosion and power of 1980s celebrations was on another level. This electrifying energy was very evident in the home ends, but more so in the away ends. It used to be quite an incredible sight when an away goal went in and the stadium was silenced – apart from one section where the celebration of away fans looked like a swarm of bees. As bad as segregation is in theory, it also allowed for that unique environment in football as a sport where a stadium is silenced apart from one end that is in utter delirium, which in itself is a wonderful piece of drama. Years later, as the seats came in, that ferocity did tone down significantly, for many reasons – one being that your knees would be smashed to pieces if you celebrated like that in a seated stand. One factor for such wild reactions to a goal is the energy from a youth culture that became ingrained in football from the late 60s, but also there were more goals per game in previous decades. As the years went on, defences got better, and when goals are fewer, the celebration becomes more.

Jimmy Hill

Along with pioneering TV coverage and abolition of the maximum wage, Jimmy Hill's biggest influence in English football was changing the law so that the reward for a win increased from two points to three. Nobody would argue against that change now, but one interesting theory against it is that when a win becomes so much more important, then so does 'win at all cost' and the prospect of more teams going a goal up and then 'parking the bus'. *The Guardian* looked into how many league title races were influenced by the ruling and surprisingly it's just the two seasons. In 1994/95 Manchester United would have won the championship on goal difference instead of Blackburn, had it still been two points for a win – and Liverpool would have finished ahead of Manchester City in 2018/19. A few years before three points for a win came in, third-placed Ipswich would have won Division One instead of Derby County in the 1974/75 season had the change been implemented earlier.

Muddy pitches have been a theme throughout this collection of photos, and some clubs in the 1980s tried to solve this problem by ripping out the grass and installing an artificial turf. QPR and Luton were most famous, or you could say 'notorious', for this as they were in the top flight, and they were joined by Oldham Athletic and Preston North End. Fans hated them; the surfaces were an American import, and used in competitions like NFL where the bounce of the ball is not a key factor in the game. On plastic pitches, the movement of the ball was harder to gauge, and players couldn't always maintain a solid footing, leading to safety concerns. Today, artificial surfaces have more depth and are softer, but in the 80s they were raw and one sliding tackle could result in a 'rug burn' that, unlike mud, wouldn't wash off in the shower. Familiarity with these surfaces favoured the home team, which was why Luton was never anyone's favourite away game, not least because you were not allowed to be an away fan at Luton. In 1986 their chairman David Evans, a Tory MP, banned away supporters off the back of the notorious Millwall riot of 85. To get into Kenilworth Road you needed an ID pass, an idea the Thatcher Government at the time thought was a great scheme and tried to introduce universally. The Football League insisted that away fans should be allowed in for League Cup games, and threw Town out of the 1986/87 competition for not complying. Luton lifted the away fan bar in the early 90s, and artificial pitches were banned by the FA in 1988.

In 1989, where this book's collection ends, two dominant forces of today's era – Manchester City and Chelsea – were competing against one another right at the very top of Division Two. They would both get promoted in the 1988/89 season, but Chelsea's relegation a year earlier was in unique circumstances. They finished fourth from bottom of Division One, yet still went down. In 1986/87 the Football League had introduced the play-offs where the third- to fifth-placed teams in Division Two had a chance to get promoted. The fourth team involved had finished fourth from bottom in Division One, and in 1986/87 that was Charlton Athletic, who managed to stay up by beating Leeds in the final. The following year Chelsea lost to Middlesbrough, meaning that four went down and three went up, which reduced Division One from 21 teams to 20. A top-tier team competing in the play-offs would never happen again.

Admiral became a victim of their own success in the company's pioneering advances in replica kit sales. They showed that there was money to be made in this business, and other companies took keen notice. As the 80s rolled on, Admiral got overtaken by bigger manufacturers

'I was against advertising and sponsorship more than anyone. I felt we would be losing a little bit of our identity but I have been persuaded the other way.'

Arsenal chairman Peter Hill Wood as Arsenal agree to a JVC shirt sponsorship worth £500,000

'Domestically this is still the glamour showpiece of the year and it's one thing that people always look forward to regardless of who's playing.'

Bobby Moore, talking to Jimmy Tarbuck in a bar during the TV build up to the 1988 FA Cup Final

including Hummel, Adidas, Le Coq Sportif, and the most visible of all – Umbro. On the kits were now sponsors, a trend that first started in the late 70s and became normalised in the 80s. Rather than being a British trend, it was something that had been more common in Europe and was causing disputes between the TV broadcasters and the clubs in England. The BBC was a non-commercial broadcaster and so issues arose as to the ethics and legality of this new culture. Liverpool had a two-year deal with Hitachi between 1979 and 1981 in which the contract stated they would not wear sponsored shirts for televised games. In contrast, when you look at TV coverage today, every single inhibition about advertising has gone straight out the window.

Spurs had similar success in the 80s as they did the 60s, albeit with no league title. They won a European trophy, were strong contenders in the league, and celebrated glory in the FA Cup. In the 60s they won the cup in 61, 62, and 67, and had a chance to repeat that success after winning the cup in 81, 82 and getting to the 87 final. Their opponents, Coventry City, had never been in a major cup final, even though they had been in the top tier since the 60s. In a decade of classic finals Coventry caused an upset, winning 3-2 courtesy of a famous diving header from Keith Houchen. A year later Wimbledon caused a bigger upset against Liverpool, making for a trilogy of underdog winners as West Ham from Division Two had beaten Arsenal 1-0 in 1980, their last trophy to date – and the last time a club outside the top tier has won the FA Cup. Another underdog should have been on that list of 80s cup upsets: in 1983 Brighton had been relegated from Division One, yet had the chance for FA Cup glory against Ron Atkinson's Manchester United. The score was 2-2 with 120 minutes on the clock. Brighton striker Gordon Smith had scored the game's opening goal but he would not be remembered for that. In the dying seconds, Smith was put through, one on one with the goalkeeper, in what represents the most classic 'sliding doors' scenario in football. If Smith puts the ball past United's Gary Bailey, he forever becomes known as the scorer of the winning goal in a cup final giant-killing. The Brighton bench at Wembley go crazy with joy as Smith runs towards the fans in glory. Brighton win a major trophy for the first time in their history. Instead, Smith struck a weak effort into the goalkeeper who collected the ball with relief. The Brighton bench looked utterly devastated and sat back down in disbelief and Smith got forever associated with the biggest miss in FA Cup Final history. The favourites won the cup. Sliding doors, in just one moment the whole future of Smith's legacy is cemented as the quintessential 'what if'. What if Manchester United had not appointed Alex Ferguson in 1986 after Atkinson departed? He was supposed to go to Arsenal, but they didn't like the idea of him taking Scotland to the 1986 World Cup in Mexico, so rejected him. Fergie's Manchester United and the 80s was a story of frustration and failure, producing no trophies and not even an appearance in a major final. In this age, Fergie would have been sacked long before he won the first of his 25 major trophies at Old Trafford.

The league title over the years became the most prestigious domestic honour, but the FA Cup had not been diminished, and its glamour was very much intact. No manager would think about resting players for a League Cup tie, let alone the FA Cup. Whereas now, TV coverage for the FA Cup Final starts an hour before kick-off, the 80s was known for its lavish build-up from the morning. The aura of occasion was huge, almost feeling like a royal wedding, with both the BBC and ITV airing the game. To take the 1988 final as an example, the ITV coverage featured the legendary duo of Saint and Greavsie. Ian St John wore the red rosette of Liverpool, his former team, and Jimmy Greaves the blue rosette of Wimbledon, and the features included Greavsie travelling to America to interview heavyweight boxing champion Mike Tyson, followed by an overview of the Final courtesy of 'Loadsamoney', the comedy creation of Harry Enfield. There was also an interview with Frank Bruno and a celebrity football match on the Wembley turf featuring some of the biggest names in

'I've got a funny feeling about Wimbledon, Jim.'

Terry Neill, also with Moore and Tarbuck in the same bar

UK sport and entertainment. Most of the crowd were already in the stadium as the likes of Nigel Benn, Rod Stewart, Eddy Grant and Daley Thompson played what essentially was a warm-up to the main event. Cup final coverage would typically have a reporter on each team bus as they made their way from the hotel to the stadium. The players always seemed to be happy and relaxed in the presence of the reporter, but that feature petered out as players got richer, more protected and emotionally distant.

The parity of competition of the 1980s was a paradox. Liverpool dominated, but predicting the other places was more of a lottery as Southampton, Watford and Ipswich all finished runners-up during the decade (twice in the case of Ipswich along with winning a UEFA Cup). The branded 'Big Five' were Liverpool, Everton, Manchester United, Arsenal and Spurs, but they didn't all finish in the top five every year, they were just considered the biggest names in the country. Liverpool's dominance was a wholesale change in English football history. Huddersfield Town had won three league titles between 1923 and 1926. Arsenal repeated that feat from 1932–35; the common link between these two great dynasties being the manager Herbert Chapman. Such dominance was unrepeated until Liverpool won three titles in a row between 1981 and 1984, and a total of six in the decade. That paradox of parity was well summed up by the winners of the League Cup. Liverpool won four in a row from 1981–84. That was then followed by total outsiders winning the trophy as Norwich City, Oxford United and Luton Town all won silverware at Wembley. The 85 final between Norwich and Sunderland was particularly telling, as both finalists got relegated from Division One that season, a scenario that has not happened since in any final. One outsider might get to the final, as Sunderland did in 2014, but their opponents that day were the billionaires of Manchester City and the Black Cats lost 3-1.

The 1980s would end how the 1950s began, with no European football; for English clubs anyway. The hooligan problem dating back from the late 60s reached its most horrific moment yet, as 39 fans of Juventus died after a wall at the end of the terrace collapsed, after they had been chased by Liverpool fans prior to the 1985 European Cup Final at the Heysel Stadium in Belgium. All English clubs felt the wrath, as the punishment was a five-year European suspension with immediate effect. English clubs had comprehensively dominated European competition and now they were not even allowed to compete for the rest of the decade. Bobby Charlton was asked his opinion on the ban and put up no defence for English football. No one did; 39 people were now dead. The general feeling was that this was a problem of our making and we'll just take the punishment and get our

'I still wonder what Everton did do to get kicked out of Europe for five years? We were champions, we'd just won the Cup Winners' Cup, and we had conducted ourselves in the right way so what was that ban going to teach us?'

Neville Southall, Everton and Wales goalkeeper

house in order. Everton and Arsenal were big losers in this as neither team got to play in the European Cup after winning the league. Nor did Liverpool, but they had already won the trophy four times though a huge question loomed on how their legendary 1987/88 side would have fared against the great AC Milan team of that era. Luton Town, Oxford United, Wimbledon and Coventry City wouldn't get the chance to play in Europe, and unlike the bigger clubs this was a chance that hasn't come their way since. The 80s had started with Nottingham Forest and Aston Villa reaching the pinnacle and becoming champions of Europe, then halfway through the decade every club in the country was banned from even playing.

'The Liverpool players are down abject. Aldridge is down. Barnes is down, Dalglish just stands there. Nicol's on his knees, McMahon's on his knees.'

ITV commentator Brian Moore – Liverpool v Arsenal 1989

Everton were well placed to have been a force in the European Cups of 1985/86 and 1987/88 and to this day they still harbour resentment that they were denied this chance. If ever a decade was bittersweet for a club, it was Everton in the 1980s. They were brilliant and very successful, yet at the same time totally overshadowed by their neighbours. They won trophies, yet will look back on the 80s and believe they should have won more. In 1985 they had the chance to achieve the double, and be only the fifth team ever to do so, but the Toffees were beaten 1-0 by Manchester United with a goal from Norman Whiteside. To twist the knife further, Everton were chasing the double the following year, in the first season since the 50s where not one English club would compete in Europe. Instead of an Everton double, Liverpool won the league and FA Cup; the open wound for Everton being they were the beaten team in that FA Cup Final, losing 3-1 after Gary Lineker had given them a first-half lead. To date, the all-Merseyside FA Cup and League Cup finals of the 1980s have been the only such finals to feature any of English football's most famous local rivalries.

The second all-Merseyside FA Cup Final was repeated in 1989 under the saddest of circumstances. Liverpool's route to Wembley had come off the backdrop of the Hillsborough disaster, the most wretched moment in domestic football history along with the Bradford fire of 1985. The two sets of fans didn't need segregation at Wembley, as the blue and red halves of the city stood in unity in what was the last cup final in England where supporters watched from the terraces. Gerry Marsden sang 'You'll Never Walk Alone' on the Wembley pitch before the game in the most classic example of cup final pageantry and sense of occasion. Shortly after Hillsborough, the two clubs had played a league game at Goodison Park in a moving and emotional night where Liverpool fans watched from all ends of the stadium in a throwback to when there was no segregation. How things had changed over the years. At the start of this book rival fans mixed in the same terraces but by the end, steel fences were put in place, culminating with 96 fans being crushed to death when the terrace they were standing on became dangerously overcrowded.

Everton fans were still desperate to win the 1989 final, and their reaction to their last-minute equalising goal was electric as hundreds invaded the pitch in wild scenes that have not been seen at Wembley since. If any example could be used to sum up 80s goal celebrations it would be that one, but it didn't stop Liverpool winning 3-2 in one of the classic finals. This was supposed to be part one of Liverpool's second double, as the seventh league title of the decade looked in the bag. Liverpool's merciless rule of Division One was to make their dethroning in the final year of the decade even more cruel, dramatic and remarkable. 'Nobody gave them a chance' is a cliché, but nobody did give Arsenal a chance to win by two clear goals at Anfield which was their task in the final game of the season. In February 1989, Arsenal had been clear at the top with Liverpool down in eighth, 19 points adrift, albeit with four games in hand. With ten games to go, Norwich were, in the eyes of many, the title favourites and some even suggested a double, as the Canaries had made it to the semi-final. Millwall were also in the title race but by the final game of the season it came down to two of the most dominant clubs in English football history in the most famous league match ever played. Arsenal boss George Graham's game plan was to keep it to 0-0 at half-time, then get an early goal in the second half. The aim was then to get a late goal and win the championship, and that's exactly what happened, although the goal came far later than what Graham had in mind. Michael Thomas charged through the midfield, made it 2-0 in the dying moments, and Arsenal equalled Everton's tally of nine league championships in a fashion that is unlikely to be repeated. Manchester City's amazing Premier League win in 2012 was said to have eclipsed Anfield 89, but some pointed out the difference in opposition as City won at home against a QPR team that just avoided relegation. Anfield 89 was the top two teams battling it out, with the loser being the colossal force of football for the past 13 years, who hadn't lost at home by two clear goals for three years.

For all the bad incidents associated with 80s football, it was also a time when people decided to change things for the better. Racism never went away, but in the second half of the decade people decided to tackle it. Hooliganism was on the decline. As a youngster going to games across London in the late 80s with my dad, I never felt threatened, rarely saw trouble, never heard monkey chants; football did feel like a family game despite popular opinion that it wasn't. Every club still had a mob, but fights between rival firms were more likely to happen at train stations and pubs rather than in the stadium which was a shift in events from the 70s and early 80s. The era, for the most part, did have a good side to it, and there were nice gestures that you don't see anymore. One small example was banter between home fans and the away goalkeepers, most notably the likes of Bruce Grobbelaar, Tim Flowers and Les Sealey. At Arsenal I recall the home fans behind the goal would always applaud the opposition goalkeeper as he took his place between the sticks before kick-off. The one exception to this being the Tottenham keepers, and I recall a time when Bobby Mimms jogged towards the North Bank goal with a look of terror in his eyes, his body shaking, such was the velocity of abuse thrown in his direction. In many ways this shows the paradoxical nature of old football culture; there was so much good about it, but it also came with a dangerous edge.

1980s Domestic Honours

Division One Champions
1980: Liverpool (overall wins 12)
1981: Aston Villa (overall wins 7)
1982: Liverpool (overall wins 13)
1983: Liverpool (overall wins 14)
1984: Liverpool (overall wins 15)
1985: Everton (overall wins 8)
1986: Liverpool (overall wins 16)
1987: Everton (overall wins 9)
1988: Liverpool (overall wins 17)
1989: Arsenal (overall wins 9)

League Cup Winners
1980: Wolverhampton Wanderers (overall wins 2)
1981: Liverpool (overall wins 1)
1982: Liverpool (overall wins 2)
1983: Liverpool (overall wins 3)
1984: Liverpool (overall wins 4)
1985: Norwich City (overall wins 2)
1986: Oxford United (overall wins 1)
1987: Arsenal (overall wins 1)
1988: Luton Town (overall wins 1)
1989: Nottingham Forest (overall wins 3)

FA Cup Winners
1980: West Ham United (overall wins 3)
1981: Tottenham Hotspur (overall wins 6)
1982: Tottenham Hotspur (overall wins 7)
1983: Manchester United (overall wins 5)
1984: Everton (overall wins 4)
1985: Manchester United (overall wins 6)
1986: Liverpool (overall wins 3)
1987: Coventry City (overall wins 1)
1988: Wimbledon (overall wins 1)
1989: Liverpool (overall wins 4)

Major European Honours for English Clubs
1980: Nottingham Forest, European Cup
1981: Liverpool, European Cup
1981: Ipswich Town, UEFA Cup
1982: Aston Villa, European Cup
1984: Liverpool, European Cup
1984: Tottenham Hotspur, UEFA Cup
1985: Everton, Cup Winners' Cup

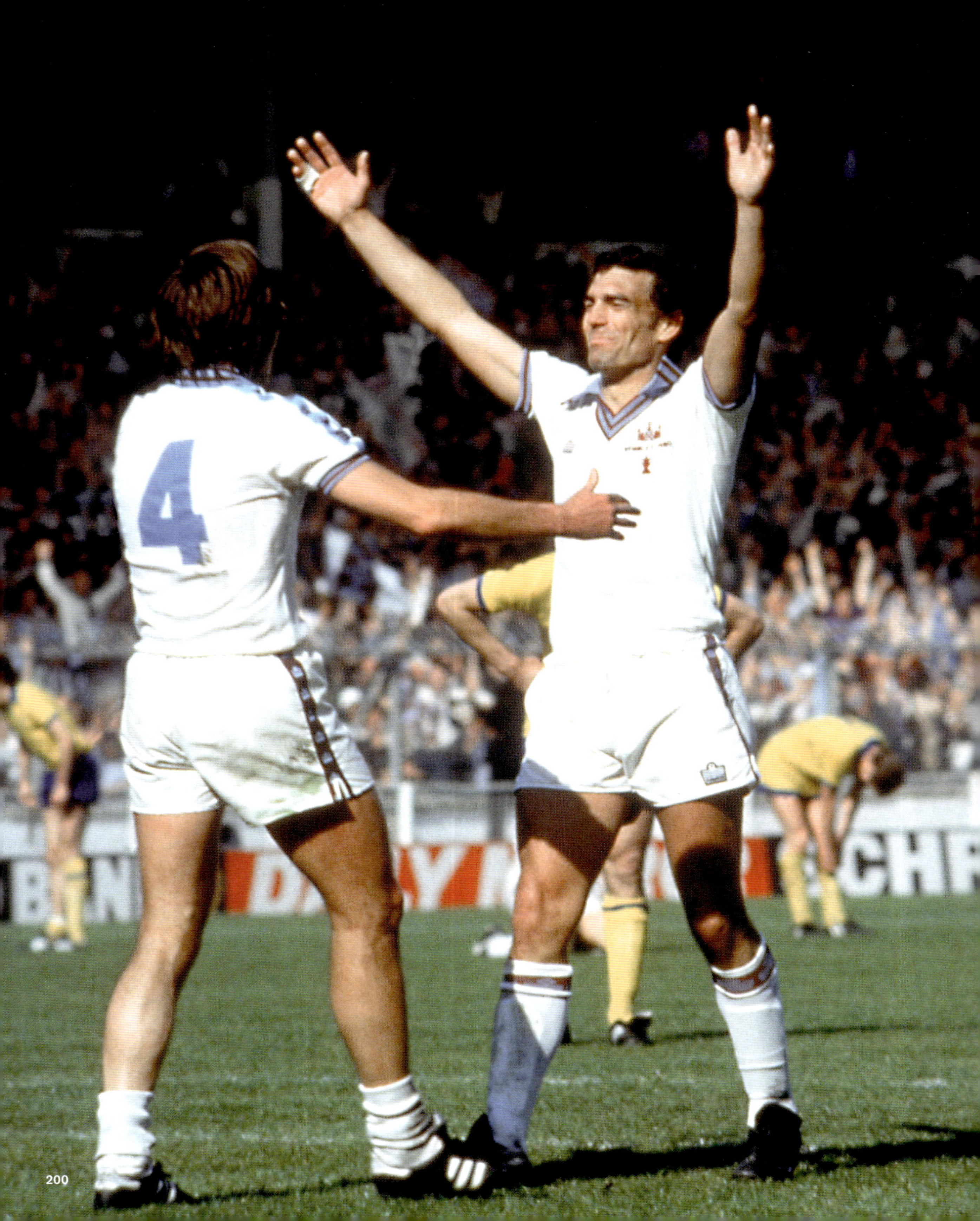

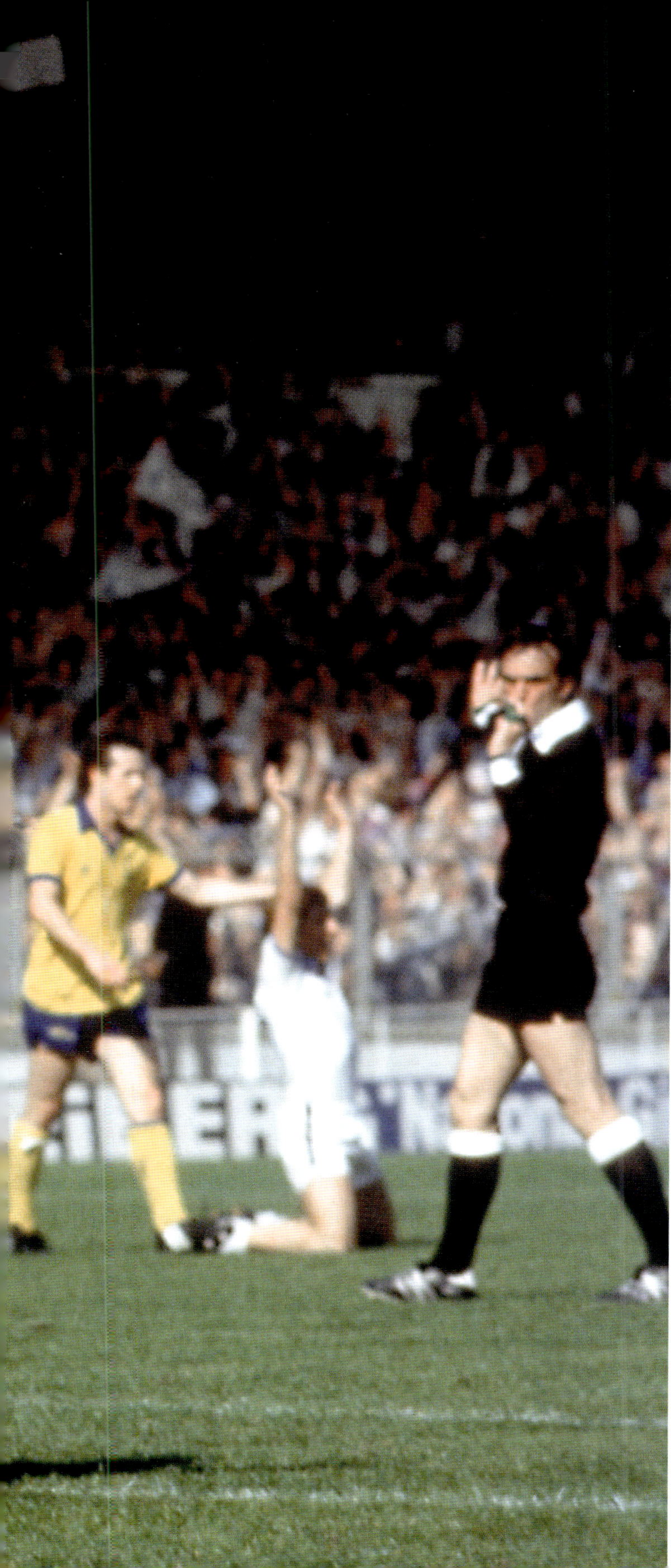

Wembley 1980
The final whistle goes in the FA Cup
Final as West Ham beat Arsenal 1-0 in
a big upset. The lone goalscorer, Trevor
Brooking, celebrates the crowning
moment of his career.

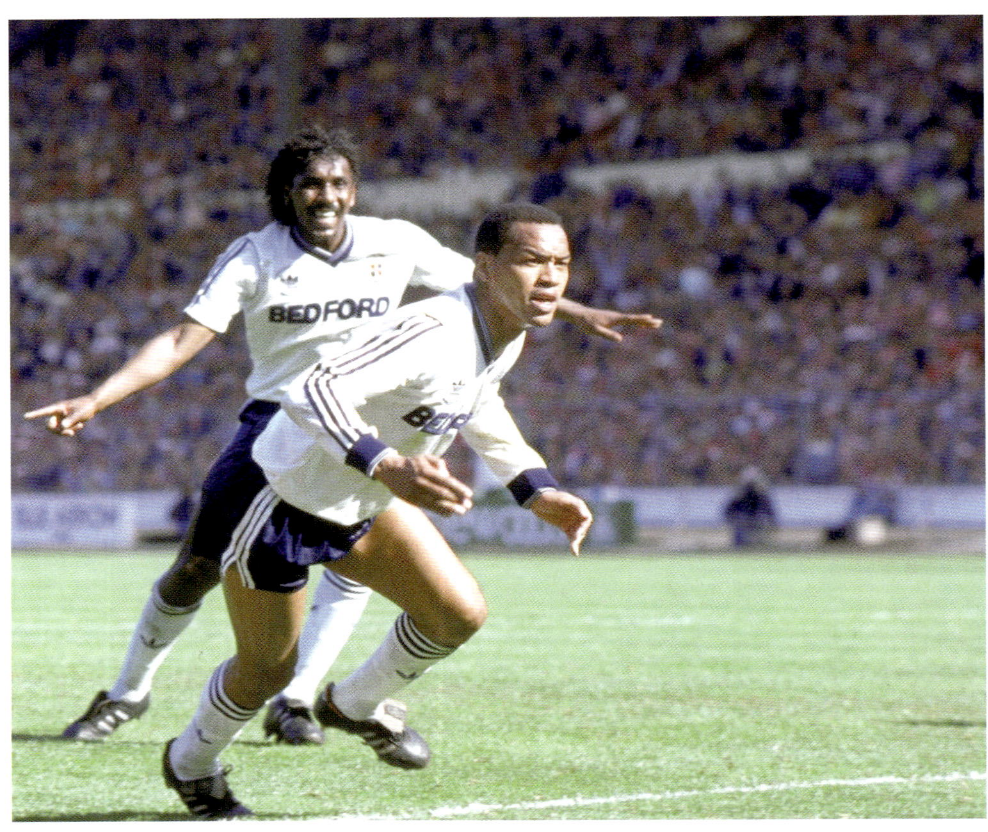

Wembley 1988
Luton Town win the League Cup
Final, as Brian Stein scores in the final
minute against Arsenal to make it 3-2.
Behind him is Ricky Hill.

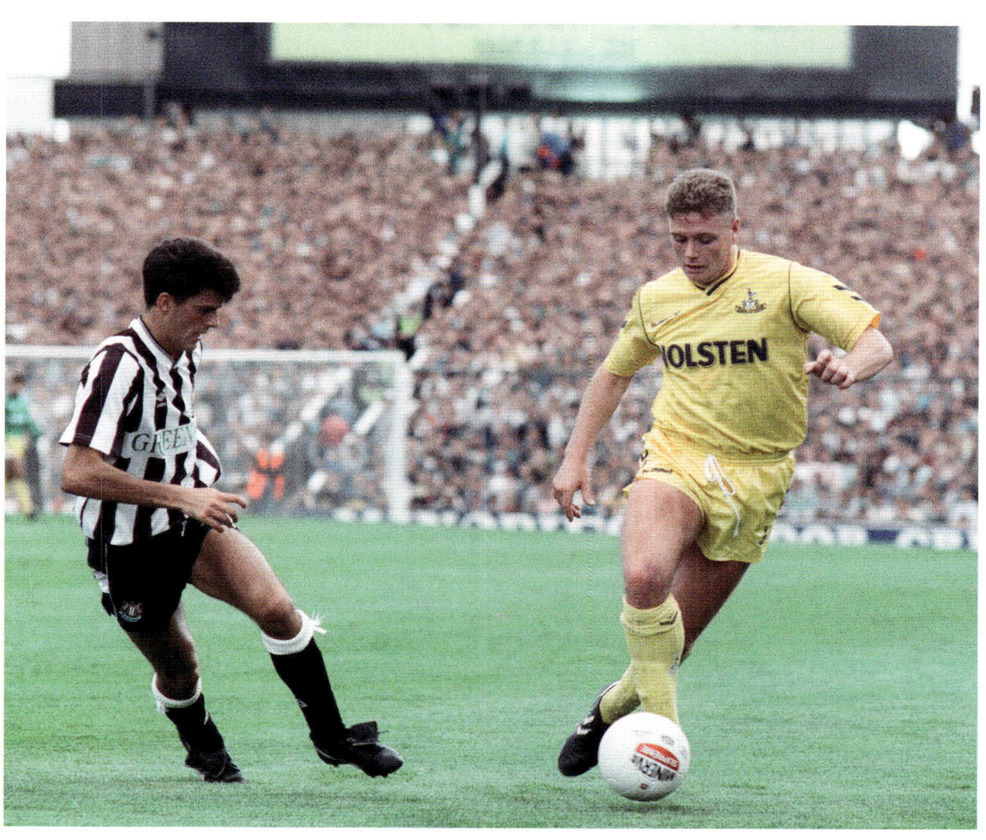

St James' Park 1988
Paul Gascoigne returns to Newcastle
just weeks after signing for Tottenham.
Newcastle legend Jackie Milburn had
described Gazza as 'the best player in
the world'.

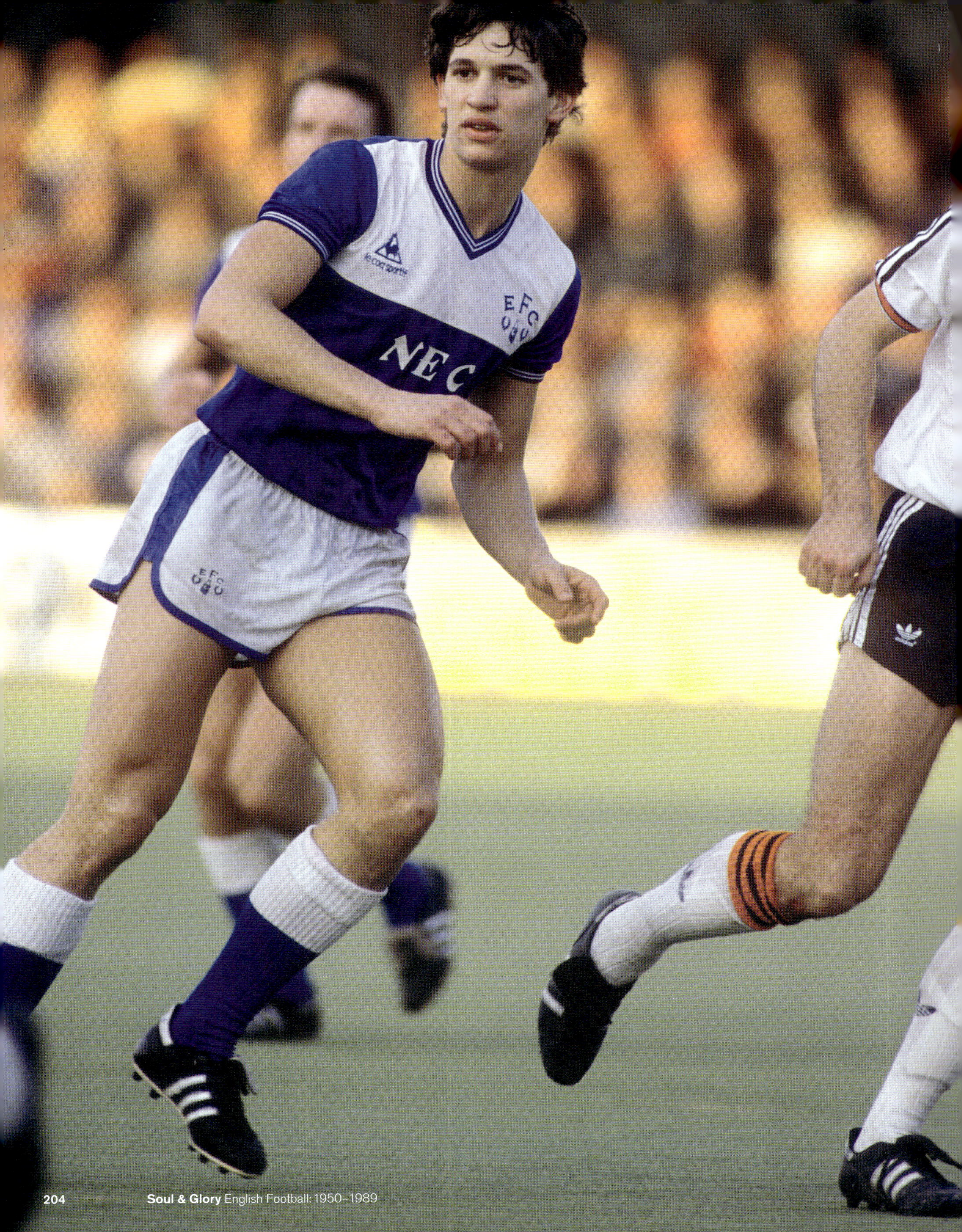

 Soul & Glory English Football: 1950–1989

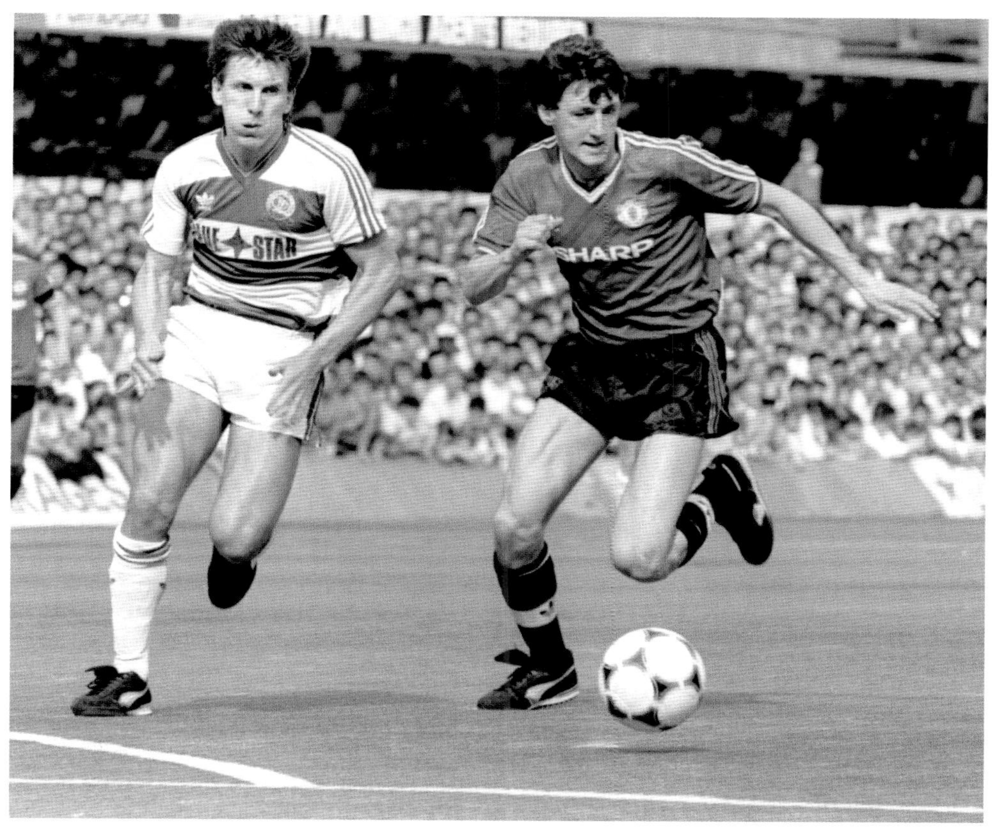

Kenilworth Road 1986

The plastic pitch meant different footwear than normal for the away team. Gary Lineker's Everton won this FA Cup tie en route to the final.

Loftus Road 1987

Warren Neill chases a through ball on Queens Park Rangers' artificial pitch with Manchester United's Peter Davenport.

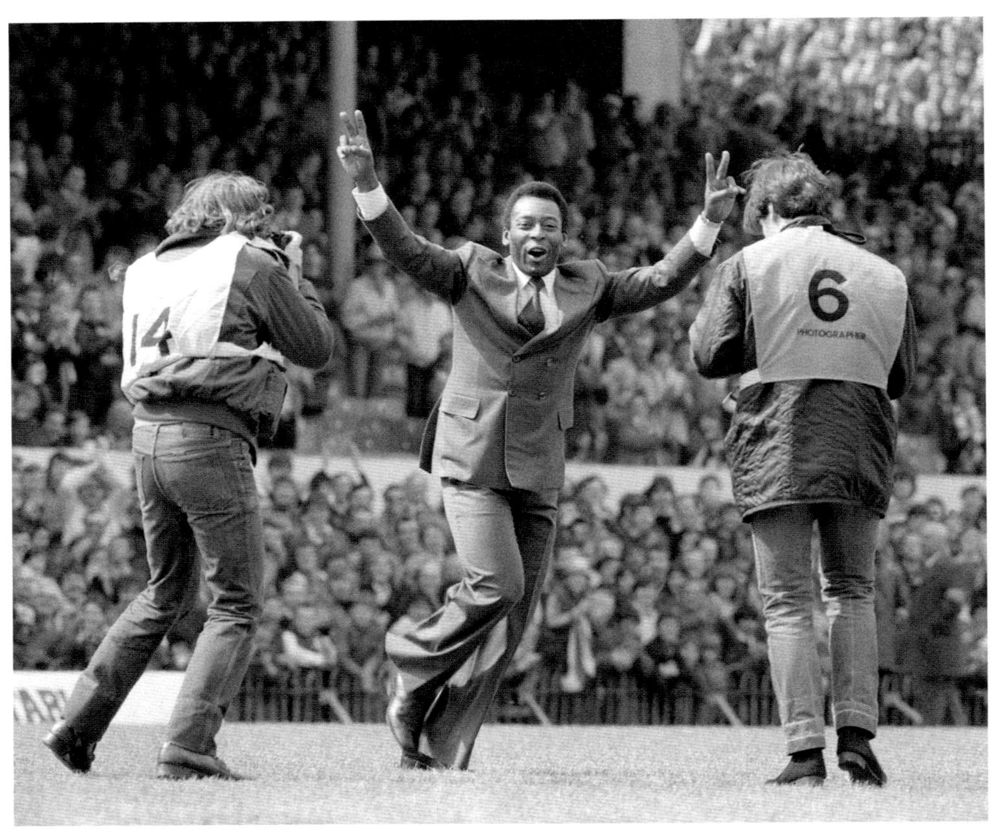

Highbury 1981
Before Arsenal v Villa, Pele is
introduced to the crowd to a very warm
reception. An eventful day; Villa won the
title and there was fighting on the pitch
between fans.

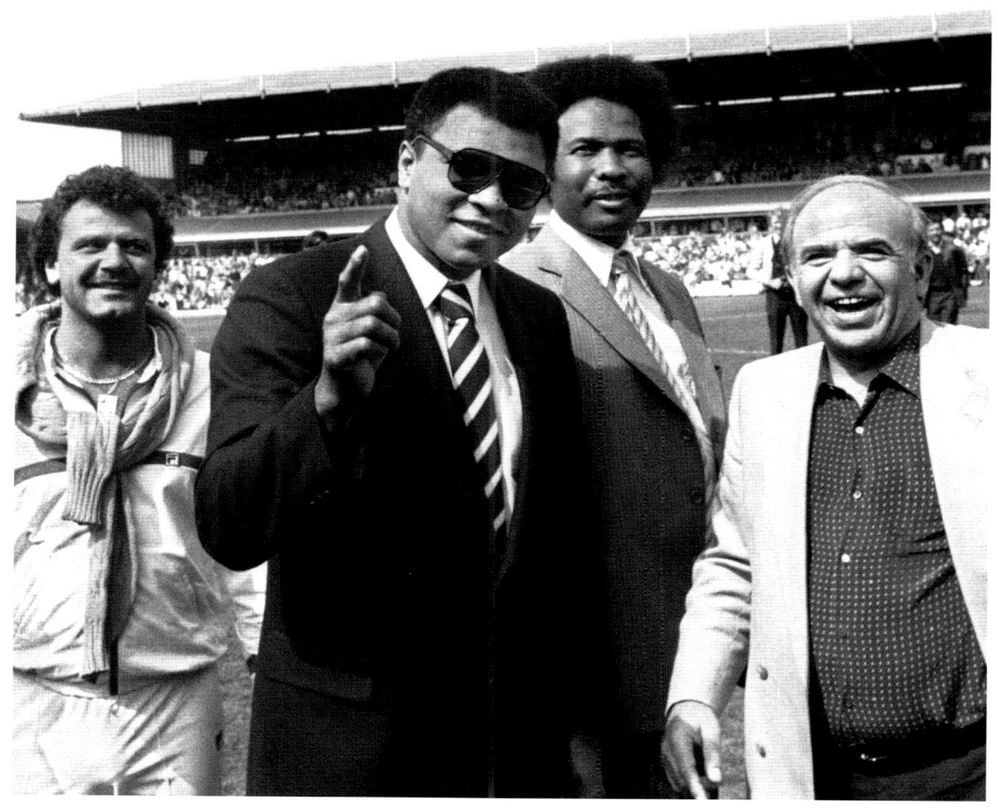

St Andrew's 1984
Birmingham City fans are treated to a
guest appearance from 'The Greatest',
as Muhammad Ali reminds everybody
who is number one!

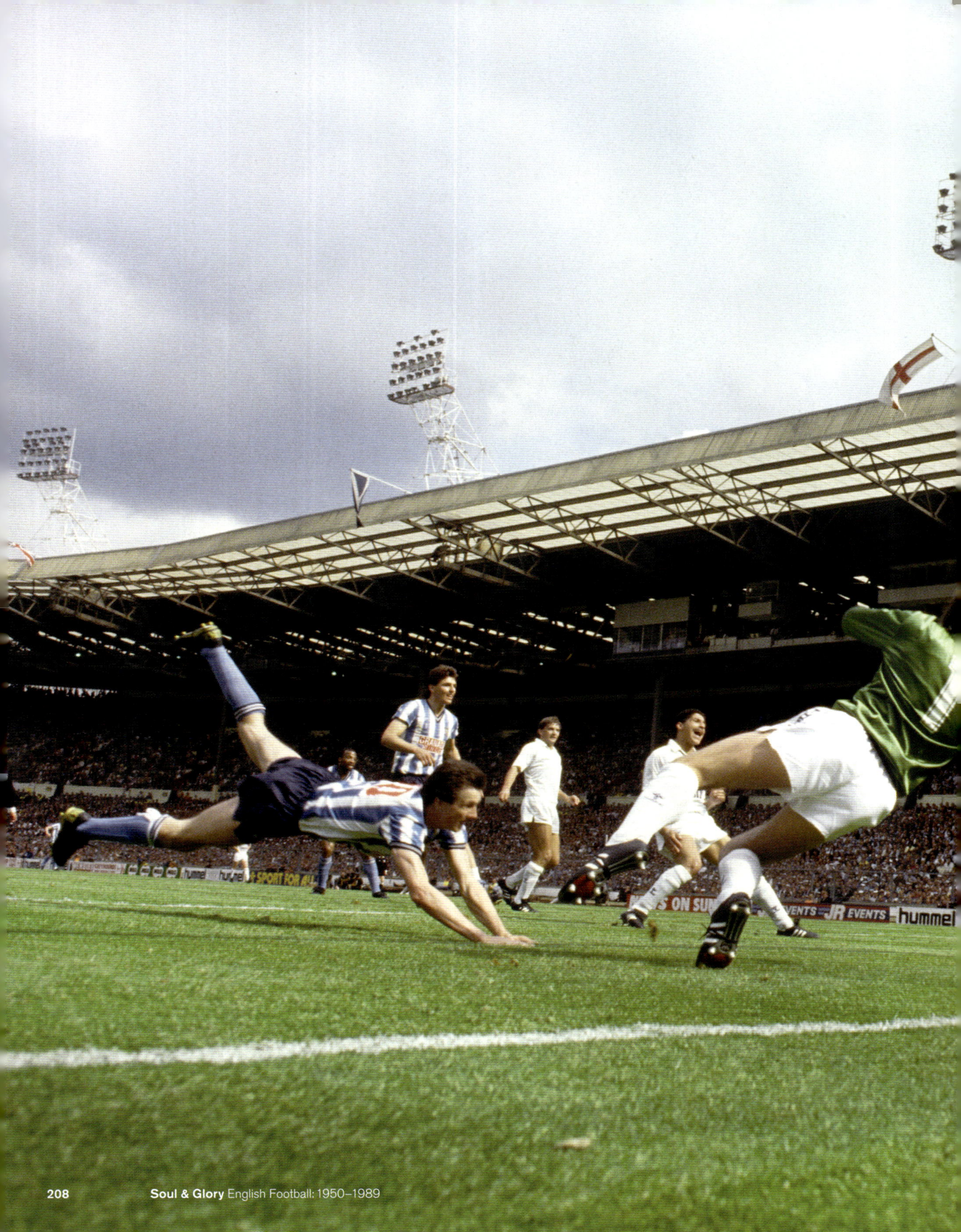

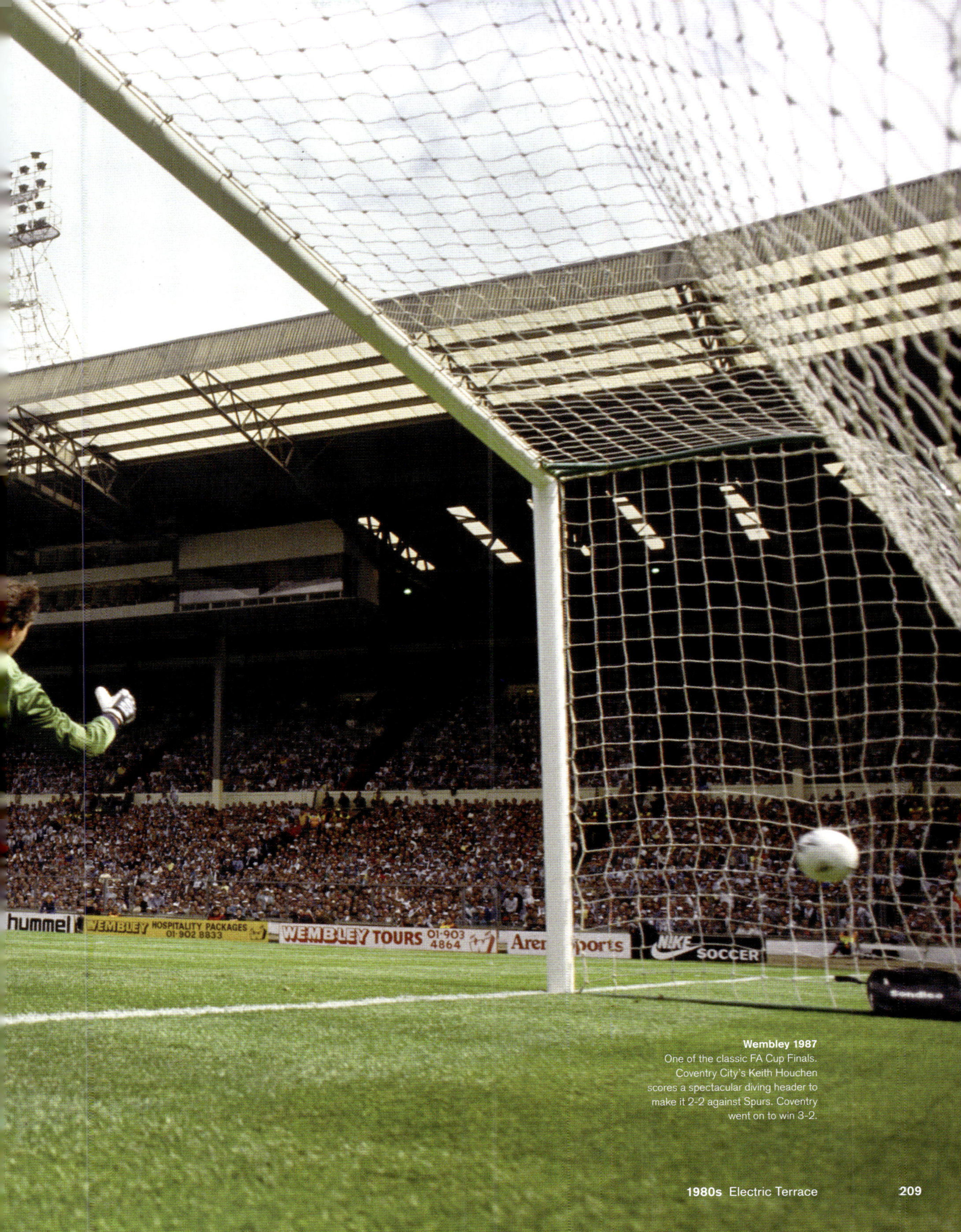

Wembley 1987
One of the classic FA Cup Finals.
Coventry City's Keith Houchen
scores a spectacular diving header to
make it 2-2 against Spurs. Coventry
went on to win 3-2.

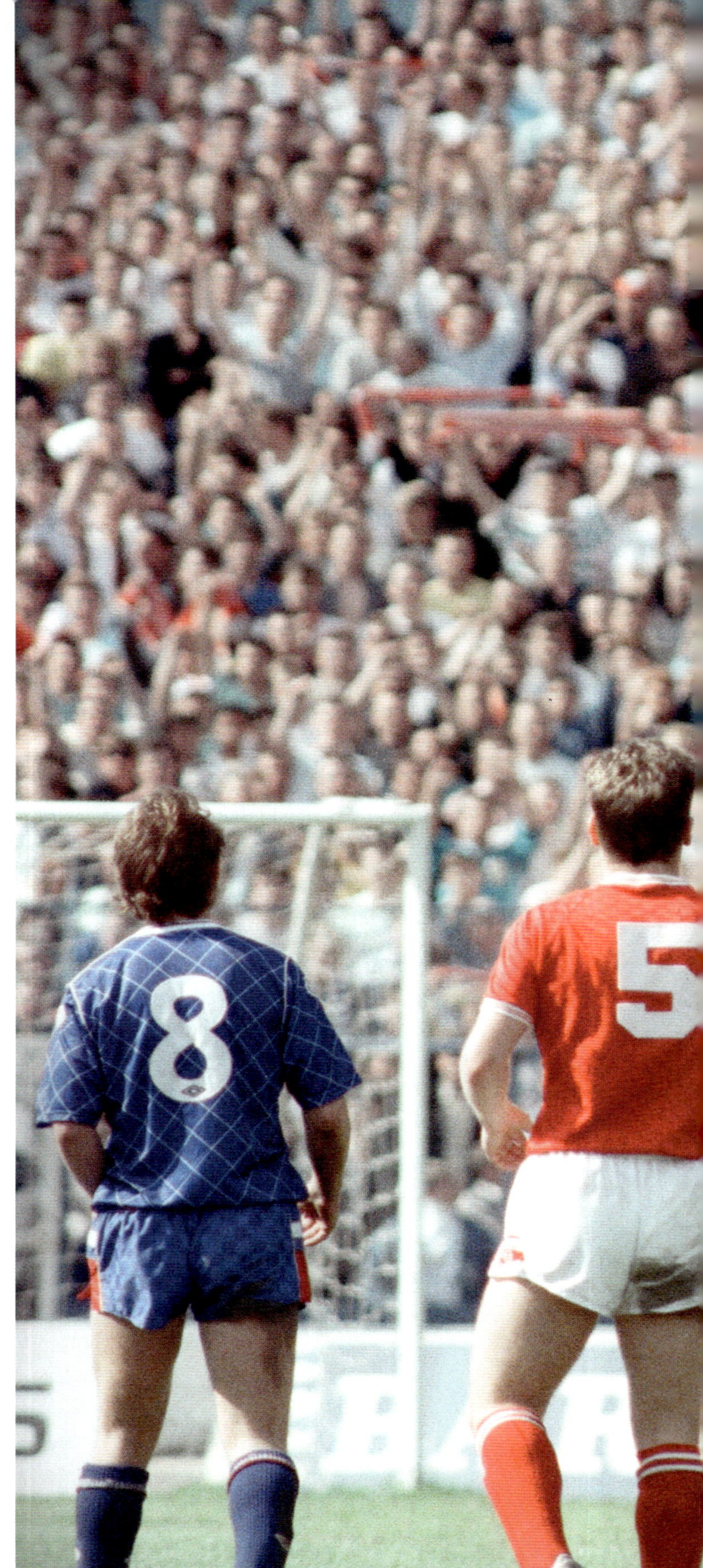

Stamford Bridge 1988
Division Two Middlesbrough take on
Division One Chelsea in the play-off
final. Boro fans in the background are
happy and with good reason. They went
up and Chelsea were relegated.

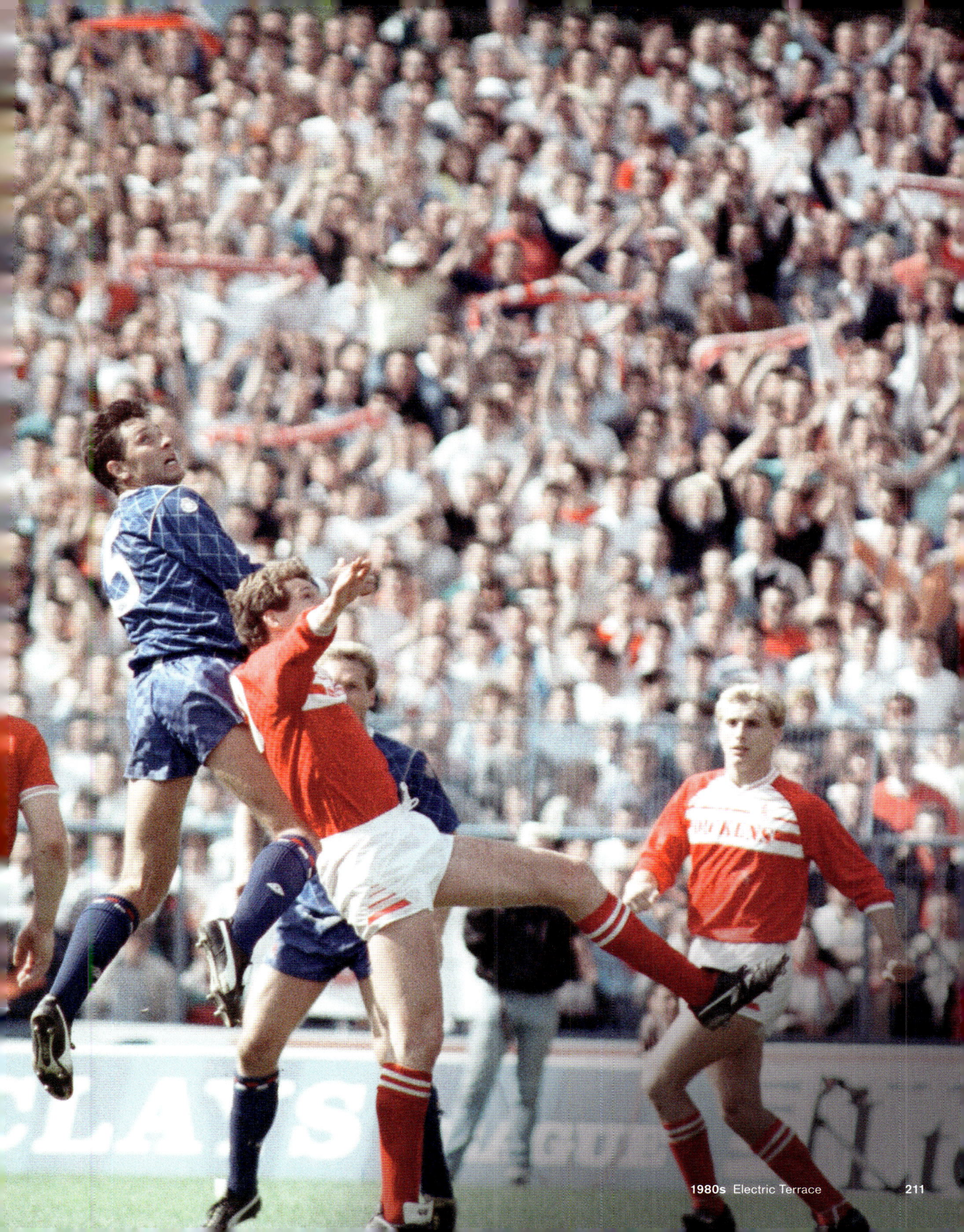

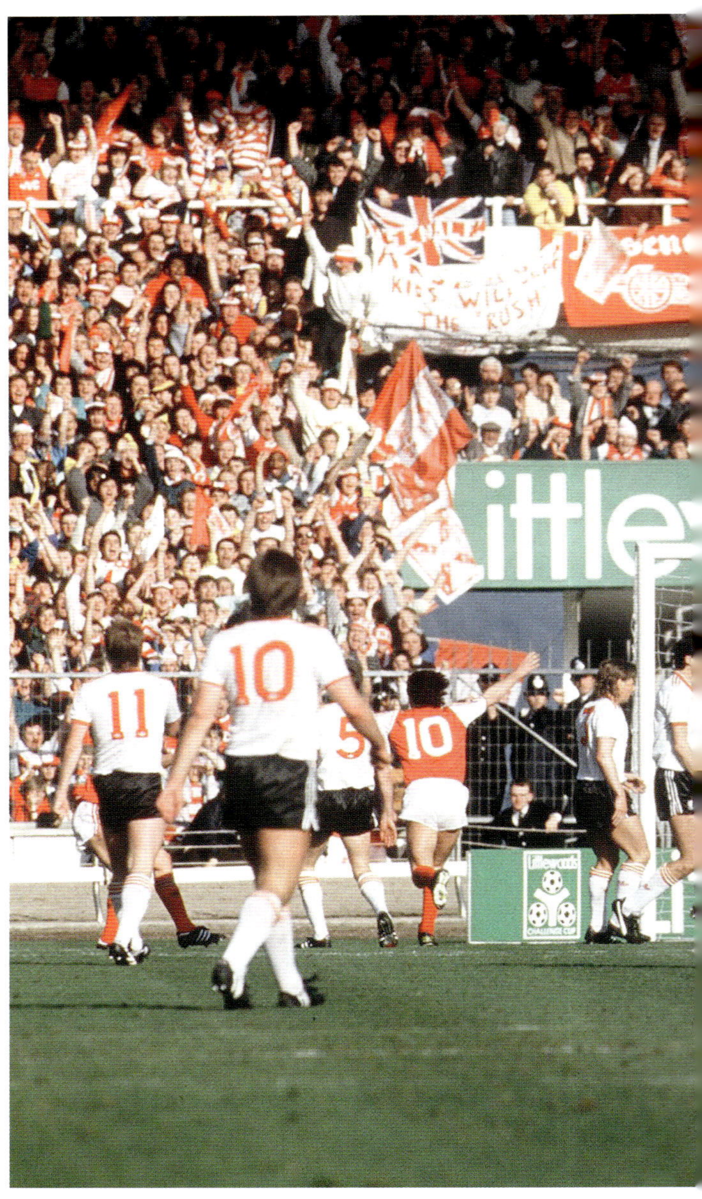

Wembley 1987
David Rocastle runs across the goal towards double scorer Charlie Nicholas (10) as Arsenal come from behind to beat Liverpool in the League Cup Final.

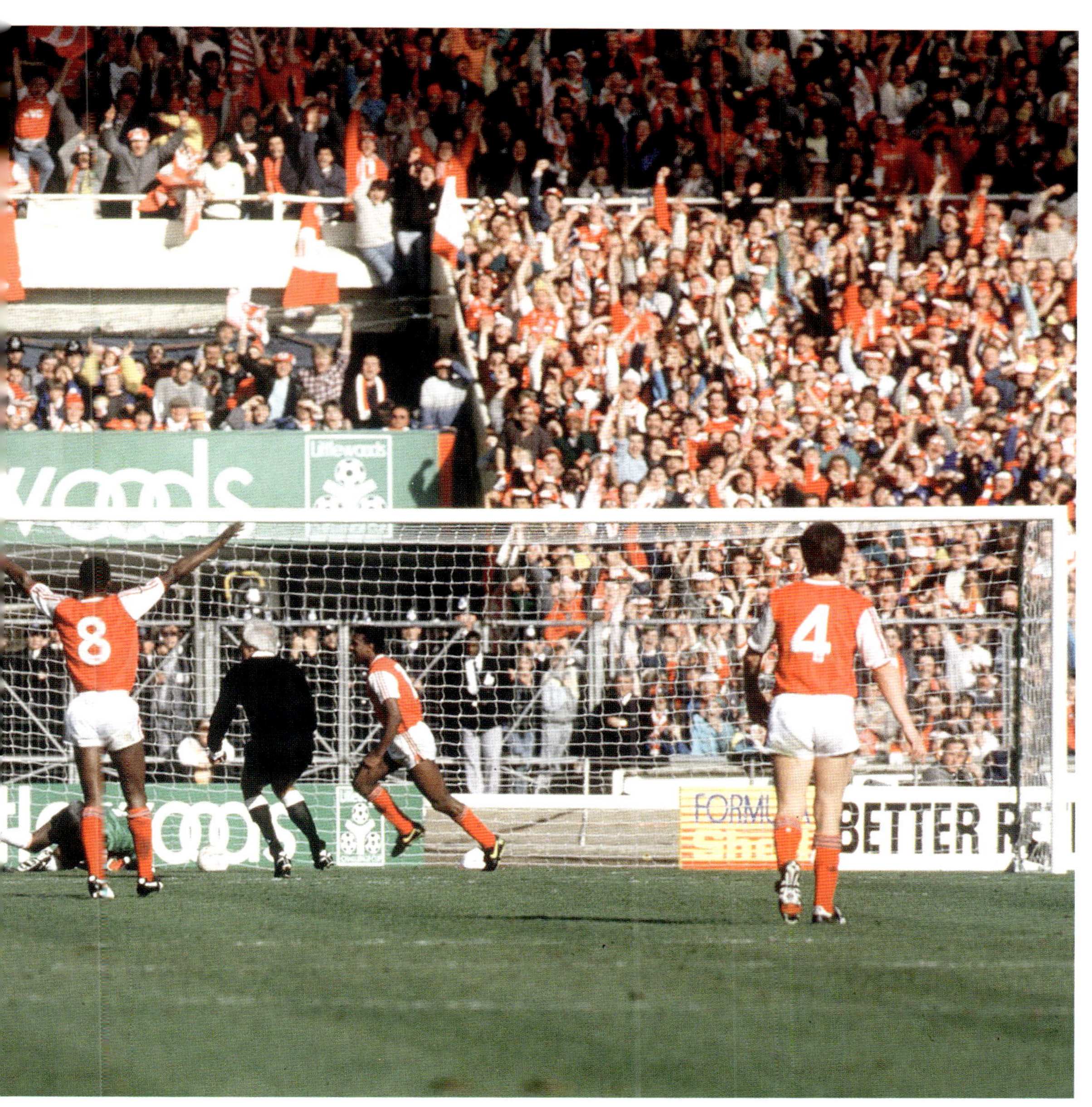

woods
Littlewoods
FORM
BETTER RE

 Soul & Glory English Football: 1950–1989

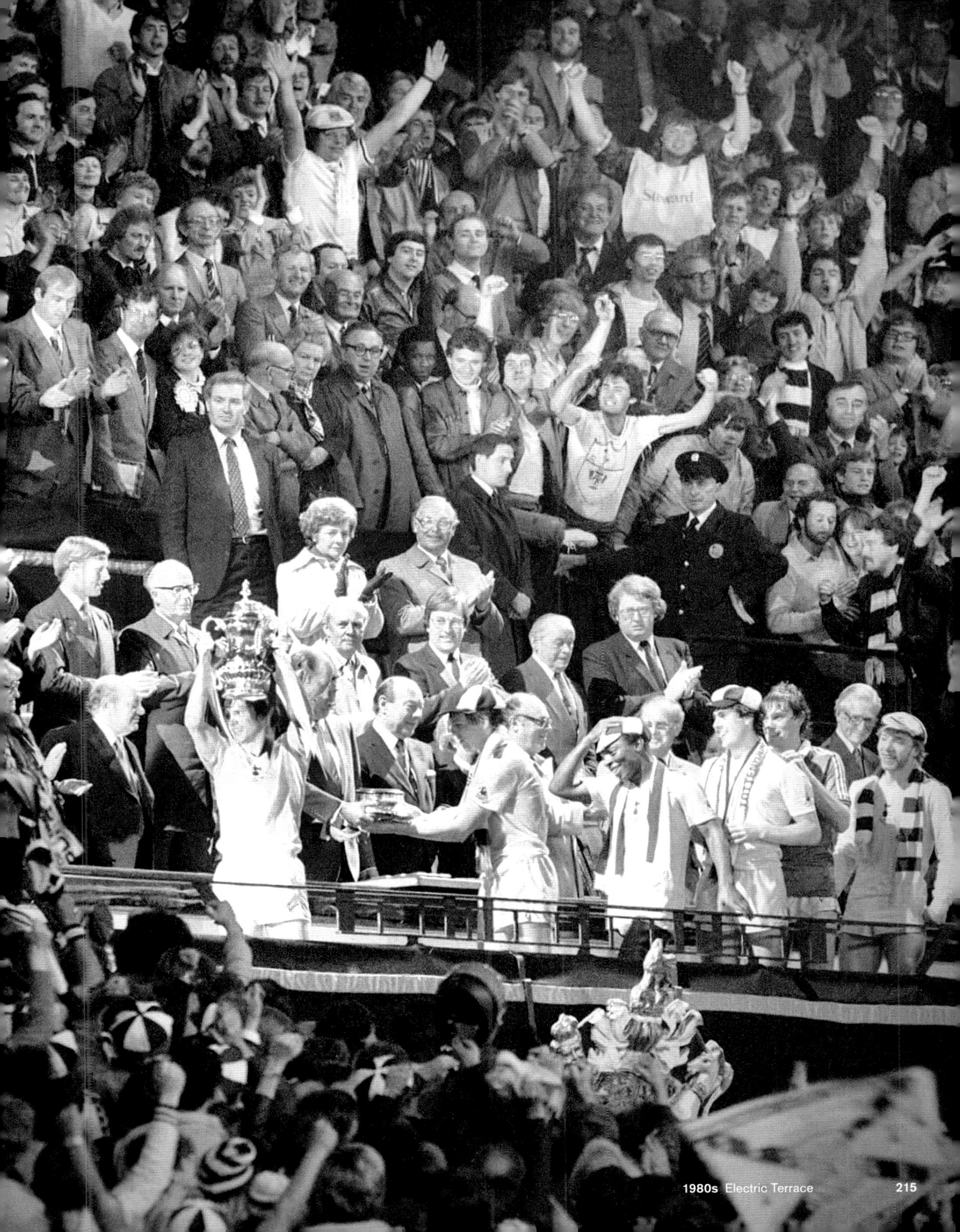

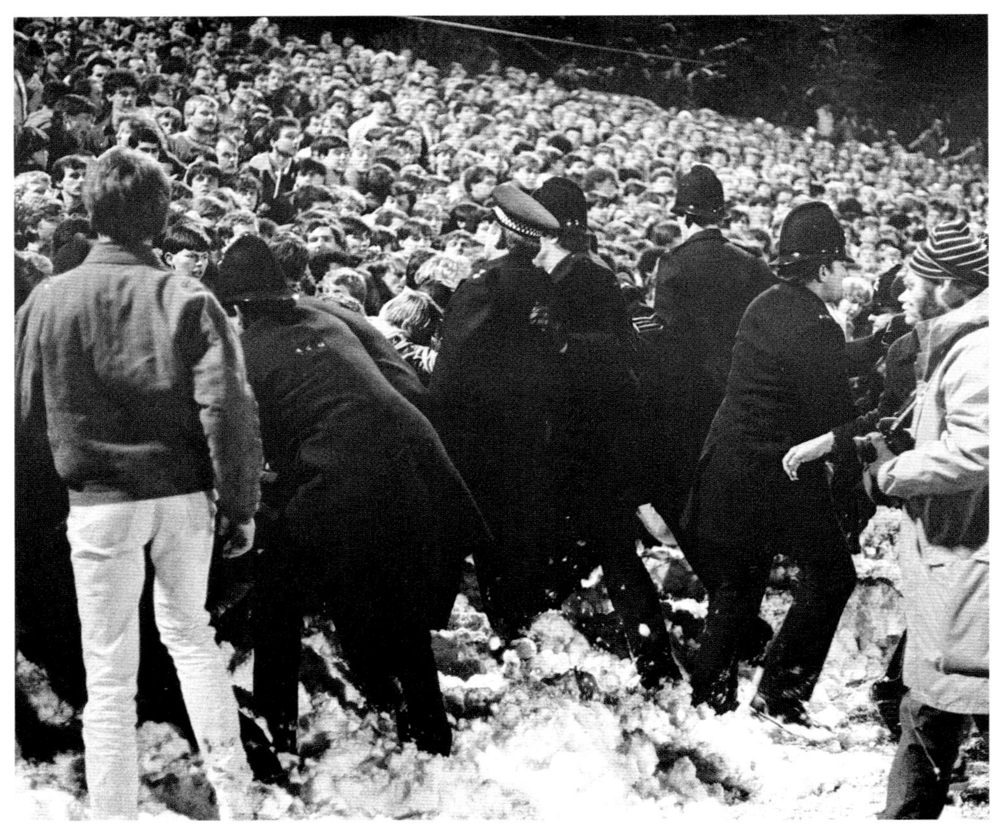

Feethams 1985
A packed away end as Middlesbrough
fans spill on to the snowy pitch in a
cup tie against Darlington.

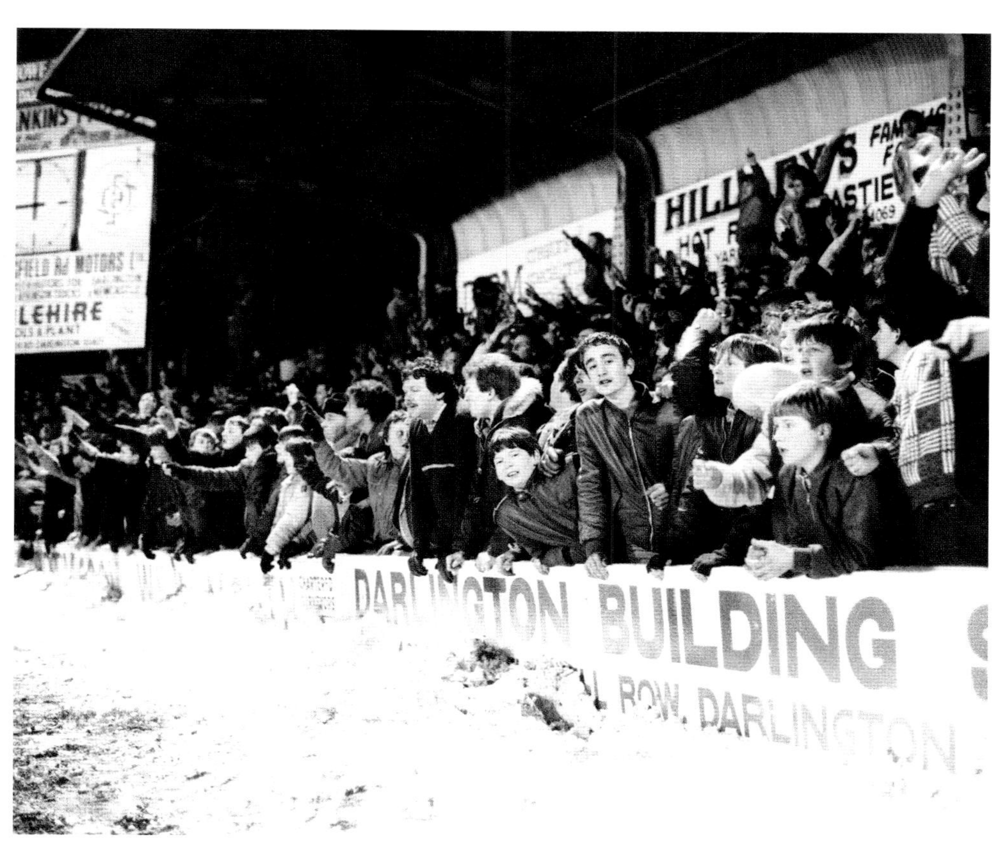

Feethams 1985

Darlington fans in the 'tin shed' end are pumped up for an FA Cup tie against their local rivals Middlesbrough. Despite being in close proximity, the two clubs have rarely met over the years.

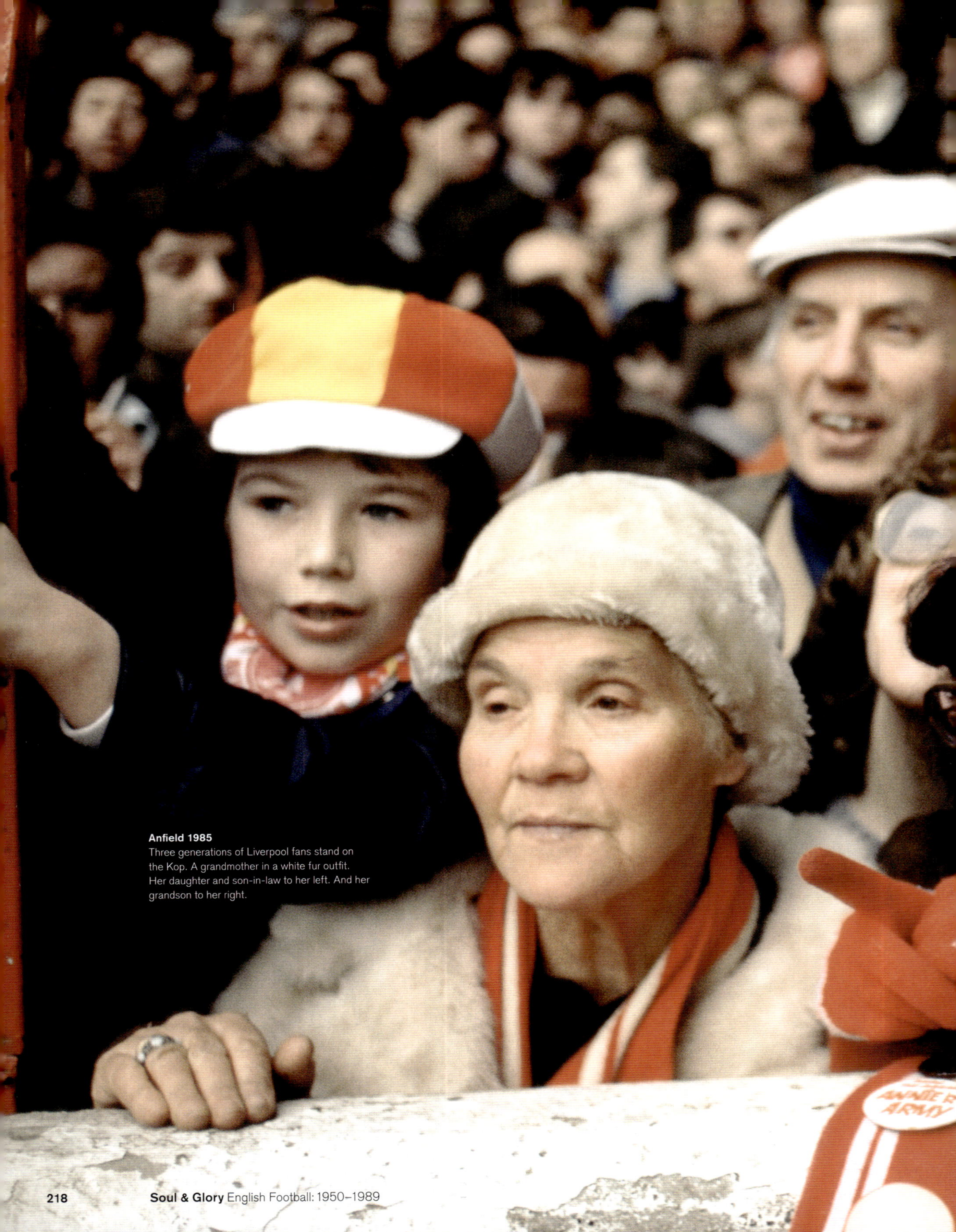

Anfield 1985
Three generations of Liverpool fans stand on
the Kop. A grandmother in a white fur outfit.
Her daughter and son-in-law to her left. And her
grandson to her right.

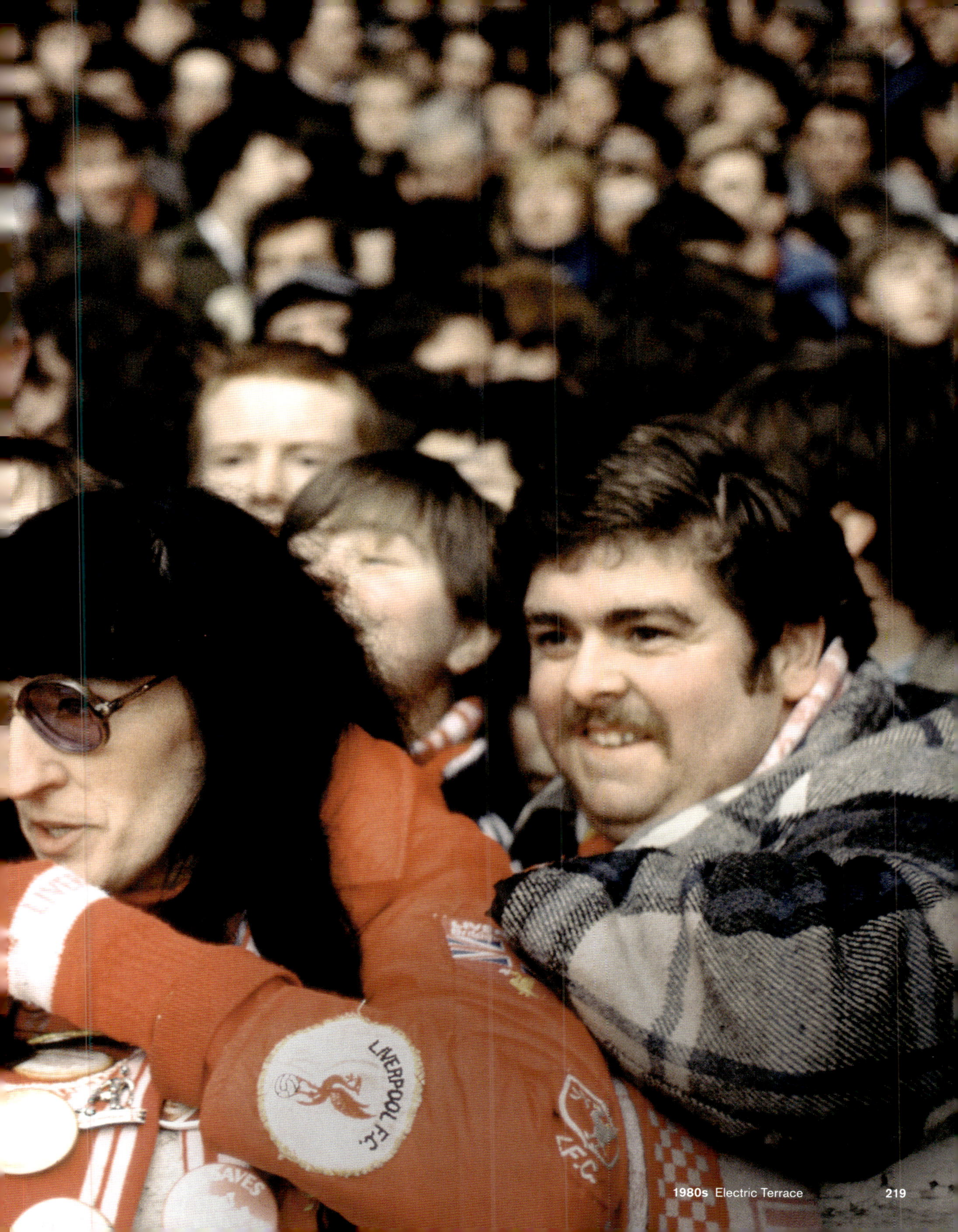

LIVERPOOL F.C.
L.F.C.

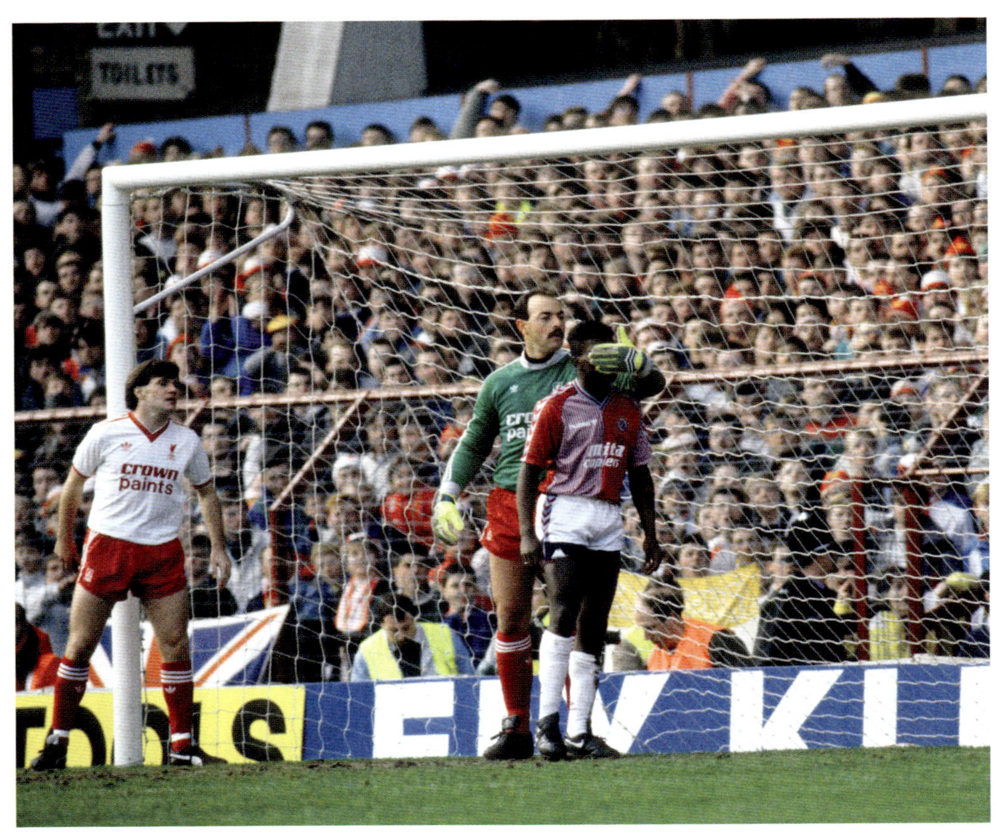

Villa Park 1988

In an FA Cup tie, Liverpool's
Bruce Grobbelaar comes up
with a unique way to stop
Villa's Tony Daley.

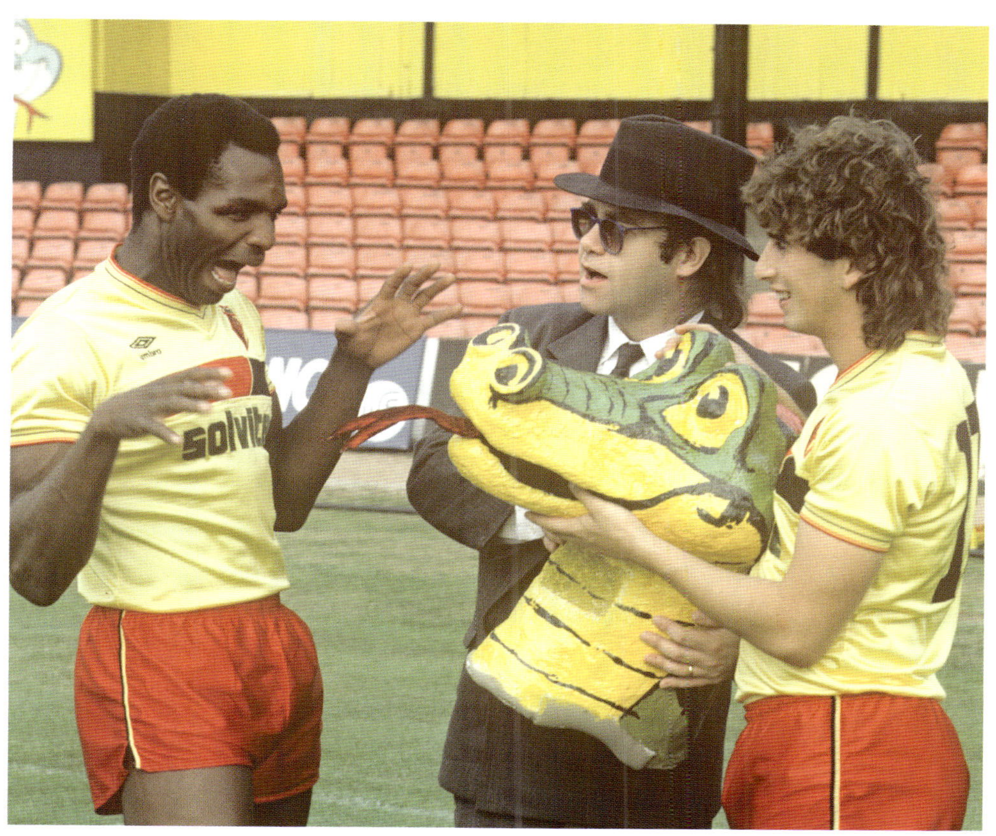

Vicarage Road 1986

Luther Blissett fooling around with
Elton John and a dragon. Not quite
sure what's going on here!

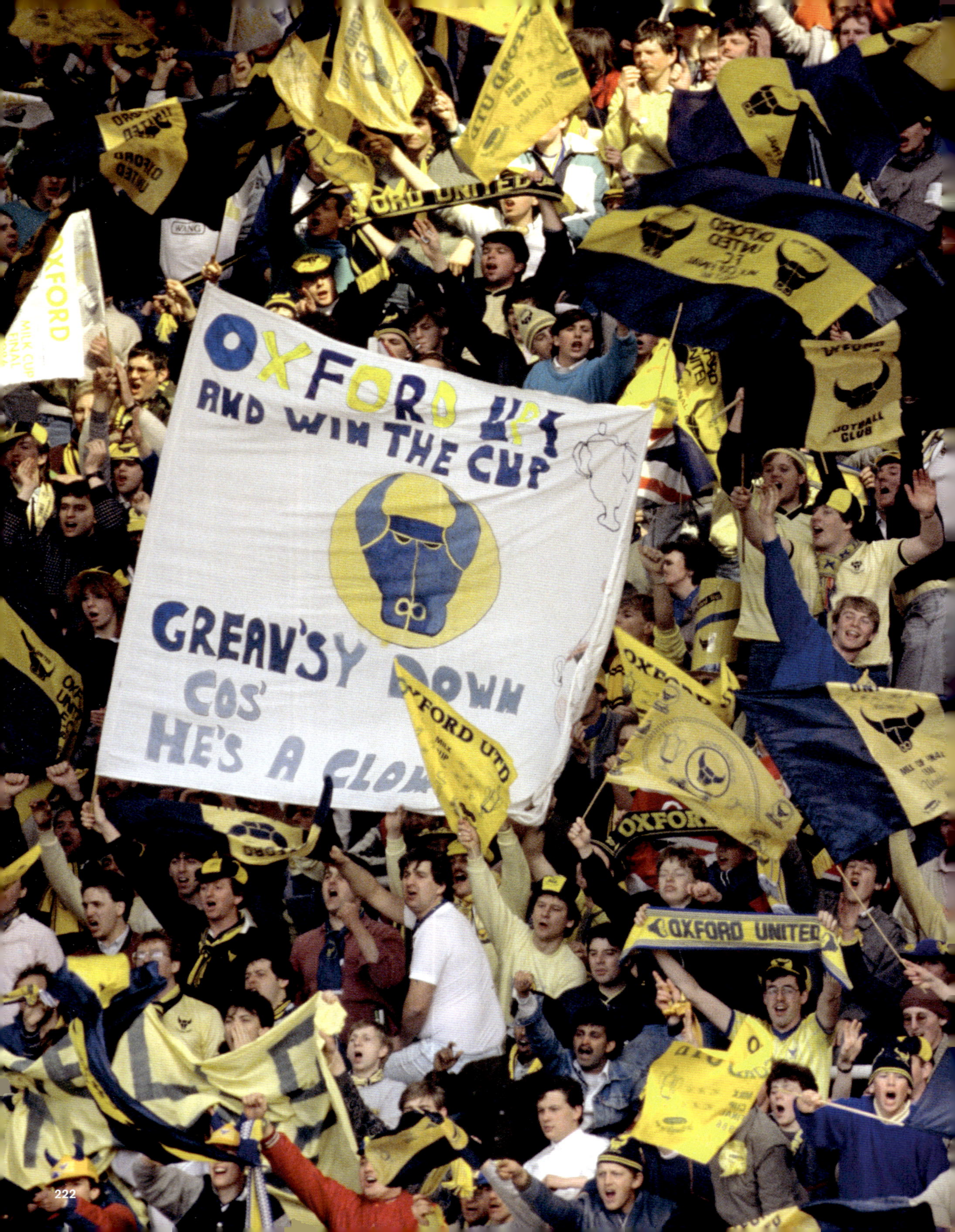

OXFORD UP!
AND WIN THE CUP
GREAV'SY DOWN
COS' HE'S A CLOW

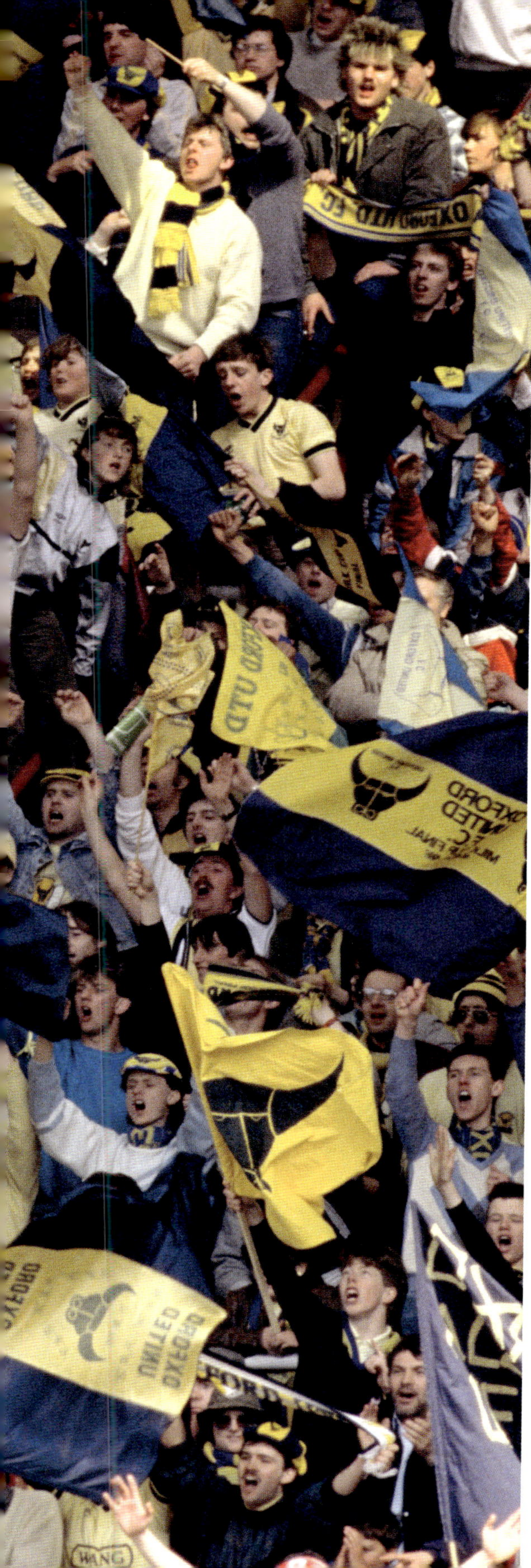

Wembley 1986
Oxford United fans celebrate winning
the League Cup in the greatest
moment in the club's history. One of
the banners is having a dig at 80s TV
pundit Jimmy Greaves who must have
tipped losing finalists QPR.

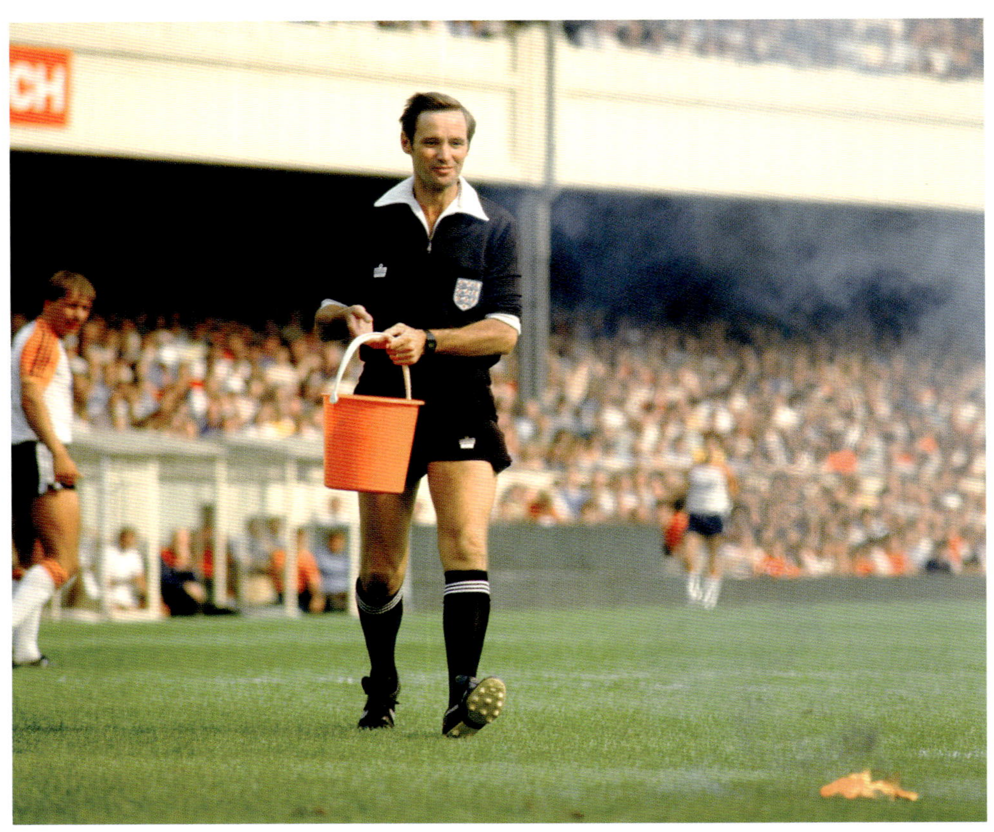

Highbury 1983
Refereeing duties in this Arsenal v Luton
game included putting out a fire on the
pitch. Most likely an object thrown from
the nearby North Bank.

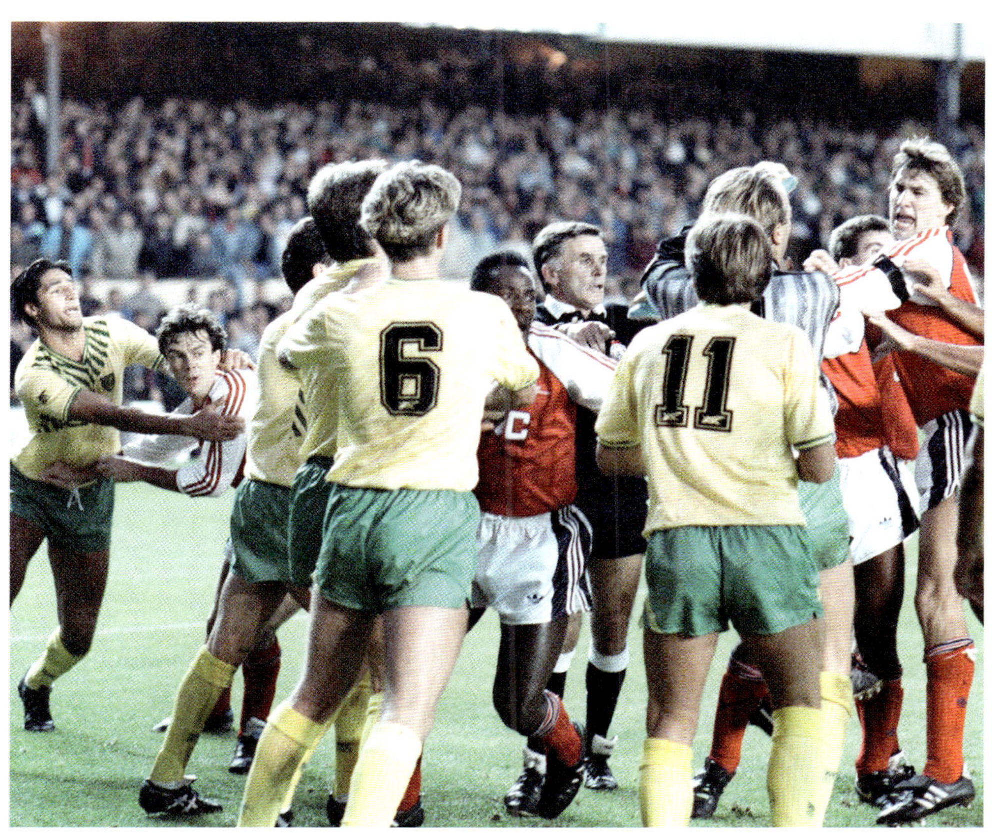

Highbury 1989
A brawl between Arsenal and Norwich players the day before Bonfire Night was branded as 'Fireworks' by an outraged press. David O'Leary (second from the left) is held back in an eventful afternoon for the Irishman. He had celebrated breaking the Gunners' appearance record and scored a rare goal in a seven-goal thriller which the Gunners won 4-3.

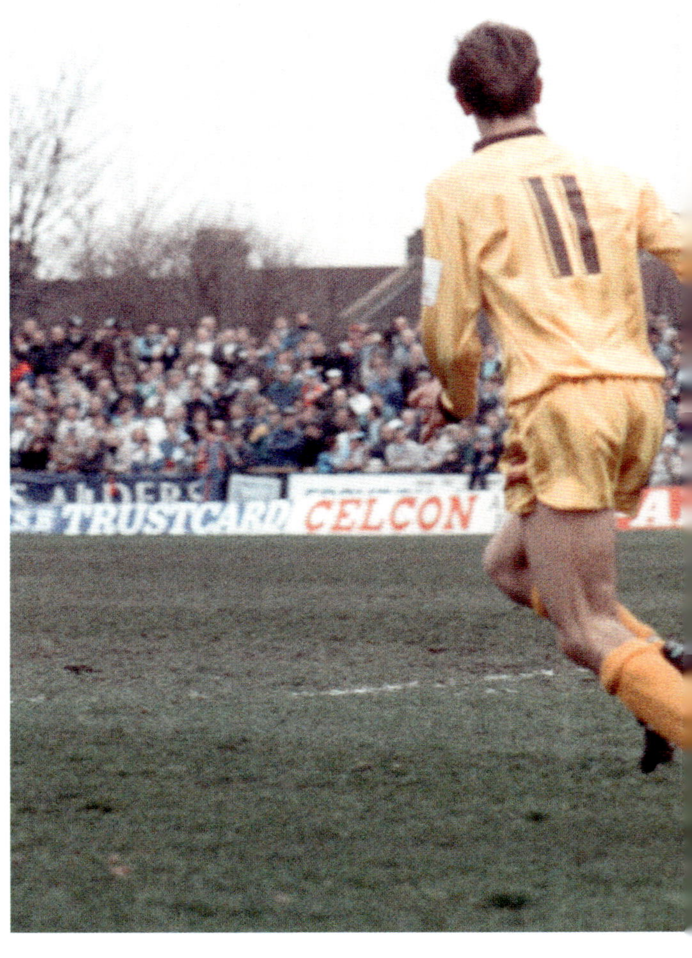

Gander Green Lane 1989
Sutton United's Tony Rains, arms in the air, celebrates scoring the opening goal in the 2-1 giant-killing of First Division Coventry City. Still one of the biggest cup upsets of all time.

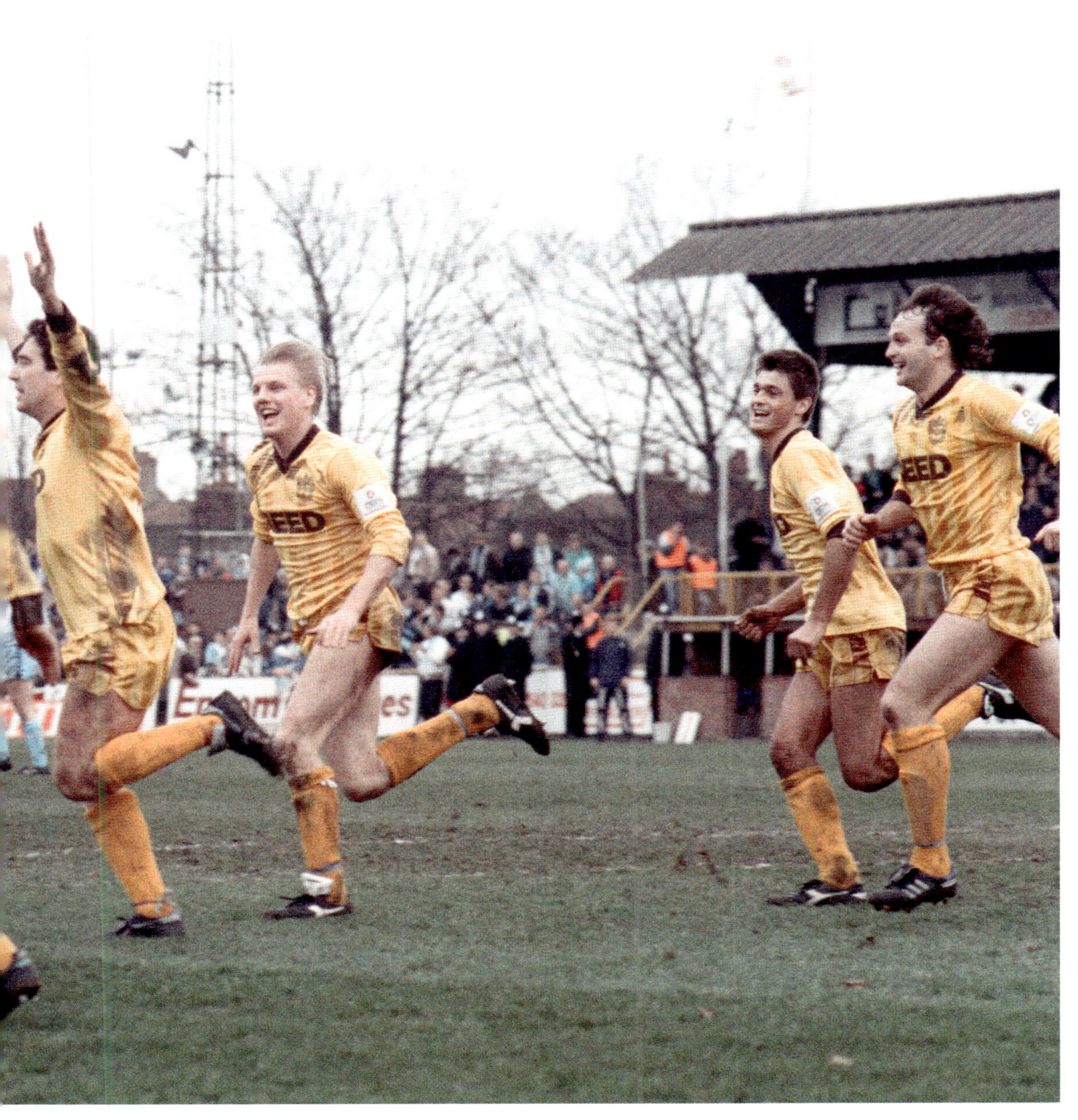

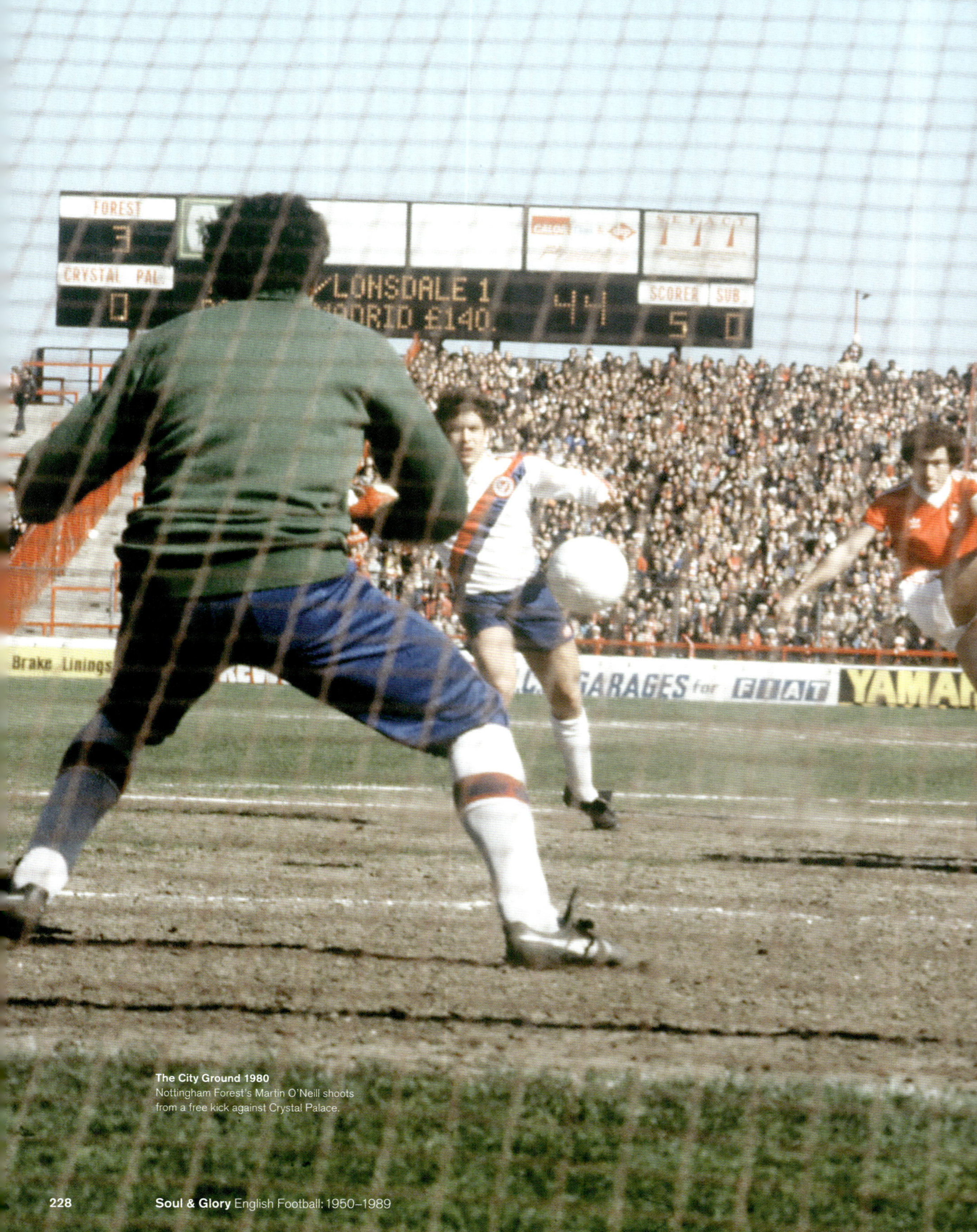

The City Ground 1980
Nottingham Forest's Martin O'Neill shoots
from a free kick against Crystal Palace.

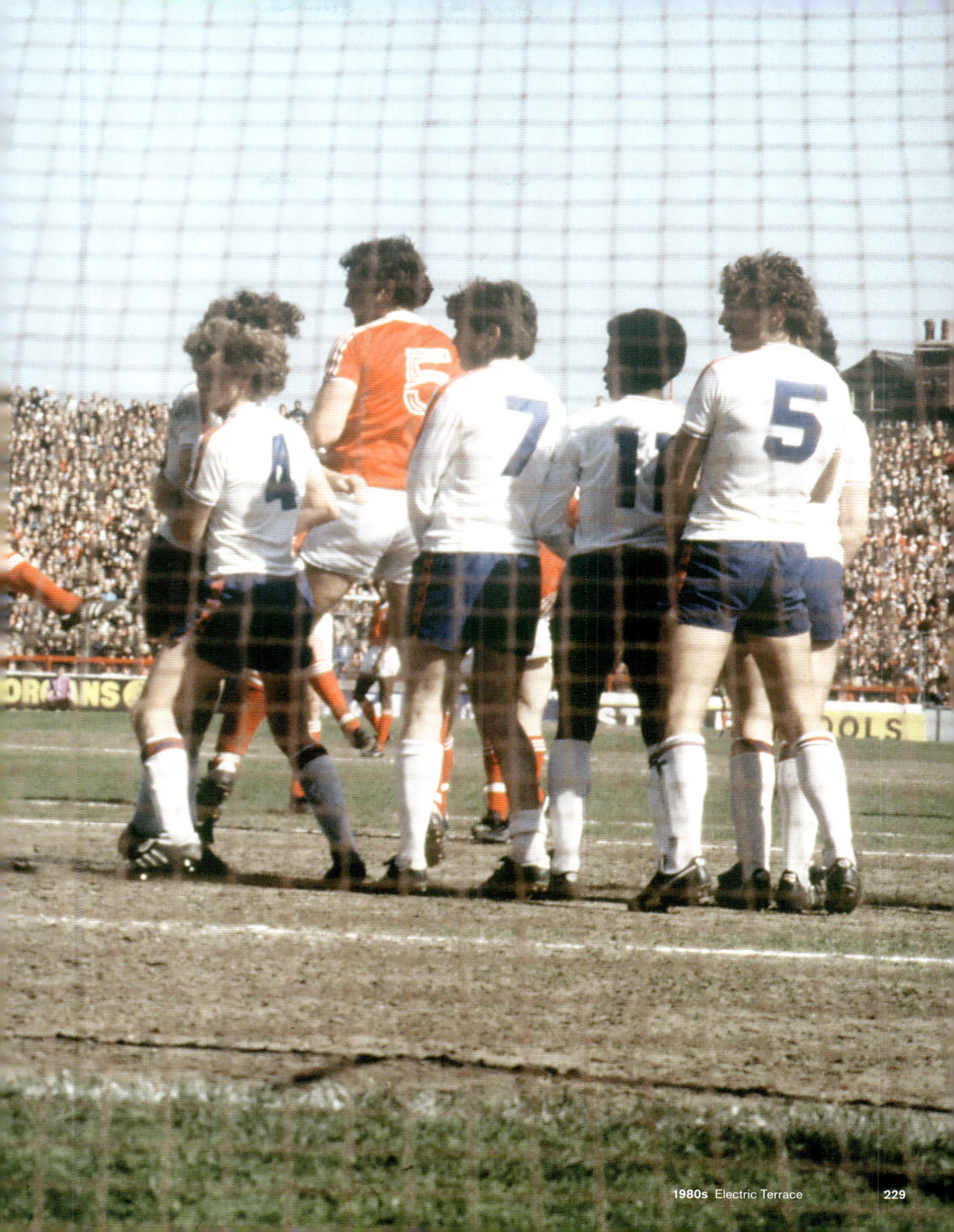

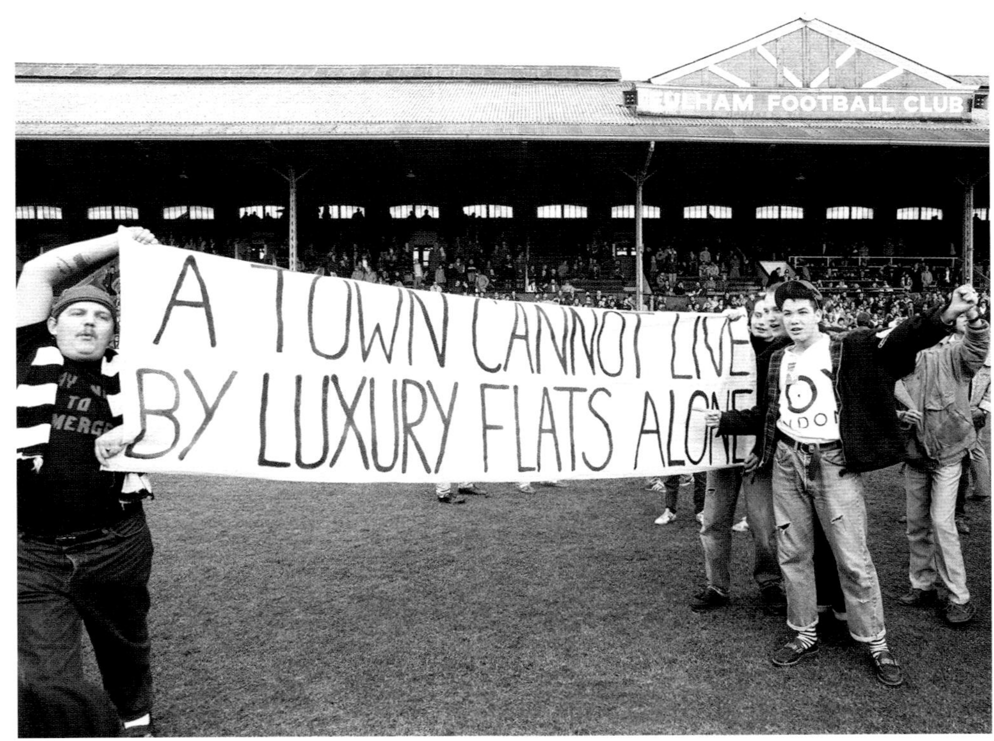

Craven Cottage 1987
During a game against Walsall, disgusted
Fulham fans made their feelings known
about the proposed merger between their
club and west London rivals QPR.

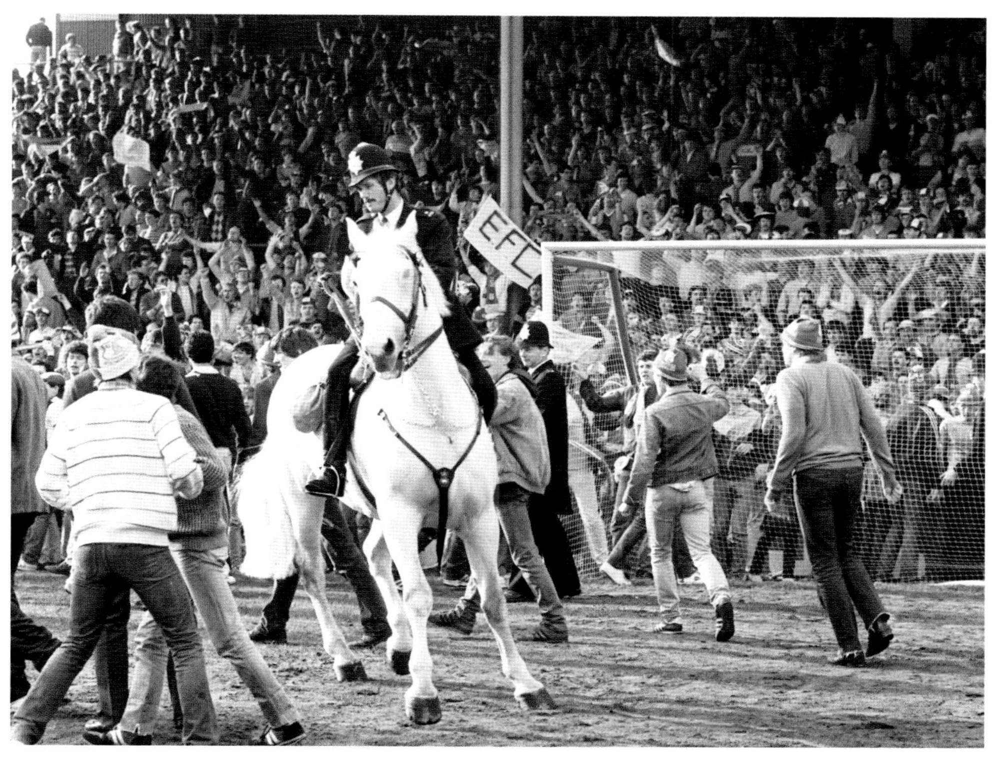

Highbury 1984
Everton fans go wild in excitement
as the Toffees beat Southampton
in the FA Cup semi-final.

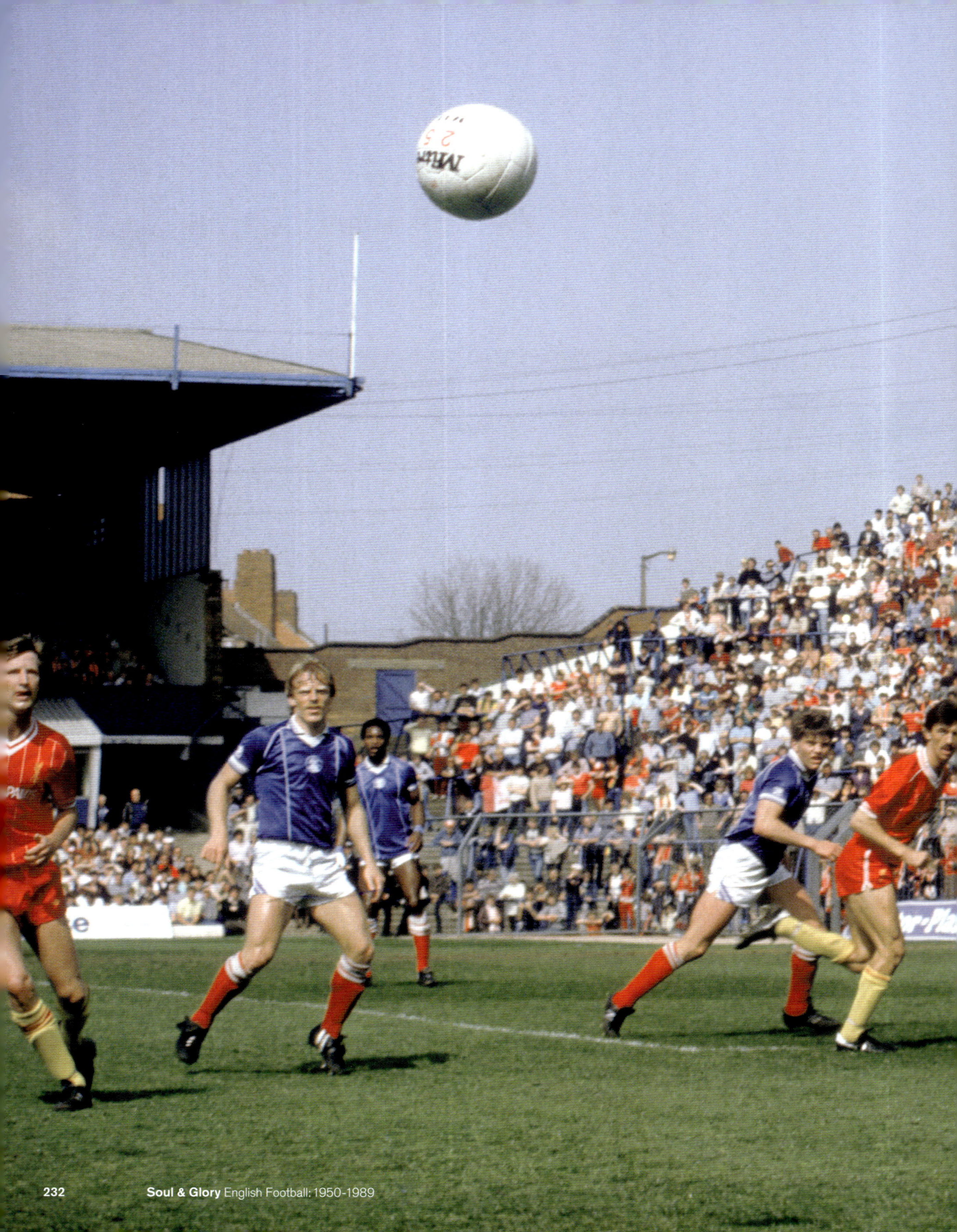

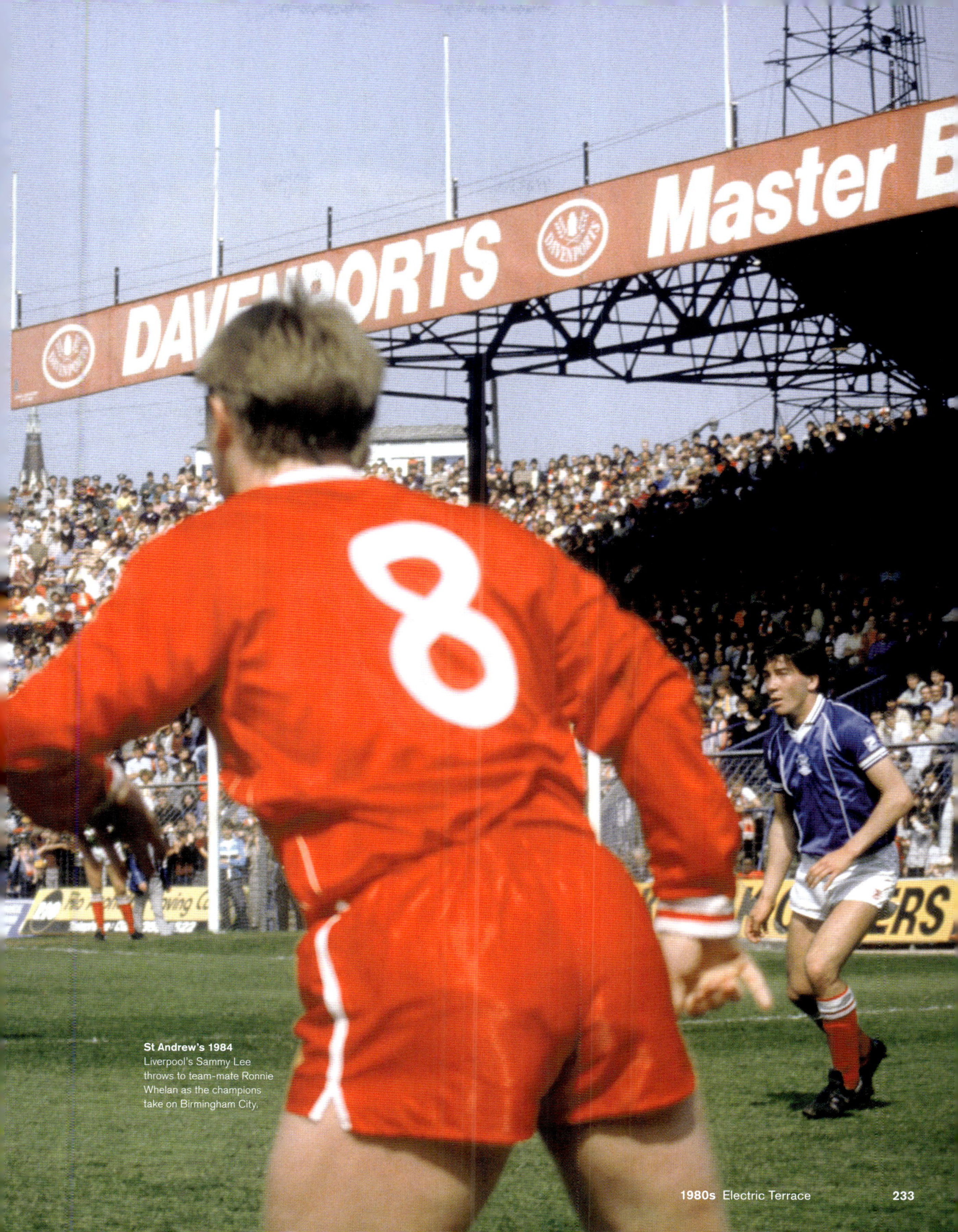

St Andrew's 1984
Liverpool's Sammy Lee throws to team-mate Ronnie Whelan as the champions take on Birmingham City.

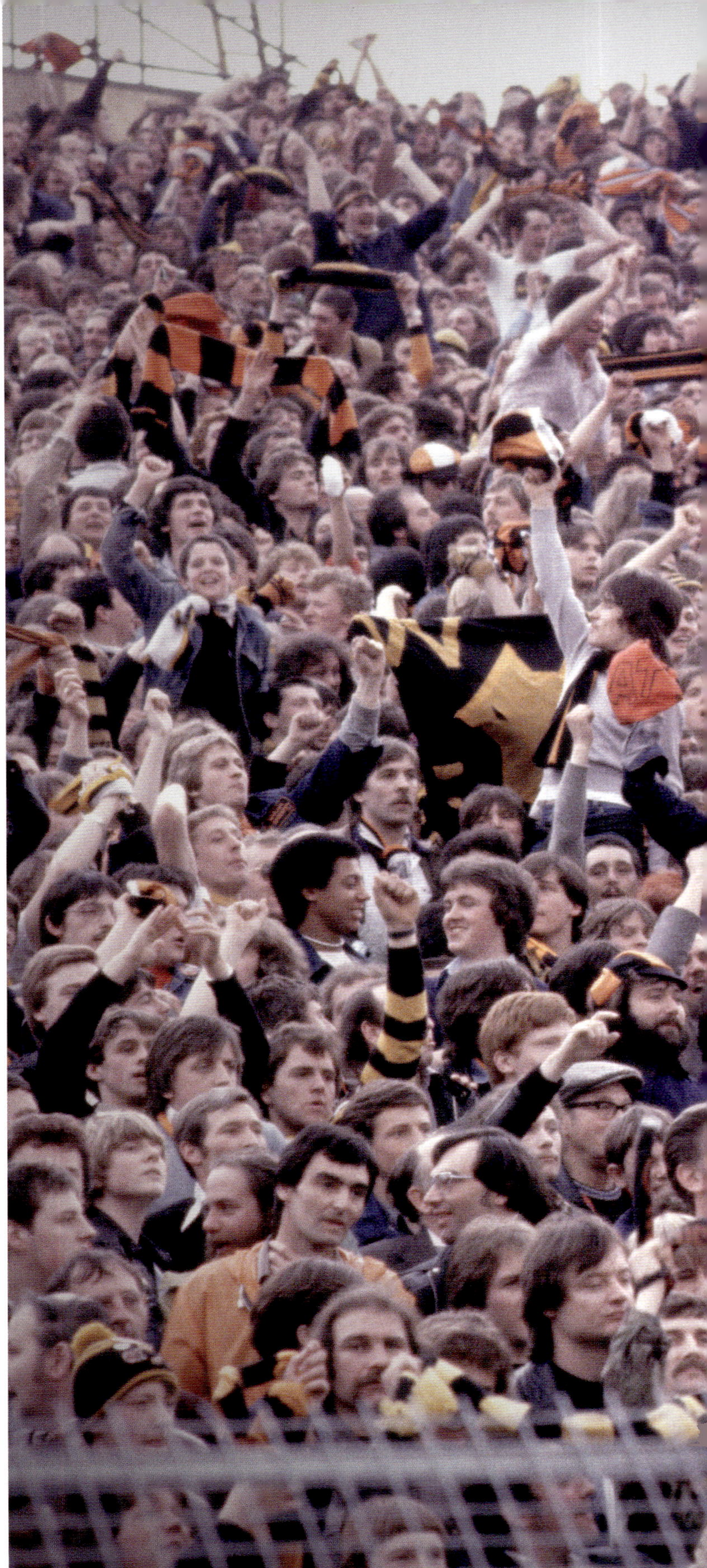

Hillsborough 1981
Electricity in the Kop end as Wolves
fans support their team in an FA Cup
semi-final against Spurs.

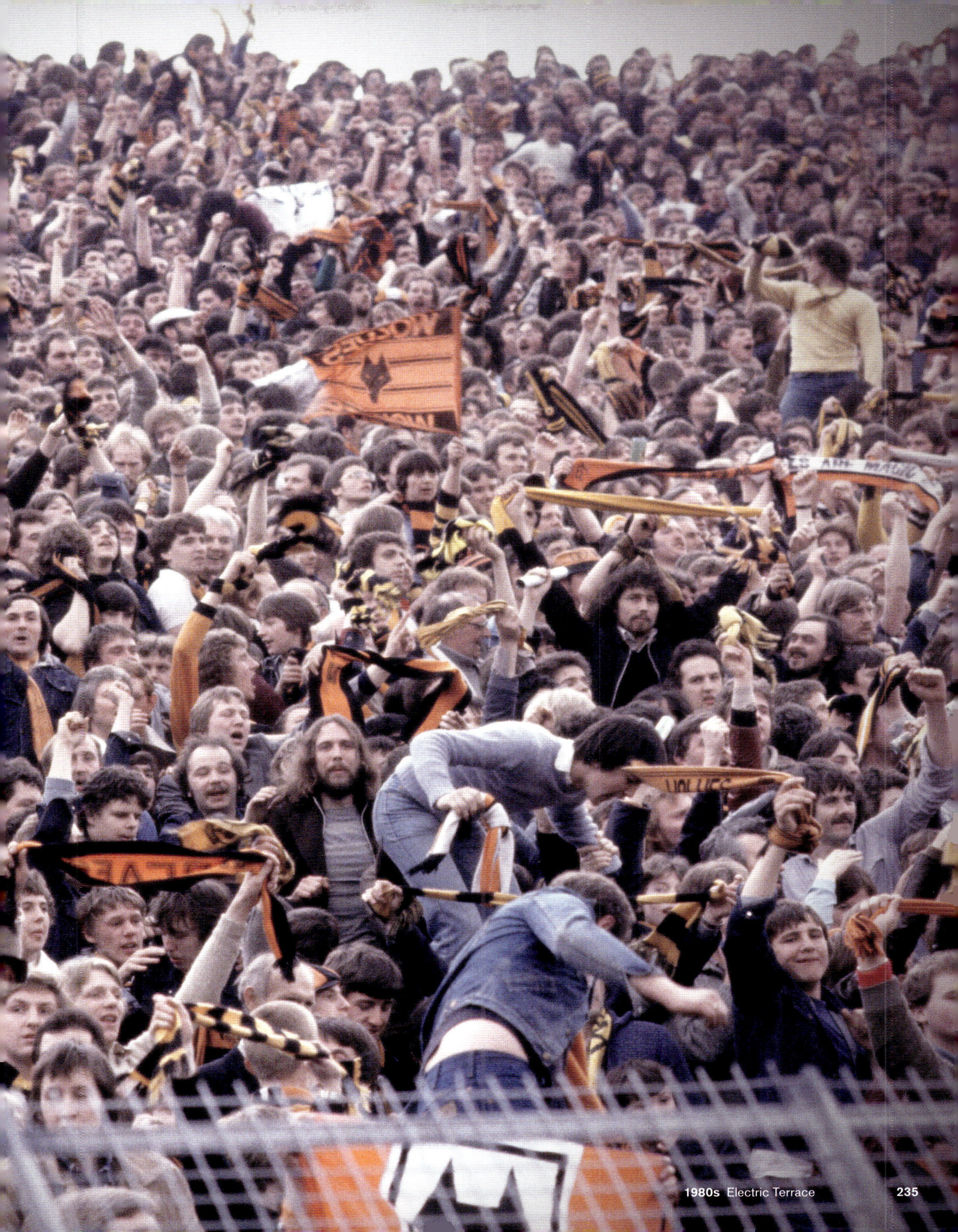

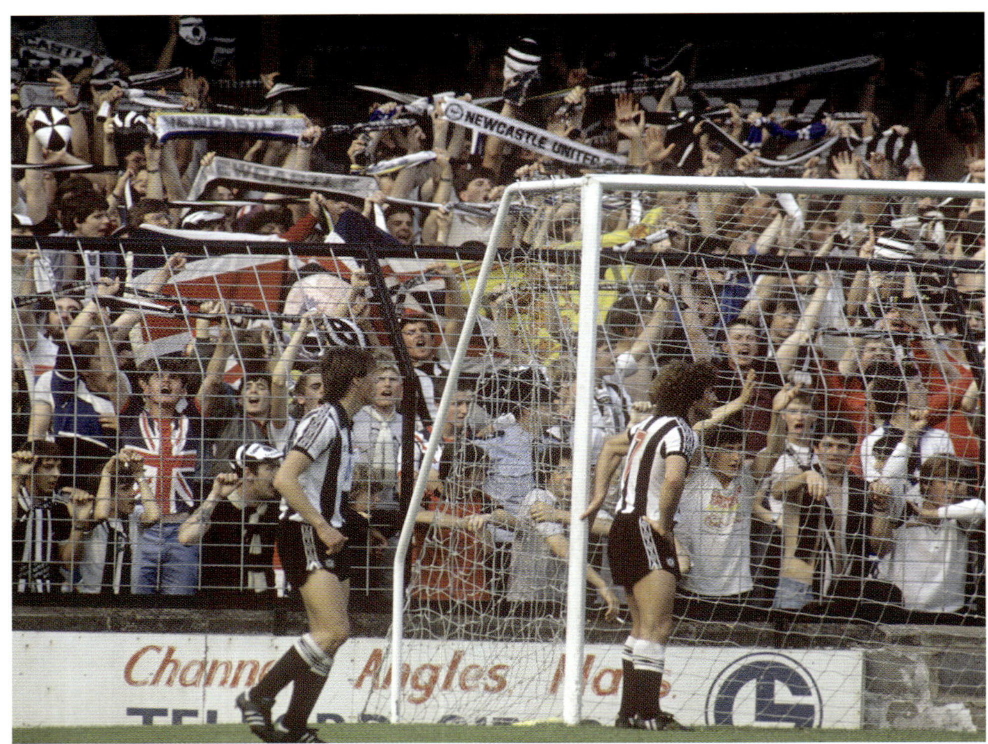

Gay Meadow 1982
Newcastle United fans in the away end are
in good spirits as their hero Kevin Keegan
defends the far post in a Division Two game
against Shrewsbury Town.

Gay Meadow 1982
Shrewsbury fans ask
Keegan for his autograph.

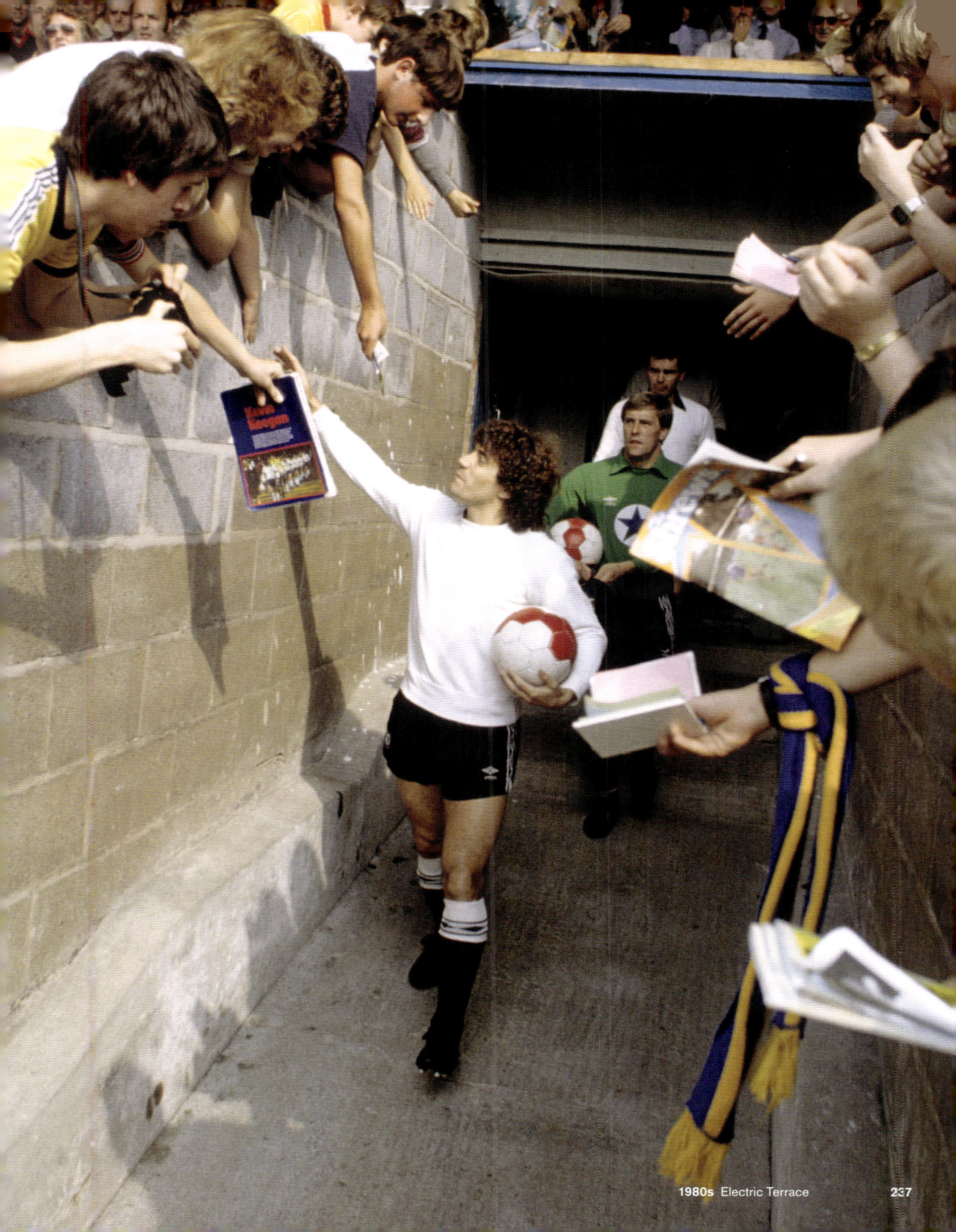

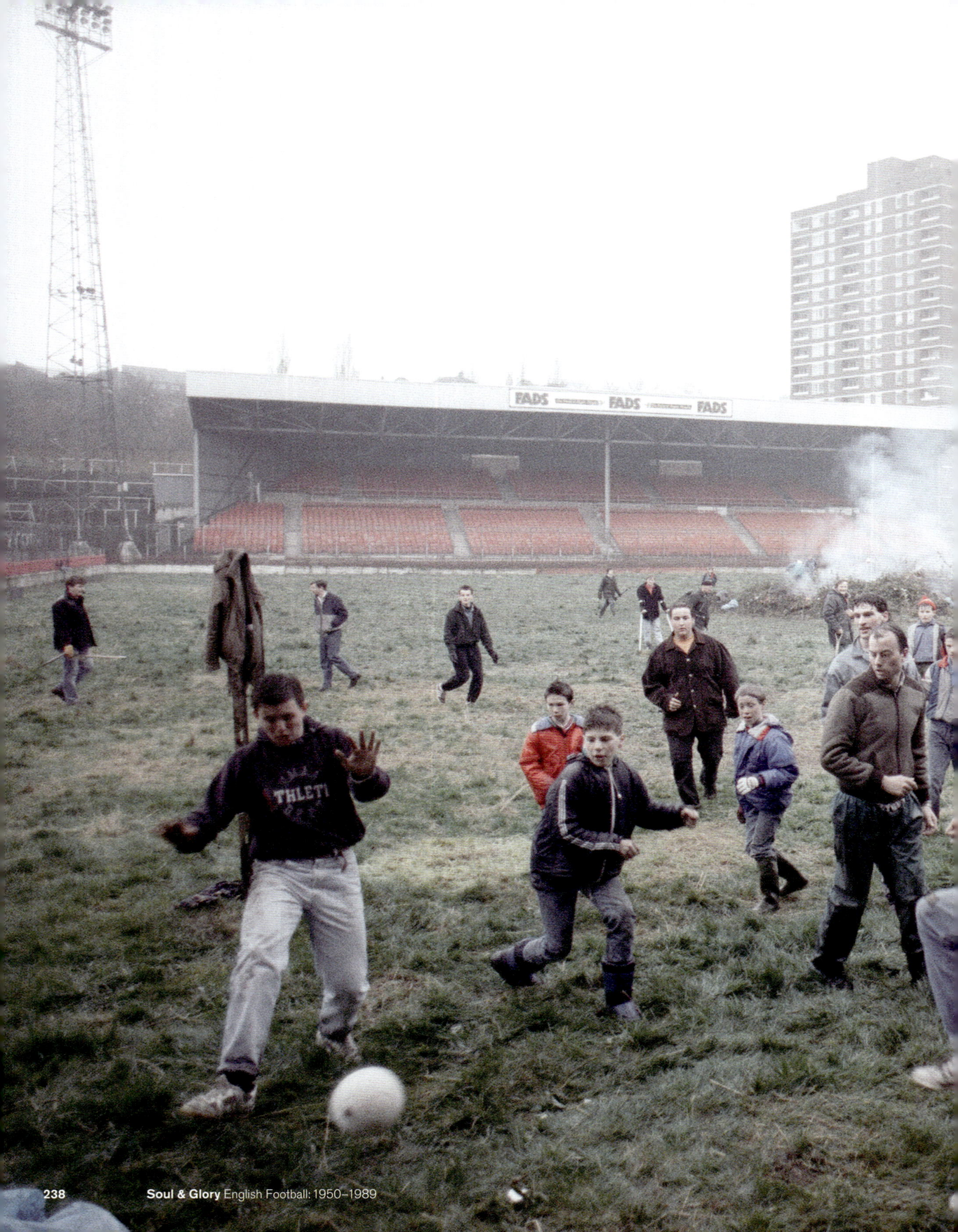
FADS   FADS   FADS

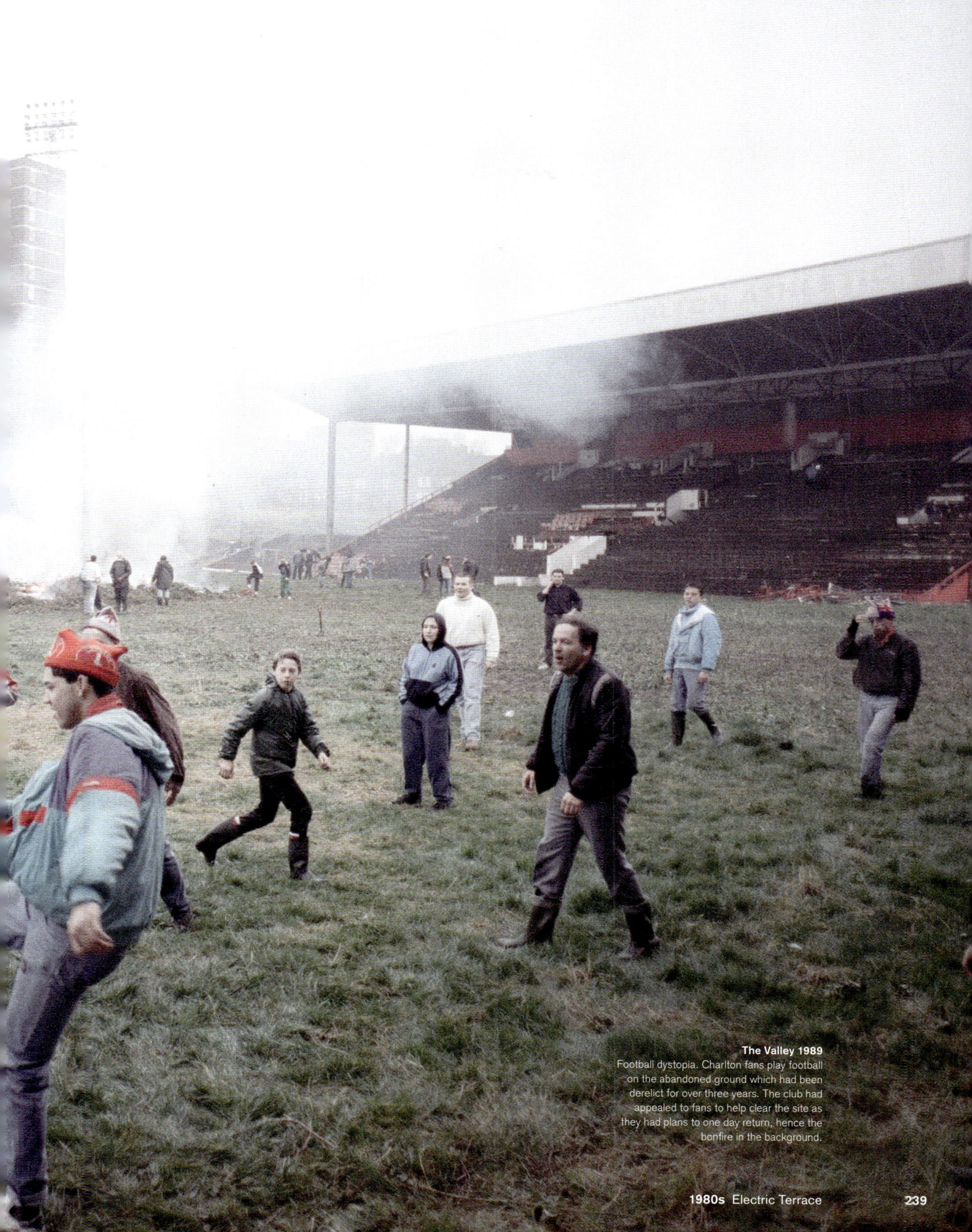

The Valley 1989
Football dystopia. Charlton fans play football on the abandoned ground which had been derelict for over three years. The club had appealed to fans to help clear the site as they had plans to one day return, hence the bonfire in the background.

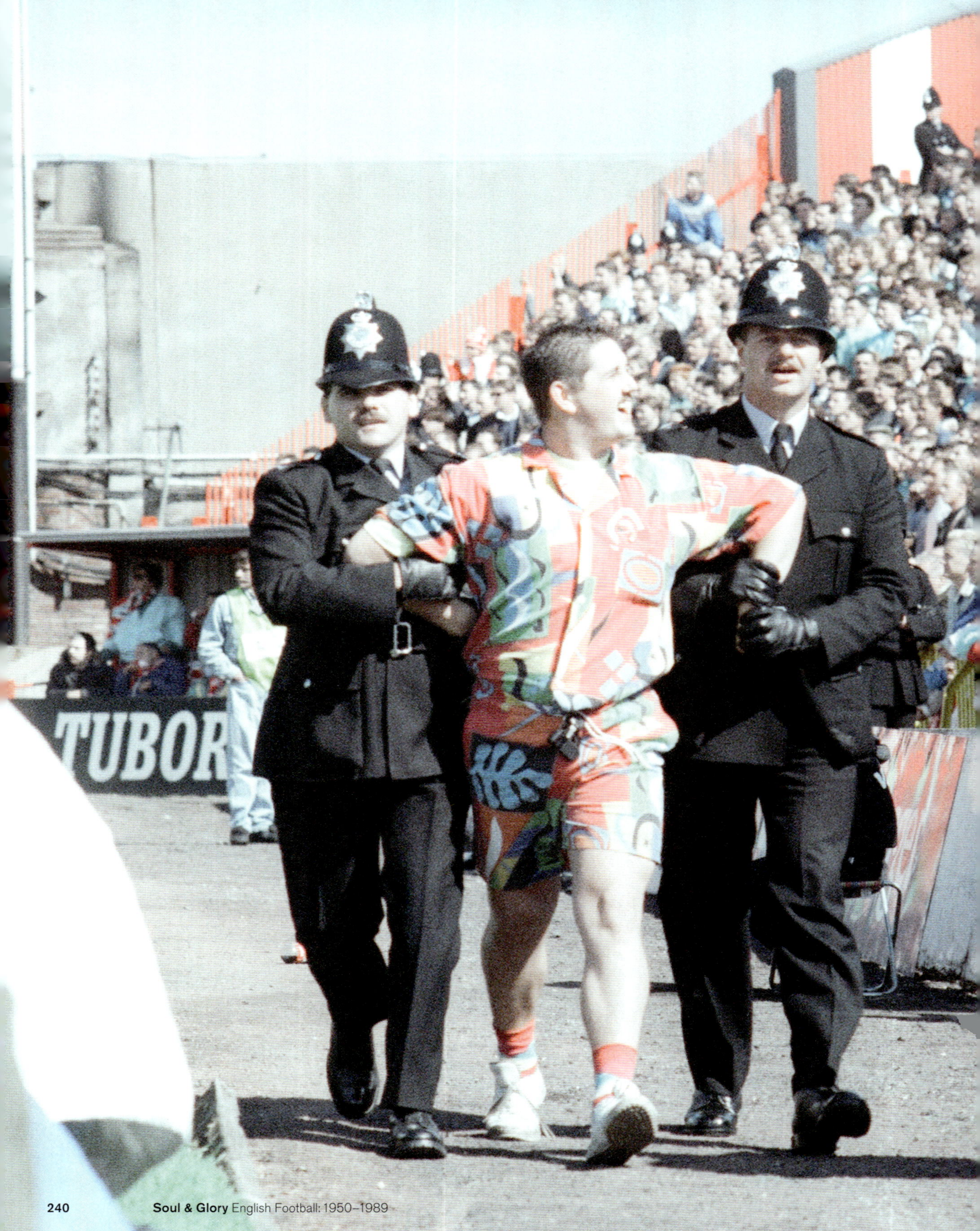

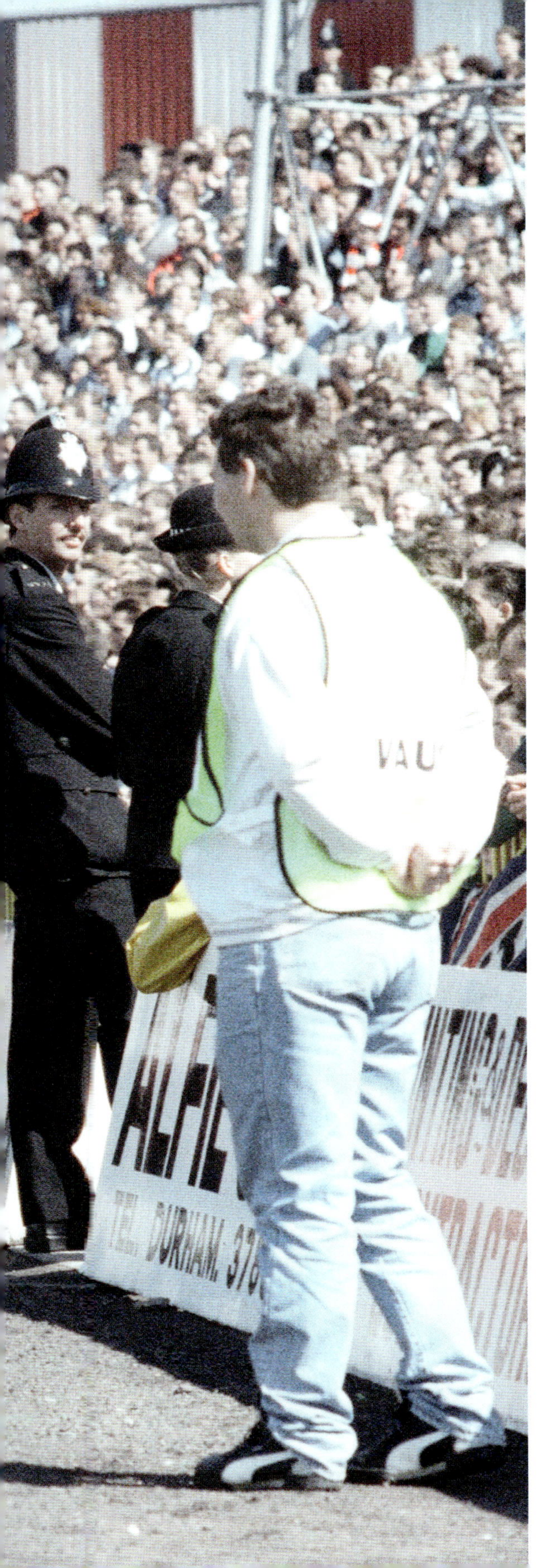

Roker Park 1989
A fan is removed from the stadium
during a Wearside-Teesside
derby between Sunderland and
Middlesbrough. Some might remark
that this was the fashion police.

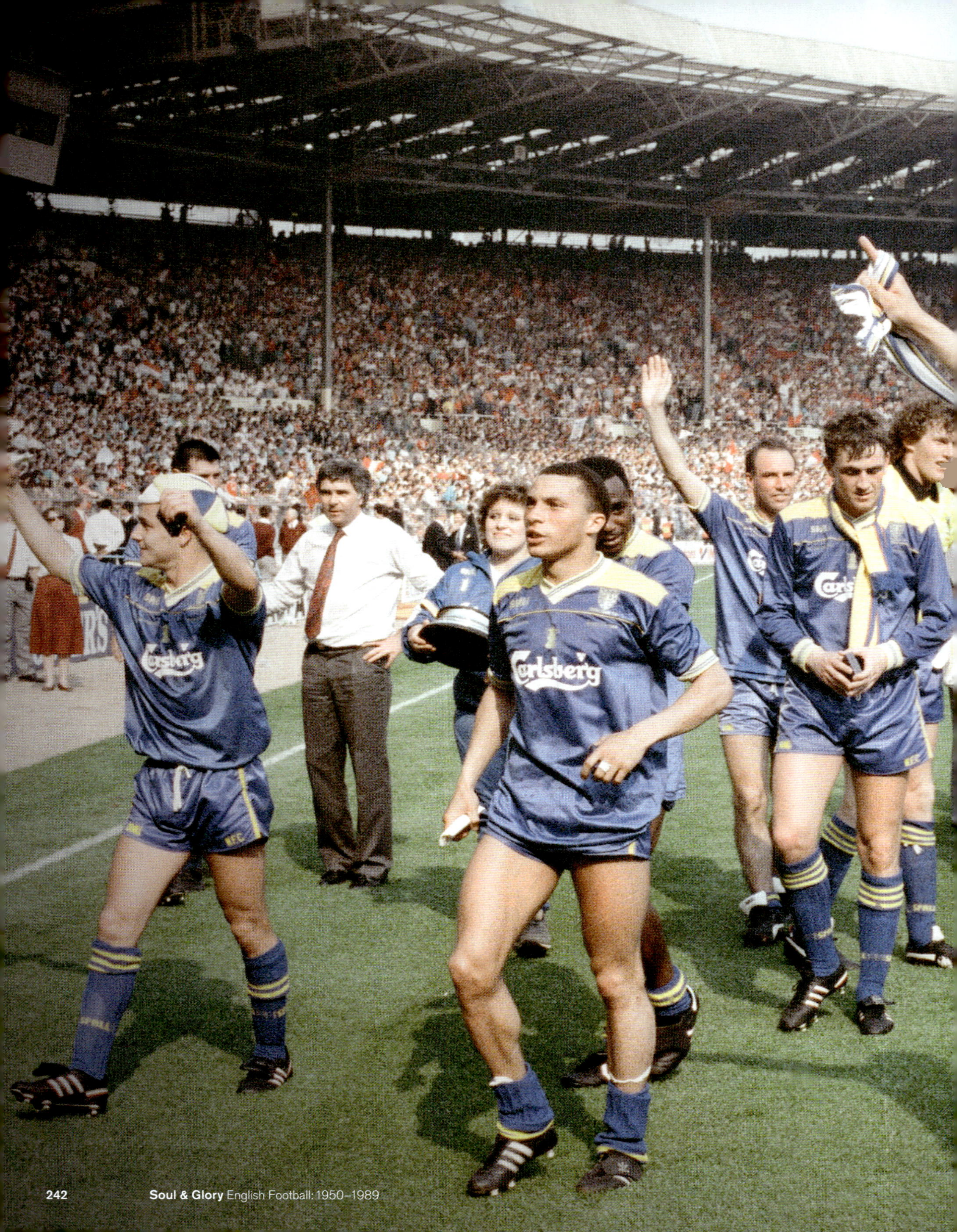

 Soul & Glory English Football: 1950–1989

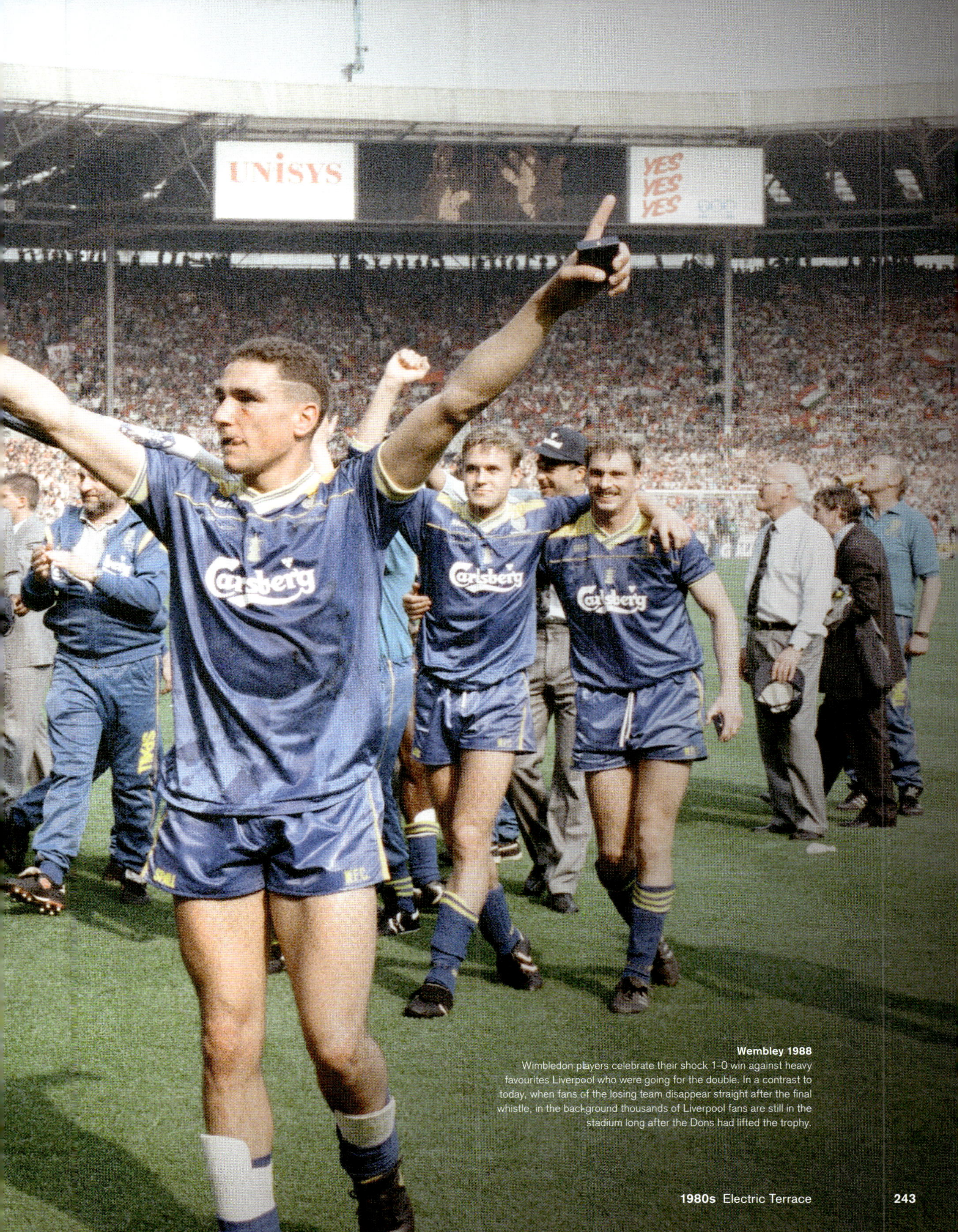

Wembley 1988
Wimbledon players celebrate their shock 1-0 win against heavy favourites Liverpool who were going for the double. In a contrast to today, when fans of the losing team disappear straight after the final whistle, in the background thousands of Liverpool fans are still in the stadium long after the Dons had lifted the trophy.

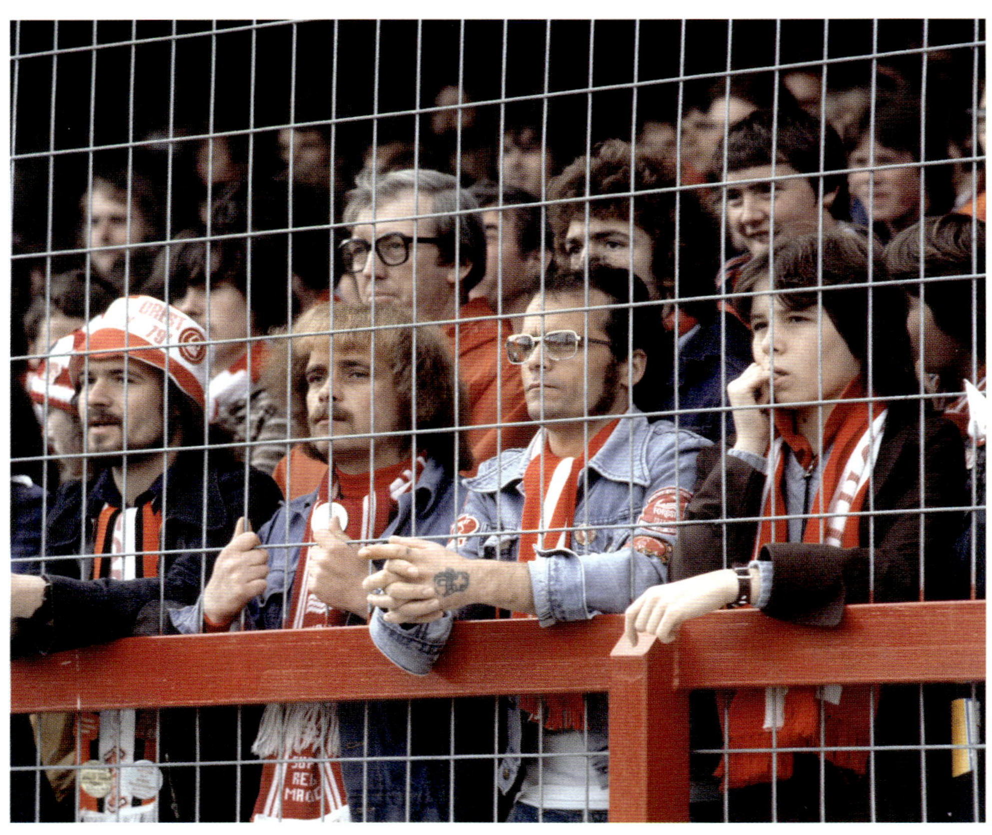

The City Ground 1983
Nottingham Forest fans watch from
behind the fences as their team play
Queens Park Rangers.

 Soul & Glory English Football: 1950–1989

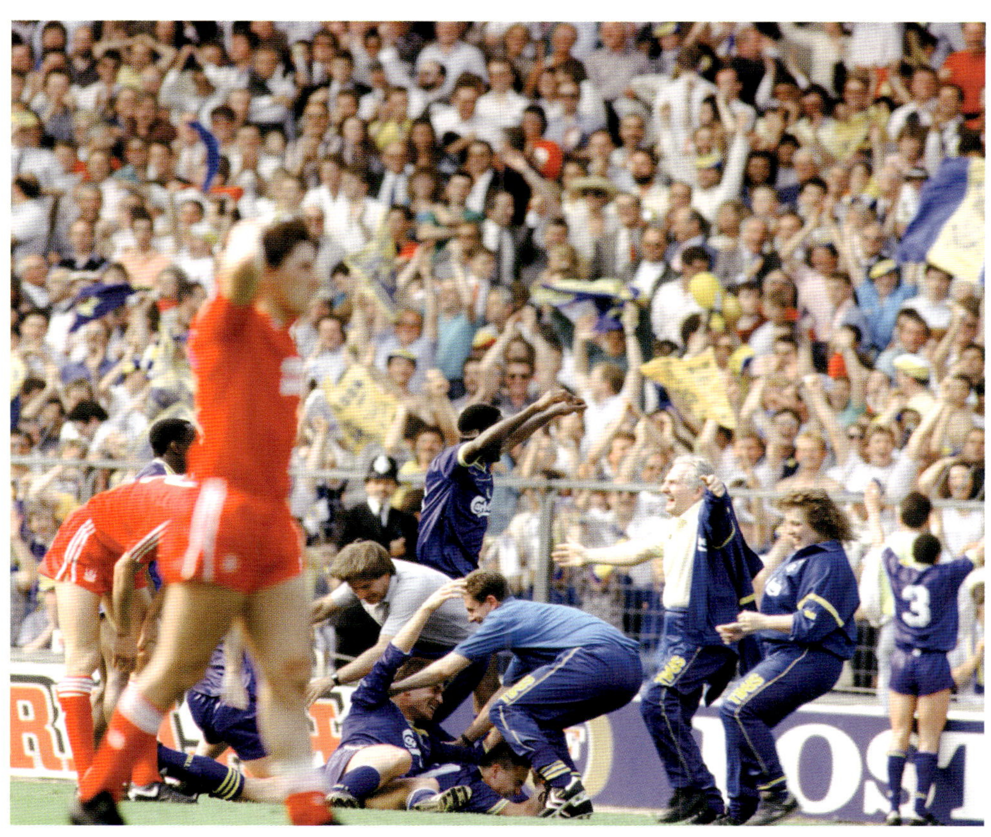

Wembley 1988

Wimbledon players and fans celebrate
upon the final whistle of the FA Cup
Final. In the foreground Liverpool's Peter
Beardsley holds his head in disbelief.

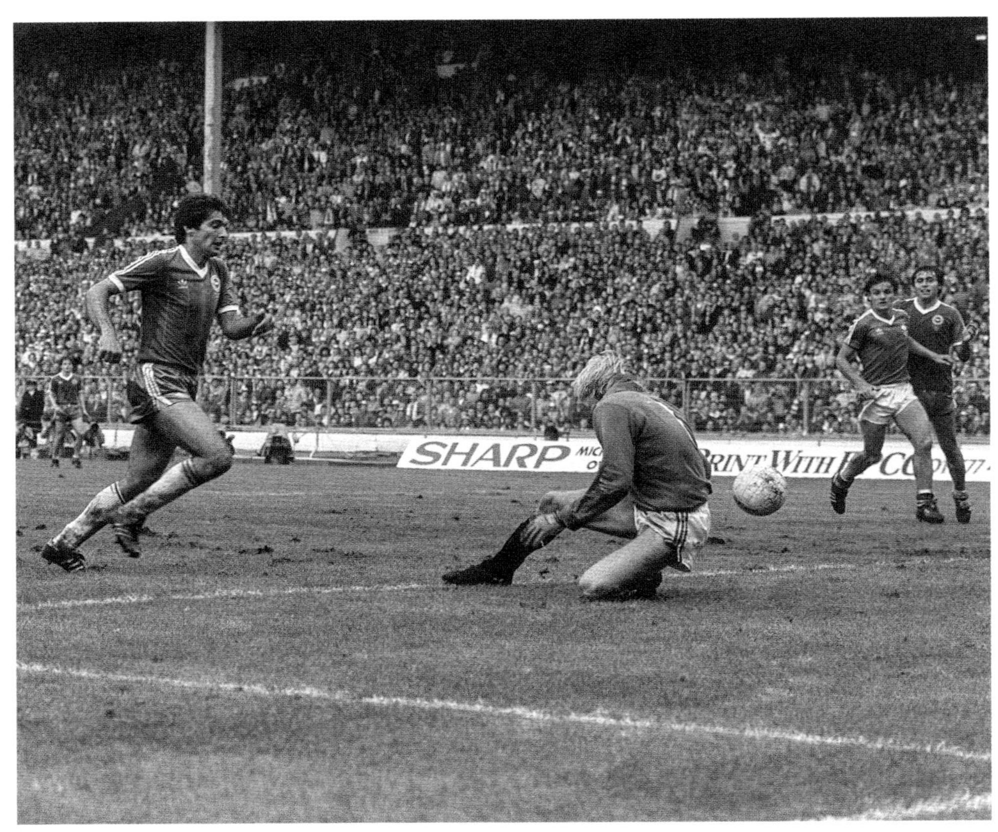

Wembley 1983
Despair for Brighton in the FA Cup Final. Gordon
Smith, with virtually the last kick of the game,
fires a tame shot to the body of Manchester
United goalkeeper Gary Bailey and the match
ends 2-2. United won the replay 4-0.

     Soul & Glory English Football: 1950–1989

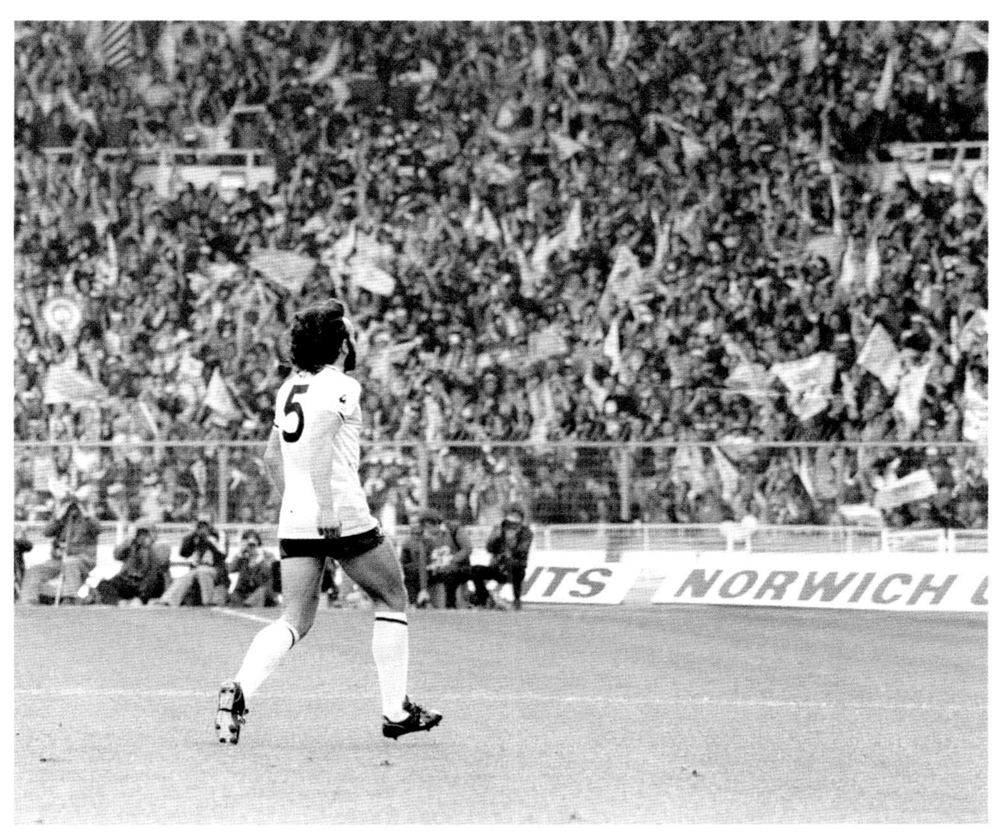

Wembley 1981
Glory for Spurs as Ricky Villa celebrates
one of the most famous FA Cup Final
goals of all time. Spurs beat Manchester
City 3-2, after the first match ended 1-1.

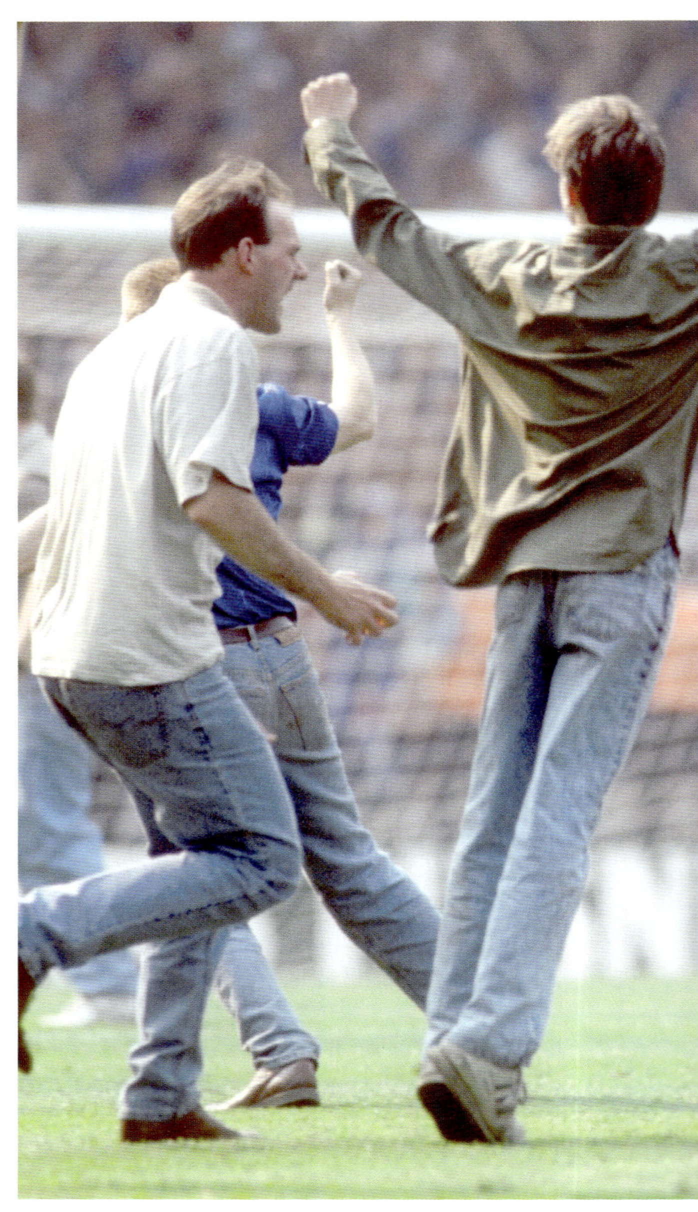

Wembley 1989
After a last-minute equaliser from
Stuart McCall, Tony Cottee (r) and
Pat Nevin (l) celebrate as the fans
invade the Wembley turf in a classic
all-Merseyside FA Cup Final.

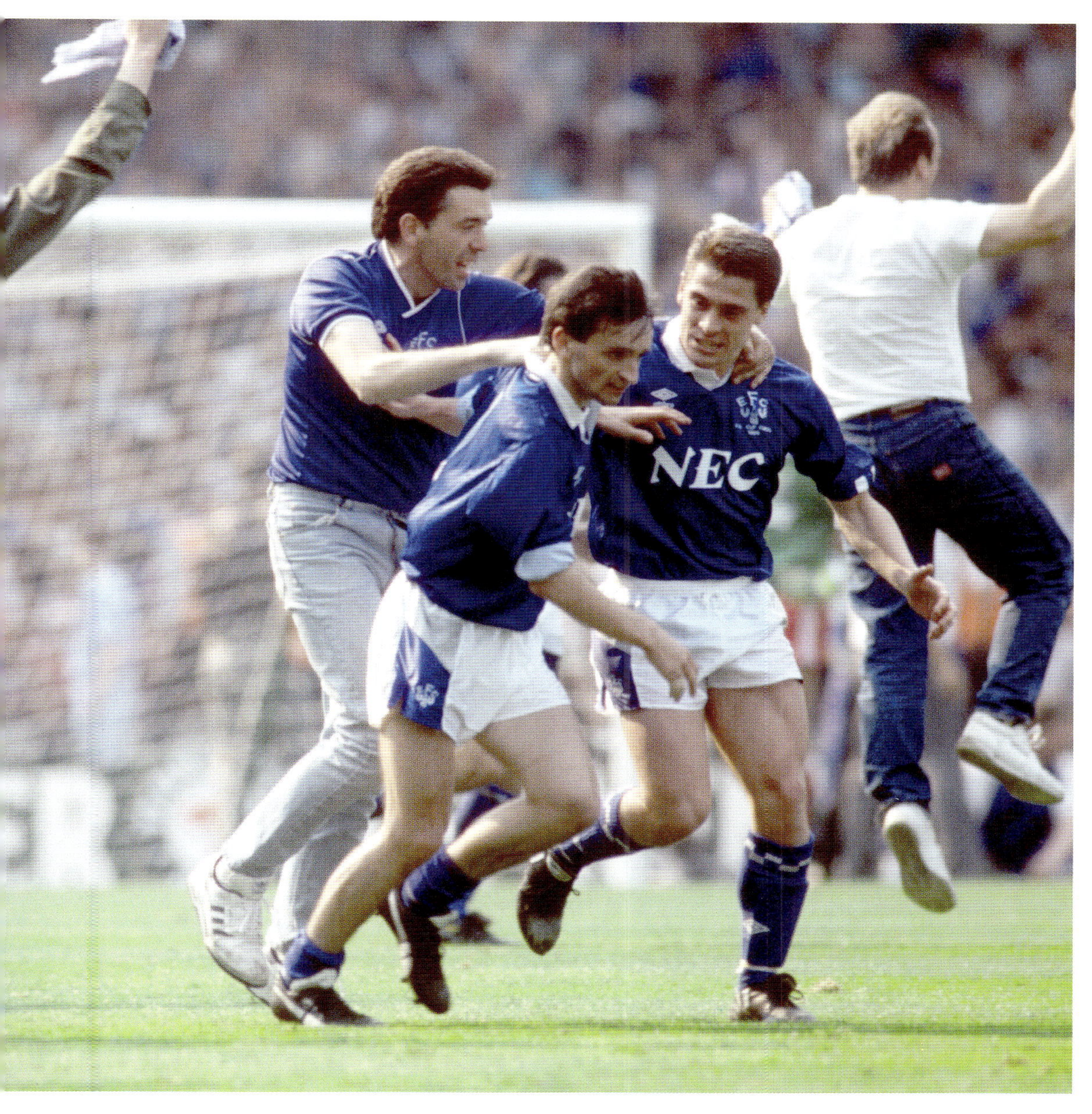

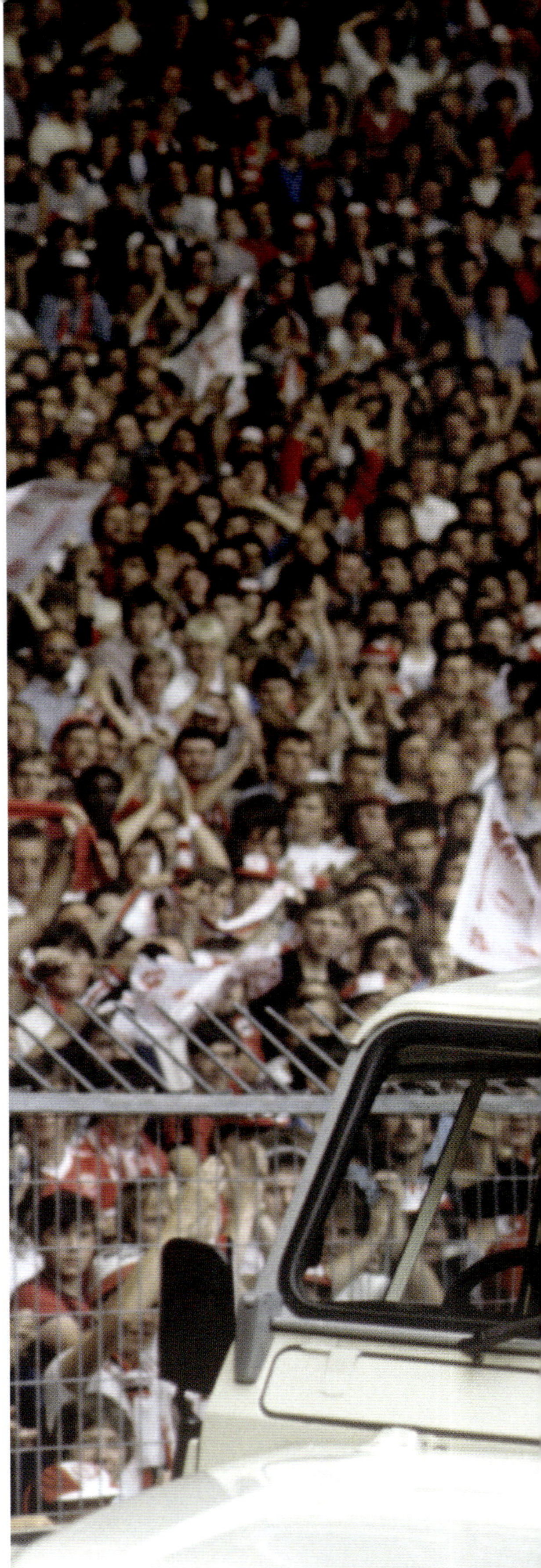

Wembley 1983

Two legends are paraded to the Wembley crowd before the
League Cup Final between Liverpool and Manchester United.
At this time Matt Busby (l) who retired in 1971, was United's most
successful manager and to this day Bob Paisley, who retired later
that year, is still Liverpool's leader in terms of trophies won.

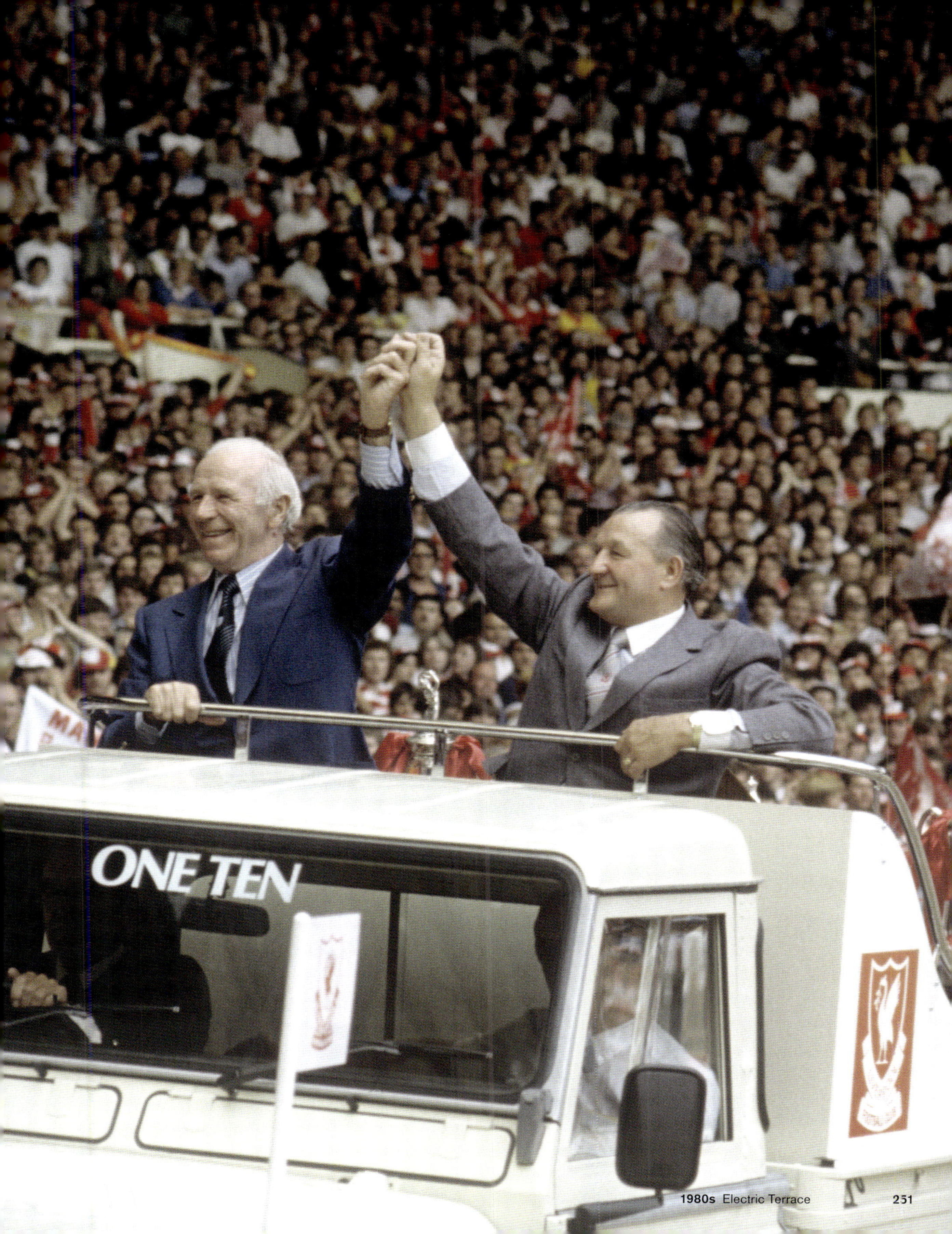
ONE TEN

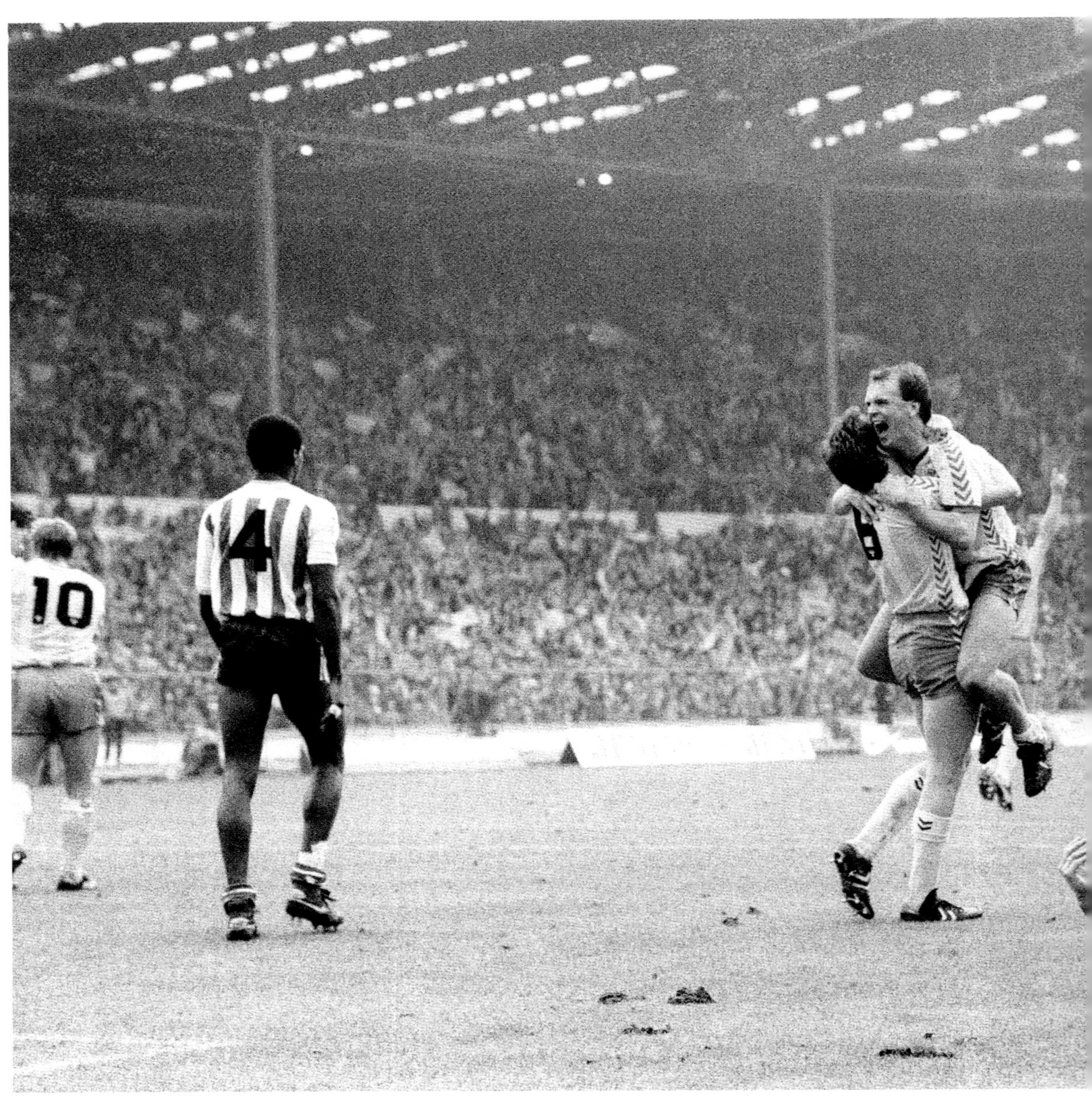

Wembley 1985
The final whistle goes in the 1985
League Cup Final between Norwich
and Sunderland as the Canaries
celebrate a 1-0 victory. Both teams
were relegated that same season.

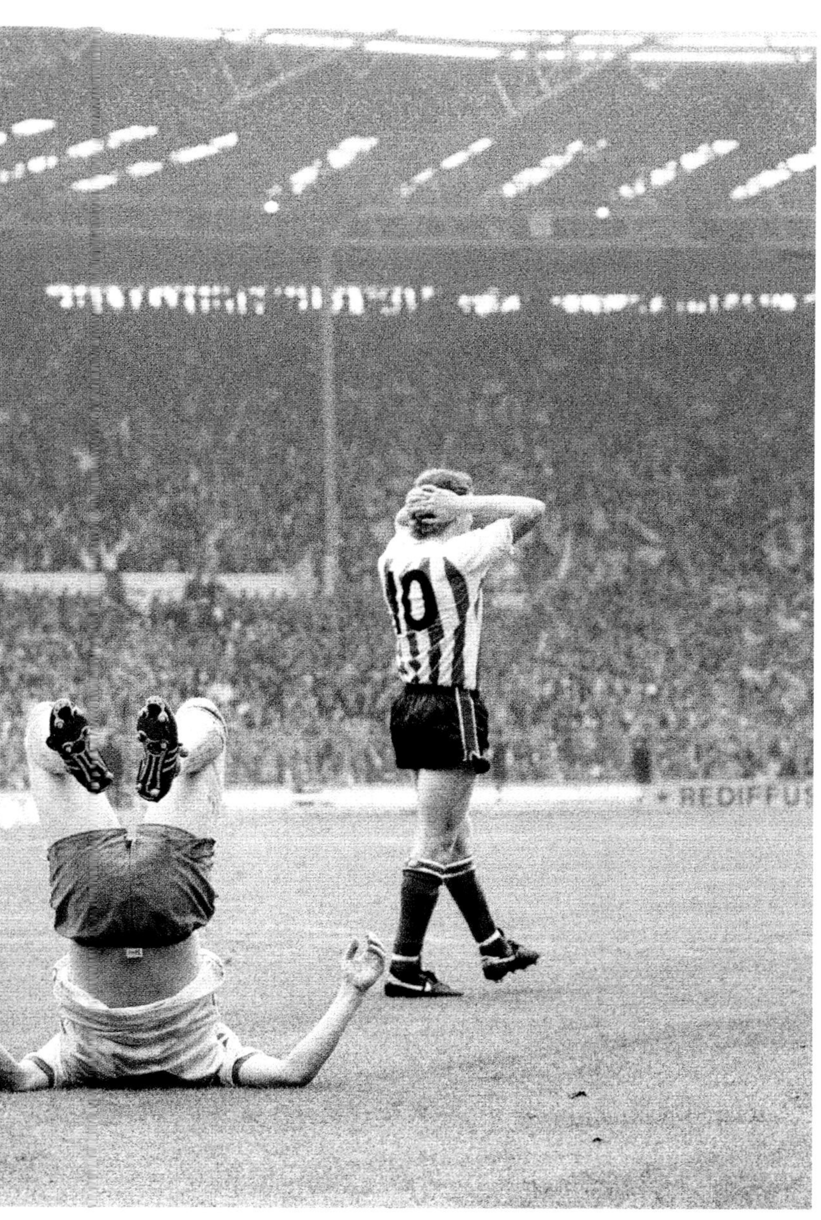

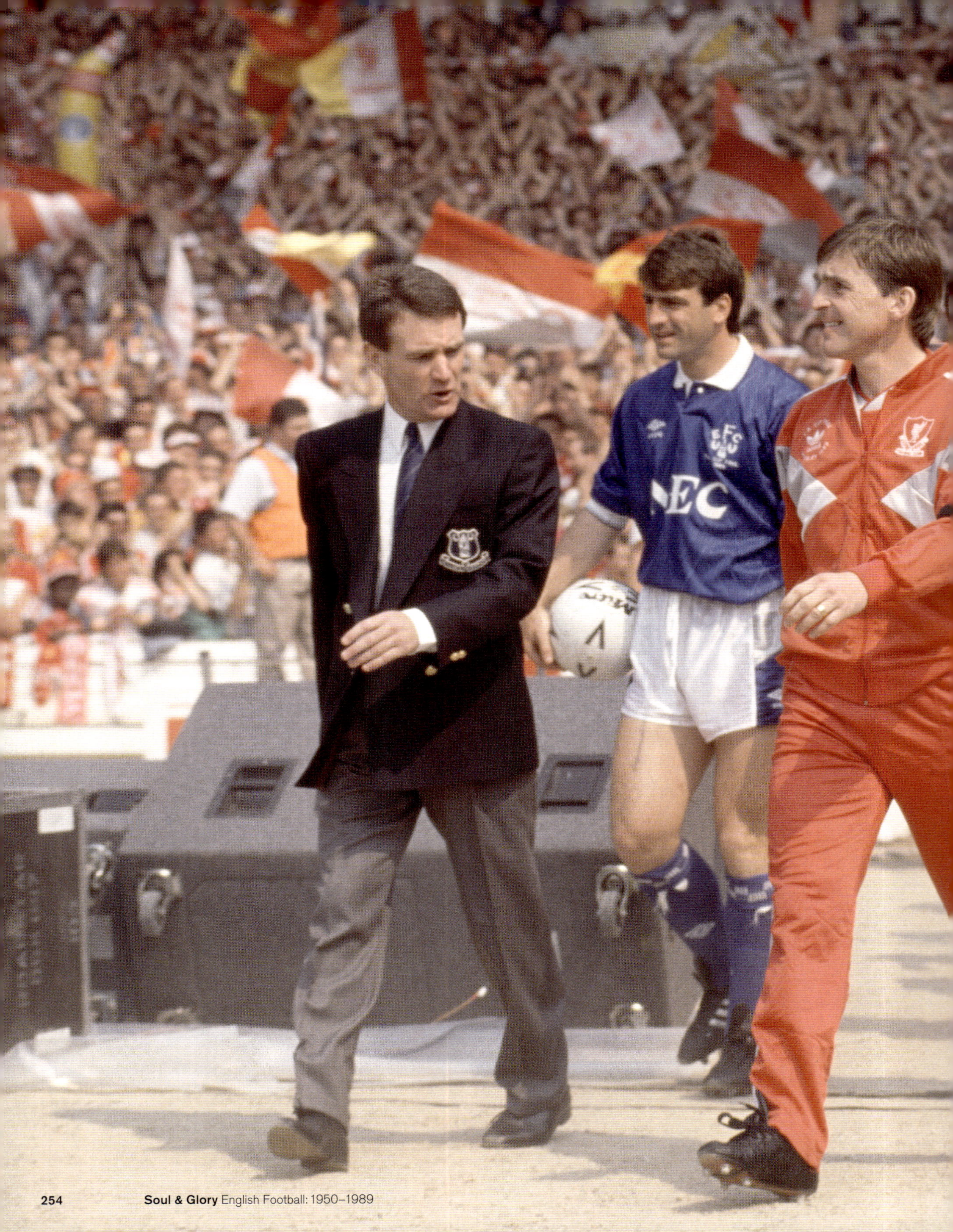

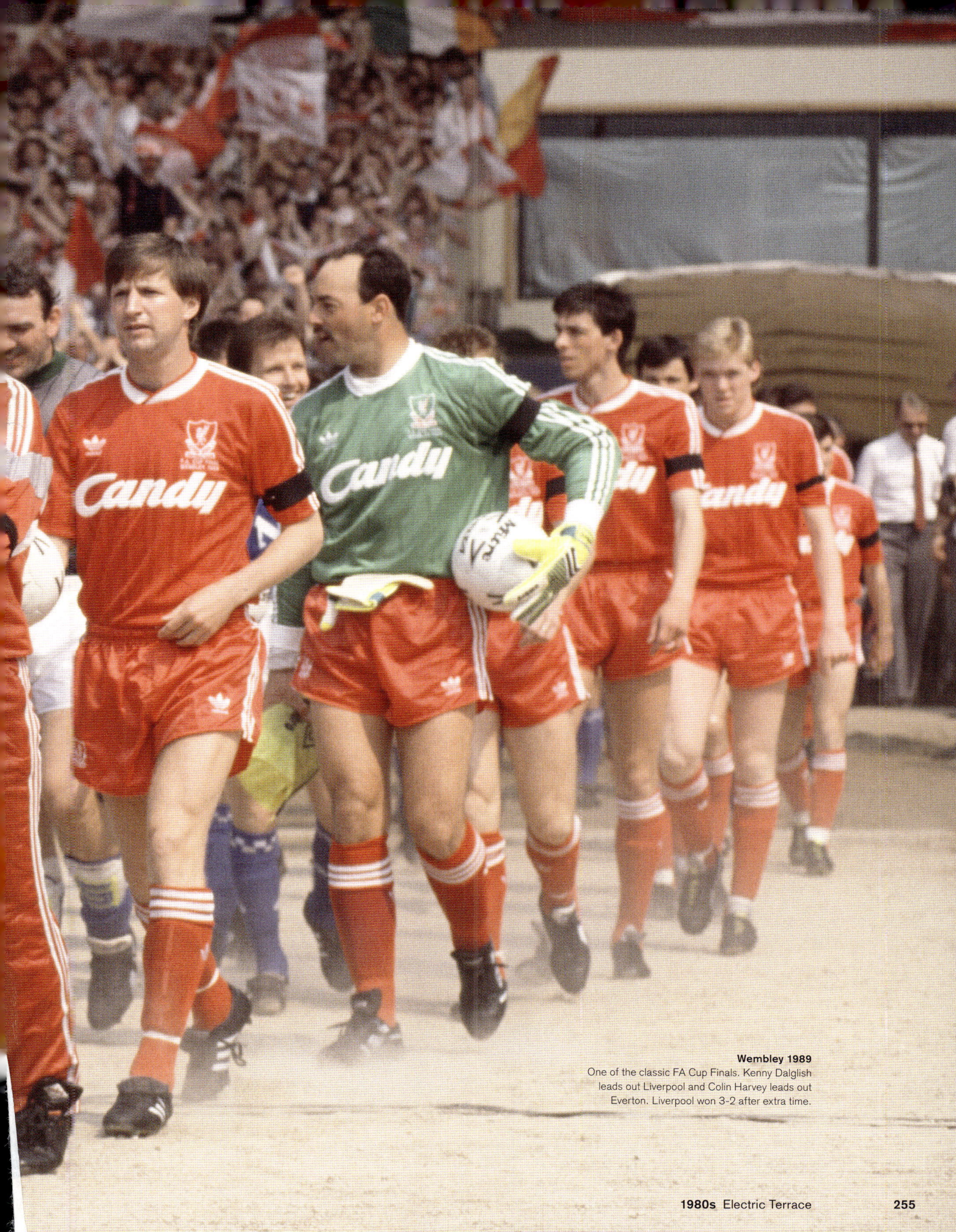

Wembley 1989
One of the classic FA Cup Finals. Kenny Dalglish
leads out Liverpool and Colin Harvey leads out
Everton. Liverpool won 3-2 after extra time.

Acknowledgements

I would like to thank everyone who bought a copy of this book for supporting authors and print media. Thanks to my parents Catherine Bazell and Ben Bazell for proof reading duties. I would like to say thanks to Paul and Duncan at Pitch Publishing for sharing the same vision of the book as I did, and for being easy to work with. I'd like to dedicate the book to my nieces the double V's....Veronica Bazell and Vivienne Delaney.

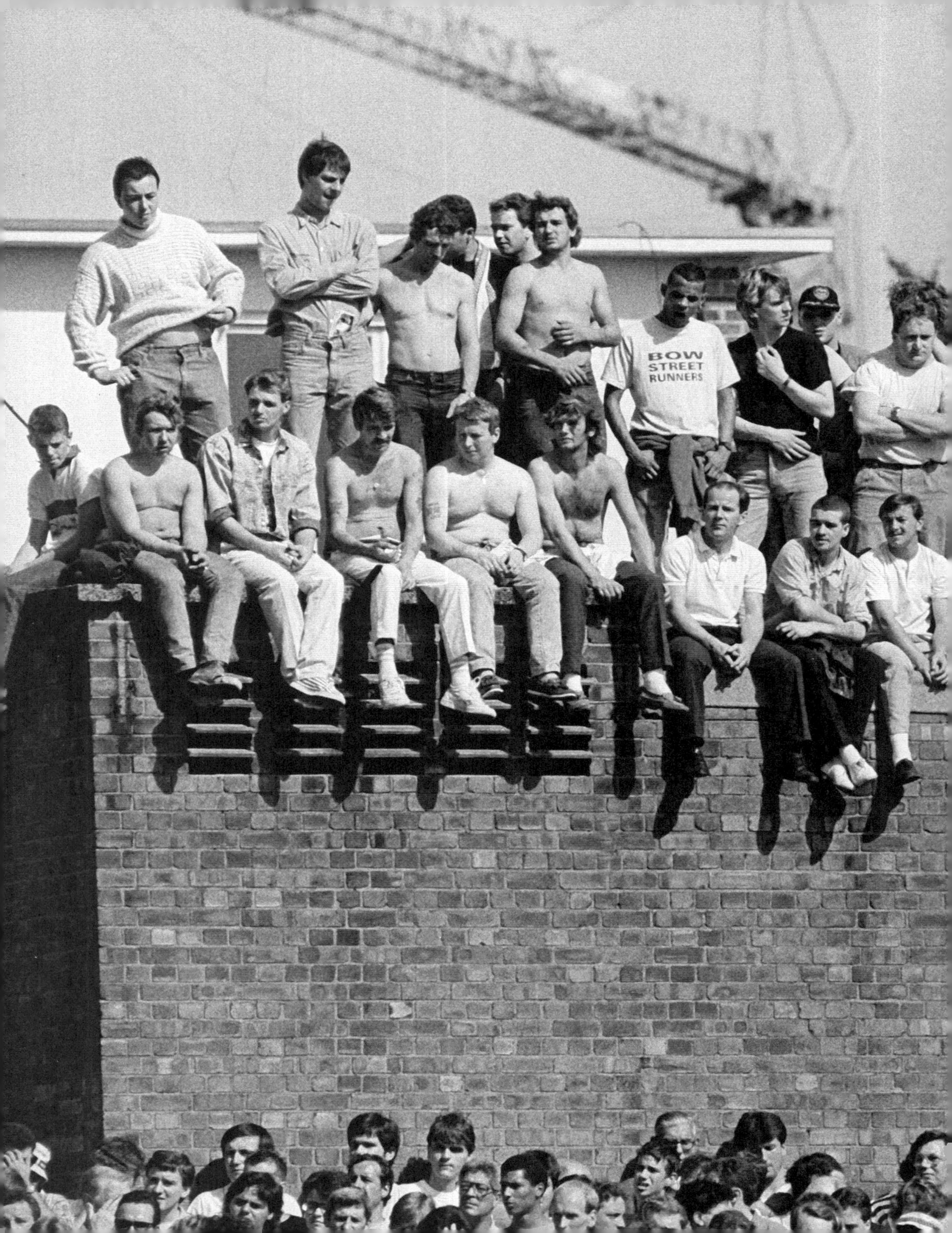
BOW
STREET
RUNNERS